MASSACRE IN MINNESOTA

MASSACRE IN
MINNESOTA

The Dakota War of 1862,
the Most Violent Ethnic Conflict
in American History

GARY CLAYTON ANDERSON

UNIVERSITY OF OKLAHOMA PRESS : NORMAN

This book is published with the generous assistance
of the Kerr Foundation, Inc.

Library of Congress Cataloging in Publication Control Number: 2019007398

ISBN: 978-0-8061-6434-2 (hardcover) ISBN 978-0-8061-9199-7 (paper)

The paper in this book meets the guidelines for permanence and durability of the
Committee on Production Guidelines for Book Longevity of the Council on Library
Resources, Inc. ∞

CONTENTS

List of Illustrations   vii

Preface   ix

ONE   The Dakota Homeland   3

TWO   The American Invasion   17

THREE   Removal, the New Reservations,
        and the First Indian Massacre   47

FOUR   Chaos, Confusion, and War   63

FIVE   The Massacre   83

SIX   Fright and Flight on the Minnesota Frontier   135

SEVEN   The Road to Retribution   161

EIGHT   Captives and the "Fate Worse Than Death"   189

NINE   Capture and Trials   212

TEN   The Executions   241

ELEVEN Deportation and Rebirth   268

Notes   287

English-Dakota Name Glossary   333

Bibliography   337

Index   351

ILLUSTRATIONS

FIGURES

Reverend Thomas S. Williamson   34

Reverend Steven Return Riggs   35

General Henry Hastings Sibley   36

Governor Alexander Ramsey   37

Farmer Indians guarding cornfields at the Lower Sioux Agency, 1862   38

Robert Hopkins (Chaska) and family   39

Wounded Man (Taopi)   40

Shooter (Wakute)   41

Charles Crawford and the Sisseton-Wahpeta delegation at Washington, D.C., 1858   42

Agent Joseph R. Brown and the Mdewakanton-Wahpekute delegation in Washington, D.C., 1858   43

Little Crow (Taoyateduta)   44

Wabasha (Wapaśa)   45

Little Six (Shakopee or Śakpedaŋ)   46

Standing Buffalo (Tataŋkanaźin)   112

John Otherday (Aŋpetutokeça)   113

Walking Galloping (Simon Anawaŋgmani)   114

Charles E. Flandreau   115

Captain John S. Marsh   116

Captain Timothy J. Sheehan   117

Refugees from the Yellow Medicine Agency, August 19, 1862   118

Big Eagle (Waŋmditaŋka) 119

Captain and Mrs. William B. Dodd 120

Gabriel Renville 121

Joseph Akipa Renville 122

Jeanette DeCamp Sweet with infant son Benjamin 123

Refugee Mrs. Leopold Sentzke and body of daughter Clara 124

Justina Krieger (Kreiger) Meyer 125

Lake Shetek survivors rescued on the Missouri River from White Lodge's
    Band in November 1862 126

Theresa Eisenreich 127

Liasa Eisenreich 128

Old Bets, mother of Taopi 129

Laura Terry Duley 130

Attack on New Ulm, by Frank Stengel 131

The Second Battle of New Ulm, by Alexander Schwendinger 132

Ambush, the Attack on the Recruiting Party, Milford Township,
    by David Geister 133

Mary E. Schwandt Schmidt, Urania S. White, and Helen M.
    Carrothers 134

Colonel Stephen Miller 235

One Who Forbids His House (Tihdonića) 236

William Duley 237

"Execution of the Thirty-Eight Dakota Men at Mankato, Minnesota,
    December 26, 1862" 238

"Scene in the prison, Mankato, Minnesota, where the Sioux murderers
    are confined" 239

Dakota prison camp at Fort Snelling, November 13, 1862 240

MAPS

Minnesota in the 1830s 20

Minnesota in 1862–1863 78

PREFACE

The research for this book started four and a half decades ago when I studied for master's and doctorate degrees. What a well-traveled road it became, resulting in the publication of *Kinsmen of Another Kind* (1984), *Little Crow, Spokesman for the Sioux* (1986), and finally *Through Dakota Eyes* (1988), the latter a collection of narratives edited by myself and Alan R. Woolworth. All of this work has one common thread: the books avoid offering a serious study of the war that Dakota Indians inaugurated in 1862. At the time, I failed to comprehend how such a tragic event could have transpired when, for nearly two centuries, the Dakota people had been at peace with, first, Europeans who arrived after 1650, and then with Americans, who began coming into their lands in 1819. The only explanation that seemed plausible at the time was a vague, but arguable "ethnohistorical" conclusion: the common kinship bonds that had cemented friendly relations for so many years broke down. But there simply is more to this terrible conflict than that explanation.

The effort before you is a comprehensive history of what has often been called an "outbreak" but was a bloody conflict that turned into all-out war in which almost everyone on both sides suffered terribly and few, if any, emerged as heroes. The scope of this conflict was unparalleled. It resulted in the deaths of more than six hundred settlers and dozens of soldiers and militiamen. Those settlers who survived the initial onslaught fled, leaving behind their cabins, cattle, and livelihoods to destruction. Nearly forty thousand of them became refugees. The aftermath of the massacre involved the ethnic cleansing of six thousand Dakota Indians from Minnesota. Finding a similar story in American history is difficult, perhaps impossible.

Years ago, I could write about the people involved, in particular the politicians, the Indians, and the many Franco-Dakota and Anglo-Dakota people (often called "mixed-bloods," using a disparaging term often intended to stereotype and stigmatize people but that simply has no synonym and at times must be used). If all these people seemed to get along relatively well, how could the seemingly friendly relationships dissolve, supposedly in a flash, resulting in terrible bloodshed, the destruction of villages and farms, and a near hysterical exodus of whites from the western portions of the state of Minnesota to safety in the east? I also struggled to explain the thirty-eight Dakota men who, at the conclusion of this conflict, faced the gallows on December 26, 1862. A young historian at the time, I thought it was best to avoid the issue, to write about people caught up in the struggle, and to think hard on what it all meant.

As I continued in my academic life, I strayed from the topic, turning to writing a book on Texas, another on the Indians of the Southwest, and several biographies, one of Sitting Bull and another of Will Rogers. With the exception of Texas—Texans did not care for my depiction of "unsainted" Texas Rangers—these were all safe topics and books that sold well. But in the many trips back to my home state of Minnesota, I continued to search for answers. Many were found in the National Archives, an incredible institution that keeps every scrap of paper produced by the government. Among the scraps was Colonel Henry Sibley's official letter book of his march up the Minnesota River and his defeat of the Dakotas who had participated in the war as well as the "District of Minnesota" correspondence (in Record Group 393), documents seemingly never before used by historians. Along the way, other archival sources revealed fascinating aspects of the struggle in Minnesota: the Wisconsin Historical Society held financial records relating to the sale of the southern part of the state by the Dakota people in 1851, revealing massive corruption, and the Newberry Library in Chicago and the Henry E. Huntington Library in San Marino, California, held diaries and letters from various participants. Finally, the massive archives of the Minnesota Historical Society, as well as other archival collections across the state, continually added to the evidence, helping to document and explain the tragedy.

The journey to this book has not been without consternation. Some of the research led to the discovery that the founding fathers of Minnesota were in fact thieves who took hundreds of thousands of dollars from the Dakota people, money that Indian leaders knew was being stolen. Dakota chiefs said so time and again. It also became clear to me that many more settler families perished in the war than has ever before been claimed in books or articles, including some written earlier by me. The violence justifies the use of the term "massacre" in the title, even though I realize it is controversial today and know that some will object to it. If numbers are a criterion—and I think they are—then it is worth pointing out that the violence in Minnesota surpassed that of the "massacre" of Indians at Bear River (1863), Sand Creek (1864), and even Wounded Knee (1890). The title also states that this conflict was the "most violent" ethnic struggle in American history; given the fact that most of the killing occurred in just four or five days, it is difficult, if not impossible, to find an equal in the history of our country.

The title's wording may be the least-controversial part of the story. A careful reading of sources led to the discovery that of the more than one hundred white women and children taken prisoner, several dozen of them suffered the "fate worse than death." In addition, I wrote this manuscript while a legal fight erupted over just who was a "loyal" Dakota Indian during the war. The term is slippery and begs the question: Loyal to whom and to what? Actually, many—some Christian Indians, other farmers, and a good many Sissetons and Wahpetans, who generally opposed the war but lost their reservation in Minnesota at its conclusion anyway. Many of these Dakotas are revealed for the first time in this book. There were also the trials of 392 Indians by a military commission. Some would argue that this form of military justice was perfectly legal and that the men who faced the gallows in Mankato were all guilty of rape and murder. Others claim innocence, and based on the evidence used to convict them, the guilt of many is questionable. Whatever the argument, most of these questions remain unsettled today and often lead to exaggerated claims in the local press. Here again, I have tried to distinguish between what is factually true and what is supposition or, worse, politically motivated hyperbole.

Some readers will, I hope, see that for the first time much of this history is told using Indian voices, especially the part that occurred in August 1862 and thereafter. Some thirty-six Dakota and mixed-blood narratives are found in *Through Dakota Eyes* alone, a collection that Alan R. Woolworth and I edited thirty years ago. Many other Indian voices come from a plethora of records tied to testimony connected with the Sisseton-Wahpeton Claims Case of 1902. Newspapers offer other accounts. Some readers may be dismayed to find the term "squaw" in some of these texts (with almost ten instances in chapter 8). All occur in period quotations, five being spoken by Dakota men and two others by white women quoting Dakota men.

Rather than debate those issues here, let me assure the reader that after years of research I believe the answers to many perplexing arguments regarding the war can be settled. Some attempt at it occurred in 1987, after the publication of my biography of Little Crow, when I met with Minnesota Governor Rudy Perpich and we designed what became the "Year of Reconciliation." Unfortunately, little was reconciled, and even today some statement regarding the events of the war appears from time to time that simply fails the acid test. The state and those who write about it, along with the various museums that try to depict the events of the war through the display of artifacts, seem more divided over the war, its causes, and its violence than ever before. When hearing of statements related to this issue or that, which are often incorrect, I think of what a great historian once said about history. The Greek Polybius, writing in about 150 BC, set a standard that we should all observe today:

> Now I would admit that authors should have a partiality for their own country, but they should not make statements about it that are contrary to facts. Surely the mistakes of which we writers are guilty and which it is difficult for us, being humans, to avoid are quite sufficient; but if we make deliberate misstatements in the interest of our country or of friends or for favor, what difference is there between us and those who gain their living by their pens? For just as the latter, weighing everything by the standard of profit, make their works unreliable, so politicians, biased by their dislikes and affections, often achieve the same results. Therefore I would add that readers should carefully look for this fault and authors themselves be on the guard against it.[1]

And so it is with the history of the Minnesota-Dakota War of 1862, a conflict rife with violence and agony, a history that involves very few heroes and that abounds with issues that scholars and writers have struggled with for decades. Polybius might shake his head and walk away from it, something I once did. But I can no longer do that. The war was and is a conflict born of corruption and magnified by extreme violence in which thousands suffered on all sides. It is as controversial today as it was a century and a half ago. The effort that has resulted in this book may satisfy no one, but the time has arrived for this student of the affair to spell out what he thinks happened and why it happened.

So many have contributed over the years to this research that it is impossible to list them all. Robert Kwasnicka, at the National Archives, was always on hand to show me pertinent documents. Bob rediscovered the

Sioux trial records in the Senate papers, seemingly lost for a time in the vast shelves of the archives. John Aubury offered the same wonderful service at the Newberry Library. Other unaffiliated scholars, including Elroy F. Ubl, Curtis Dahlin, Mary Bakeman, John La Batte, and Corinne Marz, provided useful advice and illustrations. I particularly benefited from the wonderful conversations with journalist Nick Coleman, who is no longer with us. So many helpful people have come and gone over the years at the Minnesota Historical Society that it is difficult to remember each for his or her kindness and to credit them all. I started work there with Ruby Shields in the old building across from the state capitol in the 1970s. Ruth Bauer took over at the Mississippi Street building. Finally, Debbie Miller and a cadre of others continued to help whenever necessary. And my dear friend at the society, Alan W. Woolworth, spirited me away to his office on occasions, offering access to amazing files, and then later sent me hundreds of news clippings and documents from his private collection that helped formulate my understanding of the events. Darla Gebhard, at the Brown County Historical Society, has helped me understand the struggle at New Ulm and the plight of so many immigrant families who lost everything in the conflict. Their story is important too.

The months and years leading to publication have been a learning process as well. Thomas Lebien, an editor at Harvard University Press, helped early on to define the size and extent of the manuscript. William Lass and Elliott West read the manuscript and saved me from errors. My agent in New York, Carol Mann, worked with one of the best editors in the business, Charles E. Rankin at the University of Oklahoma Press, to bring the book out. Chuck has read the manuscript several times and offered advice on a host of issues. Along the way, Steven B. Baker, managing editor at the Press, helped select illustrations, and the OU History Department chair, Jamie Hart, handled the cost of obtaining permission to reproduce them. As chapters matured, my now-retired copyeditor Sally Rubinstein, who spent many years at the Minnesota Historical Society, carefully read every page. And finally, my wife, Laura, ever the anthropologist who taught both the Dakota and Cherokee languages at the University of Oklahoma for so many years, helped keep the many Dakota names and phrases in the book in proper form. Few scholars have had such wonderful assistance.

Norman, Oklahoma
November 2018

MASSACRE IN MINNESOTA

ONE

THE DAKOTA HOMELAND

Anglo people in Minnesota called him Little Crow; his own people called him Taoyateduta (*ta*, or "his"; *oyate*, "nation"; *duta*, "red"). The Anglo name came from the dynasty that the French first identified in naming his grandfather Petite Corbeau, or Little Crow I. In 1846 Little Crow inherited the leadership of Kaposia, his father's main village, located just south of what is today St. Paul, Minnesota. The village became a standard feature viewed by passing river boats, its bark structures and buffalo hide tepees attracting considerable attention.[1] Little did the curious visitors know that one day this man, Little Crow, who welcomed newcomers with a handshake, would lead the most violent ethnic war in American history, one that nearly led to the total destruction of the new state of Minnesota.

Little Crow's father would have other male children, and some competition existed over leadership, given the fact that Kaposia sat at the center of a widely distributed complex of villages belonging to a large band of well over two thousand people called the Mdewakanton Dakota (sometimes the archaic term Sioux is used, given to these people by their enemies). And Little Crow had made some questionable decisions as a youth, marrying several daughters of the chief of another Dakota band to the south, the Wahpekutes, a people who were being pummeled by their enemies from the Des Moines River, the Mesquakie people, or as the Americans called them, the Sac and Fox. Leaving the Wahpekutes nearly destroyed, Little Crow traveled west and then took as wives the four daughters of yet another band, the Wahpeton Dakota, who lived far up the Minnesota River.

These people were closely intermarried with the more powerful Sisseton Dakota; the political chief of the band, Walking Runner (or Iŋyaŋgmani, as his people called him), Little Crow's father-in-law, ruled over a mixed Sisseton/Wahpeton village. The marriage gave Little Crow significant influence in the West, as kinship networks were the heart and soul of the Dakota nation. Kinsmen were always loyal to the extended family and often sought revenge when a relative was dishonored or killed.[2]

This new marriage might seem problematic to the parents of four young women who wanted the best for their daughters. But Walking Runner obviously thought it a good match, because the parents and brothers of the brides arranged marriages. Perhaps the decision rested upon Little Crow's lineage, or even his looks. Tall, at about five feet ten inches, he had a distinct, nearly perfect Roman nose, high cheek bones, and a very narrow face, with piercing hazel eyes. A description of him in the 1850s noted that "he was of a nervous temperament, restless and active, intelligent, of strong personality, of great physical vigor and vainly confident of his own superiority." Above all, he took great pride in his dress and offered a very distinguished look, often appearing in stylish leggings set off by a garnished necklace and carefully braided hair.[3]

Perhaps most importantly, Little Crow was a gifted speaker. He knew some English words but preferred using an interpreter. When talking to a crowd near the Washington Monument in 1858, which had just been started, he held the group of mostly Americans spellbound with stories of his war and hunting exploits, as close mixed-blood friends translated. In a word, Little Crow was a born leader, a politician who possessed an aristocratic lineage, who came of age during a period of great difficulty for his people. All of his intellectual skills would be challenged in the 1850s and early 1860s.[4]

Despite his aristocratic appearance, Little Crow had abandoned his village during one of its most turbulent periods, the 1830s and 1840s, living with Walking Runner's Sisseton/Wahpeton people. A serious decline in fur-bearing animals, which sustained the Dakota economy, led to suffering from lack of food in the winter months and conflict with traders come spring, when the hides necessary to pay debts often failed to meet obligations. Little Crow likely saw nothing but hardship along the Mississippi River, which partially explains his move west. Americans also had moved ever closer to the eastern bank of the Mississippi River, settling land in Wisconsin just across from Kaposia.

Even so, Little Crow's name, which translates to "His Red People," had a powerful, spiritual meaning and emitted a sense of influence that he wished his people to embrace. The name actually had much to do with religion and death. Dakota Indians never spoke of death to outsiders, but years later, Elizabeth Wiŋyaŋ, a Dakota woman later turned missionary, revealed that when a Dakota man or woman died, his or her spirit left the body but lingered near it for days, accepting relatives' offering of food that he or she would need on the long trek west. Once underway, the deceased's spirit finally reached a river, where a Dakota woman held sway. She looked at the body of the spirit to see if there were red tattoos and plenty of red paint, especially on the top of the head. If a prevalence of such artwork could be found, the spirit was allowed to pass to the promised land. If not, he or she was cast into the river to wander for the rest of eternity.[5]

Just why red paint became so important in displaying the identify of a Dakota person—especially his or her commitment to social and political rules or to protect relatives—is difficult to determine. Men often covered their entire heads with red when going to war, and relatives painted red on the heads of a departed person. Henry Rowe Schoolcraft, when making his historical journey through the Great Lakes and into Dakota country, noted the use of red paint, commenting that it came from iron oxide, scraped from veins and mixed with animal fat.[6]

In a symbolic sense, Little Crow assumed a name—His Red Nation—that indicated that he expected to lead his people, that he welcomed the responsibility. The name change apparently occurred after 1846. It came during a time when he decided to seize the mantle of leadership and return from the west to his native village.[7] After learning that his father had accidentally shot himself, Little Crow came back to claim the chieftainship in 1846. This did not please his two half-brothers, the oldest of which assumed that he would become the new chief. In a fit of rage, the two confronted Little Crow, and as he crossed his arms in front of him, taking a defiant stand, one brother fired, the ball passing through both of Little Crow's wrists.

The surgeon at Fort Snelling, near present-day St. Paul, suggested amputation, but the young chief declined. He would rather die than be an invalid who might be scorned as a leader. Indeed, the Dakota were patrifocal people, and men had a role to play as warriors and providers. To be an invalid, a man without hands, would be catastrophic. In a curious twist, which many in his village viewed as an omen, Little Crow lived, and while his wrists remained deformed, his hands could function, and friends supported him and killed both of his half-brothers. There would be no struggle over control of Kaposia, as other important men fell quickly in line. Becoming chief of the entire Mdewakanton band, a collection of some seven villages and twenty-five hundred people, would take even more effort than facing the musket of his half-brother, and it would entail much greater struggle.

Along the shores of the upper Mississippi River in the mid-nineteenth century, Little Crow's Mdewakanton people dominated lands that extended from what is today the town of Wabasha, on the Mississippi River, upstream to St. Paul, and thence up the Minnesota River all the way to its bend in south-central Minnesota. The term *Mdewakanton* derived from *mde,* a Dakota word generally meaning lake, and *wakan,* which means spirit, a reference to Mille Lacs Lake, the former homeland. The name itself had meaning in that the Mdewakanton people constantly asked their spirits and *Wakan* men, or medicine men, for guidance and success in war, in hunting, and even daily life.

This land offered many challenges for *Wakan* men who predicted the future. Hot summers might wilt small corn crops, tended by Dakota women, and cold, formidable winters froze hunters who failed to make it back to camp. Sometimes the weather even moved animal herds to new locations farther from Dakota camps and villages. Hunters accordingly needed and often asked for blessings from the *Wakan* men. Yet Minnesota was a beautiful land with pristine water courses, ideal for the bark canoes that allowed considerable travel, and forested regions with pines and hardwoods, found especially in the so-called "Big Woods," that provided easy access to firewood. This region, nearly fifty miles wide and a hundred miles from north to south, occupied much of the land between the upper Minnesota and Mississippi Rivers and extended south of the Minnesota River into the Blue Earth River valley. Southwest of the Minnesota River, patches of forest gave way to small prairies and lakes that occasionally attracted buffalo herds and provided ample fish and muskrats. Game abounded especially in these so-called "no-man's land"—hunting grounds contested with the Anishinaabes, or, as the Europeans called them, the Ojibwe or Chippewa Indians, to the north and the Mesquakie, who inhabited the upper Des Moines River valley to the south.

To offset these opponents, the Mdwakanton people established three centers of political power. The first, and most prestigious in colonial times—but in a state of decline by the 1840s—fell under the various succes-sive chiefs called Wabasha (Wapaśa in the Dakota language). This village, far down the Mississippi River near present Winona, Minnesota, had early contact with Europeans and obtained weapons of war. In 1837, the band fell under the leadership of Wabasha III, a civil chief, though passive in nature, who was a capable leader. His survival from smallpox left his face heavily scarred, which may have had much to do with his quiet demeanor. He spoke little in council, but most of his people respected his wisdom. His counsel increasingly led to a growing belief that cooperation and accom-modation with the ever-advancing white man, who had built Fort Snelling (the fort's early name was Fort St. Anthony) near St. Paul in 1819, would be the only reasonable position for the Dakota people as a whole to take.

Little Crow also generally preached accommodation with the advanc-ing white man, but to some degree his occasional opposition came from a need to counter the activities of another aspiring Dakota leader who lived to the west along the lower Minnesota River. Shakopee (in Dakota, Śakpe), or simply Six, as whites called him, had visions of being a great leader. Shakopee was impatient, obstinate at times, rebellious, and not accepting of the American presence. Perhaps worse, many in his band had similar views, making his village one of the most militant, nationalistic collections of Dakota people in the region, at times having minor skirmishes with the troops at Fort Snelling.[8]

Rather unexpectedly, Shakopee died in 1860, leaving his band to his son, dubbed Little Six by Americans (called Śakpedaŋ by his people). Somewhat taller than his father but slight in stature, he was boastful in demeanor and often abrupt and undependable. He had a boyish manner that sometimes fooled men who had dealings with him. As one observer thought, he looked like a "scowling ruffian, whose actions in no ways belied his looks."[9] Little Six seemed a perfect fit for the rebellious people who lived in his band—overly protective of resources, prone to outbursts, defiant at times, and generally suspicious of all Americans.

Given bilinear marriage rules, young men could join whatever band they happened to be associated with or married into. During the 1840s, Shakopee's band often became the destination of young men who wished to continue the tradition of war, especially with the Anishinaabe or the Mesquakie, acts that gave young men prestige but were destabilizing conflicts that the federal officers at Fort Snelling tried to prevent. Some men from smaller Mdewakanton villages, including those under Black

Dog, Penetion, and Wakute at times seemed sympathetic with Shakopee's young men; at other times, they listened to Little Crow.[10] But Shakopee's community came to house four to five hundred people during this period. It would eventually divide into two different villages. Some followers of Shakopee stayed with his son, Little Six, while others joined Shakopee's brother, Red Middle Voice (Hocokayaduta in Dakota), an even more determined nationalist.[11]

The Mdewakantons had close relatives in the west along the upper Minnesota River and the Blue Earth River and near Big Stone Lake and Lake Traverse. These Sisseton and Wahpeton people more closely resembled Plains Indians, who mostly hunted buffalo west of those lakes, the meat of which dominated their diet. They moved at will between the lakes and the Missouri River and had little contact with the American military and government Indian agents. Most of these bands had positive reciprocal relationships with the dominant Indian trader Joseph Renville, who had establishments at both Lac qui Parle and Lake Traverse. Yet Renville's trade houses had palisades around them for protection, as Sissetons and Wahpetons, somewhat like Shakopee's people, could demand more of traders than they were willing to give.

In the late fall of 1824, New Yorker Philander Prescott, who worked at the time with Renville under the newly formed Columbia Fur Company, took a small brigade of French and Indian voyagers into the northern reaches of the Big Woods in search of Sisseton hunters. He soon heard shots and suddenly came face to face with a hundred "wild Sisseton and Wahpeton Indians," led by the Dakota war chief Limping Devil (Itewakiŋyaŋ in Dakota). He earned the Anglo nickname from taking a wound in the knee, received in hand-to-hand combat with his Sac and Fox foes.[12]

The novice Prescott, unknown to the Sisseton Indians, feared for his life and those of his companions. Fortunately for the traders, Limping Devil soon placated the younger warriors, who considered killing the party. The chief then brought the fur traders into his camp, where they feasted on venison and exchanged goods for animal hides. Traders often got caught up in native feuds, which explains the initial reaction of the Sisseton hunters. They assumed that Prescott was trading with their enemies, the Anishinaabe bands to the north of them. Many men, traders and Indians, paid the ultimate price when caught up in these wars.[13] Such murders had happened in the past, and to prevent them, traders took Indian wives, thus becoming part of a native kin group. Family ties offered protection, as traders who had married women in other villages or camps could expect to find some of his wife's relatives in other camps or villages, who would take care of them. Prescott had married a woman from Black Dog's village, and he quickly used that relationship to soothe the Sissetons who came upon him.

The seven Mdewakanton villages were politically autonomous, and so were the dozen or more Sisseton and Wahpeton camps. Chiefs, such as Limping Devil, also had only minor authority. Despite his exploits in war, Limping Devil happened to be a hereditary civil chief, which may have given him more influence. Normally, civil chiefs, such as Little Crow and Wabasha, gained influence in a village as a counselor and adviser, introducing reason to any debate; this often controlled the passions of young warriors, because civil chiefs formed consensus while speaking with the leading men in council, as warriors looked on from the outside. But occasionally, this process broke down, especially when vengeance was necessary. Warfare on neighboring tribes, such as the Sac and Fox or even more so with the Anishinaabe, was then conducted by men who had experience in raising village war parties, rather than the civil chiefs. Such men, "head soldiers," as they were called, were also crucial in forming a soldiers' lodge. This institution was used almost exclusively in early years to control the hunt, preventing young men from scaring the game.[14] Its members were called *akacita* soldiers or warriors.

Lake Traverse, home to Limping Devil's people, often became a temporary home to much larger Sisseton bands, including those connected to Standing Buffalo (called Tataŋkanaźiŋ by his people) and the part Sisseton, part Yanktonai camp of the Charger (Waanata in Dakota). Yanktonais Dakotas had intermarried with the Sissetons and often hunted and fought alongside them. In the spring, after the winter hunt, these Plains Sissetons would return briefly to villages generally located at the two lakes, Big Stone and Traverse, or along the upper Minnesota River, where they would celebrate and perform the Sun Dance and other ceremonies often associated with vision quests, survival, and rebirth.[15]

Plains Sissetons also often visited the smaller Sisseton and Wahpeton villages—the towns and people whom Little Crow had married into—on the upper Minnesota River, south of the lakes. When this happened, villages such as those under Sleepy Eyes (Iśtaĥba to his people), Red Iron (Mazaduta to his people), and Walking Runner (Iŋyaŋgmani to his people)—Little Crow's father-in-law—were suddenly inundated with thousands of people, setting up hide tepees. Indeed, the interaction between the Plains Sissetons of Standing Buffalo's and the Charger's highly mobile camps and the more permanent village-oriented Sissetons near the Minnesota River often led to massive celebrations where dancing and courting went hand in hand.[16] Sometimes, Mdewakantons joined in these events, creating kinship bonds that led to obligations, even marriages, and, on occasion, joint hunting and raiding ventures.

While factionalism existed that revealed considerable differences, and occasional family feuds, between Shakopee's band and that of Wabasha and between Sisseton leaders such as Walking Runner and Standing Buffalo, kinship relationships did much generally to promote unity among these various groups. Every person in a Dakota camp or village had a kin name that identified him or her, the term often placing them as someone's brother, cousin, aunt, uncle, grandfather, or grandmother.[17] While this seldom, indeed almost never, led to large, united military campaigns, a common culture and language and integrated blood relationships made it possible for a Dakota man to travel from the Mississippi River to the Dakota plains and find relatives who would feed him along the way. It also allowed him to ask for help when far from the home fires.

Dakota Indians pursued warfare for a variety of reasons—to protect hunting grounds, to seek revenge for the loss of a loved one, and even to acquire individual status. Successful warriors acquired wives more easily and going to war led to acceptance in various important male societies. Some Dakota men might possess over a dozen eagle feathers in a headdress, signifying that they had counted "coup" that many times on enemies. Coup could mean killing an individual, but a second, third, and even fourth coup was allowed if, in a daring fashion, the young man dashed in to strike the fallen enemy with a coup stick. Little Crow had a headdress with seventeen feathers, hardly the symbols of a man who would shrink from war. Most no doubt came from his early years while living with the Wahpekute. After becoming "civil" chief of his village and entering middle age, he mostly retired his war club. Civil chiefs gained notoriety by speaking in council to the elders of the community.

Typically, an experienced *Wicaśta Wakan*, or medicine man, organized a war party at the village level. He controlled the cleansing ceremonies that were necessary for success, which usually included a dream or vision in which the warriors who conducted the raid would bring back scalps, the symbols of triumph. The *Wicaśta Wakan* would blacken his face, invite young men to join him, and then undertake several weeks of sacrificial ceremonies. Decorated skins were used symbolically in dances to show young men what it meant to be brave and successful.[18] Normally, a dozen or so young men joined after the *Wicaśta Wakan* selected a head soldier,or head *akacita*, to lead the group.

They departed the village with sufficient food for several weeks—guns could not be fired to acquire meat when in Anishinaabe or Mesquakie country. Great honor came from killing the enemy with a hatchet at close range. Two experienced scouts had the most dangerous job; as pathfind-ers, they led the way and sought out the enemy's village. While a small cluster of huts might become a target, where a number of men, women, and children could be killed, the usual format was to hide along trails lead-ing into the village and wait for one or two unsuspecting men and waylay them. The goal was to be successful without losing any men.[19]

When scalping a victim, successful Dakota men generally took the en-tire skin of the head, down to the nose and cheeks.[20] Warriors from all three contesting groups killed men, women, and children at will, taking scalps. Yet there were no absolute rules, and on occasion, women and children might be spared and carried off as captives. Some younger women might become wives and grow up in a Dakota village. But upon being brought into a village, their fate might be precarious, depending upon the mood. At best, captives might replace a departed young son or daughter or even a wife. If that happened, they were immediately accorded protection.

The prestige that came with wearing an eagle feather was enormous. It allowed a young man to join veterans of warfare in the War Dance. A few descriptions of this event have been recorded; one of the best came from artist Frank B. Mayer, who noted in his diary in 1851 that "none were ad-mitted but those who had taken scalps." This was very likely an exaggera-tion as warriors taking coup generally qualified. During the dance each brave would step into the middle of the circle and tell of his most daring exploits in battle. Mayer stressed that this was the only time when Indian men "were permitted to 'bragg,' & vaunt their own courage."[21]

While the War Dance might be performed before a party organized for a raid, the Scalp Dance got underway when warriors returned success-fully from such a raid. During the dance, women participated—indeed, they often controlled the dance by stretching the scalp on a hoop. A senior woman from the village would then grab the trophy and other women in the camp would form a ring around her. When the men joined, they formed a line and women opened up their circle to accommodate them. It was an exciting time. If the scalp was taken during the height of summer, the dance would resume nearly every night for a month.[22]

While the revenge motive often dominated war parties, there were rules of engagement. It was expected that an enemy would mutilate victims, even children. Gouging out eyes and tearing the heart from the body were common occurrences. Bodies left broken could not walk or see where they needed to go when they reached the afterlife; they were useless thereafter in any warfare that might occur there. When a Dakota party lost one of its own members, the dead man was propped up against a tree, decorated with trinkets and offerings of food, and left. Prescott witnessed an Anishinaabe party come upon a dead Dakota warrior. They fired a volley into his body and "charged upon the dead carcass, and scalped it and cut it to pieces and done many disgraceful acts to the dead body." Obviously, the dead man's spirit had already departed, and he had been prepared for the long voyage to the afterlife, explaining the laying on of the trinkets and food. At the same time, the departing Dakota warriors believed that the Anishinaabe warriors should not be deprived of the trophy they had earned, leaving the body in open sight.[23]

The government tried to prevent conflict by occasionally putting those who perpetrated raids in prison at Fort Snelling. Colonel Josiah Snelling even forced Shakopee's Mdewakantons to give up four young men in 1827 who, after peacefully discussing issues with the Anishinaabe just outside the fort, wheeled and fired into the delegation, killing two and wounding many more. Anishinaabe chief Strong Earth protested: "Father, *look at your floor,* it is stained with the blood of my people, shed under your walls." Snelling then threatened Shakopee, whose men had committed the crime, with troops and promised to have traders removed from his village. The chief grudgingly turned over four men, and the colonel gave the perpetrators to the Anishinaabe who, to the horror of the Dakota watchers nearby, executed them on the spot.[24] Shakopee's village elders never forgot the incident, which remained implanted on their minds and helped lead to war thirty-five years later.

Intertribal conflict continued into the 1830s, especially over the resources of the Crow Wing River valley in the Big Woods. An escalation occurred when trader Joseph Renville's brother, Victor, was killed. In the raids and counterraids that followed, nearly a hundred Indians died.[25] While revenge was a factor, the upsurge in fighting was related to the increased pressure on deer herds, which constituted the major food source for the easternmost Dakota people. One observer believed that Shakopee's village might kill two thousand deer in one year, the meat being consumed and the hides given to traders.[26] Such numbers declined during the 1830s and at times the Dakota people survived on just muskrats or fish or the small crops of corn, usually consumed green, that they grew along the banks of rivers.[27]

As the food supply became more precarious, the Dakota villagers placed increasing faith in their *Wicaśta Wakans,* who advised the hunters on where they would find deer. They often organized an *akacita* to be more successful in the hunt, selecting a head soldier to run it. These lodges often had been used by Plains Indians to hunt buffalo, as many men were needed to corral the animals in a "surround" so they could be killed. The organized hunt became necessary to an even greater extent with deer east of the Minnesota River, as the animals declined in number. Lines of hunters were often sent a hundred yards back from a river while a canoe was used to splash water and drive the deer off the bank and into the stationed hunters. Rules existed, laid down by the *akacita*'s head soldier. If any hunter fired early and spooked the deer, he suffered a "soldiers' kill," meaning his gun was broken and his tepee was cut to shreds.[28] For the Mdewakantons, this resulted in a gradual shift in power from the civil chiefs, like Little Crow, to the head soldiers in every village.

The best description of a soldiers' lodge and the *akacita* soldiers who formed it resulted from Joseph Nicollet's visit with Joseph Renville at Lac qui Parle in 1838. Renville, a Franco/Dakota person who spoke French and Dakota fluently, sensing the failures of deer hunts in the Big Woods, organized a lodge, with the help of his many Dakota relatives. Most members belonged to the Tokadaŋti, or Kit Fox Society. While its main purpose was to organize deer and buffalo hunts, the thirty members in the lodge also policed illicit traders who used whiskey to take furs away from Renville. The lodge could also undertake military missions, such as those in 1832–1833, when serious warfare with the Anishinaabe broke out.[29]

When the hunters had a good day, various lodges or families sent messengers to invite individuals to a *wakan,* or sacred feast. The feast was only for invited men—mostly successful hunters—who would bring their own dishes, sit in a circle inside the tepee, and be given portions of food. Usually, the portions were large, more than a single person could eat. If the invited guest failed to consume the food, he had to leave a gift, such as leggings, moccasins, or even a shirt.[30] The feasts reinforced kinship ties, with gift giving demonstrating the commitment of relatives to take care of each other. But they also bypassed the traders to some degree, who had nurtured relationships with civil chiefs. Nevertheless, the practice did reinforce the basic idea that to the Dakota people, generosity, rather than profit from trade, was an important virtue. When Little Crow was asked about his headdress of seventeen feathers, he responded by giving it to the person who made the inquiry. To deny anything to a person was literally a sin, and when traders did so, they were viewed as being evil people.[31]

While the Indian traders failed to challenge these rules of generosity, at least initially, the introduction of more Americans, especially missionaries, in the years to come and the decline in animals led to cultural clashes of momentous proportion. Articulation, as it is often called, led to placing prices on goods and the emergence of a market economy, which defied the rules of reciprocity that had always governed Dakota life. The conflict often had religious overtones, especially after Protestant missionaries appeared. It usually involved the most prestigious organization observed in a Dakota village, the Medicine Society. The elders who controlled the society invited members to join annually, and after being instructed on the secrets of the society, then held a large feast to honor new inductees.

While white observers never recorded much regarding the secrets in the nineteenth century, they likely included the description of the afterlife left by Elizabeth Wiŋyaŋ—that the dead must have tattoos and be painted with red ochre, all over the head, to reach the afterlife. More importantly, the society challenged the growing elements of trader capitalism that came with American invasion. Besides orchestrating the life-death cycle, the ceremony and its secrets emphasized the communal nature of Dakota society, that all Dakota men and women must practice feasting and sharing at all times.[32]

These lessons were given to the *Wicaśta Wakans* by *Unktehi* (also *Ukteri*), seemingly a mammoth-like creature who had been sent by the Great Mystery to create the earth and the Dakota people. During this creation the Dakota people believed that the Great Mystery had brought into this new land not only their own people but all animate and inanimate beings, such as rocks, birds, beaver, deer, and snakes. Given this understanding of life—the supposition that powers vested in individuals by *Unktehi* through the Medicine Society were duplicated in animals and rocks—it was easy to understand that such power was transferred to nonhuman objects. Birds, for example, caused thunder, and rocks could and did move. To preserve them for the afterlife, Dakotas often painted rocks with red ochre, a color that led to admission into the afterlife. Commonly, sacrifices of small objects—e.g., cloth, knives, hatchets—were left on such rocks.[33]

Most importantly, at induction the new members of the Medicine Society were given a "medicine sack" that held the magic ornaments that gave the inductee power, wisdom, success in the hunt and at war, and protection. These fetishes were gifts from the *Wicaśta Wakans,* who gave instructions on how to conduct the Medicine Dance. The dances occurred on special occasions. After eating at the feast, the dance began, as the members went back and forth within the confines of a brush enclosure. They held their sacred medicine bags in front of them, and when a *Wicaśta Wakan* touched them on the breast, they shrieked and fell to the ground, lifeless. But the sack and its contents saved them, serving as a symbol of the power that the ceremony had over life and death. After several minutes, the "slain" member recovered, and the medicine man supposedly extracted the shell or bean that had killed him. In many ways, the dance and its antics were a promise regarding the afterlife and its certainty. The most important part of the instructions, however, involved the need to provide feasts to feed the people, regardless of any inconvenience that an individual family might experience.[34]

The Medicine Society represented the "soul" of the Dakota people. The sacks became the most important material item that men and women possessed. The ceremony itself helped alleviate the stress and anxiety that came with life, where at any time the Anishinaabe or the Mesquakie might suddenly appear and kill members of the society, or the fact that a member might be killed in battle while on a raid. Like with rocks, raiders accordingly painted their heads red, and the Medicine Dance symbolized the resurrection. As tensions built in the 1850s, the Dakota people turned more and more to the dance. The fetish medicine bag became the one material connection that reaffirmed that resurrection.

The Dakota, then, were people with a strong religion, beliefs that had sustained them in the past, a strong sense of identity, and an economy that was, while not collapsing, increasingly unable to feed large numbers of people. This was especially true for the Mdewakantons who lived farthest east. Their belief system rested in the hands of *Wicaśta Wakans* who continued the dances and rituals that everyone hoped would sustain them. While Indian agents and army officers, and especially Indian traders, had maintained contact with the four Dakota bands for many years, they had accomplished little in the way of changing the Indians' view of life, death, support of relatives, or the sharing of life's necessities. But the twenty years following the arrival of missionaries, or the period after 1835, would bring momentous change and challenges of the sort that no Dakota warrior or hunter could ever perceive.

In his journal, Philander Prescott often wrote about what Dakota men assumed regarding their relationship with the outside world, especially with its economic challenges. Traders, many Dakota men thought, always seemed to have access to plenty of goods, and Dakota Indians believed that they should be liberal with them, much as the teachings of *Unktehi* demanded. Traders like Prescott occasionally asked Indian chiefs and hunters whether they would ever get paid for presents given out in the fall with marketable furs harvested in the spring. Prescott's description of the exchange is typical: "Time does diminish, in their view, the obligation to pay a debt, because they say the white people can get goods by merely going after them, or writing for them, and that when a trader obtains a new supply of goods, he is not in want of the debts due him, and that the Indian is in greater need of the amount than the trader is."[35] How the Dakota people would come to see this changing world that Prescott tried to get them to understand was mostly in the hands of five men—Little Crow, Wabasha, Shakopee and his son Little Six, and Little Six's uncle, Red Middle Voice. The counsel of these men held sway over the Mdewakanton people. But did they have answers when dealing with this powerful new force, the Americans? For Wabasha and even, to some degree, Little Crow, the only reasonable answer seemed to be diplomacy. And that meant speaking, arguing, and representing the Dakota people, their growing economic concerns, and their needs as civil chiefs.

Understandably, others might find diplomacy to be the path to destruction. The emerging restlessness often found among the young men who joined the soldiers' lodges, or those few who sat in the lodges as head soldiers, led to such groups more frequently inserting themselves into councils and meetings, rather than sitting on the periphery. Many such meetings, where young men spoke, were held in Shakopee's village, later to be taken over by his son, Little Six. They had no idea of the changes that were coming—of a new territorial organization sanctioned by the American Congress, called the Territory of Minnesota. Created in 1849, it would soon pressure the Dakota nation for land and resources that it was reluctant to relinquish.

TWO

THE AMERICAN INVASION

Congress passed legislation creating the Minnesota Territory in early March 1849. The act foreordained rapid change for the Dakota community; how would they get along with their new neighbors, who had visions of making Minnesota an American state, even though the name derived from a Dakota term that meant "sky tinted" water? It fell to newly elected Whig president Zachary Taylor to select the first territorial governor. He chose Alexander Ramsey, a Pennsylvania politician of Scotch and German heritage who had served two terms in Congress. Ramsey had talents as a compromiser and as someone who had a classical education, reading and writing German with ease. And he had a pragmatic view of politics, as was commonly the case with Whigs, conservatives mostly who were out of office more than in.

Ramsey arrived at his new post in May 1849. The territory had no capital and virtually no non-Indian population. However, there were fifteen hundred Franco- and Anglo-Dakota people and ten thousand Indians. Fortunately for him, the always frugal federal government made Ramsey both Territorial Governor and Superintendent of Indian Affairs. Such a position gave him authority to buy land from Indians and thus promote white settlement.[1] In appearance, Ramsey had a broad face, a pleasant disposition, and an openness that was suggestive of a brand of politics that equated building political consensus with a friendly handshake. And he was ambitious, both in a political and pecuniary sense. He soon discovered, however, that no housing existed for his family, and he readily accepted an invitation from the most powerful man in the new territory, Henry Sibley, chief factor of the American Fur Company, who likely had the only respectable beds. While politically opposite—Sibley came from a Democratic family—the two men became friends, agreeing to promote Minnesota.

Amazingly, these two Minnesota politicians seldom fought over patronage. Nevertheless, Sibley's Democratic friends seemed destined to control the territory, at least in 1849. The West was still basking in the glory of the powerful Andrew Jackson democracy—Illinois, Wisconsin, Iowa, and even California all had strong Democratic machines. By the mid-1850s, however, the new Republican Party would gain ground and Ramsey joined it. It attracted the burgeoning numbers of Scandinavian and German settlers for its stand on "free labor and free soil." With national politics somewhat in turmoil, Ramsey joined Sibley at his Mendota home and plotted to wrest the homeland of the Dakota people from them and bring those "free soilers" into the region.

To begin, they had little to work with. With the founding of Fort Snelling in 1819, the first American soldiers arrived in the region.[2] The government also sent in an Indian agent. President James Monroe selected fellow Virginian Lawrence Taliaferro in 1820. Taliaferro had high moral standards, and given his attention to duty, he kept his job for nearly twenty years.[3] A somewhat taciturn man, Taliaferro often retreated to his journals to launch complaints. He generally railed against Indian traders who dealt with the Dakota and Anishinaabe people. The men who dominated the American fur business prior to Sibley's arrival in 1834 included Joseph Rolette, Alexis Bailly, and Joseph Renville and their clerks, Jean Baptiste Faribault, Louis Provençalle, Joseph LaFramboise, and, later, Joseph R. Brown. It had become custom to give some spirits to the Indians in these early years, to encourage them to hunt or give up cured furs, and all of the above men did so even though it was illegal.

The early traders took native wives, resulting in Franco- and Anglo-Dakota families that came to play an increasingly important role, being people "in between," as they are often described.[4] Nevertheless, Taliaferro brought charges against some traders for providing liquor to Indians, but John Jacob Astor, owner of the American Fur Company, used his substantial political influence to keep Taliaferro at bay.[5] Finally, in 1834 Taliaferro's charges and the constant legal battles convinced Astor to sell out. Hercules Dousman, Pierre Chouteau Jr., and Ramsey Crooks soon joined the newly arrived Henry Sibley in taking over the trade. Sibley kept some of the traders, but he removed the most offending ones, pleasing Taliaferro.

Sibley brought economic austerity to the fur trade, limiting gift giving. Even so, he was well liked by the Dakota Indians for he also spent time in Indian camps, becoming closely associated with both Little Crow's father's band and that of Wakute. At the latter village he met the amazing Anglo-Dakota mixed-blood Jack Frazier. On a number of hunting trips, Frazier joined Sibley and the then-young Little Crow chasing down elk in southwestern Minnesota. Sibley was amazed at the stamina of his two partners, especially Little Crow.[6] And Sibley's suppression of the whiskey trade only strengthened his hand with the cantankerous Taliaferro.[7] This new rapport likely stemmed from the belief that both men were "gentlemen" in an age where appearance often identified such people. Portraits show both men posing with heads upright and shoulders back. Taliaferro is portrayed in a soldier's uniform that revealed the honorary rank of major, which agents generally were allowed to claim.[8]

Both Sibley and Taliaferro realized that the Dakota people were suffering, given the decline in the fur trade. Taliaferro wrote often of transforming the Dakotas near the fort into farmers; he even at times used some government money to hire newly arriving missionaries and former traders to break land with plows. They included the now-middle-aged Philander Prescott, who had been retired from the fur trade.[9] Prescott opened the first farm land with a plow in Minnesota in the 1830s—the Dakota people had used the planting stick to seed in the past. Given President Andrew Jackson's policy of Indian removal, which produced treaties with funds attached to support farming programs, Taliaferro suggested in repeated letters to the commissioner of Indian affairs that the Dakota might sell their claim in western Wisconsin and obtain the funds necessary to expand his modest farm program.[10]

Getting approval, Taliaferro left the agency for Washington, D.C., with twenty-one Mdewakanton tribal leaders in late August 1837, among them Little Crow's father, Little Crow II. In council, Secretary of War Joel Poinsett offered one million dollars for the Wisconsin claim, the interest of which would provide annuities for yearly distributions of food and agricultural equipment.[11] After Sibley and other traders protested, Poinsett also agreed to allot $90,000 for the payment of Indian debt, a precedent that led to further abuse later on. Even the Mdewakanton mixed-bloods—who supposedly numbered 143 families—received a one-time payment of $110,000. Despite these excesses, the treaty was a godsend to the

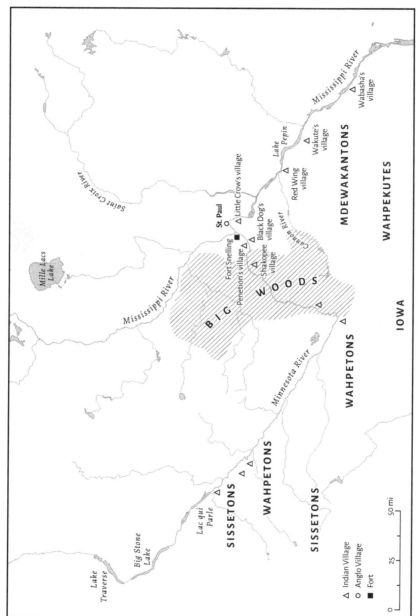

MINNESOTA IN THE 1830s. Cartography by Erin Greb.

Mdewakanton people—and promptly produced jealousies among the other Dakota bands, the Sisseton, Wahpeton, and Wahpekute. It provided yearly subsidies of food, clothing, and guns. Some 328 barrels of pork and flour (worth $5,000) arrived at Shakopee's village alone in 1838. The agreement immediately transformed Mdewakanton villages, sending populations from a mere fourteen hundred people in 1837 to roughly twenty-five hundred by the time Ramsey arrived in 1849. Many relatives who had fled west—like Little Crow—to hunt and live in Sisseton villages had returned to their Mdewakanton roots.[12]

Besides traders, another group of interested people soon took notice of the 1837 Dakota treaty. A product of the Second Great Awakening, Presbyterian missionaries Gideon and Samuel Pond and Thomas S. Williamson appeared in Minnesota in 1834 and 1835. They learned quickly that the treaty had a fund of $5,000 a year for education. Such men were filled with an enormous anxiety; they feared that Indians would become extinct before they had a chance to receive Christ's promise of heaven. The Ponds settled near Fort Snelling, doing some farming for Agent Taliaferro. Williamson, however, moved his family west to Lac qui Parle, just south of Lake Traverse, where trader Joseph Renville had a large fort. Two years later, the missionary family of Stephen Return Riggs joined the Williamsons, creating a small religious community.

Being Presbyterians, these missionaries believed strongly in simple rules—the Sabbath must be respected; dancing, a favorite Dakota religious and social activity, was considered frivolous; drinking alcohol was an absolute sin; and polygamy, of the sort young Little Crow would soon engage in, was completely unacceptable. Williamson, a tall, lanky, friendly man, seemed tolerant of some of these sins. He had little choice in the matter, given the preponderance of Indians near his Lac qui Parle mission. Riggs remained much more rigid. An Ichabod Crane sort, even his wife, Mary, reluctantly accepted his offer of marriage. She noted in an early letter to her sister that he was truly an ugly man. But she married him anyway and spent most of her adult life on the frontier. Her husband, Stephen, with a long neck, narrow face, and sloping shoulders, left letter after letter decrying the fact that he found it difficult to preach "Christ Crucified" to Indians in the Dakota language.[13] Riggs had Crane's high sense of discrimination as well, especially when it came to judging the religiosity of Indian converts, but he fell short when it came to understanding, or appreciating, human practices that differed from his own beliefs.

Progress came slow in terms of religious conversion. Indian trader Renville and his wife were admitted to the church in the late 1830s, and a number of their children were baptized, but over the next decade, the numbers attending Sunday services seldom reached twenty, and only a few of them were full-blood Indians.[14] After ten years of devoted work, Riggs summed up the efforts of the entire Dakota mission in a long report to the American Board of Commissioners for Foreign Missions, in Boston, which supported them. He noted that "at their feasts," religion "has been a subject of discussion. There are many opposed [to Christianity]." The two leading chiefs near the mission, Walking Runner (Iŋyaŋgmani) and Red Iron (Mazaduta), seemed indifferent, even though Walking Runner's son had converted. Those who opposed the missionaries often organized their "sacred feasts" on Sunday, mostly to aggravate the preaching at the church. Yet Riggs remained steadfast, believing that there was "another class still who seem to be thoroughly convinced of the falsity and deceptive charter of their own system of religion." Thus, he held out some hope even though this class of men were "persecuted as though they were Christians and threatened with being killed by witchcraft" by the opponents of the faith.[15]

While the missionaries fussed and debated, trader Henry Rice platted out town lots on the north loop of the Mississippi River in 1850. The town, located on a bluff on the left bank of the river and named St. Paul, became Ramsey's territorial capital. Within a year, it had the largest hotel north of St. Louis, the American House, and it soon boasted dry goods stores and a growing population; even so, there was no land available for settlement west of the Mississippi River.[16] Ramsey soon went to work on the land cession that he knew must occur for the territory to prosper. Congress, however, had passed a rather problematic law that stood in his way—at least the fur traders thought it a problem. It forbade clauses in future treaties that set aside money to pay for Indian debts.[17] Without the support of the traders and their mixed-blood allies, a treaty was nearly impossible to get the Indians to sign.

Another problem was the cost. Up to this point, the government had paid anywhere from half a cent to five cents an acre for lands that it wanted from Indians. While Commissioner of Indian Affairs Orlando Brown authorized Ramsey to negotiate in August 1849, he suggested a price of just two to two and one-half cents an acre for the land. Sibley and the traders said no to this—they were concerned that little money would be available for debts. Ramsey's attempts to bring Indian delegations to St. Paul in 1849 turned out to be a dismal failure.[18] Yet the governor had allies in the missionaries. Riggs thought a treaty would free up money for education, and he believed that Sisseton and Wahpeton leaders would sign an agreement. Hunting had become difficult and annuities of the sort the Mdewakantons received seemed the only answer to combat looming starvation. In informing Sibley and Ramsey of the views of these western Dakota leaders, Riggs also urged them to negotiate with the upper Indians first, and then approach the Mdewakantons, who everyone understood would likely refuse to sell their lands. They received annuities and were relative well off.[19]

After Ramsey's initial failure, the governor listened more attentively to his friend Sibley. He urged Ramsey to get the price paid for land up to ten cents an acre and told him that he would have to find a way to pay debts. Lobbying also helped, as petitions from traders sent east noted the many half-starved Indians who wandered into Lac qui Parle. There were "no buffalo" on the plains west of the river, and many bands were eating their "horses, dogs, and even Buffalo skins." Some hungry Sissetons west of Lac qui Parle dug up dead horses during the winter and consumed them.[20] While these descriptions were often exaggerations, Sibley's efforts to enlist traders such as the Renvilles, Provençalles, Faribaults, and LaFramboises, as well as their many Franco- and Anglo-Dakota relatives, began to pay off.[21] Ramsey would have to placate them to get a treaty, and a land purchase would solve the growing problem of feeding the Dakota people.

While Sibley, serving as the delegate to Congress from the territory, directed lobbying efforts there, his younger brother, Fred, issued orders to the cadre of traders and mixed-bloods who pressured various Indian leaders regarding the need to sell their land. Sibley then lifted the ban on giving credits to Indians who had been unproductive hunters, encouraging the men who still worked for him to reinforce kinship ties as best as possible. Sibley's associate, Canadian trader Martin McLeod, also worked closely with the Renvilles, especially Gabriel, Joseph Renville's nephew, to make sure that Sisseton leaders, the most important of whom were buffalo hunters in the West, knew the benefits of a treaty.[22]

Even so, the lobbying of traders seemed to have little impact on Little Crow and Wabasha. Thus, Sibley agreed with Riggs and McLeod, encouraging Ramsey to council first with the upper Indians, the Sissetons and Wahpetons, who wanted annuities and were more clearly influenced by traders and mixed-blood relatives.[23] With strong consensus among the pro-treaty group on how to handle the negotiation, Ramsey and Co-commissioner Luke Lea finally led a delegation of officials, traders and mixed-bloods, and many casual observers aboard the steamer *Excelsior* on July 1, 1851, and headed up the Minnesota River to Traverse des Sioux. McLeod, Gabriel Renville, and Joseph R. Brown, now a newspaper editor, recruited the Sisseton and Wahpeton chiefs, who lived on the upper Minnesota River, bringing them down the river to the council grounds. But all the careful preparation almost exploded when several chiefs asked for a delay, as all the band leaders were not there yet, including the important Sissetons Standing Buffalo (known to Dakotas as Tataŋkanaźan) and Sweet Corn (or Wamnahezaskuya). Then while talking in council, the often-recalcitrant Sleepy Eyes (Iśtaȟba to his Dakota friends) abruptly got up and left, which led to an outcry from a group of young men who had been waiting patiently to start a ball game, called in Dakota *takapsićapi,* similar to lacrosse. The game constituted a melee with sticks and a ball that needed to be advanced, with no limitations on the numbers of young men involved, only that the two sides needed to be roughly equal.[24]

Besides the young men, there were other distractions that tormented Ramsey, who assumed that perhaps the Indians would no longer negotiate. Newspaper reporters had come along, a concern given the fact that Ramsey had to find some way to incorporate a payoff for the traders, which was seemingly illegal. As well, Frank Blackwell Mayer, the relatively well-known artist from Baltimore, tagged along. Born into wealth, Mayer simply wanted to see the "wild west" and the treaty offered an opportunity. On his trip up the Mississippi, he also heard about this man of note, Little Crow, and as luck would have it, he convinced Captain Seth Eastman, at Fort Snelling, also a noted artist, to introduce him to the chief. Mayer took an immediate liking to Little Crow, who the artist described as being "very determined and ambitious" but with an "exceedingly gentile and dignified deportment." Mayer convinced Little Crow to sit for a portrait on July 2, 1851, as the traders and politicians tried desperately to get Sisseton and Wahpeton leaders back to the business at hand.[25]

While Ramsey failed to understand the departure of the chiefs, the traders quickly explained to the governor that the setback was temporary, a product of the excitement generated by the lacrosse game. Sisseton and Wahpeton chiefs did return and quickly signed the agreement offered. It was even read to them in Dakota, being translated by Riggs. All the "signatures," some forty in all, were made with a mark, often called "touching the pen." They included leading chiefs such as Sleepy Eyes, Good Boy (better known as Hakewaśte), Limping Devil, Extended Tail Feathers (Upiyahdayeya in Dakota), the Orphan (Wamdenica), and Little Crow's father-in-law, Walking Runner. Yet a number of very important chiefs were not there, including Standing Buffalo, the Charger (Waanata in Dakota), and Sweet Corn, men who preferred buffalo hunting to government rations. No one suggested that they needed to be present. Even Little Crow remained silent and said nothing.[26]

The delegation of Wahpeton men who signed was more representative of the tribe as a whole, most of them living along the Minnesota River from Traverse des Sioux southward to the Cottonwood River. Those who readily "touched the pen" included Cloud Man (or Maĥpiyawicaśta), Red Iron, and Walking Iron (or Mazamani to his Dakota friends). In addition, Riggs brought along a number of Christian Indians who signed the document, including Paul Mazakutemani, Simon Anawaŋgmani, and Peter Big Fire (Tapetataŋka; Walking Runner's son). These three men wrote their own names. For $1,665,000, or roughly six cents an acre—the actual figure is difficult to determine, giving the lack of discussion regarding boundaries—the Sisseton and Wahpeton leaders gave up claims to lands within southwestern Minnesota eastward to Traverse des Sioux, as well as land in northern Iowa, all of which constituted about one-third of their homeland—the rest being in the future territory of Dakota.[27]

These efforts only involved the western Dakota bands, the Sisseton and Wahpeton people, and Sibley and Ramsey both knew that Mdewakanton chiefs would be more inclined to resist any cession of land. But Sibley had opened his trade house at Mendota, feasting Indians day and night and encouraging all their leaders to consider the benefits of a deal. Surprisingly, Shakopee seemed compliant, perhaps not fully understanding the agreement. His village was far from St. Paul, and he had less contact with whites in general. While a few other lesser chiefs also seemed willing listeners, the two most determined opponents remained Wabasha and Little Crow. Wabasha spoke openly against any agreement. It included the selling of southeastern Minnesota, and his village would have to move west. And Little Crow was playing the sort of political game that increasingly made him famous; Fred Sibley noted that he seemed "very fair" regarding an agreement when at Sibley's house but talked "badly" about it when with other Indians. Without these two men, there would be no treaty and a vast expanse of land lying east of a line running north to south through

Traverse des Sioux, all the way to the Mississippi River, would remain as Indian country. This, to Ramsey, was unacceptable.[28]

Sibley realized that the key to the treaty was obviously Little Crow, who had been a compromiser in the past. And it had been Little Crow's father, Little Crow II, who had openly agreed to the treaty in Washington in 1837, a treaty that had been a great benefit to the Mdewakantons. As the negotiations got underway, the past history of the government's largess must have had an impact on some Dakota leaders. If Little Crow, about forty years of age, joined the other more compliant chiefs, Wabasha, who seldom spoke in council and thus had little influence, would have to accept the reality of a land sale.

Meeting in a warehouse at Sibley's Mendota complex, the Mdewakanton chiefs sat down with Governor Ramsey on July 29. Offering a veiled threat, Ramsey noted that the Mdewakantons could not expect to hold land "along the [Mississippi] river" with white settlers west of them. He then offered only $800,000 for the Mdewakanton lands, half of what the western Indians had received. While most of the chiefs sat silent, smoking, it was Wabasha who finally, uncharacteristically, rose. He was not a natural speaker, but at the time, he was one with an abrupt message. He wanted to know what had happened to the $5,000 yearly education fund from the 1837 treaty, which had matured to well over $50,000 by 1851. Sibley knew that the request was coming, having borrowed some $30,000 from the St. Louis office of the American Fur Company to cover this request. While he hoped not to use it, it soon became obvious that the distribution of the money would be necessary to secure a deal. Even so, for several days thereafter, the Indians simply refused to attend the discussions that had been moved closer to the river, under an open, breezy, arbor.[29]

After what appeared to be an impasse, Little Crow finally moved out in front of the commissioners and began to speak, slowly and deliberately. Dressed immaculately in a clean white shirt with collar, a bright red neckerchief, red belt with a pure silver buckle, and a pair of beaded trousers, he first expressed humility, stating that the Mdewakanton leadership had asked him to speak, but his "mouth was tied." It was his first major address as a chief as his people looked on. It was the money, he said, the education fund. "We do not want to talk about a new treaty until it is paid . . . We will talk of nothing else but the money if it is until next spring." Obviously, the Mdewakantons had learned the value of gold coin, and they knew what they were supposed to get from the 1837 treaty. Over the next few days, behind-the-scenes negotiations occurred that involved everyone except Wabasha. One issue discussed included the size of the Indian reservation that Ramsey proposed. The Indians would be confined to a strip of land ten miles wide on either side of the upper Minnesota River, a change that frightened many Indians.[30]

Finally with the promise to pay the $30,000—even though it was less than what should have been in the fund—as soon as the chiefs signed an agreement, and with Ramsey agreeing to move the reservation boundary farther east, consensus slowly formed. But the Mdewakanton chiefs were adamant about the southeastern boundary of the reservation. They wanted it near Traverse des Sioux; Ramsey ultimately offered as a compromise Little Rock River, some thirty miles to the west. Some later evidence suggests that this was not fully understood. The governor also increased the price paid for the land, making it conform more to what the Sisseton and Wahpeton had received. With these adjustments, the Mdewakanton delegation increasingly turned to many of the chief warriors, some of whom had threatened to kill chiefs if they signed.

Finally, Red Middle Voice (Hocokayaduta in Dakota), who was Shakopee's brother, a man soon to become a stiff critic of the agreement, rose and indicated that the *akacita* warriors now found the treaty acceptable. At this point, Ramsey turned to Wabasha, who had been constantly lobbied by many mixed-blood friends and relatives, including Jack Frazer, Sibley's old friend. Somewhat worn out, Wabasha finally asked the *akacitas* who should be the first to sign. At this, Little Crow's head soldier, Medicine Bottle, stood up and pointed to his chief.[31] Turning to the crowd, Little Crow spoke out in a loud voice: "I am willing to be the first, but I am not afraid that you will kill me. If you do, it will be all right." Demonstrating his expertise with literacy, learned at Williamson's mission, the chief sat down slowly and signed in big letters *Ta-oyate-duta*. Others followed. At that, the Mdewakanton people sold their homeland for a substantial amount of money for that day and age—$1,410,000, equivalent to $42,000,000 in 2016. Within hours the $30,000 in bribe money was handed out and soon found its way to the merchants in St. Paul.[32]

At the signing of both treaties, the traders urged a number of Dakota chiefs to sign what became known as the "traders' paper," binding them to pay their past debts. Ramsey hoped to finance these payments with the more than $400,000 set aside for "subsistence and removal" in the treaty. Most treaties of that period had such articles, because many tribes east of the Mississippi River were being moved west of it. But the money was supposed to be used to buy food, rent wagons, and move Indians west. From the start, however, Ramsey had few intentions of using the massive appropriations for removal; he mostly planned to give the funds to himself, traders, and others who assisted in getting the agreements. The Traverse des Sioux treaty had $275,000 earmarked for that purpose, with $220,000 given to "the chiefs" of the Mdewakanton and Wahpekute bands to be distributed as they "shall respectively request." But virtually all the Mdewakantons, including Shakopee, Little Crow, and Wabasha, perhaps hearing that a few Sisseton and Wahpeton chiefs had protested when they heard of the document, refused to sign a traders' paper. Nevertheless, Ramsey assured Sibley that traders' debts would somehow be taken care of. A jubilant Ramsey then headed east to lobby for Senate confirmation; the two agreements would open the southern half of Minnesota to settlers.[33]

Many different views quickly emerged regarding the treaties. Most initial criticisms involved the traders' paper. When its existence became known at Traverse des Sioux, the Indian agent at the time, Nathaniel McLean, felt sure that the Sisseton and Wahpeton chiefs believed they were signing a second copy of the treaty. Perhaps more revealing, the paper never even had sums attached to it, designating the amounts to be given to each trader. Agent McLean learned that Sibley's ally, Joseph R. Brown, later attached sums, totaling some $210,000 for the upper Indians, or most of the fund set aside for removal. Two leading chiefs, Walking Runner—Little Crow's father-in-law—and Cloud Man did go to Agent McLean and say that they would gladly sign the paper in his presence, suggesting that they wished to pay their debts.[34]

The back and forth regarding the payment of debts reached such a level by Christmas that Ramsey had to have several councils with various Indian groups to explain the terms of the treaties. Martin McLeod attended one with a large contingent of Sisseton and Wahpeton chiefs, in which Ramsey spoke for several hours. He assured the Indians that the "language of the treaty" was specific, in that it said that the money for removal "was to be paid to the chiefs and braves of the tribe, in such manner as they in open council should determine." And more, the funds for removal would easily support the Indians for a full year. There would be plenty of food and funds for guns and munitions, and no "agreement or contract with traders or others" would supersede the language of the treaty. Of course, he lied. Sibley had already obtained several signatures from various mixed-blood traders to act as their power of attorney when it came to dividing up the money.[35]

The next ten months proved agonizing for the Indians, the government officials who were charged with managing them, and the traders. First, the Senate, which had received the treaties in fall 1851, failed to take them up until June of the following year. Meanwhile, a great land rush occurred in Minnesota. Settlers congregated in St. Paul and quickly moved up the Minnesota River, building shanties and staking out claims to land mostly at sites that had the potential of becoming major towns. McLean notified the Indian Bureau of the obvious violation of the Intercourse Acts to no avail. When Sibley, who was back in Washington, heard of the invasion, he advised Ramsey to encourage the speculation. "Let the people go onto the purchased country in thousands if they will," he wrote. "Never in any case, will the land revert to the possession of the Indian."[36]

The next crisis emerged when the Senate ratified the treaty in June 1852 but completely cut out the two reservations for the Indians along the upper Minnesota River in the west. These had extended for ten miles on either side of the Minnesota River, from Little Rock River to Lake Traverse, well over one hundred miles. Nevertheless, the Sisseton and Wahpeton chiefs, prodded by missionaries and mixed-bloods, signed the revised treaty almost immediately. They had few villages within the ceded region. But Mdewakantons utterly refused to agree to the changes. Little Crow had become a vocal opponent. In an interview with the newly created newspaper, the *Minnesota Pioneer,* he said: "Our Father [the President] is a great glutton; he would go and shoot a cow or an ox every morning and give up the choice pieces of it." Once well fed and appreciative, the chief continued, he "belched up some wind from his great belly and poked his treaty at us." As a result, "we have neither our lands, where our fathers' bones are bleaching, nor have we anything."[37]

Given the growing anger of the Mdewakanton people, Ramsey and Sibley, who by this time were not well received by Mdewakanton leaders such as Little Crow, hired Henry Rice for $10,000, hoping that he could persuade the Mdewakantons to sign off on the changes. Sibley realized that Rice could cause trouble if not included in what was increasingly looking like a very lucrative venture. In addition, Rice, who had been involved in the Indian trade to some extent, had not been at the negotiations and was less suspected of duplicity by the Indians. He also was a silent partner with Madison Sweetser, who came into Minnesota for the first time in 1851, posing as a trader to the western bands. Not only would Rice be paid money up front, but he also was allowed to collect expenses, and he very likely participated in what became the Sweetser debt claim of some $30,000, the money coming from the removal and subsistence funds.[38]

A possible breakthrough came when Sibley and Ramsey learned that perhaps President Millard Fillmore would grant the Indians "temporary" occupancy of the designated reservations for some five years. The president had the authority to remove the land from the public domain and allow the Indians to live on it through executive action. This gave Rice the leverage he needed to get the Mdwakantons to sign the revised treaty. Later evidence shows that when discussing these circumstances with the Indians, Rice simply failed to define what "temporary" occupation really meant. Ramsey obviously encouraged Rice to argue that settlers would not want reservation land for many years, perhaps several decades.[39] The usually silent Wabasha, who had opposed the treaties from the beginning, could only remark, "There is one thing more which our great father can do, that is, gather us all together on the prairie and surround us with soldiers and shoot us down."[40] He was well aware of the vicious attack of American troops on Black Hawk's Mesquakies in 1832, where soldiers did surround part of the band and shoot them down.

When the Mdewakanton leaders finally signed off on the changes, Ramsey instructed his cocommissioner Hugh Tyler to go east and pick up a massive amount of money, the best estimate of which is $555,000. The breakdown of this money included $490,000 for removal and the remainder for what was termed immediate subsistence and education. While the purchase price for the land reached $1,360,000 for the Sissetons and Wahpetons and $1,410,000 for the Mdewakantons and Wahpekutes, this money was supposedly kept at 5 percent interest and paid out yearly for agricultural development and as cash annuities, starting in 1853 (actually, the federal government did not "bank" the principal from which this interest money would be obtained; it had to appropriate the annuity and farming funds every year).[41]

Once back in Minnesota, Ramsey honored the agreement with Sibley, paying out over two-thirds of it to the traders. Rice got a portion to cover his bribery and subsistence costs. Some $20,000 did go to Mdewakanton and Wahpekute chiefs, who then signed a receipt for all the subsistence and removal money, some $180,000. They did so only after Ramsey threatened to take the money back to Washington. The Sisseton and Wahpeton chiefs also signed a receipt, giving Ramsey power of attorney to distribute $275,000 in subsistence money. They never received a cent of this money. At a council, held at Traverse des Sioux, Red Iron, likely following the lead of the missionaries who were outraged at the removal of the reservation clause, strongly objected, threatening to disrupt the meeting. Ramsey ordered soldiers to arrest him.[42]

Where all the "removal" money went is still a matter of some conjecture. Tyler kept $55,000 for "handling" the money. This he no doubt shared with Ramsey. During a later investigation, Sibley's partner Hercules Dousman confessed that 15 percent of the removal money, or more than $70,000, was spent on bribing senators in Washington to get ratification. Other funds had to be paid to men who might disrupt the entire treaty process. Madison Sweetser had powerful friends, including George Ewing, his brother-in-law, who headed a powerful trading firm that had considerable influence in Congress. Sweetser demanded $30,000 and apparently got it because Sibley concluded that he had to be appeased.[43]

While satisfying outside parties who might cause political problems in Washington took up much of the fall of 1851, come summer, when it looked as though the treaties would be ratified, Sibley and Dousman set out to determine how funds would be divided among the traders. Sibley claimed that the Mdewakantons and Wahpekutes owed some $129,885. The Wahpekutes had signed a traders' paper, admitting to a debt of $90,000, but the Mdewakantons refused to admit to any debt. Apparently, Sibley agreed to accept $70,000 as a payoff for the Mdewakanton debts; he took $20,000 and distributed the rest to traders.[44]

The division of the funds appropriated for Sisseton and Wahpeton debts caused the most debate because there were many men involved. In a series of accounts found in the Green Bay and Prairie du Chien papers at the Wisconsin State Archives (Dousman's actual financial records), it is fairly clear that of the $275,000 set aside in the Treaty of Traverse des Sioux, $40,000 went to mixed-bloods who had helped get the treaties signed, but the bulk went to the traders. Sibley and Dousman contended that the Indians trading at the Prairie du Chien trade house owed $13,600, those at Traverse des Sioux $20,500. The Indians at Little Rock, Patterson Rapids, and the Des Moines River (LaFramboise's outfit) had a debt of $30,600, and the Big Stone Lake, Lake Traverse, James River, and Devils Lake trading outfits had a total debt of $72,633. When additional charges were added for "horses killed"—$2,457—and for the burning of the buildings at Lake Traverse—$5,000—the total debt came to $144,984.40.[45]

By the 1840s, the so-called "company" consisted of Sibley and Dousman, as Chouteau simply acted as a merchant, no longer having a liability when it came to the Indians. Dousman's records show that traders owed Sibley $33,180, including nearly $3,000 in interest. But it would be almost impossible to collect that money and keep everyone quiet. The decision was finally made to receive the $144,000, pay the traders, and have the traders pay whatever debts they owed afterward. What appears to be the final division of the money coming from the Sisseton and Wahpeton fund is found in Dousman's financial records. Alexander Faribault and his son received some $32,000, Joseph LaFramboise $11,000, Javier Frenier $2,000, Martin McLeod $18,500, Kenneth McKenzie $4,500, Hercules Dousman $10,000, and Henry Sibley $82,000. One receipt, given to Ramsey, in the Sibley Papers is for $105,618.54, which obviously included the $82,000 coming to him as well as to McLeod and McKenzie, the reason being that the first two men were likely in Canada and Pembina, respectively, and Dousman was at Prairie du Chien. Sibley may have had other obligations when it came to the $82,000, but then traders may have repaid him as well. Likely, he cleared close to $100,000 from the treaty funds.[46]

Ramsey, for his part, did live up to his agreement to pay off the traders. Even so, just a year after the treaty was implemented, the governor demanded as a reward that Sibley forgive a $1,500 loan that he had taken out with Sibley when he moved to the territory; Sibley agreed to do so. Some years before, when the loan was made, Fred Sibley had written his older brother that while the outfit in the west had brought in only 1,150 buffalo hides, he was able to report that the outfit still made a handsome profit, producing sufficient funds to provide a loan to the new governor.[47] While there might have been lean years, Sibley's reordering of the trade, which began in the mid-1830s, his refusal to allow credits to Indians, and his careful business practices had produced profits.

Sibley had initiated shrewd business practices after 1834, and the notes in the Dousman Papers suggest that the outfit had to go back to the 1820s and early 1830s to find numbers to present as debt. The supposed debts owed by the Indians in 1851 were due to astronomical price mark-ups for goods distributed in the 1820s and 1830s, numbers that likely had to be invented by the traders as they contemplated the massive payoff from the two treaties. Had a real debt for the Sissetons and Wahpetons actually been as high as Sibley argued—$145,000—it hardly seems possible that the company, and its half-dozen or so traders, could have remained solvent.[48] The entire debt scenario was a massive fabrication.

As rumors flew over the corrupt outlay of money, Ramsey faced a Senate investigation in the spring of 1853. But the governor had covered his tracks fairly well, with receipts signed by Indians and traders—theoretically, there had been no violation of law, because the treaty did not have a debt clause. Of course, the fact that the senators who organized the investigation had benefitted significantly from the treaty made any conviction unlikely. More importantly, by the time the investigation began, Ramsey had vacated the territorial governorship—the Democrats had won the presidential election in November 1852—and Sibley had declined to run again for delegate to Congress. The massive corruption simply slipped away as Minnesotans celebrated the opening of the "Siouxland," as they called it.[49]

The early Minnesota geologist and amateur historian Newton H. Winchell, in a 1911 study titled *The Aborigines of Minnesota,* pronounced the Dakota treaties of 1851 to be nothing more than a "monstrous conspiracy."[50] The treaties were at the time one of the most expensive agreements negotiated with Indians, the only others offering up such massive sums came from agreements made with large, populous southern tribes. Ironically, the circumstances surrounding the distribution of cash might have been forgotten had the terms of the treaties been honored. It soon became obvious that the roughly $250,000 that was to be expended on these Indians every year thereafter, money that would easily support them, provided ample opportunities for graft among the various bureaucrats who would implement the treaties. Money would simply disappear, much like the subsistence fund set aside for the Indians. After expecting to be fed and cared for, the Dakota people quickly became disillusioned with the agreements, and that disillusion soon led to despair.

REVEREND THOMAS S. WILLIAMSON, Presbyterian missionary.
Courtesy of Jeff Williamson.

REVEREND STEVEN RETURN RIGGS, Presbyterian missionary.
From Riggs, *Mary and I, Forty Years with the Sioux*, 1880.

GENERAL HENRY HASTINGS SIBLEY, governor of Minnesota
and later leader of the expedition against the Dakota soldiers' lodge.
Courtesy of Minnesota Historical Society.

GOVERNOR ALEXANDER RAMSEY. Courtesy of Library of Congress.

FARMER INDIANS GUARDING CORN FIELDS at the Lower Sioux Agency, 1862.
Courtesy of Minnesota Historical Society.

INDIAN FARMER ROBERT HOPKINS (CHASKA) AND FAMILY near Thomas
Williamson's mission at Yellow Medicine. Courtesy of Minnesota Historical Society.

WOUNDED MAN (Taopi), farmer Indian and protégé of
Bishop Henry Benjamin Whipple. Courtesy of Minnesota Historical Society.

SHOOTER (Wakute), Mdewakanton subchief and farmer.
Courtesy of Minnesota Historical Society.

CHARLES CRAWFORD AND THE SISSETON-WAHPETA DELEGATION
at Washington, D.C., 1858. Note the attempt at dressing in "citizen" clothes.
Standing, from left: Joseph Akipa Renville, Scarlet Plume (Waŋmdiupiduta),
Red Iron (Mazaśa), John Otherday (John Aŋpetutokeça), Walks Shooting Iron
(Paul Mazakutemani), and Charles Crawford. *Sitting from left:* Iron Walker
[Walking Iron (Mazamani)?], Stumpy (?), Sweet Corn (Wamnahezaskuya), and
Extended Tail Feathers (Upiyahdayeya). Courtesy of Minnesota Historical Society.

AGENT JOSEPH R. BROWN AND THE MDEWAKANTON-WAHPEKUTE
DELEGATION in Washington, D.C., 1858. Note the traditional dress. *Standing,
from left:* Joseph R. Brown, Antoine J. Campbell, His Iron War Club, Andrew
Robertson, Red Owl (Hiŋhaŋduta), Thomas A. Robertson, and Nathaniel Brown.
Sitting, from left: Mankato (Maĥkato), Wabasha (Wapaśa), and Henry Belland.
Courtesy of Minnesota Historical Society.

LITTLE CROW (Taoyateduta), Mdewakanton chief often seen
as the leader of the uprising. Courtesy of Library of Congress.

WABASHA (Wapaśa), Mdewakanton chief often seen as the leader of the farmer Indians. Courtesy of Minnesota Historical Society.

LITTLE SIX (Shakopee or Śakpedaŋ), leader of the Mdewakanton soldiers' lodge. Courtesy of Minnesota Historical Society.

THREE

REMOVAL, THE NEW RESERVATIONS, AND THE FIRST INDIAN MASSACRE

Steamboats docked regularly at St. Paul by 1852, increasingly discharging speculators and settlers. A few sought town sites. The choice names for these new metropolises reflected the Indian and even French heritage of Minnesota—Wabasha, Red Wing, Shakopee, Le Sueur, and Mankato—communities that had only stakes in the ground and tent structures by the fall, but places that would become small cities. A few years later, speculators preferred to use Anglo names, such as Henderson and St. Peter, and a group of German immigrants chose to honor the town in southern Germany they had left, New Ulm. Most of these towns were on the rivers, the Mississippi below St. Paul and the Minnesota from St. Paul westward into the Dakota heartland. The interior of the state would fill more slowly, as Forest City, Hutchinson, and Glencoe emerged north of the Minnesota River on the edge of the Big Woods, and Garden City, Madelia, and Jackson slowly took form south of the river.

As these throngs of newly arriving settlers and speculators flocked into Minnesota, they came with a certain swagger. Often called "settler sovereignty," this belief included the general supposition that the land was theirs, and they could take a "preemption" claim wherever they wanted. Unfortunately, the Indian owners of the land had yet to move and Governor Ramsey spent little time orchestrating removal. Complaints from citizens increasingly surfaced; some forty-four new citizens of Wabasha complaining that the "Sioux, some forty in number, threatened their families, often took boats they used for crossing rivers, and pitched their tents on the claims of the various settlers." At the new town of Shakopee, Indians were "tearing down our fences, and destroying our crops, shooting our cattle and stealing everything."[1]

While Ramsey spent most of his time in Washington defending himself, Agent McLean asked questions: Where was the money necessary to support removal? By the time the new agent, Robert Murphy, replaced him in the spring of 1853, more questions surfaced. Where was the $30,000 fund designated for breaking land for the Sissetons and Wahpetons? Willis Gorman, the new territorial governor, was livid about the situation; he likely assumed that massive funds existed from the treaty that could be plundered. Both the governor and the missionaries soon learned that of the $490,000 designated for Indian removal in the treaty, Ramsey turned over only $10,000 to Gorman. This was supposed to fed 6,000 Indians on the new reservations over the coming winter of 1852–53.[2]

While settlers felt imposed upon, the Dakota people saw the situation much differently. Whites invaded the villages of the smaller, less well-armed bands and burned them down. Wakute's village suffered such a fate, forcing the 160 Dakota people from the community into the nearby woods. Some agreed to move thereafter to the reservations after wagons appeared to carry their women and children. Wakute's people, however, left "naked and destitute," having lost their bedding and clothing in the fire.[3] The bands living along the Mississippi River were experiencing what modern-day scholars call "ethnic cleansing"; most seemed confused and outraged at being expelled from villages that they had lived in for decades if not longer.[4]

The larger Mdewakanton bands, including those of Shakopee, Little Crow, and Wabasha, proved more difficult to move forcefully. Some of Wabasha's people refused entirely to leave. Murphy requested help from the army, which at the time was busy building a new military post just east of the designated reservation, a post soon to be named Fort Ridgely. The post commander, Lieutenant Colonel Francis Lee, was somewhat perturbed by the request: "Until they positively decline to go," he responded, "I must respectfully decline to furnish a command of soldiers."[5] Samuel Pond, who visited with the aged Shakopee, found a similar determination to stay at their old village. Being in "ill humor," he wrote, "they appear determined not to be satisfied with the country assigned them."[6]

Only Little Crow seemed reluctantly willing to consider removal. In spring 1854, he marched his entire band to the new reservation. Dr. Asa

Daniels saw the caravan pass by Fort Ridgely, which at the time consisted of just four log houses. Little Crow and his mounted *akacita* soldiers, came first, with their guns. The remainder "were scattered along in the easy disorder of a long march," Daniels observed. "There were a few carts and wagons loaded with baggage on which the women might ride by turns. The ponies, with their loads of baggage and children," Daniels continued, "placed on the primitive Indian conveyances formed by two trailing lodge poles fastened to their sides, were plodding sleepily along."[7]

By spring 1854, the Indians realized that promises of food had almost all been broken. Most of the Dakota people who did reach the new reservations stayed only a few weeks. Some, including Little Crow, had returned to the vicinity of Shakopee's old village; others were still near Traverse des Sioux; most of the Wahpekute people were camped near Mankato; and a large number, including some of the Wahpeton and Sisseton bands, were on the upper Blue Earth River.[8] The only progress made came when President Franklin Pierce signed off on the promised executive order, dated April 13, 1854, which gave the Indians a right of occupancy on Minnesota River lands until spring 1859.[9] But because Agent Murphy was so frequently absent from the lands, little progress toward creating farms to sustain the Indians occurred.[10]

While the President's sanction allowed Agent Murphy to begin breaking farmland, he made no preparations to implement the treaty. A distribution system did not exist for funneling food up the Minnesota River to the reservations, where steamboats could only occasionally venture. He did send men to start construction of a few buildings at the newly created Lower Agency, a few miles below where the Redwood River struck the Minnesota. A few tepee villages under Little Crow, Wabasha, Wakute, Passing Hail, and the Wound (better known as, and always called in English, Taopi) took shape the next year south of the agency buildings. Larger villages under Shakopee and Red Middle Voice were occasionally occupied northwest of the agency.[11]

At the Upper Agency, designed for the Sisseton and Wahpeton bands, workers started constructing a second series of buildings located just above the mouth of the Yellow Medicine River. The missionaries also decided to rebuild nearby, hoping to obtain some benefits from the treaties. Williamson constructed a community later called Pajutazi a mile and a half above the Upper, or Yellow Medicine River, Agency, and Riggs collected a few of his followers at a place he called Hazelwood, located a mile above

Pajutazi.[12] But the Sisseton and Wahpeton villages along the river, under Walking Runner, Red Iron, and Walking Iron, were well to the north; other than a few Christian Indians, there were actually very few Indians at the Upper Agency during its existence. Migratory bands of Sissetons, including those of Sleepy Eyes and White Lodge, stayed well west of the Minnesota River. The much larger Sisseton bands under Standing Buffalo, Sweet Corn, and Scarlet Plume, roughly half the Dakota nation, remained out on the plains.[13]

Near both agencies, a new batch of Indian traders built houses, four at each location. Andrew Myrick kept the most extensive inventory at his two trade houses. He, like the others, employed mixed-bloods and expected to gather the annuity money that the agent would hand out each summer. This cash, usually in silver or gold dollars, would supposedly be given to individual heads of families. Unlike Sibley, who in the traders' papers simply listed the amounts owed to each trader by an individual band, the traders increasingly presented lists of individual Indians who owed them debts. As trader George Spencer later testified, "the trader generally stood right on the ground when the Indian was paid his money and he tapped him on the shoulder and he would get paid." This slowly evolved into a system where the money was handed directly to the trader without it even passing through the hands of individual Indians.[14]

By 1854 some of the promised funds, goods, and food finally arrived at the new agencies. But given the ineptness of Agent Murphy, the Indians often had to turn to the traders, buying flour, pork, and other items on credit. They could and often did pay these debts with furs, but being unable to speak to the agent or prove these payments, the traders claimed most of the annuity money as debt, roughly $80,000 in cash a year—the remaining $70,000 or so was spent on agricultural improvement, education, and the salaries of agency personnel. The system soon became institutionalized, and corruption, so obvious during the treaty fiasco, became the norm throughout the 1850s on the reservations.[15]

Men working for Murphy had opened several hundred acres of land as a "common field" by 1855. In a series of letters, missionary Stephen Riggs decried this method. He believed that the lands within the two reservations should be broken up and handed out in allotments of 160 acres per family, a new idea that became standard in most treaties of the decade. To prove his point, Riggs gathered some fifteen families at Hazelwood and purchased a small sawmill for his "Indian farmers," and they then began to build frame houses.[16] Murphy applauded the progress and allocated some funds for plows, oxen, and even stoves. Over the next few years, more than fifty of these "lower" Sisseton and Wahpeton Indian men and mixed-bloods, some converts to the mission churches and others contemplating conversion, turned to farming. A handful—perhaps a dozen—even discarded their blankets and breechcloths and donned pants and shirts.[17]

The vast majority of Sisseton and Wahpeton Dakotas living well north and west of the Yellow Medicine River Agency soon concluded that such special treatment of the farmers was unfair. The farmers became quite uneasy when large villages of Sissetons—sometimes two to three thousand people—came in from the Plains to collect annuities. The leaders of these Sisseton bands were powerful and impressive men, often feared by military officers who were increasingly called by the agent to keep order at the Upper Agency. Standing Buffalo, Sweet Corn, and Scarlet Plume had lethal reputations in war and large followings of *akacita* soldiers. While usually peaceful, some of these bands showed increasing hostility to the farmer Indians associated with the missionaries.

The hostile Sissetons included those following now-old Limping Devil, the man who had barely saved Prescott's life some thirty years before. His son, White Lodge, had assumed a leadership role, and Sleepy Eyes soon joined the band. After Sleepy Eyes's death in 1860, White Lodge became the nominal leader of this band, which often harbored men who opposed the American invasion of their land.[18] The discontented Sisseton chiefs often communed with yet another small Wahpekute band who had intermarried with them. Led by the indomitable Scarlet End (known to his friends as Iŋkpaduta), the band roamed across the open prairie between the upper Des Moines River in northern Iowa and the upper Cottonwood River, west of the Lower Agency. When these groups came to the Upper Agency, which they were attached to, they occasionally raided fields, taking potatoes and other vegetables from farmers, killing the cattle of the missionaries and their converts, and provoking no end of trouble.[19]

While progress toward what the missionaries termed "civilization" seemed possible, Riggs lamented the fact that the improvements at Hazelwood seemed difficult to replicate at the Mdewakanton villages at the Lower Agency, or Redwood. Ironically, some explanations for the lack of progress were attributable to the new, progressive Commissioner of Indian Affairs George Manypenny. Murphy had provided estimates for the cost of mills, housing, field work, and farm machinery in late fall 1854—all funds built into the two treaties—but come spring, Commissioner Manypenny informed the agent that such funds could not be spent until the Indians "were permanently settled on their reservations."[20] A virtual shouting match then erupted through the mail, with each side defending itself. Philander Prescott, who had been hired as superintendent of farming at the Lower Agency, even got into the fray, arguing that criticism of Agent Murphy's slow progress "has been very unjust." By 1856, Prescott claimed that a total of $163,500 had been withheld from the Lower Sioux alone.[21] Manypenny then exploded, claiming that some $562,000 had been spent on the Dakota Indians—he obviously included the money set aside for removal—with no results. "It is a matter of congratulation that a considerable amount of the funds for the object of education, improvement, and other useful ends," the commissioner contended, "has been retained in the treasury."[22]

The attempt to untangle and account for the funds seemed hopelessly mired in past expenditures that simply were not accounted for. The blame for the mess at the agencies, however, became apparent when the new Superintendent for Indian Affairs Francis Huebschmann made an unannounced visit to the Lower Agency in July 1856. What he found was appalling. There were four farmers employed, including Prescott. Huebschmann "saw only one farmer actually working in the field," while a second was "engaged in cooking," and a third was "lying drunk on the floor."[23] Little progress had been made toward farming and no schools had been opened. Indeed, by 1856, the agency was some $6,000 in debt, and employees, who were starting to construct houses for the Indians at the Lower Agency, had to be laid off.[24] In a meeting with Huebschmann, Little Crow openly complained that Agent Murphy "had a very long pocket into which their [the Indians] funds were slipped."[25]

While money disappeared, or languished in the treasury department, an inept distribution system also plagued the delivery of food. Major Henry Day from Fort Ridgely observed the first large-scale distribution of food at the Lower Agency in October 1854: "What few articles of subsistence have been given them are of an inferior quality . . . the flour furnished at the last payment . . . stood alone and was as hard as a similar lump of dried mortar." The pork was "entirely rotten."[26] The situation at the Upper Agency was perhaps worse. Captain John Hayden discovered that "there was neither powder, lead, guns nor tobacco among their goods," items that buffalo hunters like the Sissetons needed. Dry goods, Hayden noted, included items that went on a ledger as being expensive but not of much use, including "novel ties for young people," "swallow tail suits," and "stiff boots" that "tortured" the feet of those Indians who threw them away.[27]

A clear indication of growing trouble erupted when Little Crow and Shakopee ordered their *akacita* soldiers to break into the newly built warehouse at the Lower Agency in June 1855 and steal flour, much of which was kept for government workers. Rather than attack agency personnel, however, Dakota and Anishinaabe bands—the latter also seeing their annuity money vanish—took out their frustrations on each other. A new outburst of intertribal fighting ensued, creating a conundrum for the army. When it forced the chiefs to surrender men who had been responsible for raids and deaths, it had no authority to punish them and civil authorities did not want them either. At one point when Dakota warriors surprised an Anishinaabe camp, killing twenty-five, they paraded the scalps first at Lac qui Parle, then initiated a "scalp dance" for the benefit of the government employees at the Upper Agency. The triumphant warriors ended up in the streets of the new town of Traverse des Sioux, waving clubs and dancing. In many ways, such acts of defiance clearly demonstrated the growing anger of young Dakota men at the changes affecting their lives.[28]

Nevertheless, at Riggs's Hazelwood, besides nine male full-blood Indians who had converted, a large number of Franco-Dakota people also joined the church and took up farms. Among them were the many relatives of Renville, including John B. and Gabriel Renville. Given this growing flock, Riggs decided to declare them all independent of the Dakota Nation, giving the group the name "Hazelwood Republic." All members had renounced their Indian identity and even began petitioning territorial officials for the right to vote.[29] In a state of exuberance, Riggs traveled with nine of his Hazelwood followers to the District Court in Mankato, where he asked that they be granted voting rights. The hearing quickly degenerated, the judge proclaiming that "men with colored skin should never be naturalized"—that they could not be made "white men." In an anonymous newspaper article, one of those who had been rejected, proclaimed that "they treat [ed] us like dogs."[30]

While disheartening, the members of Hazelwood adopted a constitution. Virtually all took or were given Christian names. The republic listed Paul Mazakutemani as the "elected governor," and Henock Mahpiyahdinape as "Secretary of State." Henock was Walking Runner's son and Little Crow's brother-in-law. The so-called "cabinet" consisted of Gabriel Renville, Simon Anawaŋgmani, and Antoine Freniere. Other men of distinction who joined the movement included John Otherday (or Aŋpetutokeça), Lorenzo Lawrence (Toŋwaŋiteton), and Joseph "Akipa" Renville. Akipa, as he was often called in English, was the younger brother of the two local Wahpeton chiefs, Walking Runner and Red Iron.[31] Indeed, by the late 1850s even chief Walking Runner, Little Crow's father-in-law, had become interested in Christianity, although he did not convert.

While Riggs gloried in his converts, he also fretted about them. Christian members Henock, Otherday, Mazakutemani, and Akipa were some of the most successful Dakota warriors then living on the upper Minnesota River. Otherday had killed five Anishinaabe warriors in one battle, and Akipa proudly wore a headdress with nineteen eagle feathers. Riggs had few illusions about such men, calling Henock and Otherday "notorious" men. Nevertheless, Riggs desperately hoped that the "spirit" had entered their souls.[32] Such a belief in the spiritual change helped define Presbyterianism: being reborn in Christ could not be denied, even to men who might have been rather notorious individuals early in life. Donning pantaloons, however, was another matter, as it became a visual cultural change that most of these men resisted. As for abandoning their medicine sacks, nothing was said.[33]

Just before departing the agency, Murphy provided members of the Hazelwood Republic with oxen and plows, recognizing them as a separate "Dakota band." Murphy's report to Washington of the incident highlighted the vigor with which Hazelwood members took to building frame houses, which were nearly nonexistent at the time. Five such buildings, with lofts, appeared in the center of Walking Runner's Sisseton village, where his son, Peter Tapetataŋka, a Christian, taught school. Mazakutemani's settlement had four clapboard houses, and two were even under construction in Red Iron's village, well to the north of the missions. Gabriel Renville's house, however, might have been the most modern. It had a brick fireplace, a very progressive symbol. John Otherday's was nearly as modern as it sported carpeting in the main room.[34]

In contrast, while the houses of most arriving white settlers were made of logs, the new towns springing up along the Minnesota River quickly adopted modern features. Henderson, with a population of four hundred by 1855, had a newspaper, edited by Sibley's ally, Joseph R. Brown. Traverse des Sioux, even closer to the reservations, boasted of nine stores and three taverns, and St. Peter and Mankato were growing even faster.[35] One of the largest distribution centers emerged in the German town of New Ulm, located just south of the reservations. Its founder, Fred Beinhorn, recruited eight hundred German families to move to Minnesota, picking an ideal spot for the community just above the mouth of the Cottonwood River. The population grew to sixteen hundred by 1860, despite protests by the Mdewakantons, who believed that the Cottonwood was the southernmost boundary of their reservation lands.[36] Fanning out from New Ulm, other settlers moved north, into what became Milford Township, and west, up the Cottonwood River, on lands that literally adjoined the reservation.[37]

Considerable growth occurred in the interior as well. Captain Theodore Potter, the skipper of a riverboat, logged the many trips he made in 1855–56, taking pioneers from St. Paul upriver to Belle Plaine, where they scrambled ashore and headed west to find home sites. One group included a large number of Norwegians and Swedes, who took up land near communities called New Sweden and Norseland, then just thirty miles east of Fort Ridgely. Just northeast of them, Glencoe, Hutchinson, and Forest City had been founded. The land office at Henderson could hardly keep up with the new boundaries. At the height of this boom, good land sold for as much as ten dollars an acre, land that the government had purchased from the Indians for just six cents.[38]

The settler invasion brought growing clashes with Indians. One petition from New Ulm residents, written in August 1855, claimed that Dakota Indians were "continually committing grievous depredations upon our crops, shooting our cattle, and greatly annoying and harassing us in the enjoyment of our rights."[39] They also pulled up the survey stakes that were being set to mark property claims. The army investigated the claims, and Captain Thomas Steele talked with various Indian chiefs.[40] At the meeting, the chiefs pointed out that while Agent Murphy had made many promises, but virtually all had been broken; as a result, they had to beg for food from the settlers or starve. Colonel John Abercrombie, who arrived toward the end of the discussions, was so angry at the agent's incompetence that when a letter arrived arguing that the chiefs should be arrested for stealing from the agency warehouse, the colonel instead gave them some provisions.[41]

Fortunately for all, both Murphy and Manypenny left office in early 1857. The new Dakota agent was another Democrat from Minnesota, St. Paul lawyer Charles Flandrau.[42] A good man, he at least offered some hope for change. Captain Potter knew Flandrau extremely well. He had spent time on the reservations and had a certain swagger, often being dressed beautifully in a fringed, deerskin jacket.[43] Even so, Flandrau inherited a mess—reservations where the Dakota people had only two years left on their "lease" and promises had not been kept. In addition, government funds were still being held back.With Minnesota filling up so quickly with settlers, there would undoubtedly be cries to move the Indians farther west after it expired.[44]

The new agent was impressed with some aspects of progress when he first toured the agencies. Nearly a thousand acres of land had been broken, and the missions at the Upper Agency seemed to be setting an important example. The Indians there, including Walking Runner's band, had been very successful at growing crops, mainly potatoes and corn. So much was being produced by these farmer Indians that Flandrau agreed to purchase food from them and then give it to the nonfarmers. He paid five dollars for a barrel of corn and three for potatoes, buying up an impressive 225 barrels in total—nearly a thousand dollars' worth of food from fifty Indians, fifteen of them women. One woman, Sarah (another Christian whose Indian name was Wawiyohiyewin) sold fourteen barrels of potatoes for forty-two dollars.[45]

Hopes for a rapid agricultural revolution among the majority of Indians nearly collapsed, however, when news reached the Redwood Agency in March 1857 that Scarlet End's (Inkpaduta) band of Wahpekutes—those Indians who often communed with Sleepy Eyes and White Lodge—had massacred many settlers at Spirit Lake in northern Iowa.[46] Scarlet End's band, consisting of a mere six or seven lodges, had emerged from the diaspora that resulted from the tribal infighting in northern Iowa. It was a lawless land where in 1844, given relentless attacks from the Mesquakies, the Wahpekute nearly collapsed. A hastening of the dispersal came after a dispute resulted in the killing of the old Wahpekute chief The Cane (Tasagya in Dakota). Red All Over (Sintamniduta) assumed leadership, and then married the sister of the Sisseton chief Sleepy Eyes, merging those two bands to some degree. While being described by some as "renegades," Red All Over sought respectability, applying for annuities during the 1854 and 1856 distributions. After being denied, he returned to the upper Des Moines River. Here the band met newly arriving white settlers, who were themselves of questionable character.[47]

Surveyor Samuel Woods had considerable contact with both Indians and settlers in the upper Des Moines River region. He occasionally met with the Mesquakies as well as the Wahpekutes. Conflict seemed in the offing by 1849, when settlers formed a "regulator" corps of armed men, supposedly to deal with the many white outlaws and horse thieves who had infested the region. "To be rated as a 'horse thief,'" Woods concluded, "it is sufficient for a man to 'wear good clothes, ride a good horse, have some money and not work.'"[48] Into this mix of outlaws, settlers, and Indians came a number of vicious people, including a criminal named Henry Lott.

Little is known about Lott other than that he had a preemption claim near a two-lake complex called Spirit Lake. Woods thought he made his living by hunting, depleting the region of wolves and deer. By the mid-1850s, this brought near-starvation to Red All Over's people, who occasionally begged for food. In February 1854, Lott and others visited Red All Over's camp, telling the men that buffalo had been sighted nearby. As the men rushed out to hunt, Lott, his thirteen-year-old son, and several others used axes to murder at least eight children, two women, and Red All Over. An outraged Woods promptly wrote to Minnesota Governor Willis Gorman, demanding justice for the Indians. Gorman's response was tepid. He thought it best to report the incident to Washington where others would deal with it; of course, nothing was done.[49]

Red All Over had a brother, Scarlet End, who likely had been one of the men who left to hunt buffalo. After Lott's vicious attack, the band fell under his leadership, and he often consulted with Sleepy Eyes and White Lodge.[50] In January 1857, given the failure of the buffalo and the rejection from the annuity tables, Inkpaduta and his people fell back on the upper Des Moines River for food. As Inkpaduta's son, who had married one of Sleepy Eyes's daughters, faced starvation, the son approached a white family near Spirit Lake begging for food. As the son's wife later testified, "My husband went to the white man for something to eat. The white man ordered him away, set a dog on him, and my husband killed the dog." A group of white men then entered Inkpaduta's camp, seized as many guns as possible, and left the Indians to starve.[51]

At this final insult, Inkpaduta called his small band together. Off to one side, the chief's sister was mourning the death of a child. She later testified that Inkpaduta's son "got very excited, when hearing the children crying for something to eat."[52] The men decided to take food and weapons from white cabins, first entering the cabin of Roland Gardner on the southernmost lake. They took his gun and considerable food, and then proceeded east and north, into the narrow land separating East and West Spirit Lake.

Over the next few hours, they murdered forty-one settlers, including most of the people at the Gardner house; the bodies of twelve others at the settlements were never found.[53]

Hearing of the attack, hysteria struck the Minnesota frontier. In St. Paul it was believed that both Mankato and St. Peter had been overrun by nine hundred Indians.[54] Militias formed in both towns and scouted west, finding the winter camp of Red Iron, which had moved south, and firing into it with little effect before fleeing. A second party went up the Cottonwood River, southwest of New Ulm, and attacked Sleepy Eyes's camp, claiming to have killed six Indians. Superintendent Huebschmann, who was soon leaving office, raced to visit with various reservation chiefs, discovering that almost all of them were dumbfounded. They "could not understand at all what the panic among the whites meant." They knew nothing of the killings at Spirit Lake.[55]

Given the isolation of Spirit Lake and the muddled reports, the army sent out several patrols. Fighting deep snow and cold weather, one troop finally located Inkpaduta's camp, well west of Spirit Lake, but "the nest was there but not warm." In mid-May, the army then ordered Colonel E. B. Alexander to send infantry troops stationed at Fort Snelling after Inkpaduta. He mildly protested, suggesting instead that a force of Dakota Indians go after the "renegades." All that had been accomplished as spring broke was the burial of the victims.[56]

While the army did not know it, the Indians had taken four women captive: Lydia Noble, age 21; Elizabeth Thatcher, age 19; Margaret Marble, age 20; and Abbie Gardner, age 13. As Inkpaduta moved west, Thatcher fell into a river; young warriors then shot her. Weeks later, Roaring Cloud, a young son of Inkpaduta, perturbed at Noble's refusal to work, beat her brains out with firewood.[57] While hunting, two young Sissetons, sons of a Christian woman and the Wahpeton chief Walking Spirit, found Inkapduta's camp near Lake Herman (often called Skunk Lake). Here they bartered for Margaret Marble and later turned her over to the missionaries. Flandrau and Riggs then convinced Paul Mazakutemani, John Otherday, and a third Christian, John Grass, to go after Abbie Gardner. They found Inkpaduta eighty miles southwest of Big Stone Lake, camped with a large band of Yankton Sioux. They demanded her release, and with the support of the Yanktons, who seemed less than overjoyed by Inkpaduta's actions, Gardner gained her freedom. Gardner left a stirring account of the tribulations of all four women, in which she strongly implied that all four, while given as wives to separate men, were repeatedly raped.[58]

As Agent Flandrau and yet another new superintendent of Indian affairs in Minnesota, William J. Cullen, returned to the reservations in late June, they found a firestorm. The annuity payment was due to the Indians, but information from the rescuers of Abbie Gardner noted that Inkpaduta was "being feasted by the Yanktons," who were in league with many Sissetons.[59] Cullen, who knew little about the situation, quickly telegraphed the commissioner of Indian affairs, asking for instructions—he pointedly asked whether he should distribute the annuities, as scheduled.[60] New Commissioner J. W. Denver demanded that the Indians destroy Inkpaduta before delivering the annuities. At this crucial point, news arrived that Roaring Cloud, supposedly the murderer of Mrs. Noble, was camped near the Sissetons, just west of the agency. An army patrol killed Inkpaduta's son and captured his wife, who then described the events preceding the murders at Spirit Lake.[61] The interview, however, was quickly disrupted by a large party of Sisseton warriors from Sleepy Eyes and White Lodge's villages, who demanded her release. Flandrau, "under quite a nervous strain," as physician Daniels reported, "told them 'they could have her.'"[62]

Flandrau then sent for the army, which sent all the troops it could muster, including Major T. W. Sherman's battery and an infantry company under Captain Bernard Bee. As Cullen tried to bring some order on July 6, he soon discovered that several thousand Sissetons and Yanktons were coming into the agency, all well-armed. When they arrived, a scuffle ensued, and a soldier took a knife wound. At this tense moment, surrounded by thousands of Indians, Cullen convinced White Lodge to retreat slightly, threatening to open up with the battery. A day later the Sisseton chief handed over the man responsible for the attack. Sherman's unlimbering of his guns seemed to be the leverage that halted a massive conflict.[63]

Physician Daniels later learned that the Sissetons became increasingly leery. White Lodge expected another Ash Hollow, a conflict initiated by General W. S. Harney in 1855 in which a hundred or more Lakota Sioux were killed near the Platte River. Knowledge of the slaughter spread through Indian camps. Franco- and Anglo-Dakota mixed-bloods also assisted in quieting the many angry Sissetons. Sherman concluded that these men, "speaking their language," played a major role in preventing a "war." The major chiefs then joined Cullen in council on July 17. White Lodge and the young, and increasingly powerful, Sisseton leader Standing Buffalo (or Tataŋkanaźan) sat down with the superintendent who then pointedly asked them if they would destroy Inkpaduta.[64]

Standing Buffalo answered the superintendent, standing up erect and impressing everyone who watched him. "About forty years of age, of splendid physique, six feet or more in stature . . . in posture as rigidly erect as a pine tree," as a soldier recorded, Standing Buffalo knew how to deliver a speech. Daniels, who knew the chief extremely well—the doctor had even saved his life some years before—recorded the chief's words. Standing Buffalo found the restrictions on annuities unfair, declaring that his people had done nothing wrong: "Our Great Father has asked us to do a very hard thing. It makes my heart sad to think of it." But he was considering the offer. So too was White Lodge, who had relatives in Inkpaduta's camp. While he professed friendship, and even exclaimed that he would "call on my braves to prove their friendship by killing Inkpaduta," later evidence suggest that these were false words. His people were simply too closely related to the Wahpekutes.[65]

As the talks progressed, the intrepid and politically ambitious Little Crow arrived at the Upper Agency, swiftly traveling the forty miles northward. He quickly joined in the discussions and offered to form a party to pursue Iŋkpaduta, something that Standing Buffalo had considered but had not committed to. Being well connected with kin at the Upper Agency, Little Crow then turned to his "Christian" relatives, Peter Tapetataŋka (son of Walking Runner, his father-in-law), Paul Mazakutemani, and the various Renville brothers and their cousin, Gabriel, all of whom were members of the Hazelwood Republic. Others included Antoine J. Campbell, who was increasingly important in agency affairs; Baptiste Campbell; and John Mooers, all of whom were mixed-blood employees at the agencies. Along with nearly fifty other Sisseton and Wahpeton Indians who pledged to overtake Inkpaduta, Little Crow, well-armed and mounted, headed west into the prairie country. With plenty of information regarding Iŋkpaduta's haunts, they found his camp on Skunk Lake.[66]

Little Crow's overwhelming force immediately attacked, killing at least three men and driving others into a swamp, where two more children likely perished. Back at the Upper Agency, Little Crow exaggerated the numbers killed, claiming "a dozen or more." The party had killed another son of Inkpaduta, but it failed to get the elusive leader of the group. Upon their return, Cullen praised Little Crow, whom everyone realized had defused the situation; while a Mdewakanton, he had taken over a mixed party, quite unusual for the time, and brought some retribution for the murders at Spirit Lake. Cullen released the annuities in late August and the army slowly moved their troops and field pieces back to Fort Ridgely.[67]

Over the fall, several attempts were made to capture Inkpaduta. A patrol under Captain H. C. Pratt, with Little Crow again offering a hand, scoured the lands between the Pipestone Quarry and Lake Benton, finding nothing. The patrol met with Lean Bear, chief *akacita* in White Lodge's band. He apparently gave them false information; the southwestern Sissetons became increasingly uncooperative. On the upper Cottonwood River, however, they found the situation returning to normal. "The white settlements extended up the Cottonwood River about twenty-five miles," Pratt reported. "No one seemed to have the least apprehensions from the Indians."[68] By the end of August, while several councils revealed anger over the delays in getting annuities, calm returned to the upper Minnesota River.[69] Thereafter, White Lodge and Sleepy Eyes likely had many discussions regarding their roles in agency affairs. Annuities had been held up as a price for attacking and killing their own people, certainly an injustice, at least to them.

Inkpaduta had led one of the more brutal attacks on settlers ever recorded at that time. And worse, the Spirit Lake massacre emboldened other Indians who opposed the farm program on the reservations. Sleepy Eyes and White Lodge thereafter seemed unwilling to move to the upper reservation; instead, they joined an increasing number of discontented Sissetons who roamed south and west of the upper Cottonwood River. These Sissetons were often related to other Indians on the reservation, especially Mdewakantons living with Shakopee and his brother, Red Middle Voice. Many Indian leaders on the reservations also learned from the Inkpaduta affair that whenever the Great Father wanted to, he could and would stop the flow of food and money. Cullen had done just that during the July confrontation. This would certainly lead to starvation as game animals could no longer sustain the Dakota people.

At a time when reassurances were necessary and good men needed to be at the helm, yet another blow struck the agencies. While Cullen handled the crisis poorly, Agent Flandrau, a seemingly good man, resigned to take a judgeship not long after Little Crow returned from his mission. According to Daniels, he had been frightened to death during the confrontation over holding Roaring Cloud's wife; the criticism may have been unwarranted as

Flandrau certainly showed his mettle later during the war. With the two reservations seemingly adrift, and with Indians at both agencies openly discussing the Inkpaduta rebellion and increasingly upset with the failures of the Bureau of Indian Affairs and the massive corruption of agency personnel, the only question seemed to be whether the government could correct the problems and make good on the promises that had come with the 1851 treaties: that the Dakota people could live on their lands, remain Indians who occasionally went on a hunt, and never again worry about feeding their families.

FOUR

CHAOS, CONFUSION, AND WAR

Western Minnesota was a powder keg in the fall of 1857, with the Inkpaduta affair having unsettled everyone. Little Crow tried to mediate differences, and had some success, but even his people felt cheated and abused. The treaties of 1851 had brought immense change; even American politicians marveled at the flock of white pioneers who invaded ceded lands. Statehood for the region was in the offing, and it would come the next year. But corruption and incompetence in the annuity system abounded, and on occasion, Indians who remained off the reserves were denied annuities. Into this spiraling cauldron of anger stepped a new Indian agent, Joseph R. Brown. Hardly a novice to Indian affairs, Brown had lived among the Dakota people for thirty-seven years.

Born in Maryland in 1805, Brown reached Minnesota at age fourteen, serving as a drummer boy at Fort Snelling. He worked for Sibley in the west, cultivating a relationship with him that only grew stronger after the treaty negotiations in 1851. Thereafter, Brown edited two newly created newspapers supporting Sibley. While editor of the *Henderson Democrat* in 1856, he aggressively attacked the Murphy and Gorman administration of Indian affairs, despite their Democratic lineage. Their conduct, he wrote, "should have long since led to serious trouble with the Sioux." He praised the missionaries, however, and called for giving a Dakota man 160 acres of "land in severalty . . . independent of the rest of his band."[1] This idea had come to dominate Indian policy across the land, being written into many of the treaties negotiated by the commissioner of Indian affairs.

In intellect, Brown was surely superior to Murphy, and the new agent had endless energy. Missionary Thomas Williamson thought him as a man of "little education" but with "handsome talents, much kind feelings, and very little principle."[2] Brown had questionable moral baggage. He had taken as least two Indian wives in the late 1820s and deserted them. A traveler who reached the upper Minnesota River in 1835 described Brown as "a gay deceiver amongst the Indian fair."[3] Brown finally married Susan Frenier, a Franco-Dakota woman whom he met at Lac qui Parle in 1837. Only fourteen years of age at their marriage, Susan, a striking lass with a waistline in inches nearly equal to her age, had ten children with Brown. Perhaps more importantly, Susan Frenier Brown came from a very influential family, her mother's husband being Akipa, a prominent warrior and leader who had turned to Christianity. Susan never spoke English, but Brown spoke Dakota fluently and could count on help in the administration of the agencies from important Dakota leaders, including Walking Runner, Scarlet Plume, and Akipa's brothers, chiefs Walking Iron and Red Iron, all of whom were important upper, or Sisseton/Wahpeton, Indians.[4] He had a more difficult time with the Lower Agency Indians, the Mdewakantons, who distrusted him from the start.

Agent Brown hoped to re-create Hazelwood, albeit without the religious elements, and he turned to people whom he trusted to do it. At the Upper Agency, he hired Gabriel Renville, his wife's stepbrother, to be head farmer. At the Lower Agency, where the most improvement was needed, Brown hired the very active Andrew Robertson, a Scottish immigrant who replaced Prescott as head of farming. Robertson was popular and had married a Dakota woman. Brown brought order, then, where there had been disorder. Over the next two years, Brown's crews opened new fields, built stables and shops, and began construction on houses for individual Indian families.[5]

Brown's ultimate goal included the creation of what he called a "civilization program." But he needed more funds, especially the vast amount of money that Manypenny had held back, which was nearly $200,000. Fortunately for the new agent, the Indian bureau in 1857 fell under the leadership of Charles E. Mix, whom Brown cultivated. Mix released some funds by the fall of 1857; nevertheless, he too realized that the president's five-year occupation permit was about to expire. Brown pressed Mix for a new treaty, one that guaranteed reservations and allowed for the allotment of 160-acre farms to individual Indian families. And a new treaty could lead to "diminishment" of Indian lands, as Minnesotans especially coveted the lands on the north, or left bank, of the Minnesota River, fertile river bottom that would sell at a premium.[6]

Given these supposed positives, Brown received authority to bring delegations east from all four Dakota bands in 1858. Brown's close associate Gabriel Renville selected amenable Sisseton and Wahpeton chiefs, including Sweet Corn, Red Iron, and Scarlet Plume, the latter man being Gabriel's "uncle." All these men could be easily handled; the likes of the Charger, Standing Buffalo, White Lodge, and Sleepy Eyes, all major chiefs, were conspicuously absent. The delegation from the Upper Agency also included a group of farmer Indians—Akipa, Paul Mazakutemani, Akipa's son Charles Crawford, and John Otherday. All but one of the delegates from the Upper Agency wore pants and shirts, clear and significant symbols of change.[7]

The Mdewakanton and Wahpekute delegation looked much different. Little Crow led the group, and he helped select the rest of the delegation, which included his head *akacita,* Big Eagle (in Dakota Wamditaŋka).[8] Wabasha remained the nominal head of the group, but he lacked charisma, especially when speaking, and was, as one newspaper put it, "careless of display." Older than Little Crow and perhaps suffering from the sun blindness that often affected Indian hunters, he carried an umbrella. Others included Shakopee, Mankato, and Red Owl (known in Dakota circles as Miŋhaŋduta); although both Shakopee and Red Owl were old and would die just two years later, Mankato was young and active. The Wahpekute, with just one small village, sent Red Legs. These men left Minnesota in traditional dress—leggings, breechcloths, and braided hair, with medicine bags dangling from their waists. Several proudly wore eagle feather headdresses.[9]

The delegation reached Washington by mid-March 1858, and soon Little Crow basked in the attention given him. He had spent several weeks in the city in 1854 and offered advice to his colleagues. The trip four years before had been a reward for being the first leader to step forward and sign the treaty at Mendota in 1851. Visiting the city for the second time, Little Crow witnessed considerable change; the new Washington Monument pushed skyward and the United States Arsenal at Greenleaf Point, another impressive construction effort, was nearing completion. On an excursion to the arsenal, the delegation discovered a group of Turkish naval officers looking over naval guns. Newspapers quibbled over who looked more impressive, the Indians in their finest clothing, with braids inlaid with otter skin, large decorative jewelry, and painted faces, or the Turks, who, according to one account, "wore magnificent uniforms, the collars, cuffs, and seams of which are covered with heavy gold embroidery."[10]

The delegation passed several evenings at the theater, Dakota men quickly approving of the many women who performed. Other nights were spent in the saloons of Georgetown, where on one occasion, John Otherday retired to his hotel with a young waitress, who also doubled as a prostitute. Proclaiming that he would not give her up, Otherday, upon returning to Minnesota, put aside his Dakota wife and later asked Riggs to perform a marriage ceremony. After many months, Riggs, ever the austere Presbyterian but certainly torn by the possible loss of one of his coveted Christian Indian farmers, finally relented. Perhaps he came to believe that the church never recognized the earlier "Dakota" marriage.[11]

While the first meetings with government officials were cordial, Little Crow had much to say. "If I were to give you an account of all the money that was spilled . . . it would take all night to tell you," he began. Acting commissioner Mix brushed the comments aside, saying only that the money would be accounted for. It soon became apparent, however, that the Indians from both delegations were oblivious to the fact that the reservations were set aside for them for only another year, and that the government wanted them to cede half of this land.[12] After several weeks of what the missionaries dejectedly called "debauchery," Mix finally told the delegations that the treaty he wanted them to sign would relinquish all rights to the ten-mile strip on the northeast side, or left bank, of the Minnesota River, but it would grant them permanent title to the lands on the south side. This stunned the delegation, including the Christian Paul Mazakutemani. "Since we made the treaty we have lost a good deal of money," Paul replied, hoping to shift the argument back to corruption, and now the government wanted more land. Little Crow then reaffirmed this: "We never received half of what is promised."[13]

After the protests, Mix presented the stark reality. Once the President's five-year order ended, the newly christened state of Minnesota would assume jurisdictional authority over all lands along the Minnesota River.[14] When finally presented with the treaty, the only part the Indians found acceptable was the clause that paid traders' debts and provided some money for mixed-blood relatives.[15] In obvious ill humor, and given no other choices, the men of both delegations signed the two separate treaties and prepared to return home. The Indian bureau tried to honor Little Crow by presenting him with a new set of black clothes. But once back on the upper

Minnesota River, he quickly returned to Native dress. Worse, Congress initially refused to pay for the land, as it supposedly had been purchased in 1851. Brown had told the Indians in Mix's office that when they signed the treaty, they might get five dollars an acre. Grudgingly, Congress finally appropriated $96,000 for the Mdewakantons and Wahpekutes, and $170,880 for the larger portion claimed by the Sissetons and Wahpetons. The traders then put in their claims. Just for the Mdewakantons, Nathanial Myrick wanted $10,597, Henry Sibley $9,450, Andrew Myrick $8,757, Louis Roberts $8,387; twelve more followed with smaller figures. When the sixteen claims had been sorted out, they totaled $95,119; the government never even bothered to send the Indians the remaining $881. The Sisseton and Wahpeton received a small portion of the money earmarked for them.[16]

Meanwhile, Agent Brown got virtually everything that he wanted while in Washington, thanks in part to Mix's assistance. The funds sitting in the treasury were released by fall, and Brown hired a cadre of white men to begin a massive building program. The only remaining question was whether such an effort came too late. While the delegations were in Washington, Colonel John Abercrombie at Fort Ridgely received word that Indians had broken into the warehouse at the Lower Agency again and stolen food. Disorder was growing. While troops sent by the colonel captured three of the perpetrators and put them in the guardhouse, others taunted the American soldiers and showed signs of resistance. While the Mdewakantons at the Lower Agency were in a foul mood, Indians to the west seemed even more threatening, especially the Yanktonais and many Sisseton bands.[17]

The plains Sissetons, the people of Standing Buffalo, Scarlet Plume, Sleepy Eyes, and White Lodge, all had reasons to be angry at Americans.[18] Their leaders had not even been invited to Washington, and they frequently scoffed at agents and army officers alike. This first seemed apparent when, over the winter of 1858–59, Indian Superintendent Cullen attempted to placate them by delivering some presents.[19] But the expedition to Kettle Lake, west of the reservations, proved more difficult then Cullen ever expected. The spring had been wet, and travel by wagon was often impossible. Abercrombie, who was supposed to assist him, also dragged his feet, perhaps aware of the difficulty. An angry Cullen started on his own, only to be met by a strong party of mounted Sissetons who threatened his life if he proceeded. They claimed that no American had the right to enter the lands west of Big Stone Lake. Cullen retreated, blaming Abercrombie. Embarrassed, the colonel sent a strong force of a hundred men under Captain T. W. Sherman, but his cannon promptly sank in the mud. Sherman finally reached the stranded Cullen by late June, but Cullen, in a surly mood, thought only of using the troops to overawe the Indians. Finding a small village, he ordered Sherman to take eight unsuspecting Sisseton men prisoner.[20]

Just as the effort seemed an utter fiasco, Gabriel Renville and interpreter A. J. Campbell made contact with the Sisseton chiefs and convinced them to meet Cullen. Talking near Lake Traverse, Scarlet Plume explained that the Plains Indians thought they deserved annuities, but because they did not get any at previous distributions, they decided to prevent Americans from entering their lands. Worse, given the fact that annuities were handed out individually, rather than by the chiefs, Scarlet Plume carefully explained that "the chiefs have lost their influence" over the young men. This had led to the confrontation with Cullen.[21] Standing Buffalo then noted that most of their people were starving and desperately needed annuities. Accepting this explanation, Cullen released the captives and thereafter was able to distribute some presents. But it was far too little and too late. Standing Buffalo muttered in departing to hunt buffalo, "When we sold our lands, we were promised what we have not yet got."[22]

Both army and agency officials like Cullen believed that Sherman's troop movements had impressed the Dakota people who supposedly feared his "big guns." But Agent Brown was more circumspect. "We are now at a turning point," Brown wrote in a sober letter to Cullen in 1859. "Everything depends upon sustaining and protecting the farmer Indians this fall." A number of Mdewakantons, including Wabasha, had shown an interest in taking to the plow, and Brown's program had moved into high gear.[23] The agent purchased bigger and better sawmills and manufactured over five hundred thousand board feet of lumber. Some forty-five frame houses for Indian families had been constructed just three months later. Each family who moved in had between two and five acres of land broken for planting. While the vast number of oxen and plows that Brown then handed out to each family cost thousands of dollars, Mix allocated the funds.[24]

Superintendent Cullen applauded this frenzy of activity and even offered bribes to Dakota men who agreed to have their hair cut short, removing scalp locks. After the barbering, the men received oxen, hoes, and scythes, and especially pantaloons in what became openly advertised ceremonies. Cullen approached Little Crow regarding the offer—some in his village had accepted Cullen's offer—but he politely refused. He believed that you must change your religion if you alter your dress. Nevertheless, by 1859, about a hundred Dakota men at the Lower Agency had agreed to change. A year later, Brown slowly began replacing their flimsy frame houses with brick ones, which could withstand prairie fires. Leading men who took houses included Wabasha, Wakute, Taopi, and Traveling Hail. "This I think is a great movement," a giddy Riggs wrote to the American Board. "We have been working at it for years . . . and the government takes up the matter, and a *pantaloon band is formed at once*."[25]

Little Crow's reaction to the farmer movement mimicked what the majority of Dakota men at the Lower Agency felt. After Brown explained in council that most of the annuities would go to those who adopted the dress of the white man and took up farming, when the affair broke up, a large number of young Dakota men pelted him with rocks.[26] The factions of pro- and anti-farming Indians lived increasingly in segregated locations. Farmer Indians lived almost exclusively below the Lower Agency in clusters around Wabasha's settlement, while just north of it, two large villages refused to have anything to do with farming. Here Little Six, who had succeeded his father, assumed leadership over one village. An unassuming young man with a giddy deportment, he demonstrated little ability to lead anyone and seldom spoke in council. Nevertheless, missionary Samuel Pond, perhaps biased, said of him, "He hardly had sense enough to be responsible for his deeds."[27]

Even more opposition came from the Mdewakantons at Rice Creek. Quickly becoming the largest camp, these men listened to the council of Red Middle Voice (Hocokayaduta in Dakota). Pond thought Red Middle Voice to be an "able man," but a "bold, bad man." Plots festered in these communities, and their men began threatening farmer Indians and their families, government employees, and even Agent Brown.[28] Between these two opposition factions stood Little Crow's village, which was closest to the agency. Little Crow's chief *akacita,* Big Eagle, perhaps seeing the indecision of his chief, or even feeling betrayed by his actions in Washington in 1858, left the main village, settling with a few adherents a mile or so north of Little Crow's settlement. His decision was representative of the changing political scissions that existed within most Dakota bands—civil chiefs could no long control head soldiers or their followers. Some men tried farming, but they preferred to let the white employees do the work. To accommodate Brown—and receive a full share of annuities—some men would wear farmer clothes during the day and then don a blanket and attend dances at night.[29]

The main dance that still attracted the largest crowds remained the Medicine Dance and Feast. Christian Indian Lorenzo Lawrence revealed some of the society's secrets. He noted that Indian mentors of the dance continued to "teach him [the initiate] to make feasts." Henry Benjamin Whipple, the new Episcopalian bishop of Minnesota, who visited the reservation in spring 1862, noted the growing debate over feasts versus hoarding. It led to constant "councils . . . and a strange restlessness among the Indians." For the first time, he wrote, "Indians refused to shake hands with white men." Even worse, the Scalp Dance was on the rise: "Each day there was either a scalp dance, a begging dance, a Monkey dance, or a Medicine Dance." During the Scalp Dance, Whipple saw Indians "painted in every grotesque manner, face tattooed with yellow, red, black, green—[and] naked bodies painted with coiling serpents." At the height of the performance, "the dance is interrupted by the fierce words of a warrior whose descriptions of deeds of blood lash then to phrenzy."[30] Whipple was witnessing a regeneration movement, as well as a political revolution, one leading to trouble.

The growing factional divides at the Lower Agency seemed manageable to Agent Brown, but he worried more about the Indians at the Upper Agency.[31] Brown even convinced the army to send troops to the agency, the agent agreeing to provide barracks, which he dubbed Camp Lexington. A full company stayed throughout the summer of 1860, but dozens of farmer Indians were assaulted outside the agency, some having their pantaloons literally cut off. During that summer, four were killed, including a close relative of Henock (Maȟpiyahinape to his Dakota friends), the secretary of state of the Hazelwood Republic. Henock and two blanket Indians found the murderer and killed him. They then fled north, Henock abandoning his Christian friends.[32]

Riggs tried to put a calm face on the struggle under way, but when a shootout occurred outside his church, he had to admit that the conflict between farmer Indians and those who wore the blanket "was not at all favorable to our Sabbath services." He believed that "a retrograde movement" had taken hold, as twenty farmer Indians at the Upper Agency abandoned their pantaloons for the breechcloth. Part of the problem was the introduction of whiskey.[33] One particular place where several whiskey shops operated was Ottertail Lake, located in the no-man's-land northeast of the Upper Agency, between the Dakota and Anishinaabe villages. Brown was able to name those much closer to the reservations who sold spirits to Indians—Johnson, LaCroix, LeBlanc, Floyd, Roberts, Martin, Hartman, and the notorious "Whiskey Charley." He tried unsuccessfully to have them all arrested.[34]

The grog houses served American soldiers, settlers, and the Indians. After learning that one of their men had been killed and robbed at a whiskey house, run by a man named Hartman, soldiers surrounded the place and dragged several men out, threatening to kill them. They then burned the house down. When a carpenter from New Ulm, Jacob Pfenninger, came to the fort demanding restitution for the loss of his tools in the fire—he had been working there—the commanding officer rebuffed him, claiming it was a "frivolous matter." Major W. W. Morris noted that Hartman "kept a house of ill fame of the very worst stamp." One soldier claimed that he got "deseased [*sic*] with gonorrhea" and was accordingly on the "sick list" at the fort.[35] The army seemed to be washing its hands of the many problems associated with the new lands being opened around the reservations.

Brown welcomed reinforcements in the fight against whiskey. On one of his visits to the reservation, Bishop Whipple gave a sermon in Doctor Daniels's house on the evils of spirits and then determined to send a new missionary to the region. He selected Samuel Hinman, who would go on to have a long career of working with the Dakota Indians. Whipple was particularly impressed by such men as Taopi and Wabasha, who pleaded support. The head farmer at Wabasha's village, White Dog, also promised to become a Christian. Hinman, who arrived the next year, promptly started construction on a new, impressive church, located near Wabasha's village. Sermons included tirades against the consumption of whiskey. Useful competition erupted when young John Williamson, son of Presbyterian Thomas P. Williamson, arrived and formed his own mission closer to the Lower Agency. He preached abstinence much like Hinman. Many Indian women found the churches and their schools inviting, including the mother of Little Crow's four wives—Walking Runner's wife—who had converted and was called affectionately by Williamson "Old Sarah," another biblical name.[36] Nevertheless, the missionaries only heightened the factionalism, dividing bands and even families.

The missionaries did represent civility as did the many new brick houses that Brown completed.[37] Such optimism was not confined to the reserves, as a massive land rush occurred across central and western Minnesota. The 1860 census revealed that some seventeen thousand people had settled in the "Big Woods" near Hutchinson, Glencoe, and Forest City. Stearns County, alone to the northeast, boasted a population of nearly five thousand people, and south of the Minnesota River, Blue Earth, Cottonwood, and Brown Counties each had nearly as many people. Mankato's population swelled to fifteen hundred, and New Ulm's moved toward two thousand. While statistics are not available, within forty to fifty miles of the reservations, some twenty-eight thousand pioneers could be found in 1860, with the numbers likely reaching fifty thousand two years later.[38]

Census data are not available for the next two years (1860–62), but clearly, the most dynamic growth came along the northeast bank of the Minnesota River, incredibly fertile lands that constituted half of the original reservation. Major Morris thought some five hundred families had arrived in the region during the summer of 1860 alone; however, they were not included in the census. Thomas Williamson put the number at three thousand people, with many more arriving in 1861 and 1862. Some settled on land that still theoretically belonged to the Indians, because Congress took its time ratifying the 1858 treaty and the Mdewakantons saw no money from the agreement, as the $96,000 designated for them went to traders. These settlements upset them to no end. Indian leaders complained bitterly to Morris regarding this "invasion"; the major believed that whites had "squatted" on the land, but he claimed to lack authority to remove them. Newly arriving emigrants claimed rights of occupancy under the concept of "settler sovereignty," a right somewhat granted under the Preemption Act. Lands, then, could be occupied even before they were surveyed.[39]

As the regeneration movement grew, intertribal fighting continued unabated, with Dakota war parties becoming ever more defiant and prominent, knowing by 1860 that the army would do nothing to stop them. They organized themselves at Little Six's and Red Middle Voice's villages; others formed up at the increasingly rebellious Sisseton camps north of the Yellow Medicine River. After a successful venture, one party, consisting of two hundred warriors, marched through downtown Mankato and held a Scalp Dance for the amusement of the local population. While the officers at Fort Ridgely had on occasion put Dakota warriors in the guard house for killing Anishinaabes, or vice versa, civil authorities now consistently ignored prosecuting them.[40]

The polarized Dakota reservations hardly took notice of the inauguration of a new governor, Alexander Ramsey, now a Republican, who replaced the Democrat Sibley in January 1860. A new president, Republican Abraham Lincoln, took office a year later. As was always the case with patronage appointments, the Republicans replaced Brown as agent. He retired to the scrip lands given to his wife Susan, just north of Gabriel Renville's place, on the left side of the Minnesota River. Here, Brown, who had amassed a small fortune from his time as agent, built a three-story stone house of some four thousand square feet, furnishing it with expensive drapery, chandeliers, carpets, and a grand piano, all imported from the East. The "Indian business," as it was often called, had been good to Brown. While clearly siphoning funds from contracts, debts, and annuity payments, Brown had also employed his wife Susan, son Samuel, and daughter Ellen, at the cost of $1,200 a year. Samuel was just fifteen years old at the time.[41]

Thomas Galbraith replaced Brown as agent in May 1861. He had backing from Minnesota congressman Cyrus Aldrich, who sat on the House Committee on Indian Affairs. Aldrich obviously picked Galbraith so that he might join in the pillaging of Dakota and Anishinaabe funds. Early historian Thomas Hughes, using oral history accounts, offered perhaps the most telling assessment of Galbraith: "A red headed man and hard drinker, his excessive use of liquor had brought about a serious impairment of his mental faculties and he was really unfit to hold any official position." Brown agreed, describing Galbraith as "a gentleman who could sing a good political song, make a good stump speech and had read [James Fenimore] Cooper's novels." But that was the extent of his "Indian knowledge."[42]

Galbraith inherited the same system for distributing annuities and cash as former agents, systematically taking a share. The corruption had become institutionalized, the superintendent of Indian affairs only competing with the various Indian agents at the Anishinaabe, Dakota, and the recently moved Winnebago agencies. Contracts for food were increasingly controlled by and auctioned off by the superintendent—he, or even officials in Washington, would take a cut for awarding the contract—while cash annuities went into the hands of the agent, who took cuts from traders. Both the agent and the superintendent could pay debts, supposedly caused by Indian depredations; the agent often handled the claims of traders, and the superintendent dealt with claims, often put forward by settlers, who would employ politicians in Washington, to acquire remuneration.

The scams often went like this: A settler would claim that Indians killed some cows and horses and set fire to haystacks. There was no investigation of the claim. While Brown never revealed his "fees" for handling such claims, Galbraith stated that the standard rate was 15 percent if paid "in cash." He suggested to the new Superintendent of Indian Affairs Clark W. Thompson that they might "share" another $12,000 in debt claims that were coming in, and if any trouble occurred when trying to secure it, "Charley Mix, Jr., would aid you & I think *Old Mix* would easily go it."[43]

"Old Mix," often the acting commissioner of Indian affairs, as Galbraith called him, was a close friend of Brown, and young Charley took the job as the Winnebago agent. Brown sent his daughter Ellen to finishing school in Washington, D.C., where she became close friends with the Mix family, attending the inaugurations of both Buchanan and Lincoln with them.[44] The relationship led to joint business ventures and especially paid off when Brown, who kept messy records, had to balance his accounts in 1861—or cover up the vast sums he had skimmed from debts and annuities. He claimed to have inherited an agency debt of $41,000 from Murphy, and when he left that debt had doubled to $81,000. Galbraith soon discovered, however, that he had also not paid workers' salaries, owing them $21,000, money that had likely gone into the agent's pocket. Brown did itemize what he had spent as agent on the Dakota reservations. The total was an astonishing $339,630.12 in gold and silver.[45]

The extent of the corruption surfaced after Congress made its appropriations in 1862. Galbraith was livid, writing a "confidential" letter to Bishop Whipple in which he assured him that a schoolhouse would be built near Hinman's new church, "if it [the money] is not all *stolen*." But in fact, most of it was gone. Galbraith told Whipple somewhat later, "the Blackest '*Trick*' of Indian swindles has jest [*sic*] been revealed to me—& God only knows what will be the result."[46] Mix had apparently allowed most of the appropriations for 1861 and 1862 to be applied to debts for food, salaries, and agricultural equipment purchased by Brown.

Rumors of the corruption in the Brown-Cullen administration had actually reached the White House some months earlier, likely mentioned by Whipple. The corruption was just as bad among the Anishinaabe agents in northern Minnesota. Lincoln dispatched his private secretary, John Hay—who later served two administrations as secretary of state—to Minnesota to quietly investigate. He concluded that among the three agencies in Minnesota—Anishinaabe, Dakota, and Winnebago—hundreds of thousands of dollars had been skimmed from Indian funds in the 1850s. "The Superintendent Major Cullen, alone, has saved, as all his friends say *more* than 100 thousand in four years out of a salary of 2 thousand a year." The agents working for him, including Brown, Hay concluded, "have become rich."[47]

While the corruption of the Democratic group had reached new heights, little difference existed among the Republicans. Galbraith soon discovered that new Superintendent Clark W. Thompson and even Congressman Aldrich were sanctioning debts, one as high as $5,500 for an off-reservation robbery that Dakota Indians had supposedly committed. The money to pay it would come out of their annuities, as usual. Galbraith fumed that it "cannot exceed *three Hundred Dollars.*"[48] More problems emerged over a fight to control the school fund. A. T. C. Pierson bribed Thompson into giving him the position, rather than Riggs who had lobbied for it, and Pierson saw the position as a cash cow. He first fired many teachers and demanded control of the designated funds for the construction of schools—a considerable amount of money could be made in purchasing lumber and hiring workers. But most "funds" were long gone. Failing in his effort to gain control of the funds, Pierson threatened Thompson: "If my friends won't help me—my enemies shall—I don't believe that I am impotent."[49] Galbraith gave Pierson $1,000 in cash and a new wagon to "get rid of him."[50]

Despite quieting Pierson, Galbraith seemed befuddled by the situation. He discovered that moneys coming from Washington were being diminished considerably. Worse, he too had sanctioned a massive purchase of farm equipment in March—no doubt taking a kickback for the purchase. Galbraith then discovered that he had no money to purchase food for the Indians or to pay employees. He could only complain to Thompson, demanding that he investigate the "fix," as Galbraith put it, by Mix. Nothing came of the complaints, and the 240 cross plows, 216 corn plows, 79 yoke of oxen, 47 cows, and 88 sheep that Galbraith had ordered all had to be paid for somehow. The problem likely set Galbraith to drinking more than in the past.[51]

At the Lower Agency, rumors persisted by summer 1861 that given the disturbed state of the nation—Bull Run occurred in mid-July—the agent lacked the money necessary to pay the salaries of workmen as well as the annual annuity. While the money did arrive, the discussions regarding the solvency of the Union persisted and emerged in councils held in May of the next year. When word then arrived that the annuities would be paid in greenbacks, rather than gold, everyone—Indians, traders, and laborers—became angry, because it took $2.50 in paper to reach the equivalent of a dollar in gold. Protests quickly reached Washington, and the uproar caused a serious delay in the payment. Mix backpedaled, but it took him several months to amass a sufficient amount of gold and silver to meet the annuity obligation.[52]

More trouble erupted at the Lower Agency over who would be the speaker for the Mdewakantons. The job involved placing tribal concerns in front of the agent who usually sat in a chair and listened, with the Indians formed up in a semi-circle on the ground. Such councils occurred several times a year. By 1861, the majority of Indians at the Lower Agency—those under Little Six and Red Middle Voice—refused to attend these discussions, and it was dangerous for the agent to enter their villages. Little Crow had held the job of speaker while in Washington, but after news of the 1858 treaty reached the west, Red Owl, from Wabasha's village, took over the position. He was an angry man who knew much about the corruption.

A large collection of dignitaries, including Ramsey, Galbraith, and the then-well-known, Henry David Thoreau, visited the Lower Agency late in the summer of 1861 after Red Owl had been selected as speaker. "A dark, sinewy man, of intelligent countenance," as one newspaper described him, Red Owl assailed government authorities for what seemed like an eternity. In particular, he noted that just before leaving his post, Agent Brown had shipped large quantities of goods from the agency warehouses to an unknown location. The chief asserted that "much had not been returned, and he feared they would never see it." The newspaper reporters also noted the "half a hundred new plows, exposed to the weather, rusting." Ordered by Galbraith, he had no funds to hire white farmers to even retrieve them. As one newspaper reporter rather wryly observed, "injustice and fraud, probably alas, too well founded in fact."[53]

Yet a second political upheaval occurred when Rec Owl died over the winter of 1861–62. This time, the now mostly farmer-dominated council, which represented a small minority of the Mdewakanton people, selected Traveling Hail as speaker, once again bypassing Little Crow. Little Six and Red Middle Voice ignored the entire political process. Traveling Hail had spoken out against the 1858 treaty after Little Crow returned from Washington, but he was a farmer and not necessarily opposed to "civilization."[54] Given the failure of Little Six and Red Middle Voice to even come south to the agency and participate, Little Crow surprisingly began attending services at Hinman's still-uncompleted Episcopal church. The older leaders from Wabasha's, Taopi's, and Traveling Hail's bands were being listened to by the agent and his employees, and they had access to goods and food, and thus some patronage.[55]

With few funds to purchase food, however, starvation became increasingly acute over the winter and spring of 1861–62. Galbraith knew of the problem, begging Thompson for $5,000 in emergency funds. By Christmas, Jane Williamson, a teacher at the mission, reported "a camp of starving Sissetons near us, who, after having impoverished the farmer Indians, then devoured all they can get from government officials."[56] Settlers northeast of the Minnesota River found Indian women digging "pomme de terre," which they called *tipsiŋna,* a small, wild turnip. Others tried to harvest marsh grass, which, though eatable, caused sickness. Sarah Wakefield, the wife of the doctor at the Upper Agency, noted the growing number of deaths from such "food." Come spring 1862, Little Crow, acting as intermediary for some Indians, went into the settlements and pawned or sold guns and farm equipment for a few head of cattle.[57]

By July 1862, several thousand Indians gathered at the Upper Agency, waiting desperately in the hot sun for Agent Galbraith to feed them and looking ever so cautiously at the two companies of American soldiers who rested in the shade near Camp Lexington. When the agent refused to feed them, trouble erupted on August 4, as several hundred desperate warriors broke into the warehouse. They took twenty sacks of flour. Young Lieutenant Timothy Sheehan, with what one of his soldiers later noted was "a face that looked like a dead man," ordered his troops on line and turned a howitzer on the crowd. But the Indians stood their ground, "crowding up around" the soldiers, as Private Orlando McFall later recalled: "They would push and jostle us around and slap us in the face." Only Sheehan's preparation to light the fuse of the cannon forced the Indians to disperse. During the time this standoff was occurring, Galbraith cowered in a nearby house and "showed the white feather," as McFall put it, a classic nineteenth-century description of cowardice.[58] Galbraith had few provisions, and he knew that no funds existed to replace what he did have.

Agent Galbraith, scared and shaky, finally agreed to come out and council after Captain John Marsh arrived with more American soldiers three days later. Seeing an opportunity to reignite his reputation, Little Crow also appeared, traveling north to the Upper Agency after hearing of the troubles.[59] Galbraith anticipated the arrival of annuity money, most of which would go to the traders, but he had no hope of replenishing the warehouses. The traders had a different goal: they wanted to break Indian resistance and ensure that they had their debts paid in full thereafter.

As the council came together, Sissetons Standing Buffalo and Red Iron immediately demanded that food be distributed. The agent had little to offer and finally turned to the traders. They then huddled with their spokesman,

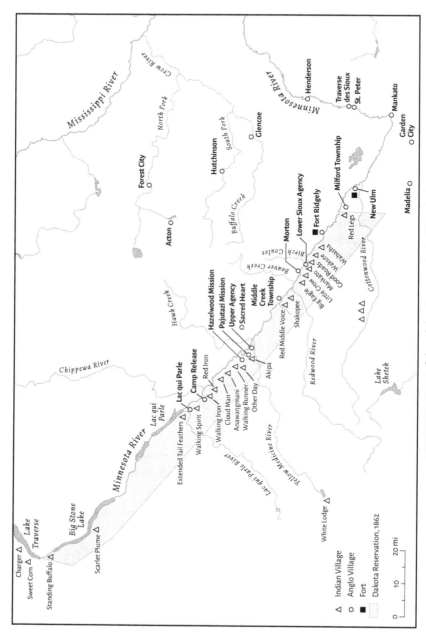

MINNESOTA IN 1862–1863. Cartography by Erin Greb.

Indian Village
Anglo Village
Fort
Dakota Reservation, 1862

Mississippi River
Crow River
North Fork
South Fork
Buffalo Creek
Minnesota River
Henderson
Traverse des Sioux
St. Peter
Mankato
Garden City
Milford Township
New Ulm
Madelia
Red Legs
Cottonwood River
Wabasha
Mankato
Good Roads
Little Crow
Big Eagle
Birch Coulee
Beaver Creek
Morton
Lower Sioux Agency
Fort Ridgely
Glencoe
Hutchinson
Forest City
Acton
Hawk Creek
Hazelwood Mission
Pajutazi Mission
Upper Agency
Sacred Heart
Middle Creek Township
Red Middle Voice
Shakopee
Redwood River
Lake Shetek
Chippewa River
Lac qui Parle
Camp Release
Red Iron
Walking Iron
Cloud Man
Anawangmani
Walking Runner
Other Day
Akipa
Extended Tail Feathers
Walking Spirit
Lac qui Parle
Minnesota River
Yellow Medicine River
Lac qui Parle River
White Lodge
Charger
Sweet Corn
Standing Buffalo
Lake Traverse
Big Stone Lake
Scarlet Plume

0   10   20 mi

78

Andrew Myrick. Once back at the council, Galbraith demanded an answer. Myrick rose slowly, as if to exit, and then turned and said, "as far as I am concerned, let them eat grass." Little Crow sat stunned, as young John Williamson translated the message. A general cry came up from the group as they left in a huff.[60] Marsh quickly ordered the warehouse to be opened, and what little food it held was distributed. Nevertheless, most Indians left hungry and in a bad mood.

Meanwhile, troubles of this sort were quickly expanding at the Lower Agency. In early June, given the lack of food, warriors from Little Six's and Red Middle Voice's villages had been gaining ascendency, contemplating expelling all traders from the reservations. But they lacked leadership and discipline. Realizing this, they formed one large soldiers' lodge, with well over a hundred young men. While western Lakota Sioux bands kept a soldiers' lodge throughout the spring, summer, and fall, this had never been done before in the summer by eastern Dakota bands. The organization of the lodge itself is a testimonial to the degree to which civil chiefs had lost control of the young men. The *akacita* soldiers intended to deny payments to the traders, or anyone else. Indeed, a large contingent of *akacita,* or soldiers, visited Fort Ridgely on July 2, identifying themselves and demanding that Captain Marsh remove the traders from the pay tables. "We are the braves [the actual term used likely being *akacita* soldiers]," they told the captain. "We have sold our land to the Great Father. The traders are allowed to sit at the pay table and they take all our money." Marsh saw that no leading chiefs were among them, and he refused to act, lacking, as he said, authority. But the young Dakota warriors seemed intent on usurping the farmer-oriented civil chiefs and had begun to speak in place of them. The revitalization movement had led to the virtual dissolution of traditional tribal government, at least in the Mdewakanton villages of Little Six and Red Middle Voice.[61]

The *akacita* soldiers had determined even before they made their demands of Marsh to take whatever credits they could get from traders, and then utterly refuse to pay for them when the annuity money arrived.[62] When two members revealed the scheme to the traders, the *akacita* chiefs caught the traitors, ripped off their clothing, tore up their tents, and killed their horses—a soldiers' kill. The *akacita* lodge was taking charge of Indian affairs. This happened just as Lieutenant Sheehan had marched his troops through the Lower Agency on June 28, headed north to quell the riot at the warehouse at the Upper Agency. His men witnessed a massive demonstration near Little Six's village, "where about seven hundred Indians were having a 'Big' Medicine Dance."[63]

They had been stirred to a frenzy by the medicine men and reassured of their own salvation by the leaders of the Medicine Dance. They were now poised to confront the traders. Increasingly fearful of retribution, the traders at both agencies had mostly cut off all credit. Hoping to salvage some profit, Andrew Myrick had devised a scheme to subvert the *akacita* warriors. He openly offered Galbraith and Thompson a deal in writing. If they agreed to pay the trade debts before meeting with the Indians, Myrick would reimburse the government officers "12 to 15 percent on the gross cash business of the year, which could net the officers from 7 to 10,000 dollars per year."[64] This must have looked inviting to Galbraith, whose salary was a mere $1,500 a year.

As Myrick schemed to force Indian payment, shouting matches between traders and Indians reached new heights.[65] Myrick often responded by telling groups of Indians that they might as well "eat grass." This phrase "eat grass" was commonly used by traders well before the confrontation at the warehouse at the Upper Agency on August 4, so it came naturally to Myrick as he left the council. It obviously referred to the harvesting of swamp grass by Native women, which caused dysentery when consumed without protein.[66] All that prevented an all-out war at that moment was the contingent of troops. To a lesser extent, some Anglo and Franco-Dakota men of influence preached calm, but the Renvilles, Robertsons, Campbells, and Prescotts were at times under siege, and a large contingent of Mdewakanton men continued to dance into the night.[67]

By August 11, Galbraith had heard that the annuity money, some $69,000 in gold and $2,000 in silver—not all that was due, but at least a substantial payment—was on its way to the agencies.[68] As a pastime, he had used his influence to recruit thirty mixed-blood men at the Upper Agency for the Union Army. Another twenty joined the group at the Lower Agency. Calling his force the "Renville Rangers," Galbraith then departed for New Ulm, where on the night of August 16, the entire company got gloriously drunk. As Galbraith departed for the east the next day—with the intent no doubt of meeting the courier with the annuity money—events at the Lower Agency spiraled out of control.[69]

Nightly secret councils, organized by the head *akacitas,* occurred at both the villages of Little Six and Red Middle Voice. The talk included revenge for trader insults and even all-out war.[70] The secret councils also included discussion of the Civil War. The Union had lost battles in the East and seemed destined to be defeated. Settlers noted the interest that Dakota men took in the engagements and "how quick they were to put together the string of defeats." Dakota men asked why so many young men were being sent east, and they questioned whether the Great Father would prevail in the war. When word arrived that even Galbraith had left for the East, they wondered if the annuities would ever be paid. It was his job to pay them, and the money was still in St. Paul. Some even thought that "the people of the South have been wronged and cheated," much like they had been, leading to the growing supposition that the Great Father was in fact cruel and mean.[71]

While awaiting the annuity money, twelve Indians left the reservation to hunt in the Big Woods. A small party of four separated from them on August 17 and went to visit the cabin of Robinson Jones, near a small settlement called Acton. Jones, who a neighbor later wrote, "often sold whiskey to the Indians," charging ten cents a glass, refused credit and then, fearful of retribution, fled to another house nearby.[72] Moving on, the four young men then stumbled onto a chicken coop and began gathering eggs, provoking a discussion over whether they should steal from farms. Soon charges of cowardice flew, and they moved on to the house that Jones had fled to. Employing a ruse, they proposed a trade for a gun. To test the new piece, several men, including Jones, went outside. Then suddenly, the Indians wheeled and killed Jones and four other settlers, two of them women. The Dakota party then fled back to the Rice Creek village, where at midnight, they told their story to Cut Nose (Mahpiyaokennaźiŋ in Dakota), who had emerged as the nominal "head soldier" of the lodge. Little Six and Red Middle Voice soon joined in the discussion.[73]

A serious debate then erupted and continued nearly to dawn. Some of the older men recalled that back in 1827, Colonel Josiah Snelling had convinced Shakopee to surrender four young men who had killed a number of Anishinaabes at Fort Snelling.[74] The colonel then handed the four men over to the Anishinaabes, who killed and scalped them in front of their relatives. Would the army not treat the young men who had killed whites in Acton the same way, and could the head *akacitas* allow such a thing to happen? Yet another argument suggested that "the Great Father had a hard fight on his hands" and was "getting short of men." Was it not a good time to go to war and push the whites off their land?[75]

What happened next is confusing. Sources suggest that the leaders of the soldiers' lodge collected their followers and headed south along the road that connected the two reservations. Along the way, they woke up both Big Eagle and Mankato, men who had become increasingly critical of the farming movement. They all then headed farther south to Little Crow's village. At the time, Little Crow seemed resolved to work with the Americans; he was even flirting with Hinman and his church and had moved into a new government frame house. But what could this visibly rejected leader say to prevent a conflict? What could he possibly offer to hold back the young men who were bound and determined to start a conflagration? The *akacita* soldiers seemed all powerful, even persuasive. Would it not be best to join them?[76]

Little Crow certainly saw the divisions within his nation, with a few farmers who had given up their scalp locks and medicine bags, thus attaining some degree of influence with the Americans, and another small group of farmers who mostly pretended to be progressives. The *akacitas* had become a powerful force, however, and with young men shouting in his ears and realizing that two important men somewhat connected to his village, Big Eagle and Mankato, had joined the *akacitas*, Little Crow's belief in accommodation became increasingly tested as the debate in his house turned into a shouting match.

Yet the chief still tried to calm everyone down. Because the house was relatively small, he approached the few angry men with a reasonable argument, a tactic often used by civil chiefs. Yes, he noted, American soldiers had departed for the East, but the Great Father had many soldiers, more than any Dakota warrior could fathom. This brought shouts, likely from the younger men outside, that Little Crow was "a coward." The chief's son, sixteen-year-old Wowinapi, finally heard his father say, "Taoyateduta is not a coward, and he is not a fool! Braves [referring directly to *akacita* soldiers], you are like children: you know not what you are doing." He then spoke of the Civil War, noting that it was far off, and that if the young *akacita* soldiers were to travel to the fighting, "all the way your path would be among white soldiers." Threatened, embarrassed, overwhelmed by the number of young men present, and dejected by the rejection of his people, Little Crow finally, reluctantly relented, saying "I will die with you."[77] Some general consensus had emerged for war among the vast majority of Mdewakantons.

FIVE

THE MASSACRE

August weather along the upper Minnesota River had been humid, with intermittent showers and even a few displays of lightning. It had little impact on the crucial meeting of the soldiers' lodge at Little Six's (Śakpedaŋ in Dakota) village; men came and went from the main *akacita* tepee where the discussions continued. By 6:30 A.M. on August 18, after conferring with Little Crow, as the sun broke out, a decision had been reached. Later evidence demonstrates that a few men and women went to warn relatives, and even a few white friends living nearby, of upcoming trouble. While the *akacita* soldiers prepared for war, no clear consensus existed on how to prosecute it. This was typical of Dakota warfare: small parties usually forming around seasoned leaders they trusted. But who was the leader? Little Six was a newly anointed chief with little experience. And his uncle, Red Middle Voice, was too old. This gave the soldiers' lodge authority, perhaps much more than it normally would have.

One goal seemed to solidify the group. The young Dakota men all believed that the hated traders needed to die, and the *akacita* chief soldiers assigned certain men and their followers to each of the four trade houses at the Lower Agency. As the daylight brightened, warriors marched southward down the road that led to the agency. The men from Red Middle Voice's and Little Six's villages dominated the group, but others from Mankato's, Big Eagle's, and Little Crow's smaller camps slowly joined them. Big Eagle, like Little Crow, had argued against the war early on, but because there was no stopping it, both he and his chief joined the crusade, the advocates overwhelming those who opposed it. Most of the *akacita* soldiers had danced all night, the drums being heard by white settlers across the river. Working themselves into a frenzy, they had painted their faces and heads for war—red paint dominated, with black and white streaks intermittently smeared in vertical lines across the face. They all bared their chests, wearing nothing but a breech cloth. The warriors stationed themselves near the trade houses, often just on the other side of the road, and waited for the order.[1]

Suddenly, the young *akacita* Tawasuota ran forward and screamed: "Now, I will kill the dog who would not give me credit." He shot James Lynd, who stood in the doorway of Myrick's establishment; others with him sprinted over Lynd's body, gunning down George W. Divoll and the cook "old Fritz," who were at the counter. Myrick took two balls, one in the arm and one in the side, but ran upstairs to what everyone knew was an arsenal of guns. Two mixed-blood brothers, A. J. and Hippolite Campbell, who had worked as teamsters for Myrick, watched anxiously outside the building as the affair unfolded, bewildered and panic stricken. One of Myrick's Dakota wives hid behind the door and escaped unharmed. Dakota warriors warned them all to leave, and they sprinted to the main Campbell residence, where their wives, children, and other relatives watched in confusion and horror.[2]

The killing continued, with Francois LaBathe being gunned down at his store despite his Dakota heritage. At Louis Roberts's store, while Roberts was gone, his three clerks, Patrick McClellan, Joseph Belland, and Antoine Young, all took a barrage of bullets. Finally at William Forbes's store, a standoff ensued after the young warriors had wounded George W. Spencer and allowed William Bouratt, a mixed-blood, to escape.[3] Spencer, like Myrick, struggled to get upstairs. Just as the soldiers contemplated an assault on the attic, a veteran warrior, Wakinyantawa, publicly proclaimed that anyone who harmed Spencer would answer to him. The two men were "kodas," or close friends.[4] Spencer and Bouratt survived, but few others did. Myrick, when hearing of plans to burn him out, exited through an attic window and ran for the cornfields, but he was gunned down. Warriors severed his head and stuffed his mouth with grass.[5]

Nearly a thousand yards of intermittent, tree-covered ground separated the trade houses on the north side of the agency from the government buildings. A large, two-story stone warehouse had been built, along with houses for the superintendents of farming and education, the interpreter, the physician, the carpenter, and the blacksmith. Common laborers lived in a boardinghouse, although given the lack of funds, most had left the year prior. In all, the traders and their clerks consisted of just seventeen men; sixty-five other government workers and their wives and children lived at the agency.[6]

Most of the government buildings were located around a large public square where agents held councils with the Indians. While many warriors who attacked the trade houses proceeded to plunder them of flour, barrels of pork, clothing, whiskey, and guns and ammunition, a few others moved south, focusing on the easternmost stables, which housed valuable live-stock. Here, Little Crow joined them when a confrontation occurred with three government workers who tried to prevent the theft of horses; the chief angrily shouted, "Kill them." Unarmed, A. H. Wagner, John Lamb, and Lathrop Dickinson were the first to fall. Philander Prescott, watching the carnage, ran for his house. Prescott had lived with the Dakota people for forty years, and he had a Dakota family. Warriors shot him as he ran and severed his head. Fortunately for other white employees, the struggle over the horses warned many to flee down the bluff of the river to the ferry, or in wagons along the road, south, toward New Ulm.[7]

While panic drove the employees from the agency, most who lived owed their lives to the ferryman. Oliver Martell had built the ferry some years before, hiring one Jacob Mauley (or Hubert Millier) to operate it. Both stayed at the ferry for some time, helping people cross to the east side of the Minnesota River. They saved boardinghouse proprietor J. C. Dickinson, his family, and several others. As Indians finally crossed the river in pursuit, Martell mounted his horse and raced eastward toward the fort. Mauley stood by his job, becoming "the hero of Redwood Ferry" to those who survived. Warriors soon killed him and shut the ferry down.[8]

Little Crow then moved south toward Wabasha's and Wakute's villages, perhaps to inform them of the carnage underway. Here, Little Crow sud-denly encountered Reverend Hinman. The chief had been in church the day before, but now he had a sullen look. "Crow, what does this mean?" Hinman inquired. The chief said nothing, only displaying a "terrible fierce-ness" that left Hinman in a dither. Realizing the danger, Hinman fled by buggy, being one of the last to make it over by ferry, abandoning a young teacher, Emily West, in the confusion. She and another young woman reached the ferry, but they were met by painted warriors on the other side, likely the men who had just killed Mauley. To West's surprise, the Dakota man in charge was White Dog (known in Dakota as *Śuŋkaska*), who had been the nominal head of the farmer Indians but was recently deposed by Taopi. He moved forward and, courteous to a fault, shook hands with the "missionary," as he called her. He then urged her to run to the fort. Just as fortunate was schoolteacher Joseph Reynolds, carpenter John McNarin, and their families, all of whom were well-liked by the Indians, escaping at times certain death and ultimately reaching the fort.[9] The selective killing of people seemed to be the order of the day at the agency. Those perceived as enemies, either by insulting Dakota religion or medicine men or refusing to provide assistance such as food, were killed. This included the agency physician, Dr. John Humphrey. The doctor, his wife, and three children made it over the ferry before Mauley was killed, but given Mrs. Humphrey's illness, they stopped at a cabin some four miles below the ferry. While son John went to fetch water for his mother, Indians appeared and set the house on fire, killing the Humphreys and their two small children. In all, some twenty employees and nine traders and clerks lost their lives in one short hour, while forty-six escaped.[10] But the killing had just begun, and it escalated to new levels in the hours that followed.

The erratic behavior of the *akacita* soldiers is indicative of the confusion that abounded, as no one seemed to be in charge. The explosion at the agency took on the vestiges of a slowly moving regeneration movement, clapping on a sail like a man-of-war, turning back time, and urging young Dakota soldiers to become vicious provocateurs who increasingly embraced traditional Dakota war.[11] This slowly included the severing of heads and the mutilation of bodies. One of the first to feel the escalating mood was Mrs. Jannette E. DeCamp, whose husband ran the mills a few miles south of the agency.

After hearing gunfire and being nearly paralyzed—her husband was in St. Paul on business—Mrs. DeCamp saw the approach of Wabasha's mother, who quickly admonished her in the Dakota language: "Fly! Fly! They will kill you, white squaw." Gathering her three children she fled toward the river but suddenly ran into Wabasha himself, who was at the head of several dozen warriors. The chief "was sitting on a large, white horse . . . dressed in a chief's costume, a head-dress of red flannel adorned with bullock horns." DeCamp later professed that he looked like a "Catlin picture." When Wabasha's followers lurched toward DeCamp brandishing tomahawks, Wabasha leaped from his horse, drew two pistols, and stood between his men and DeCamp. After being brought into the chief's village, she and her children were rushed into his house for safety.[12]

After being removed to Wakute's house that evening, Mrs. DeCamp soon witnessed other captive women being ushered into the darkened single room. With the killing spree now being some twelve hours old, one of the young warriors who delivered the captives expressed great jubilation regarding the many white men who had been killed: "They all ran away and left their squaws to be killed." One Indian, he blustered, "could kill ten white men without trying."[13] Indeed, in the following five days, the killing of hundreds of virtually unarmed white men, women, and children became commonplace, acceptable behavior in the purely Dakota world that was reemerging. The perpetration of these crimes reached such proportions that every Minnesotan believed that killing on all occasions involved severing off heads, cutting off arms, and disemboweling men.

The descriptions of this mayhem spread rapidly back east into the more settled regions of the state, producing panic. While some accounts of it were accurate, others were embellished. The United States was entering a period of sensationalistic fiction, which often influenced journalism. It would soon be produced by the volume as the so-called dime novel. While earlier "captivity narratives," written by women taken captive in the eighteenth century, had become standard reading by this time, they were readily enhanced by a more violent fictional element, presented by authors such as James Fenimore Cooper, who invented the savage Indian Magua, who was completely devoid of any redeeming characteristics. Not completely unlike Magua, the movement into the settlements by Dakota men initiated a new phase of the massacre, one that became unbelievably brutal and nearly doomed the entire Dakota nation in the end. For sure, regardless of the truth, all Dakota men in the days that followed would become Maguas in the eyes of Minnesota newspaper editors, especially after the slaughter expanded to the new settlements on the north side, or left bank, of the Minnesota River.

Many Dakota people felt that the left bank of the river still belonged to them and had been illegally overrun by settlers. This was a delightful land, with rich meadows and fine, clear water. A series of creeks, separated by four to six miles, ran in a leisurely direction from the northeast to the southwest, discharging into the Minnesota River. They offered water and rich forage for cattle and horses. Birch Coulee was just northeast of the agency, followed by Beaver Creek, some six miles to the north. Middle Creek was six miles farther on, and roughly eighteen to twenty-four miles from the agency, there were the settlements called Sacred Heart on Hawk

Creek. According to the army officers at Fort Ridgely, five hundred or more families had reached these lush lands between May and July 1862, some simply staking claims and others building crude log houses.[14]

While white settlers inhabited the vast majority of farms along Birch Coulee, at least one farm was owned by the Dakota mixed-blood family of Andrew Robertson. Andrew had passed away two years earlier, leaving his wife, young son Thomas, and Thomas's younger sister, who had recently married. At roughly 7:00 A.M. on August 18, a friendly Indian named Katpantpanu came to warn them that "a party of Chippewas [Anishinaabes] was nearby." This became a common ruse that, very likely, Dakota warriors had agreed to use when planning attacks in the soldiers' lodge. They would disarm settlers with the lie. Katpantpanu, who was from Little Six's band, had heard it from the *akacita* soldiers, perhaps even believing it. Now alerted to danger from his friend, Thomas Robertson heard gunfire. He knew that the gunfire only meant trouble, and it came from the agency, not areas to the north where Anishinaabes might be lurking.[15] He went to warn people of the oncoming trouble.

The reports from the agency also attracted the attention of young Benedict Juni, who was just eleven years old at the time. His father took up lands at the mouth of Birch Coulee in the fall of 1859. Being so close, Juni often played with Dakota children and knew their parents. Early Monday morning, after talking with his father about the reports, the Junis decided to gather their stock, mostly oxen and horses that ran free in a time before barbwire. While trying to bring the animals closer to their log cabin, Benedict met white-faced neighbors who said that the Indians were killing people at the agency. Now concerned, the family loaded their belongings into a wagon and prepared to leave. But both young Benedict and his father became separated from the women and children, who joined another family in flight. Dakota warriors soon overtook the party and shot the two men with them. At that point, the near-hysterical women and children noticed that the Indians went into council. After a few minutes, they let the women and children proceed, and the Juni family members rejoined their father at Fort Ridgely.[16]

While young Benedict Juni became a captive, the experiences of his family and those of the Robertsons suggest that as early war parties crossed over the Minnesota River, many were still debating what to do with Anglo and Franco-Dakota people and settler women and children. There seemed to be no compulsion about killing men, however. Katpantpanu moved the

Robertson family to a house near the agency, and Thomas Robertson too returned safely after warning many settlers to flee.[17] At the outset of the killing, even in the settlements, it seemed that settlers who had developed some relationship with Dakota warriors might be saved—the Juni family being a prime example. Reciprocity and demonstrated kindness still remained a Dakota virtue. This applied especially to Anglo-Dakota people like the Robertsons, but it could also apply to settlers who had been especially attentive to assisting Indians. Even so, at least a dozen families perished on Birch Coulee, leaving no narratives; only a few survived.[18] At times, warriors spared no one, not even children.

The various groups of Dakota warriors who crossed the Minnesota River to attack settlers moved quickly from Birch Coulee northward into the Beaver Creek settlements, where even fewer whites had developed relationships with Indians. Here, none of the settlers had heard the reports of gunfire at the agency, some eight miles away. A half-dozen eyewitness narratives have survived from settlers on Beaver Creek, which can offer a better sense of the evolving mayhem. A few, given within a few months of the outbreak, provide valuable insight, whereas others, written thirty or forty years later, must be viewed cautiously, as they were considerably influenced by subsequent events and newspaper hyperbole that included exaggerations of the severity of the killing. Several surviving narratives focus on a family group living a few miles up Beaver Creek: the Earles, Carrothers, and Hendersons. The group included twenty-seven people in all, twenty-three of whom were women and children. After hearing conflicting news regarding fighting and seeing Indians trying to steal their horses, they debated just what to do.[19]

The group collected at the Earle cabin, bringing in oxen and horses and hitching them to farm wagons. The wives threw feather beds, food, and some household goods into three such vehicles. Just as they departed, four Indians appeared, assuring them that it was the Anishinaabe who were causing the trouble. Although this small party of Dakota men had entered Jonathan Henderson's house and tried to take a musket from him—to fight the Anishinaabe, so they said—Henderson concluded that they were mostly friendly. The settlers hesitated, and given the fact that Mrs. Henderson was terribly ill, they turned back after starting along the road, only to suddenly face thirty or forty more *akacita* soldiers.[20] Henderson negotiated a second time and agreed to give up the oxen and horses, keeping one wagon for his ill wife. The Indians demanded the five guns that the party had; Henderson refused. After this, the whites left, pulling a small wagon with the suffering Mrs. Henderson and her two small children, ages one and three. The Indians, meanwhile, talked among themselves.[21]

Once one hundred and fifty yards down the road, the larger party of Indians suddenly turned and fired at the settlers, killing a man named Wege who had joined them. Henderson rushed to the side of his wife, who gave him a white cloth to wave in surrender. It was met with another volley that tore off Henderson's finger; he turned and ran, as some of the women and children scurried away in what became a mile-long flight. The women, carrying children, soon tired, and when the Indians reached them, one warrior grabbed Mrs. Earle's hand and shook it vigorously in a sign of friendship. Seeing the display, David Carrothers, whose five-year-old son was trying desperately to keep up with him, "turned the little fellow around and told him to go back to his mother." The boy sat crying in the road as Indians, racing after the men and larger boys in the party, approached. One tomahawked the boy outright, and others dispatched three other children who could not keep up. At the Henderson wagon Indians heaped the feather bed on top of the mother and two small children and set the wagon on fire, killing them. Five women and three small children, who fell back from the fleeing men, were captured and carried to the Indian camps across the river. The men—Earle, Henderson, White, and Carrothers—and several of the larger boys all ran, some for nearly forty miles; seven of them finally reached safety.[22] Fifteen victims lay strewn along the bloody path that led east.

The men, while fighting, had separated, with some going to the fort and others running until they reached Hutchinson. David Carrothers ran into the town late on the evening of August 18 and penned an excited letter to Governor Ramsey, noting that he had survived only by "leaving my wife in the hands of the Indians."[23] Reaching St. Paul, he then gave an interview to the newspapers, only fanning the flames of hysteria that quickly swept across Minnesota. Exaggerated newspaper reports became standard; one noted that the frontier town of Glencoe had been burned to the ground and that "horrors indescribable" were being committed by the Indians.[24] Scalping, mutilation, and rape became commonly used terms in these reports.

While some of these reports were true—the killing of the Carrothers' boy and the other children near him being witnessed by several people—narratives of such violence soon fed on themselves to the extent that it often becomes difficult to separate fact from fiction. As the rumor mill grew, the attack on poor Mrs. Henderson and its violent nature was retold in many different ways. Mrs. John Carrothers, one of the women who was captured, gave a rendition when providing testimony before the Sioux Commission, established by Congress in 1863 to investigate claims. She reaffirmed most of the details given by her brother-in-law, David, but when it came to the death of Mrs. Henderson, she said that after being captured, "they [the Indians] would not let us return by Mrs. Henderson." She only learned afterward of the wagon being burned with the victims in it.[25]

Forty years later, when penning a second narrative of the event, Helen Carrothers related how she had witnessed an Indian, who approached a Henderson child, "a pretty girl" of nearly three, "and beat her savagely over the face and head with a violin box, mashing her head horribly out of its natural shape." He then picked her up and "dashed her against the wheel of the wagon." Grabbing the one-year-old, an Indian held her up by the foot and "deliberately hacked the body, limb by limb, with his tomahawk, throwing the pieces at the head of Mrs. Henderson."[26]

Obviously, Mrs. Carrothers saw no such abhorrent violence, but as the conflict grew newspapers and publishers sought ever more gruesome accounts of killing, often exaggerating their descriptions. This became the case especially in later years when selling books led to gross exaggerations. Such publications attracted readers and supposed firsthand accounts of this sort became commonplace. Whether Mrs. Carrothers simply made up the descriptions of children being hacked to death later in life or heard such stories handed down from person to person and came to believe them or a creative editor manufactured them is impossible to determine. Certainly as the murders escalated in Minnesota, in county after county, there was little doubt that even people in positions of authority came to believe the worst.

The incident that started at the Earle cabin was repeated over and over again as war parties proceeded up Beaver Creek and to its north, reaching Middle Creek by late morning. Many new settlers in the region received a warning and fled; others were caught in their fields or in their cabins. Justina Boelter, her husband, and three children arrived on Middle Creek in June 1862, settling eight miles north of the Carrothers family. They joined a mostly German community that contained many of her relatives. Hearing of the killing of whites to the south, Justina's husband went to gather the cattle; she never heard from him again. After quickly leaving her house, her brother-in-law took her baby and ran into the woods. Justina, trying to flee with him, fell behind and returned to her house. She found all of the inhabitants dead, her mother-in-law had "her head severed from her body." While her brother-in-law reached Fort Ridgely, she stayed hidden in the woods for nine weeks, an older child dying of starvation before her very eyes. When Justina was finally found, she could no longer walk, but she and one of her children survived.[27]

A half-mile north of the Boelter cabin lived Gottfried Buce (also Busse). They had arrived in the summer of 1860 and helped organize the first German Lutheran Church in the region. By spring 1862, as Gottfried's daughter Minnie later noted, "so many people came into the country that we did not know half of our neighbors." The church had over a hundred members, all from the families along the upper portion of Middle Creek. The startling news that the Boelter family and others had been killed reached them at about 3:00 P.M. The Buce family had hardly gotten out of the house when Indians approached and killed both of Minnie's parents and her two sisters. Yet they allowed Minnie and her brother to live. As captives, they were even allowed to visit the Boelter house, where Minnie witnessed the terrible carnage. "Grandma Boelter" was on the floor of the cabin "with every joint in her body chopped to pieces." Although Minnie was just seven years old and told her story forty years later, which suggests possible exaggeration, there is no doubt that of the over one hundred members of the Lutheran church, at least seventy perished in one afternoon.[28]

By the end of the day, at least forty-nine dead settlers were strewn along Beaver Creek, and another thirty-seven died along Birch Coulee. At least seventy fell along Middle Creek. Because the burial parties failed to reach the region until over a month later, when the count was made, many of the dead were never found, including, for example, the husband of Justina Boelter. In other words, the count likely reached two hundred or more. While the evidence is surely incomplete, the surviving narratives suggest that some men fled, leaving their families behind. Perhaps this explains why a young Indian warrior who had been drinking told Mrs. DeCamp later on the evening of August 18 that white men "ran away and left their squaws to be killed."[29]

Just which Dakota warriors committed the carnage is difficult to determine. Some were undoubtedly from Little Six's village, which seemed to be the place where the soldiers' lodge formed and contained many discontented men. But the soldiers at Little Six's village certainly coordinated their attacks, to some degree, with soldiers coming from Red Middle Voice's Rice Creek village. The authors of the narratives could not easily identify them, although Justina Boelter apparently thought one was Cut Nose (Maĥpiyaokennaźin in Dakota), who was the nominal head of the soldiers' lodge. And because Cut Nose and Little Six were identified as working together, and later seen in Sacred Heart, they were certainly involved.[30]

Many of the newly arriving German- or Scandinavian-born settlers had learned only a few Dakota words and knew little regarding the character of the Indians they encountered. Samuel Brown, the young Anglo-Dakota son of Joseph R. Brown who was himself captured, indicated that many young men from the soldiers' lodge called the German settlers *"eyaśića,"* or those who spoke a "bad language." Brown, while being herded to Little Crow's house, heard a Dakota warrior scream, "The Dutch [Germans] have made me so angry, I will butcher them alive."[31] The ethnicity of certain people obviously had something to do with survival. Families like the Hendersons parlayed with their attackers, in Dakota or English or perhaps a little of both. While language was often a barrier, it also allowed for some interaction, even negotiation, at least at first. The narratives of many different settlers indicate that those who were warned could understand the Dakota word for "flee." This was more difficult for the Germans, who spoke a language seldom heard before by the Indians. Kinship, reciprocity, and language went a long way in preserving the lives of those who survived.

While Dakota warriors cleared Birch Coulee, Beaver Creek, and Middle Creek of settlers, others from the various villages moved south. They crossed the line separating the reservation from Milford Township, just northwest of New Ulm, at about 11:00 A.M. Here, just beyond the reservation boundary, new settlements had sprung up with farms claimed by Germans, such as Carl Pelzl, Athanas Henle, John Zettel, Max Zeller, Casimir Hermak, Florian Hartman, Franz Massapust, and Joseph Stocker. While most did not have good relationships with the Indians, a few did, including the family of Margareta Holl Hahn. The Hahn log cabin had a dirt floor and one window, five head of cattle, and a milk cow. Hahn, who was just fifteen in 1862, noted that on more than one occasion they "had befriended an old Indian in need of food." They freely gave "corn [and] potatoes, with some salt." This was also true of the Thomas family. When confronted with twenty hungry Indians at their house just north of New Ulm, the women of the house asked for their arms, which were freely surrendered, and then fed all of them at a large table. The arms were returned, and all left happily. Accordingly, on the morning of August 18, well before warriors arrived, the old Dakota man came back to the Hahn house and, "gesticulating excitedly," warned them to flee. While it is unclear how the Thomas family was warned, they, along with the Hahns, escaped to New Ulm, likely driving their cows ahead of them (many were later reported in town).[32]

Meanwhile, in New Ulm, the town awakened to a nice, sunny day after a night rain and some celebration. Indian Agent Thomas Galbraith had arrived a day before with his fifty recruits, known already as the Renville Rangers. They invaded the saloons but generally behaved themselves; Galbraith gave a rousing patriotic speech, something that, as Joseph R. Brown noted, he was quite capable of doing. Soon a brass band appeared, and tables were set up to recruit more soldiers for the Union Army. Eighteen signed up to go to war, and the town fathers decided to form a recruitment committee that would fill out a company (usually one hundred men). Not finding them in town, fifteen men agreed to travel to Milford and recruit others. On the morning of August 18, around the same time the Hahn family was packing to flee, the fifteen men in three wagons, waving a large American flag, left for Milford.[33]

Unlike the Hahn family, the settlers living along the southern boundary of the reservation received no warning. A war party of thirty Dakotas descended upon the region just after 11:00 A.M. Sheriff Charles Roos of New Ulm later claimed "it was . . . Wabasha's band," but others from Little Crow's and Wakute's villages had joined them, strongly suggesting that even in the villages where farmers lived, some young men held deep seated resentment against Germans. In a rather startling fashion, Roos later noted that "a negro" was leading them. This man was Joseph Godfrey, a runaway slave. While living on the upper Mississippi River, he had married into Little Crow's band, professed an interest in Christianity while living near Williamson's mission in 1850, and later took a second wife from Wakute's village. He later testified that warriors had forced him to join the group, but he seemed to be at the forefront as the party moved south.[34]

Godfrey's leadership role, which is very suspect, at least confirms the obvious failure of these young men to convince Wabasha, Little Crow, or Wakute to join them. The raiders did seek plunder, for the young men involved had missed out on ransacking the trade houses and most hated the German settlers living just south of them. They first attacked the farms of Athanas Henle, Franz Massapust, John Zettel, and Benedict Drexler. While Henle and his wife fled to safety, the others were mostly killed, men, women, and children.[35] Moving farther south along the road, the warriors reached the traveler's house of Anton Henle, where they found his wife

Theresa, her father and mother, and a hired girl in the field. They killed three of the four and severed the head of the hired girl; Theresa fled to the wheat shocks and survived. Going into the Henle house, the Indians hacked two children to death; a third later died in New Ulm after being rescued from the house.[36]

The noise made by the New Ulm recruiting party quickly distracted the raiding party. The three wagons were crossing a small bridge that led to Henle's traveler's house. Once across, the Indians ambushed the caravan, firing mostly into the lead wagon; three men were killed. Reversing course and abandoning the lead wagon, the surviving Germans fled back to New Ulm. While the attack as well as the appearance of numerous other refugee families in town brought consternation, Sheriff Roos seemed unconcerned. He initially believed that a small party of Dakotas had obtained liquor and were simply on a rampage.[37] He began organizing a posse of thirty men to bring the Indians to justice.

Rather than follow the fleeing recruiters, the Indian raiding party turned west. They found easy prey as the killing along the road had left no one to carry a warning. Looking up from his farm work, Joseph Stocker, who had a place at least three miles west of the road, noticed that the farmhouse of his neighbor, Martin Fink, was on fire. He quickly ran to help and suddenly noticed a boy lying in the doorway, "with an arrow in its chest." Almost simultaneously, he saw a wagon approaching, flying an American flag; it was the lead wagon of the recruiters. He noticed that some men were in white men's apparel, but others, running along the ground, were clearly Indians. Confused, Stocker raced back to his house. A young servant girl who lived with the family noted that Stocker instructed his wife to continue with lunch "in order to give the impression that we were unafraid." Just as they sat down, an Indian demanded that Stocker come outside. He refused, and several Indians fired a volley through the window, killing Mrs. Stocker.[38]

Fearful that Stocker might be armed, the Indians then set fire to the house, rather than invade it. Stocker and the young servant girl fled to the cellar and began to dig. Soon they could see daylight and raced into a cornfield nearby for cover. Along their flight to New Ulm, they saw farmhouses ablaze in every direction. At John Zettel's house they found the father dead in the doorway and three children tomahawked to death. More mayhem was discovered at the homestead of John Fisherbauer, where the survivors of the Schilling family had fled. Mrs. Schilling had miraculously survived a hatchet attack, but she had terrible cuts along her head. Her son had fled with a knife in his back; Stocker pulled it out, and he miraculously survived. Walking and hiding, the wounded and the foot-able finally reached New Ulm and safety.[39]

After burning the Stocker cabin, most of the Indians turned to consolidating the plunder that they had assembled. They loaded the goods onto wagons and moved leisurely in a northward direction. By mid-afternoon, they reached reservation lands and observed another party in a wagon fleeing to the south. Dakota riders quickly surrounded the wagon. The whites included three young women: Mary Schwandt, Mattie Williams, and Mary Anderson. They had worked for Joseph Reynolds at his school. Reynolds had left three trusted men—Francois Patoile, L. Davis, and an unidentified Frenchman—to escort them to safety. Patoile had been on the reservation for some time and seemed amused at the thought of an Indian outbreak. After being warned at John Mooers's house to turn north, Patoile ignored the advice and circled around the south side of the agency, heading for New Ulm. It was here that they met the war party.[40]

Although the Indians were agitated, Patoile was still convinced that they would not be harmed. Nevertheless, "they seemed to be all drunk," Mary Schwandt later wrote of the encounter, and virtually all of them rode in farm wagons with "barrels full of flour, and all sorts of goods and pictures." Their bodies were all painted, scaring Davis and the unidentified Frenchmen, who darted from the wagon and were quickly shot down. Patoile, sitting still, took four balls in his chest and fell dead on the road. The women, meanwhile, tried to flee, and Mary Anderson was shot in the side and fell. Mattie Williams was grabbed and her dress was ripped from her body, but she was not sexually assaulted. Brought back to the wagon, Godfrey drove the three young women to Wakute's house, which they reached in the early evening. Here they met Mrs. DeCamp and Wakute, who tried and failed to remove the ball in Anderson's side. A gritty young woman, Anderson, wincing in agony, dug it out herself but lost considerable blood in the process.[41]

Meanwhile, Sheriff Roos, still convinced that the war party was only a group of "drunken Indians," armed a posse that left for Milford in the early afternoon. The group soon discovered dozens of victims and a handful of children who managed to flee the tomahawks and hid in sloughs. Mrs. Henle also came out of hiding. As the posse entered Milford Township, they saw nothing but burning houses and haystacks and slaughtered cattle. Most of the dead had been tomahawked to death, as the Indians early on had few firearms. While hardly any had been scalped, a few had been beheaded, and the condition of the children who survived tomahawk attacks brought grown men to tears. One little girl "was cut across the face, breasts, and side." Another boy "was dreadfully cut up." A child's body had been recovered that had "its head cut off and sixteen other gashes upon its person." Many of the victims brought in had severed heads as a result of their throats being cut. The killing had left pools of blood.[42]

Late in the afternoon, Sheriff Roos realized that he had completely underestimated the attack on the recruiting party. He penned an urgent letter to Governor Ramsey, explaining the circumstances and asking for "1,000 men, well-armed." At that time, he estimated that thirty people had been killed; the number would grow to forty-one and finally fifty-three, when all the victims were found just in Milford.[43] While the people in New Ulm began organizing a militia, they could hardly know that other events gave them a brief reprieve from the violence.

After Reverend Hinman, ferry owner Oliver Martell, and others had fled into Fort Ridgely, Captain John Marsh called out the garrison, the eighty-five men of the Fifth Minnesota Regiment. Marsh had only assumed command of the troops on April 16; his second-in-command was nineteen-year-old Thomas Gere, a sergeant who had just been promoted to second lieutenant. While the majority of the troops were unseasoned, Marsh was a veteran who had fought at the First Battle of Bull Run. Being wounded, he returned to Minnesota and, after recovering, took a commission. Just ten days earlier, Marsh had handled the tense situation at the Yellow Medicine Agency, when the Sissetons had rushed the warehouse, extremely well. He likely had confidence in his ability to defuse the situation at the Lower Agency. The Mdewakantons, he assumed, were more "civilized" than the Sissetons. Once his men were in formation, Marsh handpicked forty-six and, with the interpreter, the Anglo-Dakota Peter Quinn, headed north toward the agency.[44]

Marsh should have been prepared for trouble. Hinman had informed him of the killings at the agency, and so had Martell, although the ferryman likely wasted little time at it, given his fright. Even more telling, the troops passed a number of dead bodies, including poor Mauley. But Marsh rushed ahead, even failing to put out scouts or skirmishers. At noon, his force entered the marshy bottoms of the Minnesota River, where grass and trees could hide several companies of troops. Still in ranks, the company stopped at the ferry and bunched up in a line. The boat was docked nearby, but Marsh and Quinn were first distracted by a man "dressed in citizens clothes" who began to speak.[45]

The Indian man was White Dog (or *Śuŋkaska*), who had once headed the farmer element.[46] He had saved Emily West hours earlier and was considered a friendly Indian by all at the agency. John Magner, whose house had been the scene of the Humphrey family murders, had joined Captain Marsh's command and knew White Dog well. He later testified that White Dog stood on the rising bluff on the western side of the river, not more than fifty yards away, "with a big tomahawk." He was, at least along his face and head, "all painted over red," a clear indication of a willingness to die in war. Quinn asked him why he seemed so out of character. White Dog replied that he brought the tomahawk "to smoke," and he encouraged Captain Marsh to cross over and parlay with the Indians at the agency. Meanwhile Marsh asked Magner to look upriver for movements. Moving above the command, he saw both in the river and in the weeds just north of Marsh's troops that "the place was red with their heads"—warriors painted for war. Marsh ordered a retreat just as White Dog signaled the Indians to open fire. The first volley was devastating, killing a dozen troopers and wounding many more.[47]

Marsh remained unscathed although Quinn fell dead. Worse, Indians had moved around the file of infantry, firing from the right flank. More troopers fell as Marsh retreated south along the river, finding some relief from the high brush. But this cover soon disappeared, and Marsh elected to cross the river. Mid-river, he went under, suffering from a cramp. His men tried to reach him, but the captain drowned. Fortunately, the Indians stopped pursuit, likely fearing the counter fire. Twenty-five American soldiers had been killed, including Marsh, and five had been wounded. The survivors staggered into Fort Ridgely at nightfall. If Dakota Indians had viewed the army as the main obstacle to recapturing the Minnesota River valley, such thoughts evaporated after defeating Marsh's command. Fort Ridgely, now commanded by an inexperienced nineteen-year-old lieutenant, had but four dozen troops to protect all of western Minnesota. And the fort was nothing more than a collection of buildings, without any palisade to fight behind.[48]

Given the easy victory, other Indians who had resisted the *akacita* at first abandoned their white clothing and took on native dress and war paint. The overwhelming power of the moment—the plunder, the whiskey, the captives being herded into camps—made for an alluring opportunity that Mdewakanton Dakota men could not resist joining. What the women thought of the confusion and conflict is mostly unrecorded, but they always supported their men when at war. A general belief emerged that they could drive the whites out of the Minnesota River valley: ethnic cleansing in reverse. More parties went out, ten or twelve in a group. At about 5:00 P.M., war parties moved north of Middle Creek, reaching the settlements near Sacred Heart, a region some twenty-five miles north of the Lower Agency.

A number of German families in the region had relatives south of them on Middle Creek. Late in the evening of August 18, a visitor to the home of Mary Schwandt's parents—young Mary had already been taken captive near the agency—came rushing back excitedly, exclaiming that the entire Schwandt family and other neighbors were dead. August, John Schwandt's son, had witnessed the killing from afar. August's father had been shingling and was shot from the roof of the cabin. His wife ran from the house; she was overtaken and killed in a field. Justina Kreiger, who later testified about the killings, noted that John's wife had "her head severed from her body," although she never witnessed this. She then claimed that John's pregnant married sister was "cut open." The child was then taken out and "nailed to a tree." While August never confirmed such a heinous crime, and Mary Schwandt later claimed it to be a fabrication (she certainly had talked with August about the event later), the story soon reached the newspapers, and the nailing of children to fences and trees became commonly accepted newspaper rhetoric in Minnesota.[49]

By midnight, some thirteen families, sixty-two people in all, had come together and decided to flee. Kreiger and her brother, Paul Kitzman, were among them. They all left in several lumber wagons, first heading east, and then south toward Beaver Creek. Two hours after sunup, on August 19, they encountered eight Dakota warriors, who, as a sign of friendship, "put down their guns and made signs not to fire." They advanced slowly, and a Dakota man who had hunted with Paul Kitzman talked with the settlers. With a smile he said: "What Johns run for? We are best friends. The Chippewa [Anishinaabe] they kill every place."[50]

Kitzman seemed convinced that the rumors of Anishinaabe war parties were true, despite what had apparently happened at the Schwandt cabin, which Kreiger learned of later. Kitzman knew the Dakota man and the Indian spoke relatively good English, saying repeatedly that "the Sioux did not kill anybody." The Dakota warriors then shook hands with everyone in the party, and the settlers turned their wagons around, deciding to return to their homes. It was late August and crops in the field had to be saved. When other Dakota warriors joined the party, the men in the Kitzman party became concerned. Within a mile or two of the Kitzman house, the Indians demanded money, and when it was furnished, as Kreiger later reported, "the Indians immediately surrounded us and fired."[51]

In the mayhem that followed, the *akacita* soldiers killed all of the men. The warriors then turned their focus on the wagons. They reached in and "beat with the butts of their guns" as many of the fifteen or twenty children they could reach. Some, blood streaming from their faces, jumped from the wagons and ran. A few made it to a slough nearby; the Indians mostly did not pursue because they plundered the wagons and nearby cabins. At this point, the leader of the war party—apparently the man professing friendship—made it clear that women and children who surrendered would not be killed. Justina Kreiger, grabbed by a warrior and told that she would become his new "wife," refused and was shot in the back. He then took her dress off; it became a trophy that would be given to Dakota women back in camp. Justina later exclaimed, "When I was shot the sun was still shining, but when I came to myself it was dark." For fourteen days, Kreiger wandered, eating berries to survive. She finally saw American soldiers who brought her to a camp on Birch Coulee, a fateful decision because it too would soon be attacked.[52]

The massacre of the Kitzman group constituted one of the worst killings in one spot during the conflict. Twenty-seven people were found dead near the wagons, and seven small children, apparently unable to run, were burned to death in a house. The Indians took twenty-two captives. In other locales in the Sacred Heart Region, fifty more victims were later found and buried, bringing the total number of people killed to seventy-seven. The high mortality rate in this region can only be explained by the fact that most of the settlers were ethnically German and recent arrivals in Minnesota. They did not have the time to develop a "kinship" relationship with the Dakota people, although this is not a guarantee of safety, as Kitzman apparently knew one of the warriors.[53]

News slowly surfaced at the Upper Agency, nearly thirty miles to the north, of trouble below. A Sisseton Indian warned George Gleason, the clerk at the agency office, who in turn laughed. The Mdewakantons were farmer Indians, not warriors, he exclaimed. Gleason had promised to take Sarah Wakefield, the agency doctor's wife, and her children to visit friends, and in mid-afternoon they departed. Near Reynolds's cabin, a few miles north of the Lower, or Redwood, Agency, they met two Indians who allowed them to pass. One then turned and shot Gleason in the back. His body tumbled from the wagon. He also sought to kill Wakefield, but his partner, Chaska, saved Wakefield and her children, who soon entered captivity.[54]

With rumors swirling at the Upper Agency, seventeen-year-old Samuel Brown and his sister, Ellen, knew not what to do. Their father, ex-agent Joseph Brown, had left for the East to promote a project called the steam wagon. Their elaborate three-story house was eight miles southeast of the Upper Agency on the east side of the Minnesota River. While the Brown children initially dismissed the rumors and went home, this changed at 4:00 A.M. on August 19, when teamsters banged on the door. The rumor of an outbreak was true, and now the large, extended Brown family considered options.[55]

Some two or three other families came together at the Brown house in the early morning hours of August 19. Some of these people had just moved to the region, because young Samuel Brown hardly knew them. Hitching oxen to farm wagons, they took to the road that led to Fort Ridgely, making it just three miles before encountering "swarms of Indians." Samuel Brown, who left a narrative, remembered the war party well: "the awful Mahpiyakenaźin, or Cut Nose, the terrible Shakopee, or Little Six, and the impudent Dowanniye, three of the worst among the lower Sioux, came to us shaking their bloody tomahawks menacingly in our faces."[56] They were fresh from the killing fields below on Middle Creek and at Sacred Heart. Some came with "blackened faces and bloody hands." Just then, one of the warriors raced forward to protect the Browns, noting that Susan Brown had saved his life one winter when he nearly froze to death. The war party then formed a council; they decided to kill all the whites who were not part of the Brown family. They "vowed . . . to spare no white man." Should they do so, "Little Crow and the soldiers' lodge would have them all shot!"[57]

At this point, Susan Brown rose in the wagon and, speaking eloquently in Dakota, demanded that the war party not harm anyone. Cut Nose replied: "Are you not grateful that your own life is spared." Susan then warned: "Remember what I say, if you harm any of these friends of mine, you will have to answer to Scarlet Plume , Ah-kee-pah [Akipa], and Standing Buffalo." Her speech constituted the ultimate promise of kinship revenge, as all of the Indians from Little Six's village understood, including the leader of the soldiers' lodge, Cut Nose. Brown won out, and five white men in the group were allowed to leave unharmed. Four young women were not as fortunate, and they, along with the Browns, were dragged into captivity.[58]

Back at the Upper Agency, a heated council of a hundred Sissetons and Wahpetons began at 11:00 P.M. on the evening of August 18. Some chiefs suggested that the Sissetons should join the uprising and "kill all the whites." But John Otherday, a fierce warrior who had taken a white wife while in Washington, countered them. "You might kill 10 or a 100 whites," he argued, but many American soldiers would soon follow. Otherday then heard that White Lodge was on his way to the meeting. This meant trouble, and Otherday and other Christians quickly gathered together the sixty-two whites at the agency, among them the wife and children of Agent Galbraith. At dawn, Otherday quietly moved them across the Minnesota River. Rather than reach Fort Ridgely by going south as the Browns had done, he guided them east to Hutchinson and ultimately St. Paul.[59]

Other Christians came forward to aid missionaries Riggs and Williamson and their families. Gabriel and Michael Renville, Simon Anawaŋgmani, and Paul Mazakutemani went to the mission houses and convinced them to leave. They first hid the mission families on an island in the Minnesota River. On the afternoon of August 19, the men sent the families eastward over the prairie. They continued for days, mostly walking, until they finally reached Henderson.[60] This left only a group of Anglo and Franco-Dakota people under Gabriel Renville, several Christian Indians led by Paul Mazakutemani and Solomon Two Stars, and several small bands of Sissetons and Wahpetons, living well to the north of the agency, with the latter having chiefs and young men who could not agree on what to do about the conflict underway forty to fifty miles to the south.

Well to the south of this debate, the survivors from Milford and the Cottonwood River valley came streaming into New Ulm on the evening of August 18. Hotels, such as the Erd House, the Dacotah House, and the Union Hotel, offered shelter; one spacious room in the Dacotah House was used to treat children with hatchet wounds. Some of those who had reached town questioned whether other neighbors had made it out. That evening, men from the Cottonwood valley and the small settlement called Leavenworth formed a militia of sixteen men, intending to go to the aid of their neighbors. There had been little news from the upper Cottonwood valley, where considerable settlement had occurred.[61]

They left New Ulm at sunrise, quickly covering the six to eight miles that led up the Cottonwood River. Here they found burned cabins and dozens of victims. Surprisingly, a few children who ran for cover survived, and a few men and women emerged from the sloughs where they had hidden themselves. The survivors were rushed back to New Ulm, but the carnage had been substantial. Several adults "were stripped of most of their wearing apearals [*sic*]." The ripping off of garments, especially from women, had become commonplace, yet it is likely explained by a warrior's wish to bring back a present for a female friend or mother.[62]

After penetrating thirteen miles into the interior, the group turned back toward New Ulm, dividing into two parties so that they could cover more ground. When the first party approached the town, Dakota warriors ambushed it and killed five men. The second party, just a half-hour behind, suffered the same fate, losing six more men. They brought back the news that the Cottonwood River valley had been cleansed of settlers, with at least nineteen people confirmed dead and likely many more unaccounted for. They also discovered that Indians were in the process of surrounding New Ulm. The founding fathers held a meeting and elected Jacob Nix, an old army officer, to take command of volunteers, twelve of whom had rifles. Nix ordered his men to build breastworks, consolidating a defense around the three to four city blocks with brick buildings.[63] It was a momentous decision that likely saved the community.

Several dozen Dakota warriors pranced on horseback on top of a meadow north of New Ulm at 3:00 P.M. on August 19. An observer with a glass could see them from atop the Erd Hotel, "naked and covered with war paint." Burning a few houses on the outskirts, the Indians left their horses and tried to assault the barricades, sniping and wounding a few defenders. They then saw some twenty-five men ride into town from St. Peter just as a driving rainstorm broke out. This forced the Indians to give up the field, and at least for the time being, New Ulm was saved.[64] While small raiding parties probed farther and farther out from the agencies, destroying farms and seeking plunder, the *akacita* leaders had yet to devise a strategy for taking either New Ulm or Fort Ridgely, which became places of refuge for fleeing settlers.

The Indians who committed these smaller raids often knew more about the unfolding events than the settlers. Dakota men traveled from village to village, spreading news of the outbreak into the western prairies and northward to Big Stone Lake. It soon reached the camp of those Sissetons associated with White Lodge. They became more radicalized following the trouble in the aftermath of the Spirit Lake affair of 1857. The band may have fielded fifty to sixty warriors, including a few men from the very small following of Iŋkpaduta. Another sub-band included the followers of Grizzly Bear, who frequently camped at a beautiful lake in southwestern Minnesota called Shetek.

Lake Shetek, nearly five miles long and located some forty miles southwest of New Ulm, attracted its first whites in 1855, desperate men with shady characters. Two men named Clark and Charles Wauben had fled after stealing goods in Mankato, and John Wright, who joined them, apparently had then killed Clark. Wright, John Jacques (or Jacobs), and William Everett built houses on the south end of the lake and began bottling something called "Jersey Lightening Whiskey," selling it to the Indians. Other, more reputable families reached the lake after 1858—at least they were not murderers, horse thieves, or whiskey peddlers. Among them were Aaron Meyers, Andreas Cook (or Kock), A. Rhodes, Watson Smith, Charles Hatch, Thomas Ireland, William J. Duley, and John Eastlick. The last three men had large families with many children. Most settled along the east-central portion of the lake and to the north.[65]

All seemed calm until the afternoon of August 19, when several of Grizzly Bear's young men began breaking down the fences and trampling the cornfields at Aaron Meyers's house at the north end of the lake. Meyers asked them why they were doing it and got no answer. As he approached the home of his neighbor, Andreas Cook, he found him dead outside his cabin. Meyers then packed up and fled with his family toward New Ulm. Charley Hatch, coming onto the scene, saw the dead man and rode south to warn other families. The remaining settlers congregated at the house of James Wright, who had traveled east on business. A dozen or so Indians then appeared, led by an old man called Pawn by the settlers. He had been instrumental in warning those at the lake in 1860 of a possible attack by Inkpaduta's young men, and the men in the settlement trusted him.[66]

The settlers tried to make Wright's two-story house defensible, even receiving assistance from Pawn. As other Sissetons appeared, Pawn then called for a parlay, convincing the settlers that two hundred warriors were on their way. They had to flee or be killed. Agreeing, a party of thirty-four people, nineteen of them children, piled what food and goods they could into wagons and fled east. After traveling a mere two miles, a large war party suddenly appeared, led by Grizzly Bear and Pawn. They fired into the wagons. At the first shots, Smith and Rhodes deserted the group, even as several of the men hollered for them to return. Knowing they could not escape using lumber wagons, the remaining six men ordered everyone into a massive slough to the north of the route. With tallgrass as protection, they were soon surrounded by Indians shooting down into the slough. Mrs. Lavina Eastlick, who survived to write a narrative, noted that the "balls fell around us like hail."[67]

While John Eastlick managed to kill Grizzy Bear, making some of the warriors more cautious, more and more men, women, and children were being wounded. After two hours, Pawn offered a diplomatic solution. Those who were alive could surrender. Most of the women and children accepted and rose from the slough, while the men remained hidden. As they left for captivity, an Indian woman beat Lavina's son, Freddie, to death while others shot her other son, Frank. Lavina, who had been wounded in the heel, then realized what would happen to the women—one warrior took Mariah Cook "as his prisoner," while another seized "one of Mr. Ireland's daughters," and a third, Pawn himself, claimed her and Mrs. Duly. As Pawn pushed her forward and she increasingly failed to keep up, Pawn shot her in the back, smashed the butt of his gun into her head, and left her for dead. The surviving captives, four women and seven children, several of them teenaged girls, were marched westward toward the Missouri River, entering a terrible captivity.[68]

While fourteen settlers perished in the slough at Lake Shetek, three of the surviving men waited patiently for nightfall. The fourth, William Duley, deserted the party early, following Rhodes and Smith, directly after ordering his family and others into the slough.[69] Another providential rainstorm then broke out, making further pursuit by the Indians difficult. Indeed, Pawn ordered Mrs. Wright to go into the slough and determine if any of the men were alive. Either she convinced them that all were dead or the Indian warriors feared going after them. The three remaining men quietly slipped away that night, reaching safety and telling the story of the massacre at "slaughter slough."[70]

Lavina Eastlick, wounded and left for dead, recovered enough to walk eastward toward New Ulm. Along the route, she encountered the Meyers family. Smith, Rhodes, Hatch, Bentley, and Everett soon joined them. When a rescue party reached them, Hatch and Bentley, assuming they were Indians, ran and hid in a slough. Amazingly, young eleven-year-old

Merton Eastlick, unaware of his mother's fate, emerged from the slough at night and brought along his fifteen-month-old brother, whom he put on his back. Harassed by wolves, Merton carried his brother for fifty miles and was brought into Mankato by the same group that found the adults. Upon entering town, he, and not the men who survived by abandoning the women and children, was rightly hailed as a hero.[71] In the days after the attack at Lake Shetek, the raiding parties diminished in size. But a pattern emerged: settlers who had failed to help hungry Indian visitors suffered terribly. They simply never understood the elements of reciprocity that were at the foundation of Dakota society. And even those who had been helpful, if they encountered Indians who were enraged at the treatment of their people, suffered death and destruction.

This was especially true at Norwegian Grove, a community of a dozen families who had built homes fourteen miles northwest of St. Peter. C. C. Nelson, who later wrote a narrative of their community, said of the Dakotas, "We didn't find them very pleasant or agreeable." When Indians came into the region on hunting expeditions, they were not welcome.[72] These settlers heard of the trouble by August 20 and had sent scouts out on patrol. Even so, that evening several men, while in a meeting at the Norwegian church nearby, were completely surprised when a rider came in from the west telling of an Indian raiding party. Most of the families quickly evacuated to St. Peter, but Eric Johnson and L. J. Larson went to rescue their families who were at home. Reaching their houses, they hitched wagons, and the two families quickly raced south. Even so, a handful of Indians on horseback gained on both families, and Johnson and his wife and children finally abandoned the wagon for a nearby cornfield. The Dakota warriors soon found Eric's wife, his fourteen-year-old daughter Ingar, and his son Pehr. Eric's wife rose to her knees and said simply, "Lord Jesus, receive my soul." The attackers then shot her in the breast.[73]

Turning on young Ingar, they seemed dumbfounded as she fell into a trance, not moving. Her father later tried to explain the scene: "They dragged her about on the grass, until the skin was torn and lacerated from the hips to the feet." They then felt her pulse and tried to open her eyes. Leaving the young woman, they turned to Pehr, who refused to follow them. After killing the boy, they burned a dozen houses and departed. In this small raid alone, some twenty settlers, almost all of them Scandinavians, lost their lives. When the troops finally did arrive, they assisted a man who was returning home to find his family. "He went back with us," one of the officers wrote, but he found nothing but a burned-out house. And there he was last seen, a "weeping man" who had lost everything.[74]

Other Scandinavians who suffered had settled in the north-central portion of the state on Norway Lake, some thirty miles northwest of the post office at Forest City. The thirteen families in the region were completely isolated, and two families, the Brobergs and Lundborgs, were surprised; all but two children were killed in the attack, mostly by tomahawks. As news spread of the attack, some congregated at the house of Asbjorn Rykke. Late in the night of August 20, Indians surrounded the house, saying they "came in peace." Rykke and others inside did not believe them. The next morning, the raiding party assaulted the house, wounding most of the men inside. This time, however, the women took up guns, holding off the attackers. Soon thereafter, other Norwegians in the area fled to an island in Norway Lake, where they remained until troops arrived. Thirteen of their fellow settlers perished, however, and several young women were carried off, never to be seen again.[75]

The killings at Norwegian Grove and Norway Lake were done by small unidentifiable war parties, unlike those that killed in Milford or Beaver Creek. This was so primarily because on the evening of August 19, Little Crow pleaded with the leaders of the soldiers' lodge to bring in the raiding parties and consolidate forces to attack Fort Ridgely. Those connected to White Lodge's Sisseton band never heard the plea, and some of his young men likely killed twelve more Norwegian settlers along the upper Des Moines River in Jackson County on August 24–25. Small groups of Dakota men killed another dozen people in Watonwan County, twelve more in Blue Earth County, and others on lands northeast of the Lower Agency, in Kandiyohi, Meeker, and McLeod Counties.[76] Reports of the attacks near Jackson County suggest that the Indians came in groups of no more than four or five men, and they often sought horses and plunder.

By late August, the massacre had reached such proportions that thousands of settlers were abandoning homes, crops, and livestock, fleeing to security in the new cities along the lower Minnesota and Mississippi Rivers. The horrific nature of the killing, only accentuated by the newspapers, brought absolute panic to the state. Typical of the stories that appeared was the graphic description of the murder of the Brown family, which lived just south of Leavenworth in Brown County. Several different descriptions of the murders have survived, some coming well after the event. While some are clearly sensationalistic in nature—products of the yellow journalism of the age—the most gruesome details of the killings are what most Minnesotans came to believe as fact.

The Browns lived south of the Cottonwood River. A few miles beyond their homestead, Robert Zierke, better known as "Dutch Charley," had a cabin. Most all the refugees from Lake Shetek reached the Zierke cabin, and then moved on to the Brown cabin, where they were rescued. Meanwhile, Aaron Meyers left the group, seeking help, as several of these people were wounded. He headed for New Ulm, swam across the Cottonwood River, and saw the Brown family, noting that a woman "about 30 years old" had been "horribly mutilated."[77] Zierke also tried to reach New Ulm. Along the way, he saw the Browns, an old man, a younger man, and a "daughter" who appeared to be about thirty years of age. She "was brutally disfigured, and had been ravished by the red devils after death."[78]

Given the terrible nature of the killings and their impact upon the Minnesota settler population, amateur historian Harper Workman interviewed as many people who were on the scene as possible, including Luther Ives, a respected resident of New Ulm and later a constable in the town. Workman recorded the following from Ives's testimony in the early twentieth century: "Miss Brown showed she sacrificed her life trying to preserve her honor. She was found with the handle of a tomahawk thrust through the vagina into the abdomen."[79] Other stories, coming from the same area, only enhanced the demonic nature of the Brown family murders. Meyers claimed to have seen yet another dead family: "One little girl had been nailed to the side of the house." The wife of Robert Thul left an account in 1925 that corroborated Meyers's description. Supposedly reaching town in a slow-moving ox cart, with Indians all about—suspicious in itself—Mrs. Thul saw "Indians all about us a mile or so away and settlers fleeing." Upon passing a rail fence, she noticed "the bodies of two young girls with the scalps removed and sticks thrust through the chests." They were "fastened together and hanging over the top rail" of the fence.[80]

Whether it was one girl or two who were nailed to the fence, or house, seemed not to matter. Captain E. Jerome Dane rescued the Lake Shetek survivors, including Lavina Eastlick, Smith, Bentley, Everett, and the others on August 26. A month later, as the story regarding the fence incident escalated in the press, Dane gave his version of it to George W. Doud, apparently on September 25. One young girl, Doud later reported, "was fastened to the side of a house by driving nails through her feet and her head was downward." Another young "lady was found scalped and all her garments were gone & both of her breasts were cut off." Finally, a woman "soon to be a mother" had her baby cut from the womb, "her offspring had been severed from her & an owl was deposited in its stead."[81]

The descriptions left by Dane, Ives, Thul, and Meyers proved remarkably useful in arousing the hatred of Minnesotans to the killing of settlers. Yet most were obvious exaggerations. Eastlick and the others from Lake Shetek moved from the Zierke house to the Brown house nearly a week before being rescued. She was with the party that buried "the bodies of four men and two women," including Mr. and Mrs. Brown (Eastlick believed that the woman was Brown's wife, not his daughter). "Near the wagon, we found the body of Mrs. Brown," Eastlick wrote. "Her head was spit open and a few feet from her lay a tomahawk."[82] There is no mention of her clothes being torn off or a suggestion of rape or a hatchet being thrust into her vagina.

While Captain Dane likely did order the burial of the Brown family—while not participating in it—he actually never led the largest burial party that scouted the lands north and south of the Cottonwood River. R. B. Henton, a resident of Brown County and later president of a major bank in the region, was ordered to form the burial party by then-colonel Charles Flandrau. Henton brought along Doctor Asa W. Daniels, a respected physician from St. Peter. Daniels examined all the bodies found, just over seventy in number. While the Browns had been buried, Henton and Daniels interred large numbers who had been killed. Of those, Henton later reported that "not one was scalped and only one mutilated." There is absolutely no mention of any children being nailed to a fence. Dr. Daniels later verified Henton's assessment.[83]

Perhaps an even more pronounced testimonial came from Ignatius Donnelly, lieutenant governor of Minnesota and later a prolific writer and representative in the U.S. House. Donnelly spent time at New Ulm surveying the destruction and reported from St. Peter on August 28: "The atrocities committed by them [the Dakota] are horrible. Strange to say, they take no scalps. Nearly all the dead bodies found have their throats cut." Donnelly, Daniels, and Henton were all highly respected individuals, and the Eastlick account is believable. This leaves open many questions regarding the accounts given by Dane, Ives, Thul, and Meyers. Atrocities certainly occurred—the tomahawking of children, viewed by many in New Ulm, being an obvious example—but the description of the brutal nature of at least some of the reported attacks, especially on women and girls, reached highly exaggerated levels.[84]

Regardless of the accuracy, the reports of terrible mutilation were believed in Minnesota and often restated, emphasizing their most horrible elements. And they escalated in nature the farther east they spread. Electra Carrier, living in Eden Prairie, far from the scene of the killings, wrote to her brother on September 12, 1862, that parents were finding their children "stretched to the sides of their houses," others with "arms cut off . . . legs cut off." The hamstringing of women and the almost universal belief that they were then raped, the cutting of children from wombs, and the nailing of children to fences became common descriptions of Indian brutality. Citizens who heard them seemed not to question their authenticity, with the exception of men like Daniels, Henton, and Donnelly.[85] By late August, the Mdewakanton Sioux people were perceived as being brutal demons who committed horrendous crimes.

While the descriptions of murder and mayhem created outrage in Minnesota, the killings closely resembled the intertribal warfare that had existed in Minnesota for centuries. Warriors gained more honor for killing enemies in hand-to-hand combat than at a distance with a rifle. The use of the tomahawk is explained by this basic belief as well as, to some degree, by the lack of firearms in the initial attacks. But mutilation, if it occurred at all, was something that Dakota warriors would do to enemies they expected to meet in the afterlife. A man without eyes or arms could hardly be a threat in the world to come, where intertribal warfare would supposedly continue. White settlers had no place in that afterlife—a belief that missionaries had reinforced time after time—making it unnecessary to mutilate victims when dead. However, using a knife to sever the throat was an ultimate victory to a warrior, and it could easily result in the actual severing of the entire head, which Daniels, Donnelly, and others readily reported. In other words, most reliable evidence regarding mutilation suggests that it was rare. But Minnesotans could hardly be convinced of that as the stories of brutality escalated.

The last settler killed in Minnesota by Dakota Indians was nine-year-old Frank York on May 7, 1865. The circumstances of his death went mostly unreported. But the documentation for the killing of over six hundred people—the majority of whom were women and children—does survive in the archives, diaries, and letters of those who witnessed what became the most horrific and destructive ethnic massacre in American history.[86] Many of those who lost their lives or their livelihood in those frightful days in late August were newly arriving European settlers. Mdewakanton Dakota warriors cut a 150-mile swath across Minnesota from Alexandria in the north to Jackson in the south. While the terrible calamity reached the eastern newspapers, it was dwarfed by the events of the American Civil War. But the people of Minnesota, reeling from such a fierce attack, thought of only one thing: escape the wrath of what most believed to be a demonic peril and seek revenge.

STANDING BUFFALO (Tataŋkanaźin), Sisseton chief who resisted the Mdewakantons. Courtesy of Minnesota Historical Society.

JOHN OTHERDAY (Aŋpetutokeça) is considered a hero for saving the missionaries and government employees at Yellow Medicine. Reprinted from Lucius F. Hubbard and Return I. Holcombe, *Minnesota in Three Centuries*, 4 vols. (1908).

WALKING GALLOPING (Simon Anawaŋgmani),
a Christian Sisseton Indian who saved white people at Yellow Medicine.
Courtesy of Minnesota Historical Society.

CHARLES E. FLANDREAU, a defender of New Ulm.
Courtesy of Minnesota Historical Society.

CAPTAIN JOHN S. MARSH led a relief to the Lower Agency,
where he and more than two dozen other soldiers were ambushed.
Courtesy of Brown County Historical Society.

CAPTAIN TIMOTHY J. SHEEHAN, defender of Fort Ridgely.
Courtesy of Minnesota Historical Society.

REFUGEES FROM THE YELLOW MEDICINE AGENCY, who were led to safety by John Otherday, August 19, 1862. Courtesy of Library of Congress.

BIG EAGLE (Waŋmditaŋka), a Mdewakanton subchief who joined the
soldiers' lodge and left the best account of the conflict from the soldiers' perspective.
Courtesy of Minnesota Historical Society.

CAPTAIN AND MRS. WILLIAM B. DODD. He alerted the defenders
of New Ulm of an attack from the south, thus saving the town. He was killed in
action, and his wife was later notified of his dying words by Dr. Jared Daniels.
Courtesy of Minnesota Historical Society.

GABRIEL RENVILLE, organizer of the Sisseton-Wahpeton soldiers'
lodge who opposed the Mdewakantons and their uprising.
Courtesy of Minnesota Historical Society.

JOSEPH AKIPA RENVILLE, a prominent member of the
Sisseton-Wahpeton soldiers' lodge. Courtesy of National Anthropological
Archives, Smithsonian Institution.

JEANETTE DECAMP SWEET WITH HER INFANT SON BENJAMIN.
Pregnant during her captivity, DeCamp left a powerful narrative of her experience.
Courtesy of Minnesota Historical Society.

REFUGEE MRS. LEOPOLD SENTZKE IS HOLDING HER DAUGHTER, CLARA, who had just died of disease in St Paul. Sentzke's husband was killed in the battle for New Ulm, and she lived with dozens of other refugee widows. From the collection of the Brown County Historical Society, New Ulm, Minnesota.

JUSTINA KRIEGER (KREIGER) MEYER is the survivor of the attack
on her family in Middle Creek. Although she was shot in the back, she was rescued
by the Birch Coulee Burial Party. Courtesy of Minnesota Historical Society.

LAKE SHETEK SURVIVORS who were rescued on the Missouri River from
White Lodge's Band in November 1862. *From left to right:* Roseanne Ireland,
Mrs. Julia Wright (holding daughter Eldora), Emma Duley (rear, daughter of Laura),
Lillian Everett, Mrs. Laura Duley (holding her son Jefferson), and Ellen Ireland.
Courtesy of South Dakota Historical Society.

THERESA EISENREICH, German wife of Balthasar, was taken captive after her husband and others around her were killed. Courtesy of Brown County Historical Society.

LIASA EISENREICH, daughter of Theresa, was conceived with a
Dakota warrior while her mother was a captive in the Dakota camp.
Liasa later went insane. Courtesy of Brown County Historical Society.

OLD BETS, mother of farmer Indian Taopi, was a Dakota woman who assisted white captives. Courtesy of Minnesota Historical Society.

LAURA TERRY DULEY was captured at Slaughter Slough and later rescued on the Missouri River. Courtesy of Elroy E. Ubl, original belonging to Gretchen Taflin.

ATTACK ON NEW ULM, August 23, 1862. Oil painting by Frank Stengel.
From the collection of the Brown County Historical Society, New Ulm, Minnesota.

THE SECOND BATTLE OF NEW ULM. Oil painting by Alexander Schwendinger.
From the collection of the Brown County Historical Society, New Ulm, Minnesota.

AMBUSH, THE ATTACK ON THE RECRUITING PARTY, MILFORD TOWNSHIP, August 18, 1862. Oil painting by David Geister. From the collection of the Brown County Historical Society, New Ulm, Minnesota.

MARY E. SCHWANDT SCHMIDT *(left)*, URANIA S. WHITE *(center)*, and HELEN M. CARROTHERS *(right)*, captive women who posed for a picture at a reunion. Courtesy of Minnesota Historical Society.

SIX

FRIGHT AND FLIGHT
ON THE MINNESOTA FRONTIER

Governor Ramsey learned of the events at Acton and the Lower Agency by the morning of August 19. While the news was sketchy, it grew worse. The governor drove from the capitol to Fort Snelling to assess military preparedness. The fort by this time had become nothing more than a staging area, as it lacked an experienced officer. Sensing a crisis, Ramsey jumped in his buggy and rode south, crossing the Mississippi River to speak with Henry Sibley at Mendota. Both men knew that the western forts of Ridgely and Abercrombie were unprotected, poorly manned, and vulnerable. With four Minnesota regiments already fighting in the East, Ramsey immediately ordered that troops at or near Fort Snelling be detained. He then asked Sibley, who had no experience commanding an army, to lead an expedition up the Minnesota River. This new "colonel" of volunteers agreed knowing little about what had transpired. He did realize the crucial importance of Fort Ridgely. It was the sentinel protecting the Minnesota River valley and a host of new towns and farms.[1]

Some efforts had been made to organize a defense of the west after army regulars went east. Three companies of the Fifth Minnesota Volunteers had been sent to Fort Ridgely, but the Fifth had not been federalized because the regiment failed to meet the required troop strength level of one thousand men.[2] The regiment's three existing companies were spread very thin across Minnesota. Company C, under the command of Lieutenant Sheehan, who had been a steady hand at Yellow Medicine, had left Fort Ridgely for Fort Ripley, along the upper Mississippi River, on the morning of August 17. Company D had been assigned to Fort Abercrombie along the Red River, north of Lake Traverse. This left the undermanned Company B—twenty-six of its men were killed at the ferry—to hold Fort Ridgely.[3]

Never before had an American fort been so unprepared for an Indian onslaught. Ridgely had several stone buildings, but no defensive stockade. Worse, its location invited attack; on three sides gullies and trees offered avenues of approach that the troops could not observe. Fort Abercrombie had similar deficiencies, and it was often isolated for half the year, as floods inundated the upper Red River valley. The situations of the forts seemed inconsequential in 1861 as federal troops pulled out. The senior officer in command of the district, Colonel John Abercrombie, wrote in May, "The Indians on this frontier have never been so quiet as they now are."[4] Never had a military officer been so wrong; the growing conflict at both agencies, and the need to send troops, should have been a warning.

While the early defeats of the Union in the East complicated recruitment—all three Minnesota volunteer companies had fewer than a hundred men—this may have been a godsend. The posting of new laws regarding the draft in the summer of 1862 kept many Minnesota men on their farms, rather than putting them in units that might have been sent east. County officials registered every man between the ages of eighteen and forty-five, and sheriffs posted broadsides ordering them to stay in their respective counties. They would be drafted if the county could not provide the required number of volunteers.[5] Back at Fort Snelling, Ramsey was able to turn four companies of the newly organized Sixth Minnesota Regiment over to Sibley. Sibley promptly recruited Colonel William Crooks, a West Point–trained officer, to take command of the men. Ramsey then ordered elements of the Seventh Minnesota Volunteers to return from furloughs and join Sibley. Lieutenant Colonel William Marshall, later to become the fifth governor of the state, took command of this unit. A number of volunteers also came along, including old friend Joseph R. Brown, who had no idea of the whereabouts of his family, then captives at Little Crow's house.[6]

Few of Sibley's soldiers had uniforms, and most received poorly manufactured European muskets. Some were Austrian made, called the "Augustins," whereas others were Belgian muskets manufactured in Liege. Most of these weapons had been shipped to the western frontier by the army because of their poor quality. Nevertheless, this rather motley army boarded the steamer *Pomeroy* and headed up the Minnesota River at daylight on August 20. Later that afternoon in Shakopee, Sibley discovered the flawed weapons. The barrels had different calibrations as a result of being rebored; the Augustin started at 55 caliber and could go as large as 58. When Sibley examined the weapons, he was aghast. "Many of them will not burst a cap . . . and the ammunition is too large."[7] The Belgian guns may have been even more problematic; one soldier wrote, "Out of one bundle . . . only about 20 would fire at all and only two out of the 100 hit a board eight feet long and 12 inches wide at a distance of 30 yards." Another soldier suggested that it was better to give the gun to an Indian and "let him shoot at me." Of course, "he would miss me and the musket would kick him down." After reaching St. Peter, officers and troops advised Sibley to dig in, rather than push on to Fort Ridgely, until better weapons were available.[8] Sibley agreed, being mortified by the weapons.

The march also exhausted the men, and most of his force had no tents, cooking utensils, or even blankets. Sibley then learned that the arsenal at Fort Snelling had some 1861 Springfield muskets—a fine weapon—but that the quartermaster refused to issue them "until the volunteers" were "fully organized." A mildly enraged Sibley demanded that the governor "cut the red tape," if necessary "with the bayonet of a corporal's guard." Some Springfields finally arrived on August 26.[9] It soon became obvious that if nothing else, Sibley's force at St. Peter had a calming effect. Steamboat captain Edwin Bell, who carried the troops to Shakopee, noted that "men, women, and children" were along the bank, "in their night clothes just as they left their beds." It was "a wild scene," with part hysteria and part joy at seeing the army. The news of a frightful massacre had spread east rapidly.[10]

Meanwhile, some 250 to 300 lodges of Dakota people (perhaps 1,500 in all) had assembled near Little Crow's village, on the northern edge of what had been the Lower Agency on the evening of August 18.[11] Red Middle Voice's village at Rice Creek also had a large population, but many members of the soldiers' lodge congregated at Little Crow's village after that day's raids. That evening, the various leaders of the *akacita* and the band chiefs gathered to discuss the cyclone of events that had transpired. On the periphery, some Dakota women watched, as did several mixed-bloods, including Antoine J. Campbell, who had been just outside Myrick's trade house when the killings began.[12]

The interests of perhaps fifty mixed-bloods, such as Campbell, were intense, because several had been killed during the early hours of the attacks, including Patoile, and others were being threatened. Many did have "fictive" kinship relationships with Dakota *akacita* soldiers, which could bring some protection from increasingly violent young warriors. Campbell was just such a man; his father, Scott Campbell, developed a close relationship with Little Crow's father, Little Crow II, while Scott served as an interpreter at Fort Snelling in the 1830s. Accordingly, Antoine, born in 1826, while more than a dozen years younger than Little Crow, called the chief "cousin," a term that the chief reciprocated with.[13] Yet, other mixed-bloods certainly wondered regarding their fate, even the women. Nancy McClure Faribault Huggan later wrote that one evening, while in Little Crow's camp, she heard three young Indians say "that when the half-blood men were killed one of them should have me for his wife."[14]

Campbell believed that Little Crow, at least, would help protect his family and others of mixed ancestry. He also overheard the chief berate the young men for going into the countryside. "You ought not to kill women and children," Little Crow said when he addressed the gathering. Doing so made warriors "weak in battle," or so he argued. Those who needed killing, the chief said, were "those who have been robbing us for so long." Such corruption was obviously a primary course for the rebellion itself. He then strongly suggested that the warriors "make war after the manner of the white man" and demanded that the *akacita* soldiers agree to attack and capture Fort Ridgely, which guarded the valley below.[15]

Some warriors voiced approval. Little Six and Big Eagle and others from the soldiers' lodge agreed that the fort stood in the way of capturing the entire Minnesota River valley, which Little Crow believed should be the objective of the war. But Wabasha spoke against such an attack, as did his close ally Wakute; they slyly opposed the attack without saying much about the war itself. Lightning Blanket, a young Dakota woman who was eavesdropping, later noted that the debate went on for hours. She suspected that Wabasha was jealous of Little Crow, because members of the soldiers' lodge had approached Little Crow the night before, rather than him. Even so, Little Crow offered a popular strategy: if the fort fell, Minnesota might be an Indian land once again. Nevertheless, both Wabasha and Wakute stood their ground. The next morning when a group of warriors followed Little Crow down the road to attack the fort, the two chiefs and some farmer Indians refused to go.[16] The Mdewakantons, to some degree, were divided over strategy.

The troops and mounting numbers of refugees at the fort expected an attack by the evening of August 18. After Marsh's departure, the forces at Fort Ridgely could hardly sustain picket duty. Marsh had handpicked his troop, taking the most fit, leaving Lieutenant Gere with only twenty-six soldiers—a few other survivors from Marsh's troop, some wounded, would join them. Gere, however, was a more than capable officer who was later awarded the Medal of Honor in the Civil War. Gere organized a picket around the fort, using some armed refugees—including the Anglo-Dakota Jack Frazier—but he could do little to stem the panic when one of the pickets came rushing into the fort late that evening hollering "Indians." As Gere later noted: "The scene that ensued defies description . . . women and children crying and even men in terror breaking through the windows [of the stone barracks] to get inside."[17]

Fortunately, Marsh's sergeant at the ferry attack, John F. Bishop, had pulled together the survivors from the debacle and sent off two messengers to alert Gere of the disaster. They reached the fort at about 8:00 P.M. on the night of August 18, and Gere, who at that point had no idea of what had happened at the ferry, promptly sent a fast rider after Sheehan, who had left the fort at 7:00 A.M. on August 17. Sheehan had been marching for two days, reaching a campground north of New Auburn on the evening of August 18. As his troop of fifty men sat around a fire after dinner, in the late dim moonlight they could see a rider "emerging from the dust [on] a jaded, almost lifeless horse." The rider, Corporal James C. McLean, had covered the forty-five miles in a little over three hours, an almost herculean pace of thirteen miles an hour. He handed Sheehan a dire message. "Force your march returning," Gere wrote. "Captain Marsh and most of his command were killed yesterday [Gere obviously expected the rider to reach Sheehan early on the morning of August 19, thus the use of the term "yesterday"]." Two hundred and fifty refugees were at the fort and the Indians were "killing men, women, and children."[18]

Sheehan, just twenty-four and hardly more experienced than Gere, came to America from Cork, Ireland. An orphan, he entered the army in 1861 and rose quickly through the ranks, displaying characteristics of stern discipline and leadership. He would later distinguish himself in Civil War combat, taking a bayonet in the hand. Just before midnight, north of New Auburn, Sheehan's men threw their food on the ground, doused the fire, and marched out of camp in twelve minutes. The lieutenant then rousted the citizens of New Auburn at 3:00 A.M., confiscated two wagons and teams, and began a forced infantry march in which, as one soldier put it, "the horses and mules were on the trot more than half the time." After the sun appeared, when just ten miles from Ridgely, they encountered several boys from the Carrothers and Earle families. A mile out, they could see the "stars and stripes" and only then realized that the fort had not fallen. Sheehan's men had made the grueling forty-five-mile trip—after marching for two solid days before—in just ten hours; his men entering the fort were exhausted but ready for a fight.[19]

Just as Sheehan arrived on the morning of August 19, warriors, following Little Crow, prepared to storm the fort. But a discussion ensued, likely concerning the six cannons that remained at Fort Ridgely. Sergeant John Jones had been instructing soldiers on how to use the cannons for several years, and the soldiers regularly practiced firing them, learning how to cut the fuses to the right length in order for the ball to explode, creating shrapnel. Most all the Indians with Little Crow had watched these practices; the sound of cannon fire practice could be heard at the Lower Agency. And as the Indians congregated to make an assault, Jones opened up on them, scattering a few.[20] More significantly, as Little Crow urged them forward, more disturbing news arrived; the chief was told that reinforcements had entered the fort—Sheehan's column. George Quinn, an Anglo-Dakota scout who had openly joined the rebellion, had seen the force from afar and brought the news that "soldiers were coming in great numbers." While he was not intentionally deceiving, Quinn did cause great consternation within the ranks of the soldiers' lodge.[21]

As the news spread, thoughts of assaulting the fort diminished. Some Dakota men returned to the villages to protect their families. Mrs. Carrothers, already a captive, noted that later in the evening "the Indians sat up all night long [the 19th and 20th] running bullets," expecting a possible attack by troops; Dakota women remained ready to leave at a moment's notice. Sarah Wakefield witnessed a similar scene at the Rice Creek Village.[22] Given Sheehan's reinforcements a party of perhaps thirty to forty mounted warriors broke off from the main group in mid-afternoon and reached the tableland on the west side of New Ulm. This group also witnessed the reinforcements that reached the town from St. Peter and remounted and headed back north. The first "battles" to take New Ulm and the fort had fizzled.[23]

Sheehan's arrival at Fort Ridgley came at a crucial time, and it bolstered the troop levels to nearly a hundred soldiers. Another sixty-six men among the refugee population were organized; some had shotguns while those without, as one volunteer noted, received "axes, crowbars, and the like."[24] The fifty men who had joined the Renville Rangers also reached the garrison by wagon late Tuesday afternoon. Under the command of young James Gorman, Galbraith had elected to stay behind. Gorman, son of the former territorial governor, was a good officer who served the campaign with distinction. But much like in Sibley's army, the only weapons the Renville Rangers brought from St. Peter were some old "Harpers Ferry" muskets, either the 1819 or 1841 version. Speaking to the guns' quality, one ranger said, "we raised our hammers to our guns, [and] the little caps would fall off." Perhaps worse, each man carried but three bullets apiece. The rangers departed for Fort Ridgely anyway, as some of them had family caught up in the growing conflict.[25]

Little Crow soon learned that Quinn had exaggerated. Accordingly, on the evening of August 19, he argued once again for an all-out assault on Fort Ridgely. The *akacita* warriors agreed and at noon the next day, some 350–400 Dakota men left camp intending to overrun the garrison. They divided into three groups, with bands being led by chiefs; Wabasha, who likely realized that he could not stop his young men, even agreed to lead his group. Other band chiefs included Little Crow, Little Six, Big Eagle, and Mankato. No doubt, Cut Nose led the *akacita* soldiers from the Rice Creek soldiers' lodge. But they separated from Little Crow, intending to strike the fort on its north and east flanks. As Little Crow gathered his force in the river bottom on the southwest side, American soldiers could see the chief, on a horse, urging the men onward and giving orders.[26]

Sheehan had brought his soldiers into the interior of the fort, placing them behind barricades and in the windows of the stone buildings. This strategy allowed the Indians to quickly take possession of the outbuildings, mostly wooden stables; the attackers, however, lost some momentum as they competed to acquire the horses and mules inside the stables. Seeing that these buildings provided cover, Sergeant Jones soon put the buildings ablaze with cannon fire from his position on the south side of the fort. The Indians in turn launched fire arrows at the interior buildings, most of which had shingled roofs. Soon, some buildings at the fort were on fire.[27]

While most early fighting occurred on the southwest corner of the fort, at 1:00 P.M. warriors struck the northeast corner of the fort, where another ravine hid them from view. In the center on the north side stood a large two-story stone barracks building, with nearly a dozen other log outbuildings to its north. Two howitzers, one manned by Sergeant James McGrew and a second under command of a civilian, John Whipple, who had fought in the Mexican War, protected the approach, with one located on either side of the stone barracks. The Indians soon captured some of the outbuildings, driving the troopers from them. McGrew, cutting his fuse too long, fired his cannon over the top of them, making considerable noise but doing little damage. Pulling the cannon back behind the stone building, he then cut the fuse short and fired again, placing the shot in the middle of oncoming Indians. Three warriors and one American soldier went down instantly by the cannon fire, while others were slightly wounded. The struggle on the north side of the fort produced much the same result as the one on the south side—the cannons terrified Indians who found it exceedingly difficult to hold a charge against such fire.[28]

Another assault came from the southeast ravine at 4:00 P.M., but it proved to be just as ineffective as the other two, because the Dakotas had foolishly divided their forces, preferring to fight as bands rather than as one force. The battle then reverted to a standoff where Indians and soldiers sniped at each other. Smoke soon enveloped the battlefield, making it difficult to estimate losses. While some officers jubilantly suspected that as many as a hundred Indians had died—definitely an exaggeration—the cannon fire had been effective. Some Indian burials were discovered afterward on the north side of the fort, where most were likely killed, and some wounded warriors were carried back into camp, dying later. Sheehan lost just three men, but over a dozen were wounded, with some dying in the days that followed. Realistic estimates of Dakota casualties ranged anywhere from two dozen to fifty. Sheehan had won a decisive victory, but he realized that the Indians still surrounded the fort and his ammunition was running low. That night, bar iron, cannonballs, and even the spent balls left by the Indians in the wooden buildings were recast to fit whatever guns existed.[29]

The Renville Rangers and the companies of the Fifth Regiment fought bravely in defense of the garrison. But an entirely different story unfolded with the civilians. Young Ezmon Earle, who had saved himself during the attack at Beaver Creek, fought from the stone barracks. He later recalled: "It seemed as though pandemonium itself had broken loose" as the fighting erupted. For him, "the war whoops was [sic] worse . . . it was simply blood curdling and I really think that I dodged oftener for the war whoops than from the bullets." While Earle recovered from his fright, two hundred women and children pressed into the second story of the stone barracks, most in a state of panic. "There was singing and praying & crying & screaming," as one soldier put it. Discipline collapsed among the citizens, and of the nearly seventy men who were capable of defending the fort, forty abandoned their posts and fled to the second floor to wail with the women and children.[30]

Sheehan recognized that literally hundreds of Indians had tried to take the fort and that they would likely return. His men, especially those who had marched with him from New Auburn, were exhausted, and he needed soldiers to stand guard during the night. He contemplated abandoning the garrison, but he instead called the citizens into a formation and chastised them. As Earle put it, he made a speech "in which he called us all the mean names such as cowards and sneaks, etc., that he could think of." Earle seemed not to know it at the time, but some forty of the men in rank had fled to hide with the women and children. After the lecture, Sheehan asked for volunteers to stand guard; none stepped forward. One claimed that he had no cartridge box, and thus could not do it. "I was ashamed of the company I was in," Earle wrote. While only an older boy, Earle volunteered, to which Sheehan responded, "Thank God for one man." Nine others then grudgingly joined the young volunteer.[31]

Next day, messages arrived from New Ulm, where the town was once again surrounded by Indians, pleading for a hundred men and more ammunition. Sheehan must have been amused, although the Germans had suffered eleven dead during the Leavenworth fiasco. Sheehan did get a desperate message to Governor Ramsey, carried by Jack Frazier. He could "hold this place but little longer," he wrote. Both Sheehan and Gorman had flesh wounds, placing more responsibility on Lieutenant Gere. By evening, Gere too ultimately collapsed, one arm being draped around a cannon; he slept that way for several hours.[32]

That night in Little Crow's village, there was less celebrating. Given the availability of liquor, some young men overindulged and became dangerous. Some of the farmer Indians—including Wabasha, Wakute, and Taopi—had been forced to change from their civilian clothes to breech-cloths and blankets, but they still did their best to protect captive whites. Fearing that captives would be vulnerable, Hazatoŋwin, the mother-in-law of Big Eagle, collected the Brown family from Little Crow's house. She knew them well, being called affectionately "old Aunt Judy" by Susan Brown's children. Hazatoŋwin moved them to an isolated tepee. Others were protected by women associated with the farmer group; "Old Bets," the mother of Taopi, extended her hand to a number of captives. Later, Samuel Brown concluded that his mother's close kin ties with various

Sisseton and Wahpeton chiefs saved many captives, as Little Crow realized that these much larger tribes, potential allies, could tip the balance and help take the fort.[33]

This strategy, to bring all the Dakota bands together into a war against the United States, might easily have had the same effect as that sought by Sitting Bull, fourteen years later, a strategy that brought about the destruction of George Armstrong Custer and his regiment. And the effort seemed to pay off when on August 22, over three hundred Sisseton and Wahpeton warriors arrived near the old Lower Agency. Their leading chiefs, Standing Buffalo, Sweet Corn, and Scarlet Plume, were not with them, and they seemed most intent on watching battles, rather than participating in them. For certain, the Sissetons and Wahpetons were now well aware of the conflict underway.[34]

Low on ammunition and fearful that many of the civilians might break and run at any time, Sheehan had a long conversation with "Captain" DeCamp, who had run the mills at the agency and was placed over the civilians. After the first fight, Sheehan carefully instructed DeCamp on where to place his men thereafter and warned of retribution if any deserted their posts. DeCamp dutifully obeyed: he moved to the front of the civilian corps and said, "Boys, I am ordered to shoot the first man who leaves his post without orders, and I'll do it by God."[35] At 1:00 P.M. the afternoon of August 22, the soldiers inside the fort once again saw Little Crow at the head of an Indian column coming down the road to attack the fort. This time, reinforced with several hundred Sissetons and Wahpetons, the Indian warriors likely fielded eight hundred men. This massive army surrounded the garrison and fired at every position held by the troops. The second battle for Fort Ridgely had begun.[36]

The onslaught opened again from the southwest, where Little Crow urged his charges forward. But a ball from Sergeant Jones's cannon grazed the chief's chest as it flew by and exploded, muting the charge. It was a serious psychological blow, as Big Eagle later noted, that "a few sub-chiefs, like myself," had to then lead the attacks.[37] When it became obvious that a large mass of Indians had congregated northwest of the fort, McGrew grabbed the twelve pounder, which had a long range but had not been fired, and put a shot into the middle of the group. Horses, warriors, and Indian women scurried for cover. Later, as another charge was organized from the southwest corner, Jones lowered his cannon to the ground and fired directly into the oncoming party. He later estimated that seventeen Indians were killed or wounded, perhaps a slight exaggeration. Finally, just after 6:00 P.M. the rains came in, dashing the hopes for an Indian victory. They had many dead and wounded, and enraged by the outcome, some Dakota men began killing captives back at camp; one was shot at Little Crow's village and another had her throat slit at the Rice Creek camp.[38]

At the fort, four dead bodies laid on the ground, and the hospital housed sixty-two wounded. The garrison had run out of fresh water, because the river, only a mile away, was still in Indian hands. Yet the garrison held out, due mostly to the leadership of Sheehan and Gere. A. J. Van Vorhes, who had brought the $71,000 in annuity money to the fort on August 18, noted that "Sheehan was everywhere present, cheering on the brave and stout-hearted and encouraging the few wavering." The only criticism Vorhes could muster included the thought that he was "too reckless of his personal safety." He constantly passed from "post to post giving directions," bullets "whizzing over and about him like hail." Though wounded twice, on Saturday morning, August 23, as the sun came up, Sheehan was still at his post when an Indian appeared with a white flag. He represented Little Crow and explained that if Sheehan abandoned the fort, the American soldiers and civilians would receive safe passage. Sheehan had considered such an option, but given all the wounded, he steadfastly refused.[39]

Colonel Sibley tried to keep abreast of what was happening at the fort from St. Peter. Scouts sent in the direction of the garrison came in late on the night of August 22, noting that buildings were on fire, cannons were going off occasionally, and the situation looked dire. Sibley penned a quick note to his wife: "People are absolutely crazy with excitement and credit every absurdity." He agonized over what to do. His troops were completely untrained, and many, especially the cavalry, were "not regularly enlisted." They could apparently leave whenever they wished.[40] Given these circumstances, Sibley hesitated when it came to relieving the garrison. He had come to see the ferociousness of the attack on the fort and realized that there had been many civilian deaths: "One must see the mutilated bodies of their victims," he wrote Governor Ramsey, even though he had likely seen only a few. The colonel's greatest fear was a "night attack," which could easily lead to "panic" within his ranks.[41]

Ramsey reluctantly agreed, but he nevertheless pressed Sibley to relieve the fort. On August 23, the governor wrote that more troops—the Sixth Regiment—were coming, and "your arms are more than equal in quantity to those of the Indians." It was, he wrote, "the best we can give." Neither argument placated Sibley who knew that his muskets were inferior and that a defeat of his army at that crucial stage would lead to the ruin of the state.[42] Ramsey countered two days later: "The eyes of the whole people are on Fort Ridgely. You can have no idea of the intense anxiety there is . . . if it is lost it will cause lamentation throughout the land."[43]

Ramsey's words hardly described the seriousness of the situation. There was mass chaos in the central parts of the state. News came first from those who managed to flee Beaver Creek as well as the settlements just north-west of St. Peter—an area often referred to as Scandinavian Grove. The towns on the north, or left, bank of the Minnesota River, well southeast of the fort, became instant refugee centers with thousands of people flocking to them. Much the same was true of the communities north of the river. C. P. Troxel wrote the governor regarding the panic at Henderson: "All was excitement." The town went through two or three stampedes just on August 20.[44]

The crowding along the roads east even affected the ability of military forces to unite with Sibley at St. Peter. William J. Cullen, who had orga-nized two hundred cavalry, managed to reach Shakopee—a town just forty miles from St. Paul—but found it difficult to get through the town. "The people from the country are flocking into Shakopee," he wrote on August 22, "in great alarm, and instant action is necessary to prevent the upper portion of the [Minnesota] valley from being depopulated." Just after leaving Shakopee the next day, Cullen met "immense numbers of families leaving their homes, in fact I may safely say several hundred teams, with women and children, frightened to death." They crowded the road to such an extent that the cavalry had to pass around them.[45] Some such as Julia E. Farnsworth and her family found that the race for safety was too much for her wagon to bare. It broke down, and in a panic, her entire family "went into the deep woods" north of the road. They stayed there for twenty-one days, surviving on the milk of one cow and berries, not daring to come out.[46]

Farther north the exodus continued. Some 150 families (nearly a thousand people) fled to Forest City, all vowing to keep moving until they reached St. Paul. Another seventy people lined the single street in the small town of Paynesville; they gave harrowing stories regarding the murders at Norway Lake. At Glencoe, John Stein, one of the founding fathers, reported "a general Stampede . . . every family in Glencoe left, but two." Worse, four hundred refugee men, women, and children arrived at the town from the west in search of shelter. Many had walked and physically could go no farther. At Glencoe, the footsore frantically selected high ground, dug trenches, and piled up the sod. "Fort Skedaddle," as it was dubbed, was designed to be quickly abandoned at the first signs of a large Indian force.[47]

At Hutchinson a somewhat different scenario emerged. While the town attracted hundreds of refugee families, "Captain" George Whitcomb arrived with seventy-five Springfield rifles, obtained from Governor Ramsey. While these did not stem the tide of flight, some citizens agreed to form a home guard unit. They dug a trench three feet deep and one hundred feet square, and virtually every log building in town was quickly pulled down and used to fortify the position. After getting organized, Whitcomb decided to take thirty-one Springfields to Forest City, where his family and others were holed up. This produced an ugly argument that nearly resulted in fisticuffs. But the citizens dared not defy Whitcomb's commission from Ramsey. Hutchinson then elected their own militia captain, Lewis Harrington, and Whitcomb left, quite upset over the reaction of the Hutchinson townfolk.[48]

Some settlers elected to stay and fight for their farms and homes, whereas others fled in abject terror. Women often stood up to the strain better than their menfolk. Those living south and east of New Ulm, near Madelia and Garden City, learned on the evening of August 21 that New Ulm had been attacked a day or two earlier, bringing about the first exodus from these communities. Mary Ann Marston Hallock from Garden City left a vivid account of the fright that suddenly struck all her neighbors. Come the next morning, a "Captain" Smithson, who Hallock later concluded was a great "coward," ordered the abandonment of the town. Many refugees from Madelia nearby soon joined them in flight, heading southeast toward the small settlement of Vernon Center.[49]

While preparing to leave, Hallock and other women expected the worst. "We never expected to see another dawn," Hallock wrote. Just before departure, one almost deranged woman thought it best "at the first war whoop" to "tie the babies to us and jump into the mill pond." While on the road to Vernon, the party corralled twenty-five wagons and slept on the ground. Not all the women were stalwarts like Hallock; the "smothered sobs" of women could be heard at night, she later wrote. The next day, when hearing rifle fire, the easily alarmed Captain Smithson hollered: "Break ranks, run for Vernon." When they reached the town, they discovered a stockade already in progress, filled with eight hundred people. As it turned out, the gunfire was a false alarm. Indeed, the refugees learned that New Ulm had actually held against the first, rather weak, Indian attack, and a few, including Hallock, returned to their homes, nervously awaiting the next events. Others continued east, stopping only temporarily at a camp on the outskirts of Mankato.[50]

After the first battle at Fort Ridgely, thousands of settler families packed and ran for safety, while others waited a day or two, then left and then returned, trying to salvage something from their farms. They had valuable crops to harvest and precious livestock to care for, but any news, of the slimmest kind, easily produced an exodus. This fear even emerged among townspeople well to the east, where the shock of the killings did not reach them until August 22 or 23. Those who continued to flee from the frontier often justified their actions by exaggerating what had happened, creating descriptions of Indian brutality that they had never witnessed. This occurred at completely safe locations over a hundred miles from the scene of the massacre. One of most amazing events occurred at Carver, along the Minnesota River, forty miles southwest of St. Paul.

Carver had a steamboat landing and several docks used for commercial barge traffic. As three thousand refugees flocked into town, some in a crazed state, a few crowded onto the barges; one report suggested that a majority were men. Some of the more stouthearted townsmen scoffed at them; a newspaper editor reported that they cursed them for "the cowardly act of running away and leaving their wives and children to the mercy of the savages." Some wives and children had literally been abandoned on the roads leading into Carver. But it did no good, as the men, even when kicked, refused to leave the barges. Then a boy came riding into town screaming that Fort Ridgely, New Ulm, and St. Peter had been burned. Glencoe and Young America were under attack and likely destroyed. Panic struck.[51]

The steamboat *Antelope*, which sat at the dock, had been detained "by special request" to run messages to the governor. With the news, as one newspaper account stated, a mad rush occurred "for the decks of this last harbor of safety." The rush resembled "one continuous scene of delirious people." Guards tried frantically to keep men, women, and children from boarding the riverboat, without much success. People of all sorts "jumped, clasped, and clung to her as their only hope." The captain, realizing that the boat would sink, cut the *Antelope* loose and drifted downstream, leaving people on the riverbank screaming and pleading for her to return.[52] Thomas Scantlebury and his family, people who had assisted Sheehan at New Auburn, made it on board. Packed with refugees, "there was hardly standing room," Louisa Scantlebury later wrote. After the *Antelope* landed at St. Paul, hundreds of people scrambled ashore looking bewildered and dazed.[53]

The most significant factor that fueled the panic was the exaggerated reports that came from the west. Scantlebury, while taking flight with his family, later noted the way that messengers enhanced stories of destruction, stories that he initially believed. "From all directions came news of towns being burned," he wrote. "A person who had made a clear statement of the facts would not after it has passed through two or three frightened messengers, recognize his own story, so exaggerated would it be." What most astonished Scantlebury was the fact that the farther they got from the scene of the massacres, "the greater we found the panic."[54]

A thousand or more refugees flocked into Monticello, located twenty miles north of Minneapolis along the Mississippi River. They pleaded to sleep in the homes of people and filled up the hallways of the one hotel. As the townspeople were trying to help them, "a man named Uncle Calvin" came running into town, screaming "the Indians are coming, sweeping everything before them." Dick Blanchard, who remembered the night, recalled that his aunt, in a complete panic, "ran into the pantry, got some biscuits and fried cakes and stuffed them in her bosom." Just outside "the streets were full of teams, horses, and men and women, many of whom were crying."[55] A scout quickly discovered that Calvin's Indians were a herd of whitetail deer. Uncle Calvin had seen their tails floating in the air and mistook them for Indians. Even so, the flight continued. At Clear Lake, just opposite and somewhat north of Monticello, on the left bank of the Mississippi River, an observer wrote Ramsey that the people at Monticello were "perfectly panic stricken," crossing the river to safety on barges and ferries. So many had left that the main road that led to Wisconsin was "lined with teams, filled with women and children."[56] The state government faced a crisis, and Governor Ramsey had limited means with which to solve it.

A most pressing concern included stopping the exodus—the state was on the verge of being depopulated. Ramsey issued a proclamation on August 22 to calm the citizenry. He noted that Sibley had an entire regiment in the field to deal with the crisis, failing to mention, however, the poor quality of the arms or that Sibley's force was far short of a regiment. Another three hundred cavalry were headed west, the governor proclaimed;

this was, once again, an exaggeration. He believed that relief would come to Fort Ridgely and New Ulm within a day or two, which also turned out to be untrue. However, Ramsey argued that settlers should not be duly alarmed as the murders had occurred well to the west, a far distance from St. Paul. Fleeing settlers should return to their homes and harvest their crops, or all of Minnesota would starve over the winter. "Turn a deaf ear to idle and improbable reports," Ramsey concluded. "It must be the duty of all sensible men to check the needless panic."[57]

Unfortunately, the same newspaper that printed the proclamation, the *St. Paul Pioneer and Democrat,* also published letters from the western portions of the state in the same edition on August 22. One from Van Vorhes at Fort Ridgely stated simply that "escaped citizens came in during the night, giving accounts of horrors too terrible for the imagination to conceive . . . mothers came in rags and barefooted, whose husbands and children had been slaughtered before their eyes." John J. Porter, a former state legislator from Mankato who had traveled to New Ulm on August 21, wrote in the same edition that as he left to return home, the city was burying the dead. Some bodies came from Milford Township while others included the eleven men from the Leavenworth Expedition. Porter noted that those brought in had suffered a terrible death, "their bodies most horribly mutilated."[58] Such eyewitness accounts by upstanding citizens did much to invalidate the governor's efforts, even among those who returned to their farms with an intention to save crops and livestock.

New Ulm seemed most vulnerable after the second fight at Fort Ridgely. It was located just a dozen miles south of the lower reservation. A small force of volunteers commanded by the charismatic former Indian agent and then-judge Charles Flandrau had assembled at St. Peter with the intention of relieving the town. Flandrau seemed hardly the choice; he had no military experience and had chosen the law as a career. He seemed also to have lost his nerve at the agency in 1857, when the Inkpaduta crisis occurred. Yet he did have qualities of leadership. According to one account, he struck a "picturesque and handsome figure . . . with legs like an antelope." Yet he had no authority, not even a "paper" commission from the governor.[59] As Flandrau prepared to depart for New Ulm on the morning of August 21, Sibley sent seventy-four volunteers to reinforce him under Captain Eugene St. Julien Cox. Yet Cox took his time, dallying in the river towns. Perhaps the reticence had something to do with the company's armament: they were given fifty notorious Augustin muskets.[60]

Flandrau's force originally consisted of nearly 150 volunteers. But as they marched west toward New Ulm, the number quickly dwindled to ninety. As Richard Pfeiffer, who had joined the column, put it: "All along the road . . . were the refugees . . . riding behind ox teams, a few rode horses, but mostly they were on foot, women carrying children in their arms, men bearing on their backs all they had." Doctor Daniels later reported that the fleeing refugees unnerved the men, causing a number to leave the command, some before and some after reaching New Ulm and some even after facing, as Daniels put it, "the protestations of the commander." The desertions, which Daniels viewed as cowardice, could not be reversed.[61]

Nevertheless, Pfeiffer and Flandrau's column continued on, marching in route step. Meanwhile, at Mankato the fire bell had been sounded, and a debate ensued as to whether the townsmen should defend Mankato, help New Ulm, or abandon the town in flight to the east. At this point, a German-born citizen of New Ulm, William Bierbauer, stepped forward to argue that if each town tried to defend itself separately, all would fall. He won the day, and a few townsmen joined Flandrau, then at New Ulm. A third force of some seventy-four men came from South Bend, a small town located at the southernmost bend of the river; most of the families of these men had sought protection in Mankato. As the force came together, Flandrau could call on over three hundred men by the night of August 22, when he reached New Ulm, but they were poorly armed. Being elected "colonel," upon inspecting their arms he found mostly squirrel guns and shotguns; there were only thirty rifles with any range in the entire command.[62]

Flandrau expected an attack and immediately set the men to work building stronger fortifications. Digging day and night, they soon created a four-block stronghold of trenches and barricades in the center of town. Divided by Minnesota Street, which ran north and south, the sturdy brick Forster Building provided a bulwark for defense on the west side. The Dacotah House stood two blocks east of it, and just across the street, there was the Erd Hotel, another large brick establishment. Along with two smaller buildings on the north, including the wood-framed Minnesota Haus, these larger buildings formed the defensive center.[63]

The hasty defenses did little to distill the panic of the nearly fifteen hundred women and children who had fled into New Ulm in the two days following the first attacks. A young Anna Schmitz, just eleven years old at the time, later described the scene: "The confusion in New Ulm was awful.

Women were running about screaming and wringing their hands." No one knew what would happen next. Flandrau and others finally convinced many to take refuge in the Erd Hotel. They then brought in barrels of gunpowder and placed them in the basement; though dark and damp, the basement held some two hundred women and children. The floors above held hundreds more. Mary Schmitz Ryan from Milford Township, just twenty-six at the time, the mother of two small children and six months pregnant, agreed to light the powder and kill everyone in the hotel should the Indians succeed in taking the town.[64]

Outside this perimeter of buildings stood perhaps 125 wood frame houses. A handful had been burned on the north side during the skirmish on August 19, but others still stood. The only weak point was to the south, where Minnesota Street led to a parkland with heavy grass and shrubbery sloping down to the Cottonwood River.[65] The defensive work went on at a feverish pace, especially when the cannon could be heard going off at Fort Ridgely. At night, fires could even be seen rising above the fort, which was a mere fifteen miles away.[66]

Given the fires, Flandrau concluded on the evening of August 22 that "the fort had fallen." At that point, evacuating the town might have been an option, as a number of his men and even some townspeople suggested it, but the idea, if seriously considered, quickly evaporated the next morning.[67] At 9:00 A.M. on August 23, Flandrau witnessed Indians "moving down upon the town." He foolishly sent a force of seventy-five men under William Huey across the Minnesota River to investigate. Just an hour later a massive number of Dakota warriors appeared to the north and west, estimated at anywhere from 350 to 500. Andrew Friend, who watched the display, wrote that "they made a brilliant appearance as their spears and guns and knives glistened in the sun [the guns taken from the troopers at the ferry had bayonets]." Flandrau sent out skirmishers to meet them on the prairie north and west of town. The second battle for New Ulm had begun.[68]

Dakota warriors covered the entire front of Flandrau's forces. They then spanned out, going left and right, threatening the flanks of the inexperienced Americans. "The men were encouraged by their officers to stand firm, and meet the attack," Flandrau noted. But having long rifles with more effective ranges than the defenders of New Ulm, soon the battle on the prairie seemed in question. At that point, the Indians "issued a terrific yell, and came upon us like the wind," Flandrau later wrote. His force, unsettled and taking increasing casualties, fell back, running in disarray for cover. They passed through the line of outbuildings, surrendering them to the Indians. Flandrau feared the end, "that they would rush into town and drive all before them."[69] His fear seemed ever more real as Dr. Daniels noted that some men, stricken with terror, ran and hid in the cellars of the brick buildings, and "no urging could get them out."[70]

But the Dakota warriors then stopped occupying the outbuildings and poured a murderous fire upon the retreating volunteers. It was a crucial stage in the battle, as Flandrau recognized the advantage taken by the Indians of using the outbuildings for cover. He ordered his best men to drive them out, later reporting that they "gave three cheers and sallied out with good effect." One advantage had been the windmill on the west side of town, with its high elevation. It had been occupied by a small force from Le Sueur, who, in turn, poured an accurate fire down upon the Indians. Just as quick as the battle on the prairie stagnated, news reached Flandrau of a massive assault coming from the south and east, with Indians hiding in the bottoms of the Cottonwood and Minnesota Rivers.[71]

A large group of *akacita* warriors, some on horseback, first charged up Minnesota Street, taking advantage of the massive smoke that enveloped the town to give them cover. The winds, at twenty miles per hour and picking up smoke from burning buildings, made it difficult to identify them. One of Flandrau's captains, William B. Dodd, thinking it was Huey's force of twenty-five men, mounted a horse and rode down to meet them. Instead, he encountered mounted Dakota warriors; Dodd took five balls, and his horse several more. In some ways, Dodd had saved the day, giving his life to reveal the movement, shrouded as it was in smoke. As others joined him, they met another attack by some sixty warriors who came up from the bottom of the Minnesota River. They again threatened to break into the defensive positions. Flandrau proclaimed it "the crucial part of the day," as he suspected that his men would crumble, as they had on the prairie west of town. Instead, they "sallied out" and, once again, turned the Indians back. The town had held out, and toward evening, Flandrau ordered all the remaining outer buildings burned down so that Indians could not use them for cover. The townspeople reluctantly agreed. During the fight, Flandrau had twenty-six of his men killed with seventy more wounded, many seriously. Twenty-three of Flandrau's men had died outside the barricades, mostly in the attempt to retake the outer buildings. Others, like Dodd, lived into the evening and then died. Dr. Daniels delivered to his wife Dodd's last words. She could only say: "Last—oh, shall I never ever more hear his voice?"[72]

The next morning a few Indians remained on the periphery, but they soon saw Captain Cox's relief column, which Sibley had ordered to New Ulm, crossing the Minnesota River at the ferry.[73] These last remaining warriors also then departed, but they left behind a town completely gutted; 183 buildings, including a brewery, distillery, several churches, and other shops, had been destroyed.[74] Inside the defensive position, the common area had been packed full of horses and wagons. When the battle started, as Aaron Meyers later wrote, "they all stampeded ... in many cases taking the wagons with them." Even the dogs partook of the "pandemonium, biting everything they came within reach of." In the end, Indians killed some of the horses and cattle, while the townspeople shot the most obnoxious dogs. As a result, the day after the battle, as Meyers noted, there were "cattle and horses lying dead in every direction ... [and] furniture scattered" everywhere.[75]

Flandrau and his forces had fought off a determined Indian assault that should have overrun the town. The Dakotas fielded at least 350 warriors, and Flandrau's force, while equal in manpower, lacked effective weapons. And worse, a number of his men cowered in the basements of various buildings. Dr. William Mayo, who later became famous for founding a medical clinic in southern Minnesota, found bunches of them; he "drove them out, armed them with pitchforks and told them to stand behind the barricades." The failure of the Dakota force to take the town stemmed from the root problem that consistently plagued their strategy: they seldom agreed on a leader, followed a number of important but independent "head" soldiers and chiefs, and attacked at different times from different locales, dividing their overwhelming force.[76]

Fearing another assault—and perhaps now cognizant of the unwillingness of some men to fight and having little if any ammunition left—Flandrau decided to evacuate New Ulm. There were insurmountable problems; both the Dacotah Hotel and the Minnesota Haus housed dozens of wounded men. Jacob Nix, who received a slight wound during the fighting, could hardly get into the Minnesota Haus as the floors were covered with mattresses and wounded people.[77] Flandrau ordered what wagons and animals that had survived to be organized; as this happened, people readily placed what household goods, food, and property they could into the wagons. This left no room for the wounded. Flandrau then ordered all the material goods to be thrown into the streets, and the wagons filled with wounded men.[78]

By noon, some 153 wagons headed south, down Minnesota Street, crossing the Cottonwood River on their way to Mankato. In leaving, some of the townspeople brought out bottles of strychnine and laced several barrels of whiskey with it, hoping that the new occupants—Indians—would take the bait. (The strychnine was on hand for poisoning wolves.) Flandrau, seemingly appalled, broke the barrels. With this parting gesture, the exodus from New Ulm got underway. The caravan reached St. Peter on August 27. Flandrau could only lament the situation: "It was a melancholy spectacle to see two thousand people, who a few days before had been prosperous and happy, reduced to utter beggary."[79] Albert Knight, who had been designated to help with refugees in St. Peter, was aghast at their arrival. There were three thousand refugees in town already, and the "procession that arrived from New Ulm was nearly four miles long." They were all hungry, tired, and lame, and Knight could not help them, even with the "base necessities of life."[80]

While taking care of the massive numbers of refugees only increased in the days ahead, Governor Ramsey made slow progress on the war front. President Lincoln was simply distracted by the Civil War and gave little attention initially to Minnesota's problems. Nevertheless, Sibley finally left St. Peter for Fort Ridgely on August 26; a relief column of mounted men reached the garrison early the next morning. Ramsey had also named Flandrau, whom all perceived as being the "hero" of New Ulm, as a colonel of volunteers. He was ordered to organize the defense of the regions south of the Minnesota River and west of Mankato. Flandrau had men upon whom he could depend, but he lacked arms, much like Sibley. He did order a militia captain, Jerome Dane, from South Bend to reoccupy New Ulm, as it was on the very front line of the conflict.[81]

Dane arrived back in New Ulm on August 29 amid devastation that even he could hardly imagine. Large herds of pigs had been left behind, and they rooted into everything. Stacks of flour, sugar, and other staples had been abandoned on Main Street. Furniture could be found everywhere outside, and the doors of what buildings still stood were wide open. A few residents slowly began to return, increasingly aware that the state was offering some protection in the form of troops.[82]

At the very least, Minnesota's defenders were getting organized, slowly moving back up the Minnesota River. While Sibley received more and more men at Fort Ridgely, several regiments were coming together at Fort Snelling, including the Eighth, Ninth, and Tenth. Sibley's force rapidly grew to twelve hundred men. Yet the colonel wisely recognized the men's lack of experience. When he learned that elements of Minnesota's Third Regiment, which surrendered at Murfreesboro, Tennessee, had been exchanged and were now at St. Louis, he urged Ramsey to get them back to Minnesota quickly (exchanges of prisoners between the Union and Confederacy happened quite regularly in 1862, but they came to an abrupt end as these men were thrown back into battle).[83] While their officers had not been released, the federal government sent them on anyway. They had seen action, were outraged that their officers had surrendered, and wanted to redeem themselves. As a kind gesture, Ramsey even sent Sibley a chaplain for his army: Stephen Return Riggs, the missionary who had escaped from the Yellow Medicine Agency.[84]

Even so, Sibley still had unsurmountable problems. The only food stores he received were some barrels of pork, lacking almost entirely breadstuff, the staple of any army. Each soldier armed with a new Springfield received so few bullets that he could hardly take target practice; most of Sibley's men had never fired a weapon. Worse, Lieutenant Colonel Samuel McPhail's cavalry force could not be depended upon. Some disliked McPhail, who demanded some discipline; volunteers preferred to elect their officers, and most of them refused to take an oath to serve for thirty days. Once at Fort Ridgely, a large number returned home.[85]

While supply and troop problems persisted, without a sufficient mounted force to carry out scouting duty, Sibley had little idea of what he was up against. The only good news was that the Dakota warriors who had hung around Fort Ridgely had finally withdrawn by August 26, as they saw McPhail's cavalry approach. Sibley wrote his wife that while he hoped to proceed against the Indians soon—he was still "waiting for cartridges"—he had no idea of where the largest forces had congregated.[86]

Minnesota newspapers seemed somewhat unsympathetic to the colonel's explanations, with some beginning to question his competence as a leader of the army. "Much complaint had been made that Sibley had not relieved the fort before this," the editors of the mostly sympathetic *St. Paul Pioneer and Democrat* wrote. The paper admitted that some of the ammunition sent to Sibley was "of a size that would not fit his guns," but such excuses seemed inconsequential, given the size of his army.[87] Minnesota seemed on the verge of anarchy in nearly half of its counties.

Simple law and order had disappeared in some locales. Local volunteer officers sought to establish martial law at times, which led to further problems as townspeople saw them as dictators. At the outbreak of fighting,

Ramsey had ordered that any saddle horses and wagons capable of hauling freight be brought into St. Paul and "pressed" into service. Captain A. D. Nelson, a West Point graduate, was placed in command of procurement. He scoured the countryside for horses and food, taking what was needed to supply Sibley and other militia units. South of St. Cloud, settlers openly opposed "the scoundrel Nelson," writing the governor that while he had "never been known to go where there was the least chance of encountering an Indian," he took whatever he wanted. Complaints steadily mounted, as various frontier militia units used the governor's order to acquire livestock and food required for their men.[88]

The problem seemed especially acute south of the Minnesota River. Militia captain D. R. Redfield literally demanded that Ramsey "stop these irregular companies and squads of men from coming up here." Groups of three or four were unwilling to "attach themselves to any authorized command," but they, instead, used the so-called military press to pillage the houses of settlers. At times it seemed impossible to determine who was responsible, but later evidence demonstrated that most of the pillaging was done by white riffraff, not Indians. While Dane had occupied New Ulm with troops, Sheriff Roos, who had been wounded, showed up a week later and could only lament that "our town is plundered out entirely, everything we left here taken away, every trunk broken open by *White Thieves*." Dane may have been responsible for some pillaging, especially of food necessary to feed his men, but there was also no doubt that goods taken from New Ulm were appearing in markets back east.[89]

While initial news of an "outbreak" produced an exodus, a second great panic struck Minnesota after New Ulm was abandoned by Flandrau on August 24. It broke out the next day near Mankato, spread northward into St. Paul and then into the towns all along the Mississippi River. Rumors abounded that towns like New Ulm had been burned to the ground—a rumor that was not too far from the truth. In a time when rumors overcame reality, there was little anyone could do to stop the exodus. St. Peter alone had thousands of desperate and hungry people, most of whom had not the means to travel. Henry A. Swift, who would succeed Ramsey as governor in a year, outlined the seriousness of the situation: "I cannot command language to point to you the necessities of the emergency," he wrote to the governor. And after Sibley had departed with his entire army on August 26, the town, full of refugees, was suddenly defenseless. Worse, the army had confiscated horses and wagons, making it impossible to move the people east. The refugees in St. Peter were starving, and Swift urged Ramsey to appoint a "quartermaster" to feed them.[90]

Farther southwest of St. Peter, Captain Dane reported that Flandrau's abandonment of New Ulm had led to another "general and widespread panic among the settlers." They were leaving their crops in the field, and the entire state might starve over the winter. Attempts were made to establish martial law and provide protection so that farmers might go back to their fields, but it did no good. Captain Dane, whose militia patrolled the lands between Mankato and New Ulm, noted that many settlers were simply "driving their stock, by the thousands," eastward with little hope of finding some refuge for them.[91] According to the editor of the *Mankato Independent*, such men were responsible for "promoting the excitement and increasing the alarm by the various exaggerated rumors."[92] South of the Minnesota River, Blue Earth, Brown, Watonwan, and Faribault Counties—the latter well to the east—had been literally abandoned.[93]

As the mass migration continued, established towns such as Faribault and Owatonna, both well to the east, soon filled with refugees. Some of these communities, far from the conflict, had earlier been abandoned by people who had already left for Wisconsin. As one citizen observed, those that left early "say they are leaving the state for good." The Catholic Church at Faribault, described by one onlooker as "immense," took in a large number of people, most of whom were Irish. While most of these towns were a hundred miles or more from the scenes of battle, harrowing stories circulated that led to flight.[94] A typical example was the news brought to Clinton Falls. Residents heard that "two children were found alive nailed to the side of the house . . . while others [were] fastened to the ground by stakes driven through them." The most egregious violence thought to be perpetrated by the Indians, overblown out of all proportion, had become the norm.[95]

While the lands south of the Minnesota River were being abandoned, a few townsmen attempted to make a stand, especially in the north. Sauk Centre, Hutchinson, Forest City, Henderson, Glencoe, St. Peter, and even the small berg of Maine Prairie, just south of St. Cloud, had constructed stockades. George Whitcomb had created the "Sibley Guards," a force of some sixty men. Along with Captain Richard Strout, who led forty-five men of the newly created Ninth Regiment, these two units constantly sent out scouts. Another force of fifty-three men came together at Sauk Centre under Captain S. Ramsdell. Nevertheless, some people questioned the wisdom of making a stand at places like Hutchinson and Forest City when the second round of panic struck the region in the late afternoon of August 29. While the abandonment of New Ulm had only a modest impact on the people north of the Minnesota River, news of trouble with Anishinaabe Indians soon complicated everything. Some panic even appeared in St. Paul.[96]

While the Anishinaabe Indians, or the Ojibwe as they were commonly called, had seemingly posed a threat for a few days by stealing some stock, many citizens thought they would join the Dakota in the war. Fort Ripley, on the upper Mississippi River, quickly became a refuge for settlers. Ramsey anticipated the trouble by sending two new companies of troops to the region. The area around the fort was not heavily populated, but at least a hundred or so settlers flocked to the garrison for protection. No one had been killed by these Indians, and while the situation remained tense, they ultimately remained at peace. Even so, one newspaper, the *St. Cloud Democrat,* reported on the afternoon of August 28 that "the Chippewa [Ojibwe] and Sioux have smoked a pipe of peace, and entered into a league to exterminate the whites." The story, completely unsubstantiated, did much to encourage a second exodus from northern Minnesota.[97]

Fear of a concerted Dakota–Anishinaabe attack seemed most prevalent in the town of St. Cloud, fifty miles south of Fort Ripley. Many refugees from the "Big Woods" had landed there. Most had no money or food and had lost wagons and stock, creating problems for getting any farther east. William B. Mitchell, editor of the *St. Cloud Journal-Press,* reported to Ramsey on August 28 that "a stampede to get away, as I never expected to witness," had occurred. The citizenry had become "completely overcome with the prevailing epidemic."[98] While attempting to construct a defensive position, Mitchell discovered that the lumber milling companies in town— St. Cloud had become a milling center—refused to provide lumber. Mitchell and others in the city demanded that Ramsey select an officer who had absolute power to organize and provide for defense.[99] Sally Wood, who had fled with her husband to St. Cloud from a small community called Elm Isle, wrote her brother regarding the chaos. Families were being attacked outside of town, there was no food for the refugees, and as she put it, it was "everyone for themselves, or that is the way some do that has the money."[100]

In some cases, the second panic that hit the state was even worse than the first, and it led to an even more vitriolic demand for revenge. Newspaper after newspaper demanded action. "A WAR OF EXTERMINATION AGAINST

THE SIOUX SAVAGES" was a headline in the *St. Paul Press*. Even men of the cloth lost their composure under such a barrage of terrible news. Minister Charles Galpin, founder of the First Congregational Church at Excelsior, just west of Minneapolis, had tried at times to minister to the Indians, even attempting to proselytize to the older Shakopee, who generally ignored his pleas. In late August, he no longer thought of such a solution, writing Governor Ramsey that he had a plan. Galpin proposed "to employ the Chippeways mostly to do the work for us, by giving large bounties for every [Dakota] scalp produced." Galpin, ever the preacher, ended his message with a biblical theme: "Reverses have come, and will come, until Pharaoh will let the oppressed go free." In such an atmosphere, where Galpin believed regeneration would surely come, extermination of the Indian seemed the only solution.

These thoughts increasingly entered the minds of soldiers attached to Sibley's emerging army. But could the colonel, increasingly criticized for his inaction, bring together the necessary forces to defeat what by the end of August had become seemingly a remorseless juggernaut of evil. The fright and the flight all across Minnesota, even in heavily settled communities, had become so prominent that failure to act on Sibley's part might easily have led to the utter abandonment of the state.

SEVEN

THE ROAD TO RETRIBUTION

As Minnesota newspaper editors screamed for revenge, authorities finally began putting together a massive response. Governor Ramsey used increasingly unpopular state militia laws to issue commissions, installing officers in positions of power. Confiscated grain, wagons, and horses finally began reaching the army at Fort Ridgely. A few men on their own took the initiative to organize militias, home guards, or rangers, even without the governor's sanction, yet army regulations made it impossible to muster them into federal service. Unfortunately for the governor, those in positions of authority in Washington, D.C., including Secretary of War Edwin Stanton, refused early requests to send arms, supplies, and even regular troops. Stanton seemed oblivious to the seriousness of the situation, perhaps because of a massive Civil War engagement known as the Second Battle of Bull Run (August 26–30).[1]

Ramsey did plead his case for help directly to the president, especially asking to be excused from providing men for the draft. Lincoln finally responded in a laconic fashion: "If the draft cannot proceed of course it will not proceed."[2] Fortunately for the governor, Commissioner of Indian Affairs William P. Dole and Lincoln's private secretary, John G. Nicolay, happened to be in Minnesota, investigating charges of corruption with Anishinaabe and Dakota annuities. Nicolay telegraphed Stanton, outlining the seriousness of the crisis; Sibley had a force in the field, but he lacked everything. Nicolay suggested sending six large cannons, twelve hundred horses to mount a cavalry, and five to six thousand guns.[3] Stanton must have been stunned—he had no such resources. While Minnesota would have to fight the Indians alone for a few more weeks, federal authorities now seemed to understand the need for action. But finding resources while the entire government was threatened by a confederate army was daunting.[4]

Such salvation could not come too soon. Minnesota newspaper editors published a blistering demand for immediate retribution. The *St. Paul Journal,* a sympathetic Republican oracle, contended on August 28 that "the utmost determination and energy is indicated by those in authority, to suppress the revolt," then adding, with a growing sense of optimism, "there will be no prisoners taken in this war!" The *Mankato Independent* agreed: "The Remedy. Extermination is the word!" Its rival, the *Mankato Weekly Record*, went even further: "Minnesota must either be a Christian land or a savage hunting ground—either the white man must exercise undisputed sway, or the Indian—the two races can never live peacefully and prosperously together again." The *St. Paul Press* trumpeted the same message: "We must do one of two things, *either kill every Sioux Indian within our borders or drive the tribe out of the state* . . . Let it be a war of *extermination.*"[5] Calls for genocide began to replace reports of mass murder and mayhem.

Colonel Sibley saw such headlines as a demand for immediate action. But the number of Indians involved in the attacks on New Ulm and the fort unnerved him; he had seen firsthand the Indians' ability to use stealth in warfare. Even so, he pushed on, reaching Fort Ridgely and using his supply wagons to remove the nearly two hundred civilians who had been holed up in the two-story stone barracks. The sight of these poor people moved him deeply, most being in rags and without shoes. "God knows what is to become of them," he wrote his wife. He then cautioned Ramsey: he could go no farther until American soldiers from the Seventh Regiment reached him, more mounted troops replaced those who had left to return home, and proper munitions for the guns he had arrived.[6]

Sibley's lack of intelligence regarding events at the Lower Agency only sharpened his caution. Although the many northern Sissetons and Wahpetons, who had come south and watched as the attacks went in on the fort, had departed for home, the colonel knew nothing of it. He did learn that some Germans had returned to New Ulm and seemed determined to hold it at all costs. And his northern flank was more secure as militias in Hutchinson and Glencoe had built stockades. However, any march up the Minnesota River still seemed problematic in late August.[7]

Meanwhile, Little Crow's hope of a united Indian front seemed more distant when he learned on the evening of August 23 that the Wahpeton stepfather of Susan Brown, Akipa, and his son, Charles Crawford, had appeared and demanded that the captive Brown family be turned over to them. Crawford was a close friend of young Samuel Brown. While Little Crow was not there (given his earlier wound, he likely was observing the battle at New Ulm from afar), several Dakota men taunted Akipa and Crawford for their "cowardice." They had not killed a single white man, not even a "babe," as one put it. Akipa lashed back: "There was no honor in killing helpless people." Akipa then stepped into the center of the crowd and warned: "If he had found that any of his relatives had been harmed," he would "slaughter the braves [responsible] like slaughtering a lot of beaver on dry land."[8] No one fooled with Akipa, and he spoke for many Dakota men in the villages north of the Upper Agency, men who were more concerned about their relatives than making war on Americans. The Browns and their protectors left without further incident.

Little Crow had protected the Browns with the hope they would help build an alliance with the Sissetons and Wahpetons. Akipa's response must have worried him as Akipa was the brother of Wahpeton chiefs Walking Iron and Red Iron, who had villages above the Yellow Medicine River. The incident foretold of conflict, even perhaps future intratribal feuding. Even more worrisome, Little Crow knew that the Americans were mustering their strength and might soon attack his village. Accordingly, on August 24, the village crier announced that all of the Mdewakantons would congregate some ten miles farther north at Rice Creek, uniting with Little Six's and Red Middle Voice's bands, which had remained in that vicinity.[9]

While the combined camps stayed near Rice Creek for several days, the leaders of the soldiers' lodge sent out scouts, carefully monitoring events at Fort Ridgely. Once they reported on the arrival of Sibley's army at the fort on August 27, yet another move was soon ordered. The next day, the unified camp broke up, and the *akacita* soldiers organized a large caravan that headed north toward the Yellow Medicine River. The train, according to captive Sarah Wakefield, was nearly five miles long, given the massive amount of plunder that had been brought in. "Nice coaches filled with young Indians [passed by], dressed up in all kinds of finery," as Wakefield described it. "White women's bonnets were considered great ornaments, but were worn by men altogether." Ironically, U.S. flags waved in the breeze. As Wakefield put it, "many times it looked like 'Uncle Sam's' camp." While the march resembled "the confusion of Babel," it had no difficulty crossing the Yellow Medicine River. Here, the *akacita* chiefs organized a new camp a mile or so to the west of Riggs's old Hazelwood mission.[10]

As the caravan marched past the Upper Agency buildings, a hundred or so white captive women and children trudged alongside the wagons, dressed mostly in hand-me-downs, given to them by Dakota women who wanted their dresses. Gabriel Renville, one of Joseph R. Brown's protégées who had been "head" farmer at the agency, watched the captives, somewhat aghast at the treatment of the captives. In a day and age where ladies always wore hats, Renville noted that they were "bareheaded and barefooted," an insult to their dignity. Renville later wrote: "It made my heart hot." Others standing next to Renville included Akipa, Charles and Thomas Crawford, the Brown family, and the Christian full-bloods, Simon Anawaŋgmani, Paul Mazakutemani, and Solomon Two Stars (or Wicaŋhpinoŋpi, as he was known in the Dakota vernacular). The group also included a number of full-blood friends and relatives, including chiefs Walking Iron and Red Iron, who fretted about the Mdewakanton invasion of their reservation. Along with a few others, they numbered just under twenty men, not a force strong enough to make an argument. Even so, these Sissetons and Christians determined to do something for the captives.[11]

Little Crow soon noticed the men near the buildings. He confidently rode up to Gabriel, who he knew extremely well, and, with a stern voice, demanded that he and his party leave the agency buildings, which they had been protecting, as they might one day be used by an invading American army; Little Crow intended to burn them that evening. An hour later, four *akacita* soldiers came and ordered the men at the agency to come join the Mdewakanton camp. To this, Gabriel Renville and Akipa adamantly refused, but because the Mdewakantons and the captives were moving northward anyway, Renville and the others followed them—they could easily be caught between two armies if they stayed. By the evening of August 28, the two groups were less than a mile apart, in separate tent cities; those with Little Crow and Little Six numbered perhaps three hundred tepees.[12]

Once settled, Gabriel walked to the center of his much smaller camp and called for a council, inviting the group who had been at the agency buildings and well as a handful of others from Walking Iron's and Red Iron's villages. Among the newcomers was Gabriel's cousin, John B. (J. B.) Renville, and other members of the Renville family, who had been trying to preserve Riggs's Hazelwood property. J. B. provided a young calf for the feast. Just as they were ready to sit down and eat, over two hundred Mdewakanton warriors, their heads painted red, came charging forward. Overmatched, in typical fashion, the Renvilles and Christian Indians asked them to join them in eating, an invitation that a Dakota Indian could hardly resist.[13]

Food provided the ultimate pacifier in Dakota society, but the Mdewakantons were not overtly friendly. As the Mdewakanton *akacita* soldiers prepared to leave, they made it clear that they expected Gabriel's camp to join them. But then Walking Iron rose quietly and in a sarcastic fashion said: "The Mdewakantons have many white prisoners. Can it be possible that it is their object to make the Wahpetons and Sissetons their prisoners too?" This kind of debate was exactly what Little Crow wished to avoid. Believing, however, that a crisis was at hand, Walking Iron and Red Iron sent messengers to all the Sisseton and Wahpeton camps north of the agency, all the way up to Big Stone Lake. Nearly three hundred Sissetons responded the next day, arriving at the camp of the Renvilles and the Christian Indians on the morning of August 29.[14]

The reinforcements were well armed, but they still lacked organization and leadership. Gabriel and the others then erected a massive tent in the middle of their camp and created their own soldiers' lodge. Gabriel, Joseph LaFramboise, and several noted Sisseton and Wahpeton warriors were made "chief officers." In a simple ceremony, they were "duly installed and authority given to them." Yet when it came time to select a spokesman, they quickly turned to the dynamic Paul Mazakutemani. Mazakutemani was short of stature, but he was a natural speaker, serving as president of the Hazelwood Republic in the late 1850s and making the case for "citizenship" for Christian Indians in front of a local judge at Mankato some years earlier. While he lost that battle, Mazakutemani was prepared to put the Mdewakantons in their place. "We painted our faces [red, no doubt, for war] and got our guns," Gabriel later wrote, and nearly three hundred mostly Sissetons and Wapetons warriors mounted horses and, "singing" to the top of their lungs, "went towards their [Little Crow's] camp."[15]

If Little Crow still had hopes of unifying all Dakota people against the Americans, the council that followed soon dashed them. Over a thousand people gathered to hear the debate. Iron Gourd (known as Mazawamnuha in Dakota) spoke first for the Mdewakantons, perhaps an indication that many of their leaders had lost faith in Little Crow. However, it would have been awkward for Little Crow to stand up against so many of his Sisseton and

Wahpeton relatives. But the new speaker seemed also to indicate that new Mdewakanton leaders had emerged. Besides several young men from Little Six's and Red Middle Voice's camps, they included the daring Mankato, the leader of a small village before the war; Big Eagle, who led a small faction of Little Crow's people; Grey Bird (better known as Zitkadaŋhota), who, because of his bravery, Little Crow had elevated to the position of "his head soldier"; and Red Legs (or Huśaśa in Dakota), who led the small Wahpekute contingent. Politically, it was best for Little Crow to sit quietly and listen.

Iron Gourd, who was considerably younger than the other Mdewakanton leaders, began by taunting the Sissetons and Wahpetons, something Little Crow could not do: "You men who talk of leaving us and delivering up the captives, talk like children." He then laughingly suggested that somehow those opposed to the war believed that the whites would "think you have acted as their friends." The Americans, he argued, would punish all Dakota people in the future, including the Sissetons and Wahpetons, and the only choice now was to join the Mdewakantons and fight the whites, to the death if necessary.[16]

Paul Mazakutemani answered in a condescending manner: "I am much surprised to hear that you have been killing the settlers." By doing so, "you have done us a great injustice." Had we "older men" heard of what was contemplated, "you would not have been able to involve our young men with you." Having heard rumors that the Mdewakantons considered seeking shelter in Canada, he then warned, "you must remember that the chief of the English is a woman," and warriors who "will cut women and children's throats" will not be received by her. Such men were "squaws and cowards." The only way to broker some sort of salvation, Mazakutemani suggested, was to hand over the white captives.[17]

At this turning point, some of the more passive Mdewakantons rose and spoke. Blue Thunder (Wakeeyaŋto in Dakota), representing, to some degree, Wabasha and Wakute, suggested that while "the hostile Indians had brought trouble and suffering upon themselves," and he strongly disagreed with their actions, he also believed that "the captives should have to stay with them and participate in their troubles and privations." At this, an excitement arose among the crowd of nearly a thousand Indians, indicating approval. Paul Mazakutemani then realized that rescuing the captives was futile at this time, and the council resolved nothing.[18]

As the council went on, Mdewakanton scouts continued to report on the arrival of more troops to Sibley's army at Fort Ridgely, mostly elements of the Third and Seventh Regiments. The Mdewakanton *akacita* warriors who wished to prosecute the war then considered two options. They had hurriedly departed Little Crow's village on August 24, and some wanted to go back and collect plunder left behind. Others suggested moving once again on New Ulm. But Little Crow argued that a fresh supply of flour existed at Cedar Mills, a small isolated community in the "Big Woods" just west of Hutchinson. After hitting the mill, his force could then harass Sibley's supply trains, which were headed to the fort.[19] While there had been little unity in orchestrating the attacks on the fort and New Ulm, factionalism also dominated in the confusion of the retreat to the north.

As the evening drew to a close, the younger warriors, Mankato, Big Eagle, Little Six, Red Legs, and others rejected Little Crow's argument, and a divided force emerged from the council. Just over a hundred men followed Little Crow and his former head *akacita,* the older Walker Among Stones (or Tunkaŋmani), into the Big Woods. Several mixed-bloods, including "cousin" Antoine J. Campbell, joined them. The younger men collected roughly two hundred men and mounted the road to the Lower Agency, reaching it on the evening of September 1. Scouts in the lead then came rushing back with news. As they sat quietly on a hill on the north side of the Lower Agency, they could see what amounted to fifty odd troopers on horseback, settling into a camp a few hundred yards up the north bank of Birch Coulee. The leaders of the group thought this too easy a target to pass up, and they planned an assault for the early hours of the next morning.[20]

Sibley did find two willing scouts of his own several days after reaching Fort Ridgely. George McLeod and William L. Quinn, the latter the son of the interpreter killed at the ferry, rode as far north as the Yellow Medicine River on the evening of August 29. They reported that the Indians were camped well north of the river, near the missions.[21] Sibley concluded that while he lacked the supplies necessary to move his army forward, he could at least send out a reinforced patrol to bury the dead at the agency and in the vicinity of Beaver Creek and Birch Coulee and scout the region. Captain Hiram Grant, with fifty-one men of Company A of the Sixth Regiment, joined forces with seventy mounted men commanded by Captain Joseph Anderson of the Cullen Mounted Guard. At the last moment, a number of civilians begged to go along, and Sibley turned to old friend Joseph R. Brown to lead the group; Brown had no idea what had happened to his family and wanted to go. Sibley, however, failed to tell Grant that Brown was in command; Brown did have an officer's commission in the Minnesota militia.[22]

Initially, the issue of command had little impact as the combined force marched up the road to the Lower Agency. On the first day, the troops buried twenty-eight victims, mostly in the vicinity of the ferry. Congregating at the ferry, the force then split, with Grant's company moving north into the Beaver Creek region, where it interred thirty more bodies, including Mrs. Henderson and her children. Severe decomposition had set in, and many bodies were unrecognizable. But Dr. Jared Daniels insisted in his memoir that he "saw everyone that was buried and not one was scalped or mutilated."[23] David Carrothers found his young son—the four-year-old boy who had pleaded with his father to carry him away.[24] At the northernmost point of their search, Grant's men stumbled onto a nearly famished Justina Kreiger from Beaver Creek, still suffering from the shot in her back. Daniels dressed her wound, and she quietly laid down in a wagon, bound for the camp then being set up at Birch Coulee.[25]

Brown attached himself to Anderson's troop, which had crossed the river and went into the agency. Nathaniel Myrick found the remains of his brother, Andrew, while some sixteen other bodies were found and buried. Most of the civilians returned to the fort after finding their relatives. Toward evening, Brown's forces recrossed the river and came into Grant's encampment; no thought was given to the location—a hundred yards east and extending toward the southwest was the coulee, heavily covered with trees and tall grass. The soldiers placed wagons in a circle, tying them together with ropes with the horses grazing inside. The men pitched their tents and posted guards just outside the wagons, and then everyone went to bed.[26]

At 4:30 A.M., a guard saw two figures crawling through the grass. He instantly fired, and almost instantaneously, volleys from outside the picket line tore into the camp, one after another. Brown's soldiers sprang from their sleep, sprinted out of the tents, and looked for cover. The Indians could load and fire muskets three times every minute, and they sent some six hundred balls tearing through the encampment just in the first minute. Many men were wounded or killed as they left the tents, bewildered by the interruption of their sleep. Fortunately, many balls tore into the horses that were tethered inside the ring of wagons. As the animals fell, men crouched behind them, and slowly Brown's troops began to return fire, shooting at the musket flashes that came out of the darkness.[27]

The initial fusillade killed a dozen men, with dozens of others wounded. But once the men reached the dead horses, hardly a man thereafter was killed. The sun slowly rose, and using bayonets, knives, and the three shovels they possessed, the group dug rifle pits and prepared for a long siege. While this was underway, several of Brown's men simply panicked. One, an Anglo-Dakota man named Peter Boyer, deserted to the other side, while another soldier, wrenched with fear, lay in a muddle behind a horse, screaming "O my God, My God." A young officer finally pulled out his revolver, cocked it, and said that if he did not stop, "he would blow his brains out." The scream lessened to a whimper. Jonathan Henderson, who had buried his wife and children the day before, panicked and ran crazily outside the wagons. Indians cut him down. But a cool Jared Daniels moved from soldier to soldier, treating the wounded, including Brown, who had taken a ball to the side of his neck. Daniels later berated Captain Grant, who he heard scream, "We all shall be scalped." Captain Anderson, however, as one soldier put it, "was cool and unconcerned as an iceberg."[28]

While the Indians may have considered rushing the entrenched troops, as the day passed, each side resorted to firing occasionally at targets a hundred yards in the distance. In a curious display, toward evening, an Indian bearing a white flag appeared, suggesting that any of the other mixed-bloods inside the breastworks might leave without being harmed. Young Boyer, who had ran, had apparently been killed, but a small group of men huddled to consider the offer, a number of whom once belonged to the Renville Rangers and were recruited by Agent Galbraith. They all declined, and as the white flag came down, Captain Grant fired on the bearer, striking his horse.[29]

While the command began rationing virtually everything, especially water and ammunition, hopes centered on getting relief. Back at Fort Ridgely, a picket alerted Sibley to distant gunfire, and that afternoon the colonel ordered McPhail's mounted troop of over two hundred men to check on Brown's force. As McPhail marched north toward the agency, the Indians cut him off several miles short of the beleaguered burial detail. Levering his mountain howitzer, McPhail kept the Indians at bay but dug in, facing stiff resistance. Seeking relief, McPhail sent the wiry Lieutenant Sheehan racing back toward the fort. He ran a gauntlet of Indians, spilling into the fort on a horse that promptly fell dead. Fortunately, Colonel Marshall had arrived that morning, September 3 with the last elements of the Seventh Regiment. Sibley then ordered a massive infantry force to march, first rescuing McPhail and then Brown. His men reached the burial party at 10:00 A.M., as the Indians slowly withdrew. The battle at Birch Coulee had lasted for thirty-three hours.[30]

Sibley seemed stunned by the carnage at the camp. Some eighty horses lay dead inside the enclosure of wagons; the stench was terrific. This, along with the many mounts McPhail had lost, literally destroyed Sibley's precious little cavalry. Brown had thirteen dead on the ground—five more would die later—and nearly fifty wounded. Through it all, Justina Kreiger lay still in the wagon as over a hundred bullets battered its side walls. Sibley, dutifully reporting to his wife a day later, could only lament: "These Indians fight like devils; no one has seen anything like it."[31] However, Birch Coulee had also demonstrated to naysayers back in St. Paul that Sibley's caution was warranted. While a somewhat discombobulated Sibley wrote Ramsey asking to be relieved, the governor would not hear of it. He ordered Sibley to attack Dakota forces, using whatever was necessary. But how to do it without a mounted cavalry seemed daunting.[32]

Had Little Crow stayed with the force headed south, Birch Coulee might have been an even greater disaster. Instead, he marched east into the Big Woods, chatting with his friend and relative Antoine J. Campbell as they rode on. On the second day out, September 2, dissension arose within the ranks, as a majority of the Indians with the party decided to attack Hutchinson or Glencoe, which they expected to be easy targets. They followed Walker Among Stones, formerly Little Crow's head *akacita*. While the nature of the disagreement is speculative, Campbell later noted that Little Crow had asked if it were possible to send a letter to Sibley, perhaps suggesting that the chief was looking for a way out of the war. This also may explain his intentions of moving east and south, closer to the fort. Whatever the cause, only thirty-seven men remained with the chief and his brother, White Spider (Uŋktomiska in Dakota, who had worked in a trader's store), taking the position of head soldier.[33]

Little Crow's force reached the Big Woods just as Captain Richard Strout had arrived at Forest City with sixty-five volunteers. They had been ordered to the region by Ramsey's newly appointed militia general, John H. Stevens, a prominent citizen of Minneapolis. Stevens assumed control of militia forces north of the Minnesota River, complementing Flandrau, who organized state defenses south of the river.[34] George Whitcomb still commanded some fifty armed settlers at the Forest City stockade, and a similar force held Hutchinson, but neither group had stopped the refugee flight. Whitcomb had actually counted 170 wagons of fleeing people coming through town every three or four days.[35]

Strout's company moved south from Forest City on September 2, reaching the abandoned community of Acton, where the war had started two weeks before. His troops had wagons full of food and tents for shelter, but they scoffed at the old "Belgium muskets" that had been issued to them by Stevens—they were all he could get. Perhaps more problematic, Strout's men were raw and hardly familiar with their weapons, which they had not even fired, and Strout, while a brave man, had little if any military training. As his men settled into their camp, the commanding officer never even thought of putting out a guard; Whitcomb's Forest City scouts had seen no Indians.

Ten hours after Strout's departure for Hutchinson, two of Whitcomb's men suddenly encountered Little Crow's forces, exchanging shots with them. The scouts then raced back to Forest City. The very able Whitcomb, analyzing the situation on the evening of September 2, suddenly realized that the Indians might find Strout, surprise him, and annihilate his force. Stepping out in front of his fifty men, Whitcomb asked for three volunteers to save Strout. Jesse Branham, Thomas Holmes, and Albert Sperry came forward. Leaving at midnight, they rode twenty miles through a pitch-black night, halfway expecting to meet Indians. They dashed into Strout's camp at 3:00 A.M., catching the command members snug in their blankets without any sense of danger.[36]

While Little Crow's thirty-seven men were just a few miles away, the scouts had little idea of their location. Strout, smarting for a fight, ordered his men to charge their muskets; while grabbing the minie balls from the supply wagons, they suddenly realized that the 62-caliber ammunition was too large for the 57–58 caliber Belgium guns! Quickly, the men sat by the fires, whittling lead bullets down, creating enough ammunition for twenty rounds a piece. Regardless, the undeterred Strout broke camp at dawn, marched south and suddenly engaged Little Crow's smaller force; Strout's men outnumbered Little Crow's two to one. The Indians gave way, and it looked like the volunteers, untrained, poorly equipped, but steadfast, would win the day. Just then the second Dakota war party of sixty men tore into the troops from the rear, attacking the wagons that carried supplies and ammunition.

Nearly surrounded and increasingly desperate, Strout sent twenty men back to save the wagons, as the remainder continued to fight southward along the road to Hutchinson. A lake on their left prevented total envelopment, and the men fought hard. One later confessed that he "had never fired a gun before," but he "pointed his gun at the Indians, shut his eyes, and pulled the trigger." Such volunteers might have scared the Indians, but they killed very few. Strout then had a choice: he could stand and fight and perhaps be overrun by the much larger force bearing down on him from the north or run for Hutchinson.[37] He ordered the command to fix bayonets and charge through Little Crow's smaller force. The Indians, fearing the bayonet, gave way, and the wagons raced through the opening. As they did so, one American volunteer observed, Little Crow sat "mounted on a fence," waving a blanket and encouraging his warriors on. Virtually every militiaman with a bullet in his gun fired at him. They all missed, "whereupon the chief mounted the fence [again] and made the [American] soldiers a deep bow."[38]

Racing through the gap, Strout's drivers, scared beyond belief, reached the other end and just kept going, leaving the many wounded behind. An officer rode quickly to the front of the column, drew his pistol, and ordered them to stop. Throwing supplies from the wagons and then loading the wounded, the force mounted a rearguard action and reached the Hutchinson stockade at 3:00 P.M., fighting Indians most of the way. Miraculously, the command had only three killed, but two dozen were wounded, several of whom would die in a day or two, and it had lost all its supplies. The "Battle at Acton" had ended, but the siege of Hutchinson and Forest City was just beginning.[39]

Reinforced by a band of two dozen young Sissetons and Wahpetons who were looking mostly for excitement, the Indians then divided again: one group attacked Forest City and the other went toward Hutchinson. At Hutchinson, Strout ordered everyone into the stockade; some obeyed while others stayed in a hotel that was soon under siege. Yet the Indians mostly amused themselves by setting fire to buildings, literally burning the town down. Much the same occurred at Forest City, where Captain Whitcomb could do little to prevent any conflagration. In the aftermath, General Stevens rushed whatever recruits he could find to fortify the stockades. One command included a corps of Norwegians, who when told there were no weapons for them, not even worthless Belgium muskets, went into the woods and cut spears, and then marched north to help stem the Indian assaults. Some of these men did not even have shoes.[40]

While the fighting in the Big Woods shocked Minnesotans, even worse, a few days later, riders rushed into St. Cloud with news that Captain John

Van der Horck's command at Fort Abercrombie was under siege. His troop, Company D of the Fifth Minnesota, had just sixty-five men. Fortunately, some fifty settlers had joined the garrison, most wielding squirrel guns and shotguns. Van der Horck's request, however, was not so much for reinforcements; he had discovered months before that the Harpers Ferry muskets issued to his troops took a 69-caliber bullet, but the ammunition boxes sent—containing some forty thousand rounds—were for 58-caliber muskets! Once again ingenuity saved the garrison; the three twelve-pound cannons came with "canister shot," which yielded balls that, with some whittling, could fit the musket barrels. On September 5, the Mdewakanton subchief Medicine Bottle from Little Six's band led an assault on the fort.[41]

Fort Abercrombie weathered the storm, as the cannons held back the Indians more so than infantry fire. Just one trooper was killed with a number wounded. While Captain Van der Horck estimated the number of Dakota Indians involved at four hundred, the number was likely less than half that. Mostly, the attackers wanted the horses housed in the command's stables, one building of which was fought over. When the Dakota *akacita* soldiers failed to take the stables after two attempts, they left. Outlying settlements suffered more than the fort. The fledgling town of Breckenridge, some fifty miles to the south, was burned; its one main building, a three-story hotel, collapsed. Later military patrols buried some fourteen citizens in the vicinity.[42]

The news coming into eastern Minnesota communities caused panic once again. Matthew Donahue, writing from Henderson, chastised Ramsey: "The people and farmers are all leaving . . . they say you promised them protection and failed to give it." At St. Cloud, hundreds of refugees were waiting in line to cross the Mississippi River, one hundred wagons and their teams being ferried across every day. "They are passing at all hours of day and night," resident J. P. Wilson wrote to the governor on September 6. "Such a stampede and excitement I never saw." And poor Sally Wood, who with her family did not have the means to pay the ferryman, could only write her brother in abject despair: "The Indians are upon us by the thousands. We are all expecting them every night . . . this may be the last you ever hear from me."[43]

But Mary Crowell, writing from Anoka, tried to keep a stiff upper lip, staying put in town. In a letter sent back east, she praised the "heroic little band" at Fort Abercrombie, who had "held them at bay . . . a thousand Sioux warriors!" Like many Minnesotans, Crowell exaggerated—the attacking force at the fort was one-sixth that number. But she did not overstate the fear that existed everywhere: "Pen would fail to portray even in the slightest degree the terror, the utter woe" of the last three weeks.[44] Other leading citizens tried in vain to stop the panic. An editor in Winona—far from the mayhem—realized that the exodus was fear-driven. "Panic stricken" settlers, he began in an editorial, had arrived from La Crescent. "They have seen no Indians themselves, but their neighbors have seen lots of them." Further reports, the tongue-in-cheek editor noted, told us "that Brownsville is in ruin. In Brownsville, they hear that Lansing is burned. At Lansing, people believe that Winona is destroyed, La Crosse [Wisconsin] in danger and Milwaukee threatened!"[45] Such sarcasm may have amused people, but it did not stop the flight.

Some newspaper editors increasingly blamed Sibley for the turmoil. Feisty abolitionist Jane Swishelm lambasted the whole military effort, writing Ramsey: "For God's Sake put some *live* person in command of the force against the Sioux as Col. Sibley has 100 men or thereabouts in his undertaker's corps [perhaps a reference to the necessary burials at Birch Coulee]."[46] H. J. Wakefield, from St. Peter, ranted at Ramsey for the inactivity: "The blood of . . . [Minnesota's] murdered citizens will rest on *your skirts.*" And the editor of the *Mankato Independent* had considerable fun with Sibley's strategy: "The wonder is that he [Sibley] did not entrench at Shakopee and send for siege guns!"[47] The vengeance that Minnesota editors were demanding seemed stalled at Fort Ridgely.

Many of the critics were strong Republicans who had elected Governor Ramsey. "You have either a fool, a knave, or a rebel [southern sympathizer]" at the head of the army, one wrote of Sibley. "Under the garb of patriotism he [Sibley] will dishonor your administration."[48] The editor of the *Faribault Central Republican* asserted that the reason for the colonel's failure to march centered on his fear that "a stray shot might injure the former Mrs. Sibley [the Indian woman with whom Sibley did have a child] or some of her offspring." And still others thought the reason Sibley hesitated was because of his commercial connections: "There is no disposition to exterminate the savages," the editor at the *Hastings Independent* wrote, "because they are too valuable brutes to sell bad whiskey to, and to cheat out of the annual bounty."[49]

Even close allies urged Sibley on. Sibley's friend, A. G. Chatfield, questioned the colonel over whether he had any intentions of negotiating with the Indians. Chatfield understood the need to proceed cautiously and free the prisoners, but he then added: "the desire & intention to annihilate the tribe, revenge the indescribable barbarities . . . is still stronger." The criticism hit home, and Sibley strongly denied that any negotiations were underway.[50] Others remained more supportive, including Flandrau and the new chaplain, Stephen Return Riggs, both of whom wrote the governor praising Sibley's caution. Riggs thought Sibley "had acted wisely in not advancing." He had raw troops, lacked ammunition and food, and needed the buildings in Fort Ridgely to house his men. The delay, Riggs thought, "is likely to work good in regard to the prisoners."[51]

Those poor beings, clothed in worn-out native dress and, at times, not being well fed, continued to bother Paul Mazakutemani and Gabriel Renville, who watched helplessly. By September 7, the camps separating the various groups west of the missions were only walking distances apart, and councils were occurring on a regular basis. One that brought representatives from all the bands together occurred as news spread that Sibley had sent a message to Little Crow. The two men had once hunted together, sat by a campfire at night, and enjoyed each other's company. Now, the colonel had addressed a note to the chief, leaving it in a cigar box near Birch Coulee. "If Little Crow has any propositions to make," it read, "let him send a half-breed to me, and he shall be protected in and out of my camp."[52]

Little Crow remained cautious, even though he had apparently wanted to write to Sibley several days earlier. With *akacita* warriors looking on suspiciously, he sought an accurate translation. First, he asked Campbell and David Faribault to read it. Wanting another opinion, the chief called upon young Thomas Robertson. After giving the same translation, Little Crow then dictated an answer listing grievance after grievance: the government allowed corrupt officials to steal money, children "were dying of hunger," and the traders, including especially Andrew Myrick, "told the Indians that they would eat grass or their own dung." The chief then asked Sibley for "an answer."[53] Robertson agreed to bring the letter to the colonel; he brought along a friend, Thomas Robinson. They headed down the road to Fort Ridgely in a buggy provided by Little Crow, not knowing what to expect next.[54]

As the letter campaign unfolded, a number of men in what was increasingly called "the friendly camp" noticed that some Mdewakantons and Franco and Anglo-Dakota people were defecting, quietly moving their tepees closer to this "friendly" group. Among them was Little Crow's "cousin," Antoine Campbell. On the evening of September 7, bolstered by this increase, Gabriel Renville and Mazakutemani decided to try once again to gain control of the captives. They painted their faces, grabbed their guns, and headed over to the Mdewakanton *akacita* camp, Gabriel recalled. Samuel Brown went along to reclaim property belonging to his mother. He estimated that this so-called "friendly" group now counted nearly a hundred men, including a few Sissetons and Wahpetons from the north.[55]

Mounted and armed, the friendlies rode up to the central tepee of the Mdewakanton soldiers' lodge, defiant and ready for battle. First, they demanded the property left behind by the mixed-bloods who had now joined them, including the wagons owned by the Campbell and Brown families. To this, the public crier, who seemed to be the only one present, protested: "The mixed bloods ought not to be alive, they should have been killed." Then Little Crow arrived. He seemed despondent—perhaps because Campbell had abandoned him—lamenting the fact that the war had not gone better. But he then consented to allow the mixed-bloods to look for property. A near explosion occurred when Samuel Brown found a horse that belonged to his mother. The Indian who had it threatened to shoot anyone who tried to take it. But one of Little Crow's warriors went up to the man and said, "I am a soldier [an *akacita*] do you think that I do not mean that I am one? . . . and knocked him down." Several of the friendly Indians then cut the rope holding the horse and walked away.[56]

Back at the council circle, Paul Mazakutemani then harangued a large group regarding the captives. "Give me all these white captives," he argued. "When you see the white soldiers coming to fight, fight with them, but don't fight with women and children." White Lodge's son, Strikes The Pawnee, then rose and countered: "If we are to die, these captives shall die with us." At this, a goodly number of men from the lodge nodded approval. Others even challenged Mazakutemani, calling him a coward. The group included Wabasha's son-in-law, Rattling Runner (Hdainyanka in Dakota), who had become an important *akacita* in the lodge. "The Braves say they will not give you the captives," he concluded. "The Mdewakantons are *men* and as long as one of them lives they will not stop pointing their guns at the Americans." Then Blue Thunder, representing Wabasha, quietly took Mazakutemani aside and told him "not to mention the captives again."[57]

The confusion during the struggle over the property allowed a few more white captives to escape to the friendly camp. Some *akacitas* promptly went looking for them. During a Bible meeting in J. B. Renville's lodge, over a hundred horsemen from the Mdewakanton soldiers' lodge rode among the tepees and shot at their tops. Seeing the seriousness of the situation, Lorenzo Lawrence took Mrs. DeCamp and her children, who had escaped, down to the river that night, hid them in a swamp, and then moved them by canoe toward Fort Ridgely. A few hours later, Simon Anawaŋgmani collected Mrs. John Newman and her three children and led them to the fort, arriving on September 11. Sibley's patience seemed to be paying off.[58]

A few days before these escapes, Robertson and Robinson had reached Fort Ridgely with Little Crow's letter. Sibley promptly separated the two messengers and quizzed them regarding the situation above on the river. Both confirmed that a friendly camp had taken shape, consisting of nearly one hundred tepees and well over two hundred people, but they stressed that the Mdewakanton soldiers considered both the white women and children and the mixed-bloods to be "captives," so they were watching the friendly camp intently. Sibley did send back a reply to Little Crow with the two messengers, saying simply: "Give me the prisoners and send them to my camp . . . and I will talk with you then like a man."[59] Obviously, after the debate with Paul Mazakutemani, which ended in a stalemate, the chief had no way of meeting Sibley's demand had he wanted to.

Little Crow and the *akacita* leaders quizzed the two messengers on their return, much as Sibley had done. What they learned was troubling: the American army was getting stronger, and it was very likely Sibley would soon march north. Some welcomed a final battle, even though they had not been successful at either Fort Ridgely or New Ulm. Others, however, had not been as strongly committed to the war and wished only to protect their women and children. After a quick debate on September 9, the village crier ordered the women to break camp once again, with the intent of moving northwest to the Lac qui Parle River, thirty-five miles below Big Stone Lake. The friendly Indians joined them, perhaps fearful of retribution by the Americans. Suddenly, as the combined camps approached Red Iron's village that afternoon, the front of the column confronted a hoard of mounted Wahpetons and Sissetons with Red Iron at their head. They raced down upon the column, firing their guns and demanding that it stop. They would not let the Mdewakantons pass, even if it meant war.[60]

The commotion just below Red Iron's village allowed more captives to escape as well as some Mdewakantons who had only halfheartedly supported the war effort. Among the group was Wakute, Taopi, and the only white man in the camp, George Spencer. Wabasha, however, decided against fleeing.[61] As Gabriel Renville described it, "The scattered camps caused by the halting and commotion . . . had the effect of breaking up the hostile soldiers' lodge, and to some extent the influence that it had exercised." And Red Iron's support made it increasingly impossible to coerce the friendly Indians, who proceeded to dig rifle pits and prepare to defend themselves against the Mdewkanton *akacita* soldiers.[62]

With growing desertions, Little Crow made one last attempt to negotiate with Sibley. The chief apparently went to the friendly camp—perhaps to keep his effort secret from his soldiers—and asked Antoine Campbell to compose the letter, written on about September 10. The chief gave up on listing grievances; instead, he made note of the 155 prisoners he still had—the number was probably lower by this time, but it was his only bargaining chip—noting that they were treated as well as anyone in camp. He then suggested that perhaps some resolution was possible and ended with a rather pathetic plea: "I want to know from you as a friend, what way that I can make peace for my people?" To some degree, the letter reflected the tragedy of the entire war: these two men, Sibley and Little Crow, had at one time ate together at late night campfires, talked of hunting and life, and slept under the same stars.[63]

Robertson and Robinson once again carried the letter to Sibley. Yet they barely made it out of camp, as the Mdewakanton soldiers learned of it and some threatened the chief's life. Somehow, Taopi and Good Thunder (Wakinyanwaste in Dakota), a Christian Indian who had joined Taopi's farming community, put a second letter into the messengers' hands. Written under a blanket by candlelight at the friendly camp, it claimed that many Mdewakantons were not in support of the war and that they had formed a separate camp. Just as the messengers began to leave, Wabasha, despite considerable reticence, quietly agreed to have his name attached to the epistle.[64]

After the messengers arrived at Sibley's headquarters at Fort Ridgely, the colonel quickly drafted two answers, sending one to Little Crow and the other to the friendly Indians on September 13. His note to the chief was a scolding: "You have not done as I wished in giving up to me the prisoners," he wrote. A small raiding party had also descended upon the Cottonwood River, west of New Ulm, and killed several people. Sibley blamed Little Crow, even though the chief likely had no knowledge of this raid. Sibley had learned of it after eight Dakota warriors came to ask for peace. Sibley artfully dodged their request, suspecting that they had committed the murders. While berating Little Crow, the colonel offered a poignant message of hope to Wakute, Good Thunder, Taopi, and Wabasha: "I have not come into this upper country to injure any innocent person . . . but to punish those who have committed cruel murders upon innocent men, women, and children."[65]

Just how the Franco-Dakota and Anglo-Dakota people—such as the Campbells—at the friendly camp interpreted the message is difficult to determine. It certainly suggested that those who joined the camp and protected the captives would not be punished. Big Eagle later wrote in his memoir that he believed "Gen. Sibley would treat with all of us who had only been soldiers, and would surrender as prisoners of war, and that only those who had murdered people in cold blood" would be punished.[66] With talk of extermination in Minnesota, it would have been difficult for the colonel to keep such a promise, even if he intended to do so.

Perhaps more encouraging, the messengers brought news that more and more Indians were joining the friendly camp every day. "Little Crow begins to quake," Sibley wrote to his wife.[67] In his report to headquarters, the news was, for the first time, extremely optimistic: "The Indians are very much divided in sentiment and are quarreling among themselves." And both troops and supplies were finally arriving; some 270 reached Sibley from Minnesota's Third Regiment on September 14. While the colonel still did not have a cavalry force of any size, he had received fifty thousand rounds of ammunition for his Springfield rifles. With fifteen hundred men, he expected to march soon, delayed only by heavy rains on September 16 and 17.[68]

More good news came when Secretary Stanton decided to take the conflict seriously. The secretary created the new Military Department of the Northwest on September 6, sending the somewhat disgraced General John Pope to command it. Pope's forces had been routed at Bull Run in August 1862, and the general, having a somewhat thin skin, blamed subordinates for the defeat. Not knowing what else to do with a disgraced general, Stanton banished him to Minnesota, ordering him to provide "detailed information respecting the extent of the outrages," and then "employ whatever force may be necessary" to defeat the Indians. Pope assumed that the order gave him carte blanche authority to requisition troops. Proving his worth in Minnesota, Pope believed, might help him regain his reputation.[69]

While Stonewall Jackson had bested Pope at Bull Run, the new department commander had no fear of giving orders. Once reaching Minnesota on September 16, he realized immediately from Sibley's correspondence that the crisis was real. He first ordered four regiments of Wisconsin volunteers to Minnesota; General-in-Chief Henry Halleck, back in Washington, promptly countermanded that order, sending the troops to St. Louis instead. Pope then promised Sibley one thousand "mounted men, as soon as possible," which also proved impossible; they simply were not available. Finally, he proposed a grandiose plan to reinforce Fort Abercrombie via the Ottertail Road, unwittingly telling Sibley, "I shall be glad to have your views." Sibley quietly noted the lateness of the season, and that idea also was abandoned. Pope then simply watched as Sibley, with mostly state forces, prepared to march north, encouraging the colonel to meet the Indians.[70]

As Sibley prepared to take the field, councils continued almost daily outside the soldiers' lodge, often without Little Crow. On the afternoon of September 15, the discussions were interrupted by the surprise appearance of an impressive contingent of Sisssetons, led by Standing Buffalo, the Charger, and Scarlet Plume, the latter of whom was Gabriel Renville's uncle. These chiefs were the crème de la crème of the Sisseton plains tribes, the leaders of nearly two thousand well-mounted warriors. In an obvious display of face-saving, the leaders of the soldiers' lodge—Big Eagle, Little Six, Red Middle Voice, and even Mankato and Little Crow—sat quietly. The Mdewakanton *akacita* leaders recognized that there would be little assistance from the plains Dakotas, and calling them "cowards," as they had done with the Christians and a handful of Franco and Anglo-Dakota men nearby, was out of the question.[71]

The Charger was the first to stand and address the rather large assemblage. "I live by the white man, and by the buffalo," he began. "I fear that you are going to annihilate all these for me." He then warned the Mdewakantons present that he would not allow them to advance farther north, beyond Red Iron's village. The Charger's people still had summer and winter villages at Big Stone Lake and Lake Traverse, and they did not want the struggle underway to affect those towns. The Charger and Standing Buffalo had come to send a letter to Sibley, indicating that the entire Sisseton nation had nothing to do with the war.[72]

At that, Standing Buffalo rose to speak, giving a long address. Straight and tall with a face that observers thought was strikingly intelligent, he started by calling those assembled "brothers," a usual obligatory Dakota salutation. He then said, "My father had dealings with the white people and I am afraid that you are going to destroy them all, and I dread the idea even that the connection that my father had with the white people," meaning treaties and annuities "should be destroyed." Standing Buffalo, much like Paul Mazakutemani, laughed at the suggestion that the British in Canada would come to the aid of the Mdewakantons: "They are also white men . . . and are ruled by a petticoat, and she has the tender heart of a squaw." Then raising his arm as if to point, he angrily said, "You people [the Mdewakantons] have cut our people's throats." After the meeting, Little Crow, while saying nothing in council, sought out Susan Brown and spoke quietly with her. The war was likely lost, he said, and if so he intended to go to the Big Woods and "kill as many whites as possible." He expected to die there and "it would be all right." He had long lived with such a death wish, and it was at hand.[73]

Recognizing that the time was now right—the rain had finally let up— Sibley left Fort Ridgely on September 18, moved a few miles north, and began crossing the Minnesota River. He feared an ambush, but he had his entire command of fifteen hundred men on the other side the next day. Resting a day, he then ordered the march northward, taking the well-traveled road from the Lower Agency to the Yellow Medicine Agency. He made sixteen miles the first day, a rather long hike for an infantry being fed nothing but pork and hardtack. After another fifteen-mile march on September 22, the command arrived just below the Yellow Medicine River. Here Sibley camped along the side of Lone Tree Lake—the location was misidentified as the larger Wood Lake, just to the west, and the camp and the battle that followed have ever since used the latter name. The position offered some protection, as the lake provided a shield to the west, much as Captain Strout had used a similar lake below Acton.[74]

As his troops plugged along on foot, a letter from General Pope caught up with Sibley. Pope offered his first orders and advice: move "upon the Sioux lands as far as the lake Travers [Traverse], destroying crops & everything else belonging to them." Pope had also heard the rumors of a possible negotiation: "I think it best," he wrote, "to make no arrangement of any kind with them."[75] Pope had obviously heard of a peace proposal, perhaps as a result of Little Crow's letters, promising those who surrendered without killing civilians that they would be treated as prisoners of war. Visiting with journalists from Mankato, General Pope then did a bit of politicking on his own. He left a strong impression: "Extermination is Pope's policy," as one of the editors put it.[76]

At times, General Pope expressed optimistic strategies that failed to meet the reality of the situation. While the Indians could easily flee onto the Plains, Pope informed Sibley that he planned to send a large mounted force west and then north to cut them off. But he had no troops for such an operation, and it was late in the year, as Sibley had noted earlier. Then, after making promises that he could not keep, the general did what most informed observers thought quite impossible: he overstated the seriousness of the conflict, going well beyond even what most Minnesota newspapers were reporting. He justified a request for thousands of troops to General Halleck by claiming that virtually all of Minnesota had been "depopulated, large towns and villages abandoned, and the property and crops of more than 50,000 people totally abandoned." Remarkably, with this last barrage, Halleck finally relented and released one Wisconsin regiment to join the Minnesota war effort; it was comprised of infantry troops who would take several weeks to reach the scene of battle and play no role in it.[77]

Sibley, on his own and still fearful of an ambush, remained reluctant to move north of the Yellow Medicine River. While an ambush and a rout seemed quite possible, a secondary reason was the captives: rumors abounded that the Mdewakantons would execute them when the army appeared. One captive, in a later memoir, suggested that Little Crow had ordered their murder; Antoine Campbell later categorically denied it, even stating that the chief had plans to hand them all over to him. Even so, some members of the soldiers' lodge supported killing the captives, which explains the rumors.[78] Fortunately for Sibley, the die regarding battle would be cast not by his army, but by the Indians themselves.

As the Mdewakanton *akacita* leaders learned that Sibley had reached Lone Tree Lake, a serious discussion erupted in council. Retreating farther north might cause civil war with the Sissetons, and waiting for the troops to arrive would give Sibley the advantage of choosing the field of battle, where his cannon would come into play. That evening, the *akacita* leaders ordered all capable men to march south to the Yellow Medicine River, which took several hours. Two *akacita* soldiers stood on either side of a creek and counted the warriors; they reached a total of 738, a formidable force. Even so, the Mdewakantons seemed to know that many of these men were going simply to placate the *akacita* leaders or to watch events. Then just below a knob on the north side of the Yellow Medicine River, the council resumed.

Little Crow led the way south, now seemingly convinced that there would be no peace with Sibley. Once near the river, he went to the top of a three-hundred-foot bluff to look over Sibley's army. He came back to the newly formed council with considerable exuberance, and as the light faded on the evening of September 22, he once again took the stage as speaker. Sibley's force, some two miles away, looked to be rather small, the chief argued, as it had few tents. The comment regarding tents was in fact true, as many of Sibley's men slept under wagons in blankets, if they had them. Then the chief suggested that the best option was to surprise Sibley in a night attack, overrun his camp, and kill many soldiers, much like what the Mdewakantons had done at Birch Coulee. "The plan," he concluded, "will not only secure for us an easy victory but lots of plunder, especially provisions."[79]

As the *akacita* leaders mulled over Little Crow's plan, Gabriel Renville, Simon Anawaŋgmani, Solomon Two Stars, Akipa, Antoine Campbell, and Red Iron sat quietly listening, working on a plan to counter Little Crow.[80] Gabriel Renville spoke first, berating Little Crow's night assault, especially the notion that Sibley's army was in fact small. Renville had crawled to the top of the knob as well and saw the camp. "They also have spy-glasses, and have seen the Indians coming here [to the Yellow Medicine River]." The troops had dug rifle pits for protection, Renville noted, and "they have their big guns in readiness, and are prepared for a surprise." Solomon then spoke. Such an attack would be "cowardly," he said, and "if the attack is made at night only a part of us will go, and many will not go." The Mdewakanton *akacita* leaders agreed that this was true. Solomon then suggested that it was better to wait until dawn, when the troops break camp and march toward the river where the Indians would have cover and surprise them.[81]

Renville and Solomon had feigned support for the campaign. Obviously, neither intended to join the *akacita* warriors, but only wanted to protect Sibley's forces. Solomon was a Christian Indian, the son of a Wahpeton chief, and his uncle was Paul Mazakutemani. The subterfuge seemed to work, as increasingly the *akacita* leaders could not arrive at a consensus; indeed, for whatever reason, Rattling Runner, Wabasha's son-in-law, agreed with Renville and Solomon. As they sat mostly in silence, it soon became obvious that no good option existed. As the sun slowly rose in the east, however, a small group of roughly thirty young warriors became impatient. They crossed over the Yellow Medicine River and took up positions in the grass, just above a small creek that ran northeasterly from Lone Tree Lake into the Minnesota River. Most were eager to prove themselves in battle.[82]

Sibley had planned his encampment for defense. He placed the remnants of the Third Regiment on the northern edge, near the creek bed, as those troops were the most tested. But they had only two officers, Major A. E. Welch and Lieutenant R. C. Olin, to control 270 men; the South had not released other officers. They were, in two words, unruly veterans. To the south and east of them were Colonel Marshall's five companies of the Seventh Minnesota, and below them to the west was the Sixth Regiment. Sibley had suffered continuously from a lack of food for his men, and they were running low by the time they reached Lone Tree Lake. As the sun came full in the east on September 23, a group of two dozen members of the Third Regiment, without any orders, moved across the creek in five wagons to dig potatoes, as some of the farms of the Upper Agency were just above them. The land was mostly rolling hills with spots of tall grass. A hundred yards beyond the creek, a dog's bark revealed Indians, tufts of grass woven into their headdresses for disguise. A firefight quickly broke out.[83]

At the first crack of muskets, Major Welch rallied the men in camp nearest to the conflict, who sprang to the support of their comrades. Jumping over the little creek, Lieutenant Olin led the charge, saber in hand, as a crusty sergeant hollered, "Remember Murfreesborough, fight boys, remember Murfreesborough," reminding the regiment of the disgrace of the surrender by their officers at that eastern Civil War battle. Suddenly, a full-fledged conflict had erupted. As one later report put it: "The horizon became picturesque with Indians, some mounted and some afoot, single and in squads, advancing rapidly from the direction of the Yellow Medicine River."[84] As the Americans were being reinforced, so were the Indians. Some moved to the left, trying to outflank the troops. One poetic American soldier later put it: "A retrospect brings to mind Tennyson's Charge of the Light Brigade, with Indians to the right of us, Indians to the left of us, Indians in front of us, whooping and yelling."[85]

As the firing increased in intensity, an Indian, bedecked like a chief, rode out in front of the Mdewakantons. One later account confirmed that he was Little Crow. He was "swinging his blanket above his head" and gave several "war-whoops," much like he had in the fight with Captain Strout near Acton. While the chief stayed on the field until the end, he carried only a six-shooter and supposedly never fired it. Yet the fighting had begun haphazardly, well before the Indians were able to spring their ambush.

Several hundred Indians joined in the fray, arriving piecemeal. Sibley estimated the number at three hundred, but the majority hung back. Many crossed lines and joined Simon Anawaŋgmani, who had rescued Mrs. Newman and stayed in Sibley's camp. He ran out onto the field coaxing others to desert. Walking Iron tried to join him, waving a large white flag. But he got so close to the scene of action that a cannonball blew off his leg. And the ever-ferocious John Otherday, marching north with Sibley after being hailed as a hero in St. Paul for rescuing the Upper Agency families, was at the head of American troops as they went into battle.[86]

Initially fearing a disaster, Colonel Sibley sent a rider north of the creek, ordering the Third to retreat southward. Welch at first refused it, but seeing more and more Indians appear, he relented, and the regiment slowly fought its way back to the creek where suddenly forty Renville Rangers, nearly all mixed-bloods, reinforced them and they turned north once again, ignoring the colonel. Seeing that Indians were moving into the creek to the right of Welch, Sibley then ordered Colonel Marshall to advance with five companies. Despite being green troops, they fixed bayonets and drove the Indians from the creek. The flight of the Indians became a near-rout as the two cannons opened fire, one a small six pounder and the other a twelve-pound mountain howitzer. They smashed into the retreating Indians. One cannonball struck the brave Mankato, killing him instantly.[87]

In two hours the so-called Battle of Wood Lake, misnamed and never intended by either the Indians or the Americans, was over. Seven American soldiers were dead on the field and nearly fifty wounded, with some to die later. Most were members of the Third Regiment. Dakota losses were more extreme, likely after the cannons did their work. At least thirty Indians died and many more were wounded.[88] An hour after the dead had been collected, Antoine Campbell and several others walked out onto the field with a white flag. Sibley honored it, knowing Campbell. They asked if they might retrieve their dead—Sibley's men were busy scalping the fourteen they had recovered.[89] The colonel denied the request, replying that he would bury them. Then they asked if peace were possible, and again Sibley said no—only after the captives had been handed over to him. The colonel then drafted a letter, addressed to Little Crow and the soldiers' lodge, telling them that he would wait at Lone Tree Lake for "a reasonable time for the delivery of the prisoners."[90]

Fearful that Sibley would advance quickly, the Dakota warriors escaped north to their original camp, just south of Lac qui Parle, and ordered women to pack tepees and prepare to leave. In the confusion, most of the captives held by the *akacita* warriors fled or were moved over to the friendly camp. Concerned that the *akacita* soldiers might attack them, the Christian Indians ordered everyone to dig pits for protection in the middle of the lodges at the friendly camp. The suspected assault, though, never came, and even the soldiers' lodge that had sat in the middle of the Mdewakanton camp for over a month had been taken down—the soldiers were fleeing out onto the plains. The fear of retribution was so severe that even many friendly Indians left, including some Wahpetons at Walking Iron's village and some Sissetons at Walking Runner's villages (Little Crow's father-in-law). Among them was Peter Tapetataŋka, a Christian Indian and former teacher in the village of his father, Walking Iron. The Dakota people, rife with factionalism, began to break apart.[91]

Little Crow, despondent and aware that he would take much of the blame for the conflict, sent a message to Antoine Campbell, asking him to come and see him one more time. Campbell complied, even though he knew that it would be dangerous. As he entered the tepee where the chief sat, Little Crow greeted him with the friendly "cousin." The chief then asked Campbell if he had any requests. Campbell suggested that Little Crow surrender to the Americans. The chief laughed and said that Sibley "would like to put the rope around my neck . . . if they would shoot me like a man, I would."[92] At that, he agreed to give up whatever captives still remained in camp, and they quickly moved to the friendly camp. Campbell then joined the chief as he and his small following reached an elevation well north of the camp. According to Campbell, Little Crow looked back on the Minnesota River valley and said, "We shall never go back there."[93]

As many of the *akacita* lodge members fled, Sibley began writing letters that transferred back and forth across the Yellow Medicine River. He assured Standing Buffalo that he had not come to "make war on any bands who have not been concerned in the horrible murders." Those who remained friendly should stay in their villages and raise a white flag.[94] To the Indians at the friendly camp, he, in a letter dated September 24, once again confirmed his intention of treating them fairly if they had not killed settlers. "I have not come to make war upon those who are innocent but upon the guilty," he wrote to Paul Mazakutemani and Taopi. He also let them know that he would march north of the Yellow Medicine the next day. Still cautious, he set up his camp ten miles south of the friendly camp.[95]

Finally," on September 26, the colonel marched north, passing the friendly camp and settling into a strong military perimeter a mile north of it. He then took a small contingent of soldiers to meet the leaders at the village below, increasingly called Camp Release. As they approached, the American soldiers saw nothing but white rags, attached to the top of tepee poles. "One Indian who was boiling with loyalty," as Samuel Brown put, "threw a white blanket on his black horse and tied a bit of white cloth to its tail . . . and wrapped an American flag around his body." As the two parties came together, Joseph R. Brown rushed forward to greet his wife and family, all now safe. Sibley's patience had paid off, as he counted nearly a hundred "pure white" women and children and close to 150 mixed-bloods among those who had been held captives for five weeks.[96]

Among this group at Camp Release were also a growing number of Mdewakantons. Some had been in Little Crow's camp, but they quietly joined the groups at Camp Release, mostly during the night. In the days that followed September 26, Camp Release continued to grow slowly, as Sibley allowed families that did not want to flee out onto the plains to come in. It was a devilish plot: he wholly intended to capture as many of these Indians as possible, believing most to be guilty of killing civilians. On September 27 he informed General Pope that he would use a military commission, a system of military justice then in use during the Civil War, to separate out the guilty ones from the friendly.[97]

Wakefield and the other rescued white women were taken to the military camp, where conditions were far from acceptable. They had only rags for clothes, and the troopers peered at them with a snickering that belied a massive suspicion. As the women had been turned over, Sibley made clear the speculation of his troops: "There were instances of stolidity among them," the colonel wrote of the women. "For the most part the poor creatures, relieved of the horrible suspense in which they have been left, and some of the younger women freed from the loathsome attentions to which they have been subjected by their brutal captors, were fairly overwhelmed."[98] Could they ever return to their families, or were there even families to return to? And as Wakefield quickly noticed, the women were soon "exposed to the gaze" of a hundred or more soldiers, "so we could not breath for want of air."[99] Everyone wanted to know but, in the Victorian morals of the day, dared not ask: Had they been raped?

Certainly, many Minnesotans far from the fields of battle thought they knew the answer to that horrible question. Alexander Ramsey, reporting to the state in mid-September, addressed the issue along with many others. The state had lost over five hundred settlers—his numbers were actually a bit low—and some thirty thousand people had lost homes and fled—that number was likely a bit low as well. The flight from twenty-six Minnesota counties constituted the largest forced exodus in American history. Just feeding people who had huddled in towns for protection proved a daunting task. Ramsey listed eleven counties that had been completely evacuated. He estimated that twenty-five hundred regular troops and over one thousand irregular ones had been raised. While he had needed to pass a state militia law that allowed for the impressment of wagons and horses, which made it difficult for the refugees to flee even farther east, he explained that so much abuse had resulted from it that he had rescinded the decree. Then, as he moved on to the Indians, he offered the most vitriolic condemnation of Native people ever, one that aroused a state to a level of retribution seldom if ever seen in America.

"Infants hewn into bloody chips of flesh," the governor began, "or nailed alive to door posts to linger out their little life in mortal agony." Some were even "torn from the womb of the murdered mother, and in cruel mockery cast in fragments on her pulseless and bleeding breasts." And then, as if he knew, rape of women had become commonplace. "Young girls, even children, of tender years, outraged by their brutal ravishers till death ended their shame and suffering; women held in captivity to undergo the horrors of a living death." The Dakota people, the governor concluded, "must be exterminated."[100] While newspapers had spouted such rhetoric in the past, when it came directly from the governor, it became an official, policy-driven goal. It remained to be seen whether it would become a reality.

The battle near Lone Tree Lake spelled the end of the Minnesota-Dakota War. Dr. Asa Daniels, ever sympathetic to the Indian, lamented after the battle that while the Dakota had "fought bravely," no more or less brave than "a more civilized people," such would hardly save them from a terrible revenge. And while Sibley had gained the most from the affair, being promptly promoted to general, he, ironically, had hardly given an order during the final battle and had even ordered the Third Regiment to retreat at one point.[101] But it would now fall on Sibley's shoulders to punish the Dakota, all of them, and despite his promise to treat them fairly, he had no intention of doing so. The war might have ended, but the time for retribution had just begun.

EIGHT

CAPTIVES AND THE "FATE WORSE THAN DEATH"

Confusion reigned at the Mdewakanton camp after the defeat of the *akacita* soldiers at Lone Tree Lake. The warriors and their families knew that General Sibley was coming and, like Little Crow, most expected that he would severely punish them. A few *akacita* soldiers still wanted to attack the "friendly" Indians who had fortified themselves at Camp Release. These traitors to the cause, as they viewed them, included the now growing number of white captives and their protectors, a few Sissetons and Wahpetons, various Anglo- and Franco-Dakota people, and the Christian Indians. Little Crow advised against this and instructed the few soldiers who still listened to him to give up their captives, which were very few in number by this time.[1]

A few *akacita* soldiers, most guilty of raiding white settlements, refused to surrender captives. While the number remained small—Sibley thought only a dozen—the most prized among them were young girls aged twelve to eighteen. Antoine Campbell heard of two captives, a Swedish girl of fourteen and her younger brother of eight, and he convinced several friends to confront the captors. When asked to give them up, the warrior holding them refused: "No, this is my squaw, I want her for my squaw," one of them angrily retorted. Campbell then put out his hand, and the girl grabbed it. A struggle ensued, and the Indian captor put his gun against Campbell's chest. At this point, another Indian came forward and threatened the one holding the girl captive—Campbell was, he exclaimed, "married to my cousin . . . you hurt him and you will lie there too." The man protested but ultimately surrendered the girl.[2]

Nancy McClure Huggan then told Joseph LaFramboise Jr. of another girl "of 16 or 17" being held by some "twenty or thirty" *akacita* soldiers who were preparing to leave for the plains. LaFramboise and a well-armed party confronted them, declaring that "they were going to have the girl or have a fight." It looked like civil war. The Dakota man who had claimed her as a wife shouted back that "he would shoot her," rather than give her up. LaFramboise's group then leveled their guns, and after a major shouting match, the Indians released her.[3] Huggan, perhaps ten years older and safe in the friendly camp by this time, took the young girl in and spoke with her. She was "nearly heart-broken and quite in despair" over her ordeal.[4]

Campbell and LaFramboise likely did not save these young women from "the fate worse than death." They had been "wives" of Dakota men for nearly five weeks. But were these simply aberrations, incidents in which young girls had been adopted into various families as wives, or did the events somehow represent a more nefarious explanation, such as forced marriage and rape? As the story of the captives unfolded, the latter explanation becomes increasingly the obvious one.

While Sibley counted 94 "pure white women and children" when he first received the captive group at Camp Release, the final number grew to 107, as other captives were rescued in the days that followed, such as the three teenagers described above.[5] Of the entire group, roughly thirty-five, or even forty, were either young girls of tender age—twelve to nineteen—or relatively young and middle-aged married women, most being from eighteen to forty years old. They were the sort of hearty, adventurous women the frontier attracted. The fear that many of these women and girls had been badly treated first surfaced when Simon Anawaŋmani, Lorenzo Lawrence, and the women and children they had helped escape, including Mrs. DeCamp, reached Fort Ridgely around September 11. Both Sibley and the missionary Riggs interviewed them, with the hope of finding out something related to the condition and number of captives.[6]

Mrs. DeCamp confirmed that while she had not been molested—she was in her sixth or seventh month of pregnancy—many other women were not so fortunate. After meeting with her at the fort in early September, Sibley wrote his wife: "The brutes in human shape have fearfully abused their white captives, especially the young women and girls of tender age." Riggs probed DeCamp even further, learning much about the fate of other specific captives such as Mrs. Earle and Mrs. White. "Mrs. Earle has one grown daughter and one small one. They are used hardly," Riggs concluded. The same was true with Mrs. White, whom also had a teenage daughter. DeCamp noted that yet another captive mentioned by Riggs, young Mattie Williams, "has a hard lot," signaled language of sexual abuse.[7] A better sense of the situation regarding the captives came from Anawaŋgmani himself, who was interviewed by a newspaper reporter on September 20 at Fort Ridgely. "Most of the white women are taken by the Indians as wives," Anawaŋgmani told him. They were "treated in every way like their squaws." The confrontations that both Campbell and LaFramboise had experienced seemed increasingly to confirm this: white women, especially girls, were being forced into what Dakota Indian warriors perceived as marriage.

Many of Sibley's officers and men strongly suspected that massive rape had occurred—it is often a product of war. Yet most studies of the Dakota War have given little attention to this issue. Isaac Heard, one of the first participants to write a full account of the conflict, simply noted that the captives "wept for joy" at their escape.[8] William Watts Folwell, in his comprehensive state study, written in the 1920s, noted that when released, some of the women "had been so wrought upon by the scenes through which they had passed that they seemed dazed and stolid."[9] Being "stolid" hardly constituted rape. More recent works, most of which focus on the battles rather than events in Indian camps, where rape would have occurred, fail to mention the issue or suggest only that rape became a vastly exaggerated talking point in newspapers.[10] While a few recent scholars have analyzed the captivity narratives left by women, they too found little evidence of rape, mostly pointing to statements that might include a reasonable deduction that a few women had suffered some form of sexual abuse.[11]

Rape is a common element of ethnic conflict historically. It comes as a result of the breakdown of the state and its legal institutions—even American Indians have them—and the general physical differences between men and women. Rape is used to forcefully convince groups belonging to the "other" to flee and abandon land or to humiliate them and emasculate their menfolk.[12] Some of the most obvious and brutal violence occurs when there is gender inequality, situations where women are clearly vulnerable and expected to be subservient to men. Men might even "justify" acts of sexual abuse as being a "reward" for success in war.[13]

The Dakota conflict was hardly different from other such wars fought in Africa, Asia, or even Europe over the past few centuries. Sexual abuse and rape become extremely prevalent when the society is patriarchal, such as with the Dakota people.[14] In Africa, in regions with patriarchal tribes, rape has often led to competition over women, especially virgins, whose conquest is frequently considered a good omen in battle. Such conquests can also be viewed by the male participants as an act that solidifies "marriage," despite the level of violence inherent in them. At times, nationalistic concerns convince men that raping the "other" will deprive the "other" of its future offspring. Finally, in its most violent form, rape can become "gang rape," which some scholars suggest can be a measure to promote "socialization" among troops, or warriors, encouraging camaraderie during times of peril.[15]

Scholars who have studied American Indian captivity narratives, in particular those written by white women taken during colonial times, generally conclude that American Indians seldom engaged in rape, even during times of war. In most narratives, women deny sexual abuse once repatriated. In some American Indian societies, taboos existed to prevent rape, especially while on the war path, because it could emaciate the powers bestowed upon young men by medicine men. Henry Schoolcraft, who spent decades among the Indians of the Great Lakes prior to the Civil War, noted the seriousness of the taboo: "The cause of their [Indians on the war path] being chaste on these excursions, they say, is that they may bring vengeance down upon their own heads; that is, displease the spirits."[16] Most Native societies in the East were matrilineal, however, and women had powerful positions in the social and political structure of these tribes. Nevertheless, given this literature as well as statements like Schoolcraft's, it hardly seems peculiar that this argument has been made in recent years in relation to the white captives taken all across the continent; incidents of rape were rare, if not in fact nonexistent.[17]

Such arguments may be valid for colonial history, but some new research suggests that young girls, especially young Indian women, were often traded for sex, which led to what one scholar has called the creation of a "racial hierarchy."[18] When it comes to the regions west of the Mississippi River, Susan Brownmiller's considerably older assessment offers a sweeping survey of what evidence she found regarding rape or, as in the case of the two young girls above, being taken "as a wife" by Plains Indians. Brownmiller argues that while repatriated women often denied rape, they did so from fear that it would preclude their chances for marriage in the future.[19] That is not to suppose that rape did not occur. Captivity narratives coming from the plains region more frequently than not emphasis violence toward white women by Natives.[20] This was certainly true in the case of the three women taken by Ute Indians after the Meeker massacre in Colorado in 1880. It became a common saying on the plains for white men to "save the last bullet" for a woman who was in danger of capture given the fact that she would obviously prefer death to captivity.[21]

For their part, Minnesotans had a clear understanding of the definition for rape in 1862. It was considered the "theft of a woman's virginity," especially when it came to girls just emerging from puberty. For a married woman, the issue was somewhat different as it constituted a violation of the victim's "honor," given the lack of virginal status. Generally, death was preferable to the disgrace of rape. At the beginning of the nineteenth century, the onus of a rape charge in the emerging parlance of American law was often placed upon the woman. So-called "libertines," or Anglo-American elites, often thought they had a presumed privilege of sexual access to women, particularly those of a lesser class, such as lower-class women or slaves. This changed somewhat as the century progressed, with women acquiring some degree of protection under the doctrine of "consent." Yet such a claim could only be judged valid when clear evidence existed that the woman's character was good—which, of course, given the racism involved, excluded slave women—and that she had resisted.[22]

When it came to white men and Native American women in the mid-nineteenth century, a standard emerged that clearly reverted to libertinism, with white males being convinced that they possessed some degree of "entitlement" to use Native women.[23] On the two Minnesota Dakota reservations prior to the conflict, such views were held by most white males, including carpenters, blacksmiths, Indian agents, military officers, Indian traders, and even an occasional superintendent of Indian affairs. While the numbers often changed, there were easily a hundred such white men on the Lower Sioux reservation in the late 1850s, the number falling somewhat to sixty-five or so by 1862. There were also many visitors who came and went. These men thought nothing of purchasing the favor of a Dakota woman with food or merchandise. Missionary Stephen Riggs found the situation quite appalling: "The men connected with the trade, and I must say also the greater part of the government employees, have squaws."[24] While it is impossible to determine the actual numbers involved, if Riggs is not exaggerating, it could have easily reached well over a hundred Dakota women, with some men keeping Native females for weeks, months, or even years, and others having brief liaisons with several over periods of days.

Temporary relationships may have been more frequent than longer lasting ones. Thomas "Mark" Gere, then just a nineteen-year-old soldier, took advantage of such a situation when at the Upper Agency in July 1862. During a dance observed by the troops, in which large numbers of Indians participated, "One young squaw wore around her the Stars and Stripes & wanted to marry a white man," Lieutenant Timothy Sheehan reported. "Mark Gere took her to a tepee, stay'd all day." Other soldiers presumably did the same, because Sheehan readily reported that the "Ind's [were] prowling about camp begging of the soldiers for something to eat." This occurred in the days just before the "bread riot" in which the warehouse was broken into. James Gorman, the son of the superintendent of Indian affairs who had in 1854 purchased the favors of a Dakota women while handing out annuities, visited the Upper Agency a few days later. He reported that many Indians were virtually "starving to death." The situation was ripe for the sexual abuse of Native women.[25]

The most visible "libertine" at the Lower Agency was Andrew Myrick, who fathered two girls and one boy by Dakota women—as far as can be know.[26] Big Eagle later wrote that such abuse was duly noted by all Dakota men: "white men abused the Indian women in a certain way and disgraced them." Traders such as Myrick made no attempt to hide abuse; it was socially permissible in the white society of the frontier. Indeed, they occasionally flaunted their abuse, because it was an example of their manhood, allowing their employees to sexually abuse Indian women at will. Myrick's rejection of one of his wives motivated her brother to kill the trader when the attack occurred on his trade house on August 18. At least one of Myrick's former wives, and maybe more, then fled to Canada. When faced with starvation in 1864, Catholic priests at Fort Garry purchased two of the children, and one of the wives surrendered in Pembina. The Dakota woman who was with Myrick at the attack on his trade house was later deported to Crow Creek, carrying her baby, which survived.[27]

The impact that these relationships had on Dakota society is difficult to determine. They certainly angered Dakota men. With a population of roughly 2,500 Indians in the vicinity of the Lower Agency, some 500 were easily younger or young adult women. Of them, 150 were likely of marriageable age, or roughly between thirteen and twenty. But if seventy to one hundred became entangled with white men, the number of eligible wives dropped significantly. Worse, many senior Dakota men had more than one wife; Little Crow having four, all sisters. This dropped the number of eligible Dakota women even lower. It is extremely likely that one-third of the young Dakota men at the Lower Agency—a hundred or so—could not find a suitable woman to marry. Such a circumstance became a motivation for at least some young men to raid white settlements and physically procure a wife; it may even explain why intertribal feuding with the Anishinaabe escalated after 1855. Native Indian women might be taken and brought back as wives.[28]

Young Dakota men brooded over this situation. As early as 1857, when Riggs took his Christian Indians to Mankato to apply for citizenship, the secretary of the Hazelwood Republic, Henock Maȟpiyakinape, gave an interview to a newspaper editor, with Riggs translating. Henock was particularly upset by the fact that Americans were critical of Dakota morality, given the large number of white men who took Indian women. Henock countered: "There are some [white] men who come up and live among the Dakotas who desire to have many women, some take two and some three." Where was the morality in that, he wondered?[29]

Young Mdewakanton Dakota men simply found it difficult to acquire a wife through a traditional arranged marriage and many went without. The power of gifts, offered by traders, and food, given out by government employees, soldiers, or even occasional white visitors, led often to what Big Eagle called "disgraced" women. Or as one young Dakota man screamed to Andrew Myrick just before the conflict began: "If we could, like our women, give ourselves up to you, we could get all the credit we ask for; since we are men, we cannot."[30] There is no doubt that the corruption on the reservation, the trade system, and the moral degradation suffered by Dakota women emasculated Mdewakanton Dakota men at a time of considerable hardship and near starvation.

This had not been the case in the past. Fifty years earlier, Dakota villagers had welcomed traders into their towns, and many, indeed almost all, married Dakota women. Whites with Anglo and French names like Renville, Provencalle, Faribault, Campbell, Robertson, Mooers, and Prescott married Dakota women and, for the most part, stayed with them throughout their lives (the one exception being Joseph R. Brown, who was a libertine).[31] These men nurtured respectable families, following the social guidelines necessary when entering the province of Dakota matrimony. The proper format included having a mentor—such as a friend or uncle or, on some occasions, the chief of the village—approach the brothers and parents of a young woman to see if she was inclined to accept the young suitor. Goods such as a horse, a gun, metal implements, and even clothing were assembled and left at the entrance to the parents' tepee. If the parents brought them inside, the marriage had received sanctification.[32]

A proper marriage also included protection of a young girl's virginity. Samuel Pond, who wrote a lengthy social history of the Dakota people as they were in 1834, noted that the Mdewakantons around Fort Snelling at that time still practiced the ceremony of the "Virgin Feast." Each spring, as Pond noted, "the Dakota have a custom of making a feast . . . to which all [young virgins] were invited who had not been guilty of a breach of the laws of chastity." They sat in a circle, and anyone who might challenge the virginity of a particular young woman could do so. In the 1830s, Pond only observed two occasions when challenges occurred, and girls had to depart in disgrace. Pond believed that very few fell into this category. Chastity and modesty were important in Dakota society, at least in the early years of contact with whites.[33]

Just when the Virgin Feast ceremony fell into disuse among the Mdewakanton people who had moved to the Lower Agency is difficult to determine, but it occurred irregularly, if at all, after 1853. One clear indication of the fleeting nature of the ceremony is found in the papers of Dr. Asa Daniels, the physician at the Upper Agency. He had heard of the ceremony, but he did not see it until 1857, when the Plains Sissetons at Big Stone Lake announced that they were having a "Virgin Day Feast." While it took at least two days of travel to reach the lake, Daniels felt compelled to observe the spectacle. Moving over a bluff, he first saw a pole, ten feet high with flowers at the top. Daniels noted, "Coming near, I looked upon the most impressive ceremonies that I ever witnessed." He counted "137 maids whose virginity was not questioned as it had a right to be by anyone in the audience." The young girls were dressed in "the most attractive costumes their hands were capable of producing . . . as white as snow having been made so by the use of white earth." Then Daniels, after lauding the Dakota mothers who had protected these girls, added: the Sissetons, who remained mostly on the Plains away from the reservations, were not affected by "that vice that destroys the morals of a people [such as] . . . those at Lower Sioux Agency."[34]

Why did Daniels have to travel so far to see the Virgin Feast Ceremony, and what had happened to it at the Lower Sioux Agency? The number of young women eligible for the ceremony on the Lower Sioux Reservation had diminished to a point where Native mothers apparently no longer organized it. Many had been "disgraced," as a young women's willingness to give up her virginity for food increasingly took precedence over the opportunity to obtain a good marriage, and such a possibility deteriorated appreciably after having children with a white man. Some disgraced women might find a man who would take them in afterwards, much like Dakota widows who cohabited with men without going through the negotiation involving "bride price." While Daniels never mentioned such a ceremony occurring at the Yellow Medicine, or Upper, Agency either, this is likely explained by the lack of villages nearby—most of the Sissetons and Wahpetons connected to the Upper Agency lived well above it near Lac qui Parle, at Big Stone Lake and Lake Traverse, or well west of the Minnesota River.[35]

Given the inequality, one of the principal motivations for raiding the new white settlements in August 1862 became acquiring new wives, especially young girls of marriageable age. At times, when war parties appeared, after killing the men, settler women were actually given a choice: would they come along and join the Dakota camp to become a wife or would they prefer death? Justina Kreiger faced just such a dilemma. Once her husband, as well as many others around her, lay dying, "The Indians then asked the women if they would go along with them, promising to save all that would go and threatening all who refused with instant death." It was obviously a choice! Trying to comfort her dying husband, Kreiger refused: "I told them I chose to die with my husband and my children." A Dakota warrior then shot her in the back, leaving her for dead.[36]

An almost identical situation emerged just to the south of where the Kreiger family was assaulted on Beaver Creek. Here, the Carrothers, Earle, and White families were attacked, and the men mostly ran. As the women, carrying children, tried to keep up, they were soon overtaken. "When the Indians came up to us," Helen Carrothers noted, "they shook hands with each of the women and said we were going now to live with them."[37] While Mrs. Earle was an older woman, she had two teenaged daughters. Mrs. White also had a teenaged daughter, Julia. When they arrived at Little Crow's village and entered the chief's house, Carrothers reported that the chief's brother was there. While he was not identified, it was likely White Spider (Uŋktomiska in Dakota). He sat down next to a "German girl," who Carrothers did not identify, and, "putting his arms around her in a loving manner," said, "this is my squaw."[38]

When Carrothers gave the narrative account of the event in front of the Sioux Commission the following year, she realized that the reputation of any young girl was permanently damaged by the admission that she had been taken as a wife by an Indian. Given the fact that there were no other captives there at the time, it seems logical that the "German girl" was the daughter of either Mrs. Earle or Mrs. White.[39] Yet Carrothers seemed less concerned about her own reputation during her testimony. After the incident with the German girl, a fight over her involving four young warriors ensued. "The reason alleged was," she told the Sioux commission, "that four Indians wanted me for a squaw, and as they could not agree, Little Crow, unable, as umpire, to decide the quarrel, had intended to settle the difficulty." Just who got her is never recorded, but there can be little doubt that Carrothers too joined the ranks of new wives.[40]

The taking of captive women frequently came after their men had been killed. Sometimes it even involved taking mixed-blood women, as was the case with Marian Hunter, the daughter of Andrew Robertson. She and her husband fled from the Lower Agency on August 18. But her husband, who had frozen his feet some time before, hobbled along the road south to Fort Ridgely as best as he could, trying to reach safety. The couple were met by Walks Clothed As An Owl (Hinhanshoonkayagmani in Dakota). The Dakota warrior promptly shot Miriam's husband and, "claiming his wife as a captive," then threatened to cut his head off if Marian refused to cooperate. Despite his obvious guilt, Walks Clothed As An Owl surrendered at Camp Release and was later executed.[41] While Hunter's brother, Thomas Robertson, ultimately rescued his sister, as she was among the group turned over at Camp Release, Robertson says nothing about her capture and time as a "wife" with Walks Clothed As An Owl.[42]

Anglo- and Franco-Dakota men generally cooperated with *akacita* soldiers to protect their families. Nancy McClure Faribault Huggan, a beautiful young woman, married David Faribault in a well-documented ceremony at the Traverse de Sioux treaty grounds in 1851. Both were mixed-bloods, and David came from a well-known trade family. At the time, an artist did a tasteful portrait of Nancy, who went on to live with David at the Lower Agency. As the killing started, they fled, like everyone else, toward the ferry. When they arrived, they saw a "young white girl of about sixteen or seventeen years of age," standing in a boat trying to navigate it across the river. Just then, several young *akacita* warriors arrived and told her to bring it ashore. She initially refused, and as Nancy tells the story, "my husband told her they would kill her if she did not do as they ordered." She obeyed, came ashore, and "when it [the boat] touched the bank a young Indian made this girl get on a horse behind him and he rode away."[43]

Perhaps the most illustrative example of the degree to which young Mdewakanton men saw the conflict as an opportunity to acquire wives came with the capture of the Brown family. Samuel Brown, just seventeen at the time, left a vivid account of their attempted flight to Fort Ridgely and their meeting with Little Six (Šakpedaŋ in Dakota), Cut Nose (Mahpiyaokenźin in Dakota), and *akacita* men from the soldiers' lodge. The group included Susan Brown and her ten children as well as members of "six or eight" neighboring families; two of the young girls in the group, Amanda and Jennie Ingalls, aged fourteen and twelve, respectively, likely had been working at the Brown house. In three wagons, the Browns and their neighbors hoped to reach the fort before dark. But once the wagons were stopped by a war party, Susan Brown did everything in her power to save the group from death, warning the warriors that they would answer to her powerful Sisseton relatives should anyone be killed. This saved the lives of everyone in the group.[44]

Once surrounded, the Anglo men in the party were quickly threatened. Cut Nose finally agreed to let the white men in the party go if they departed quickly. Leopold Wohler, who had just married his young wife of nineteen or twenty, nearly refused, but after kissing her goodbye, he ran with the others, including Charles Holmes and two or three other men whom Brown did not even know. This left Charles Blair, who had married one of Samuel Brown's sisters, and a hired man who the Indians agreed would help drive the three wagons as the only white men in the party. While Blair was safe for the moment—Little Crow later assisted in his escape to Fort Ridgely—the warriors in the group promptly began looking over the women. As Samuel Brown noted, "The white women—Mrs. Wohler and the two Misses Ingalls—were then parceled out among the Indians and ordered to follow them." Later evidence in Brown's account shows that there were at least two other women besides these three who were taken.[45]

While Cut Nose had been busy threatening the men who were fleeing, he returned to the wagon to claim one of the young women who had been overlooked. Brown did not even know her name. "One beautiful young girl of about 17 years of age refused to alight from the wagon," Brown recounted. "Cut Nose had told her he wanted her for his wife, and to get out of the wagon and follow him. She screamed and resisted, when he drew his knife and grabbed her by the hair and threatened to scalp her." Seeing she had no choice, she got down and followed Cut Nose while young Brown, his family, Blair, and the hired man sat quietly. "Presently," Brown continued, "the Indians came back with the women and ordered them all to get into one of our wagons." The party then continued on their journey to Little Crow's village.[46]

What happened while young Mrs. Wohler, the Ingalls girls, and the young women described by Brown were gone is open to conjecture, but Brown's description of the events strongly suggest rape. Indeed, there can be no other explanation for the halting of the wagons and the removal of the young women and their eventual return.[47] The evidence suggests that other women were treated this way after capture, the incident perhaps being a form of claiming possession. Brown's account fails to explain it, but sometime thereafter, perhaps even that very night, the women and girls taken by Cut Nose and his party were separated from the Brown party and made into wives. Proceeding farther south, the Browns ultimately reached a point just a half mile from Little Crow's camp, where they encountered other captives. One small group was being herded by a highly painted warrior: a "poor white women with six children, the oldest not more than ten." They stopped to see if she would accept a ride. But the Indian in charge quickly threatened them and ordered them to move on. "He said the woman was his and [he] would do as he pleased with her." Brown thought the man "so fierce and ugly" that the entire party feared he would soon attack them.[48]

While Dakota men culturally believed that they legitimately had a right to the sexual favors of captured women, to make them wives—who would also do familial work around the tepee—those very same captive women often later tried to disguise facts regarding sexual service, if they could do so. Mary Schwandt, just fourteen when captured, along with Mattie Williams and Mary Anderson, who were four to six years older, were all taken to Wakute's house after they had been seized from the wagon driven by Francois Patoille. There they met Mrs. DeCamp, who was in the same house with her children. That evening, after Wakute had left to attend a council, a large group of young Dakota men, including two of Wakute's sons and very likely Wabasha's son-in-law, Rattling Runner, forced their way into the house. Mrs. DeCamp, whose husband was well-liked by the Indians, giving her some influence, realized that they meant trouble, especially as most of them were intoxicated. "How they scoffed and jeered as they swung their rifles and tomahawks around their [the womens'] heads," she later wrote, "aiming to strike as near as they could without hitting."[49]

The group quickly cast their eyes upon the three young women, leaving Mrs. DeCamp alone. "I screamed," Mary Schwandt later testified in a sworn deposition in front of the Sioux Commission, "and one of the fiends struck me on my mouth with his hand." They then took her "to an unoccupied tepee . . . and perpetrated the most horrible and nameless outrages upon my person. These outrages were repeated, at different times during my captivity." One unsubstantiated report coming from a mixed-blood in Little Crow's village outlining the violence at Wakute's house later stated that "one of the girls of fourteen" was raped "by seventeen of the wretches." Because many of the Indians were drunk, this seems an exaggeration. And the source for the information comes secondhand. Regardless, Schwandt was the only girl of that age at the house, and her story was undoubtedly revealed soon after her rescue.[50]

The other two young women stayed in the house with Schwandt and Mrs. DeCamp for three days, as the warriors went off to fight at Fort Ridgely and New Ulm. They too were abused in a similar fashion at the same time that Schwandt was attacked. Laying Up Buffalo (Tazoo in Dakota), who captured Williams, came and got her on the fourth day, after the battles had come to an end. While Mary Anderson suffered terribly from her wound, her captor came to retrieve her as well. When Mrs. DeCamp protested, Anderson's captor simply said, "She is better than two dead squaws yet." What he meant by this is open to conjecture; he likely believed that having a wounded white woman as a wife in his tent was more prestigious than having two Dakota women. Mattie Williams and DeCamp lifted Anderson into a wagon, and her captor took her away. The taking of captive women then had become honorable for young warriors. Mary Anderson was incapable of resisting, and suffering terribly from her wound, she died a day or two later.[51]

Laying Up Buffalo, who had been with the party that attacked Milford, collected Mattie Williams shortly after Mary Anderson had departed. He took her to a tepee close to that of Cecelia Campbell Stay, the daughter of Antoine Campbell, who left several vivid narratives. Williams was constantly raped. She frequently pleaded with the Campbell family for help, explaining that she had offered her captor money "to kill her rather than to live with him the life she was leading, but he wouldn't do it."[52] As the pleading continued, Stay's mother finally said, "Mattie, please don't tell me that, you hurt my feelings so; we can't help you." Mrs. Campbell feared openly for her family's safety, as Anglo-Dakota people, such as her husband, were constantly being threatened in the camps. The Campbells did have close kinship ties with Little Crow—the chief and Antoine Campbell called each other "cousins"— but in the camp controlled by the soldiers' lodge, they had little chance of preventing a warrior from taking a white captive as his wife.[53]

As the pleadings went on day after day, Iron Elk, a close relative of the Campbells, declared that if Williams showed up again, he would protect her. When her captor went away with a war party, Williams escaped, remaining with the Campbell family. She was ultimately turned over to Sibley at Camp Release, giving her story to Reverend Riggs. Given her constant complaints that many people were well aware of, she likely had little to lose by testifying at the trials that commenced some days later. When her captor, apparently oblivious to the possible implications of the charge of rape, admitted that he had "ravished her" (these words might have been invented by the court), she was then called upon to verify the charge. Williams openly identified Laying Up Buffalo and said, "The prisoner committed the crime charged against him upon me. He repeated it."[54]

Given the attempts of women to hide such abuse, Mattie Williams's testimony shows considerable pluck. One other captive, Margaret Cardinal, captured at Birch Coulee, also testified against her captor, One Who Forbids His House (Tihdonića in Dakota). One Who Forbids His House, like Laying Up Buffalo, generally believed that he had done nothing wrong and would not face punishment for taking a wife. Accordingly, at his trial, he seemingly declared his innocence, stating only when it came to Cardinal, "I slept with this woman once. I did bad towards her once . . . Another Indian may have slept with her [as well]." When One Who Forbids His House came to understand that forcing sex upon Cardinal was a criminal act under American law is not clear, but he obviously thought it "bad" by the time of the trial. Once again, given the exposure, Margaret Cardinal had little to gain by denying the charge. While perhaps not pleased at being placed in front of the court, she kept her composure and stoically said, "The prisoner has slept with me. He has raped me against my will."[55]

A few observers believed that the universal charge of rape, levied by most newspapers in Minnesota, was overblown. Thomas Robertson, who carried letters back and forth between Sibley and Little Crow, when interviewed at Fort Ridgely on September 10, claimed that most of the captives fared as well as other females in camp. "The Indians use them as hewers of wood and drawers of water," he told Sibley during his interview, "making them do all the small jobs around the camp." Robertson claimed to have seen no instances of cruelty "and scarcely any of [sexual] violation, and those by rowdies, unsanctioned, and unapproved by the chiefs."[56] While something of a disclaimer, the implications were that when Indians had too much whiskey, they then looked for white women.

Over the years, Robertson wavered regarding the issue of rape, perhaps after learning more about the abuse of his sister, Marion. In his *Reminiscences*, he wrote, "Many of the women were outraged, but not in any other way abused." The statement suggests that being taken as wives and "outraged" was, in his view, quite different from being physically beaten or "abused." Later, in 1923, he concluded in an interview with Marion P. Satterlee by saying the following: "I think the violation of women prisoners was done to some extent but not as much as has been represented by some." Satterlee later noted that he had interviewed several women captives with mixed results. Regarding one woman, Satterlee simply said: "Of course I could not ask her flat out" what had actually happened. Obviously though, he concluded that most women had been sexually abused.[57] The curtain that came with the Victorian age regarding sex made it difficult for male researchers to sort out fact from fiction; indeed, most ignored the subject, rather than get mired in it.

The most paradoxical ongoing discussion of the events of fall 1862 came from the many different narratives of Mary Schwandt. These include her initial testimony in 1863 in front of the Sioux Commission, in which she stated nearly as clearly as possible that she had been sexually abused; her later published narrative in the Minnesota Historical Society Collections; and at least three other addresses and narratives thereafter, some given in the early twentieth century. In later years, she increasingly emphasized her rescue, rather than the terrible events of her first night in Wakute's house—or subsequent nights when abuse occurred, as she herself stated. She never testified against the young men who assaulted her, yet at least one of them was executed, suggesting that knowledge of her treatment became commonplace. Schwandt did consistently report, however, that when she was about to be dragged off by her captor, Blows on Iron (Mazzaboomdu in Dakota), he announced that because he did not have a tent—he was obviously a young unmarried man—he "had no use for her." Schwandt concluded that he preferred to shoot her "for sport."[58]

At this point, a young Dakota woman named Tinkling (Snana in Dakota) stepped forward and asked her uncle if she might purchase Mary, offering a young colt. Tinkling and her husband, Good Thunder (Wakinyanwaste in Dakota), had been married in Hinman's Episcopal church, and she had recently lost a young daughter. The fourteen-year-old girl served as a replacement. Given Blows on Iron's greater interest in fighting, the arrangement was made quickly. While Mary never suffered any abuse thereafter, in her second typed narrative, completed some years after her release, she did note that one night, while asleep, three or four young Dakota men tried to "drag her out" of the tent. The noise awoke Tinkling and her husband, who then drove the men off. The two women, Mary and Tinkling, were united later in life and remained close friends.[59]

Falling into the hands of Indians who were either Christian, such as Tinkling, or even somewhat opposed to the war provided protection for a number of other captives. Sarah Wakefield, the wife of the doctor at the Yellow Medicine River Agency, contended that she had never been abused, nor had she seen any white woman who had been. One German woman with whom she spoke, apparently while at Rice Creek, declared that "she had not been abused by the Indians. She said they were very kind." Wakefield's husband had been on hand when Anishinaabe warriors had attacked Shakopee's camp in 1858, and he had treated many of the wounded men. The doctor later fled with the missionaries to Hutchinson and saved his own life. Given his compassion, the Indians generally thought highly of his wife. She was taken directly to the Rice Creek camp, where most of the Indian men were involved in fighting American troops. These Indians included those whom her husband had treated. The women in the camp promptly "spread down carpets for me to sit on, gave me a pillow and wished me to lie down and rest." While a captive, she was quickly taken under the care of Chaska, who had been near the wagon when George Gleason was killed. Chaska's family protected her throughout the five-week ordeal that followed.[60]

Wakefield's narrative has the feel of honesty. Her savior, Chaska, however, had a problematic brother-in-law, one Hapa–which may have been a nickname, because it translates to "bad." Hapa had shot George Gleason. Trouble with Hapa continued over the next five weeks, as he constantly tried to take Sarah "as a wife." One night, while drunk, Hapa invaded Chaska's tent and asked outright for the "white woman." Once he found Wakefield, he came toward her with a drawn knife, proclaiming "you must be my wife or die." A debate then ensued over who should have Wakefield. Chaska argued that Hapa already had a wife, Chaska's sister. But because Chaska had no wife, he should be the one. After more debate, Hapa demanded that they consummate the so-called marriage. "You must let me lie down beside you or he will kill you," Chaska told Sarah. Once that happened, Hapa went to sleep.[61]

Thereafter, everyone in camp, including several white captive women, assumed that Chaska and Sarah Wakefield were man and wife. Wakefield even encouraged the idea, acting as if she enjoyed her new relationship. While the various groups moved north to Yellow Medicine Agency, more trouble erupted over Wakefield's status. One day, Paul Mazakutemani came and offered ponies to Wakefield and her children so they could ride, rather than walk. Wakefield, somewhat suspicious, consulted with Chaska, who said it was fine with him, but that Mazakutemani, as Sarah put it, "wanted me as a wife, and has been for several days trying to get a white woman." The offer was tempting because Chaska's family remained with the main Mdewakanton village and its soldiers' lodge, while Mazakutemani and the Christian Indians camped separately. Even Mary Renville, the Anglo wife of John B. Renville, encouraged Wakefield to take up the offer, suggesting that the offer had more to do with saving Wakefield from abuse than anything else. Wakefield still declined, telling Mazakutemani she was ashamed of him for asking, as he had a wife and was supposedly a Christian.[62]

Other women had stories similar to Wakefield's. Mrs. N. D. White and Mrs. J. W. Earle were often in the same house as DeCamp and later lived near Little Crow's tent. White left a narrative, whereas Earle did not. Both had children, teenaged girls. White's narrative praises the old Dakota couple who initially adopted her, noting that they called her "big papoose [baby]." As the Mdewakantons moved north, first to Rice Creek and then beyond Yellow Medicine Agency, both women increasingly saw Little Crow as a protector. Little Crow later gave both women to Antoine Campbell just before he departed for the plains. Campbell wrote of Mrs. Earle that "both herself and family were not subjected to the outrages endured by the others. Mrs. White and her family were equally fortunate." Campbell, who acted at times as Little Crow's "secretary,"—as he called it—does seem overly apologetic regarding the actions of the chief throughout the entire five-week period, but he certainly knew what had happened to Mattie Williams and did nothing about it.[63]

The early period proved a far different experience from the later treatment of these women. After it seemed that the *akacita* warriors would not prevail, captives were generally treated better. But on the day Mrs. White and Mrs. Earle were taken captive, their daughters, both aged fourteen, went along with them into captivity. The young girls were taken from them, and they were not recovered for well over a week, if not longer. White would later conclude the narrative of her ordeal with the following jubilant statement: "And Oh, how pleased we were that so far we had been spared not only from death, but, worse than that, the Indians' lust." What she did not know is that during the trials, Thomas Robertson testified that "Miss White," her young daughter, had been for many days "in the tent" of Wind Comes Home (Tatayhdedon in Dakota). John Moore, another Anglo-Dakota, further sealed the fate of Wind Comes Home, testifying that "he had a horse and a girl whom he took prisoner. He was in the massacre at Beaver Creek." Thomas Robertson then testified that "he had Miss White in his tent." Wind Comes Home was later executed, despite the fact that he claimed to be a "coward" and never killed anyone. Once again, he seemed obvious to the fact that forcing a young girl to have sex was a crime.[64]

The narrative of Sophia Huggins, the wife of missionary Amos Huggins, provides yet another example of protection by Dakota people, yet she too feared being taken as a Dakota wife. She and her husband, Amos, worked as teachers in Red Iron's village, just below Lac qui Parle. On the afternoon of August 19, three men came into the camp, and one killed Amos. While the men then fled, Huggins and her two small children went through five weeks of torment. Fortunately, a nearby Franco-Dakota family as well as Red Iron took turns sheltering Huggins and her children. But while at the village, various men tried to "purchase" Mrs. Huggins, including one Good Day, who was apparently from Yellow Medicine. Good Day, supposedly a Christian, may have been trying to rescue her, or perhaps fearful of the *akacita* warriors, he might have been acting like Paul Mazakutemani, trying to protect her. Friendly Indians, including the trustworthy Christian Indian Robert Hopkins, finally arrived to take Huggins and her children to Camp Release, ending her ordeal.[65]

The difficulties that Wakefield had in dodging the affections of Chaska's brother as well as the fears expressed by Huggins and White do provide several insights into the treatment of captives. As the conflict widened, it became commonly accepted practice among young Dakota men that captured white women would become wives, one way or the other. Older Dakota men mostly had wives or failed to join war parties where they were captured. They seemed less likely to participate in the competition that evolved in Dakota camps over these women. The fact that Christian Indians tried to rescue women does not necessarily suggest that they wanted them as wives, despite the open efforts of Paul Mazakutemani and Good Day. As the arrival of Sibley's army seemed eminent, the Franco- and Anglo-Dakota men as well as the Christian Indians at Camp Release were concerned about the reaction of Sibley's soldiers to them. The more white captives they had in camp and protected, the more secure the group obviously felt.

In contrast, a few other women received virtually no protection, leaving narratives that can only be described as brutal, similar in nature to the attack on Mary Schwandt. The most descriptive cases of such treatment—testimony that seems at times difficult to describe—came from the female captives taken at Lake Shetek by the Sisseton–Wahpekute group connected with White Lodge. Some of the young Dakota men among them vividly remembered the treatment of their people at the hands of settlers near Spirit Lake in the 1850s, where family members were hacked to death by white settlers, and they saw the conflict that had erupted as an opportunity for revenge.

As news of the war reached the relatively isolated region called Lake Shetek—the lake was some fifty miles southwest of New Ulm—a small gathering of Indians under a Sisseton leader called Grizzly Bear was soon reinforced by several dozen more Indians who had determined to force the settlers to leave the region. After rendezvousing at a settler's house, the Anglo men of the community agreed to leave, and the party of thirty-four headed east. Indians followed, however, and soon attacked them, killing several of them. As the settlers fled into the slough nearby, only three men remained alive. While Grizzly Bear had been killed, an older leader called Pawn convinced the women and children to surrender. Mrs. Lavina East-lick, who left the most vivid and accurate account of the attack, described what happened next: "One Indian started taking Mrs. Cook [sometimes the German "Koch" is used] as his prisoner; another took one of Mrs. Ireland's daughters [Rosanna, a girl of eleven or twelve], while a third started off leading by the hand Mrs. Duley and myself, neither of whom made any resistance." After Eastlick bolted, returning to her dying husband, she was shot and left for dead, only to recover and leave a long narrative of the eventual rescue of some of the Lake Shetek people.[66]

The captured party soon connected with other members of White Lodge's band and headed west. Years later, Mrs. Duley provided revealing testimony to physician Herbert Workman as to how the women and girls were treated. While their surrender occurred at 4:00 P.M. in the afternoon, as rain descended upon the party, Pawn took Mrs. Duley and Mrs. Cook into his tepee. Pawn then told the Dakota women inside to take the clothes off of the two women. Then, according to Mrs. Duley, "Pawn attempted to rape Mrs. Cook and she managed to strike him on the scrotum with her knee and grabbed his genitals with one hand." Cook severely damaged Pawn, who was apparently in his fifties, injuring him to such an extent that when the party started to travel the next day, Pawn had to "ride on a *travois*."[67]

The next evening, other Dakota men took the women to separate te-pees and "tied their wrists and ankles together." Mrs. Duley noted that as "other squaws [were] holding her knees apart," they "accomplished their purpose." When the women tried to pull away from the young warriors who were assaulting them, the Dakota women "poked hot sticks under us." Because Duley passed out, she could not tell how many young men were involved in the gang rape. The Dakota women in the Sisseton camp seemingly participated, almost in a ritualistic fashion. As terrible as the event seems, it resembles a rite of passage for the young men, designed, so it seems, to reinforce warrior relationships. What makes this all the more likely is the fact that in the nights that followed, as Mrs. Duley noted, "we were not mistreated by other bucks [young men]" again. The gang rape was a one-time event, with Dakota women actively joining in it, much like they would have participated in a Medicine Dance.[68] The three women became wives of various Sisseton leaders and, as members of a family, were pro-tected from assault by the young warriors.

The ordeal of these three women continued into the fall. Cook, who had been held by White Lodge himself as his wife, eventually escaped with the help of several Dakota women in his camp and reached Camp Release in late September. It seems ironic that the Dakota women who likely par-ticipated in the ritualistic rape of these women would then help one to es-cape.[69] Wright became the wife of Cross River, and Duley was kept by the young son of Sleepy Eyes, who had thrown in his lot with White Lodge. Yet unlike Little Crow and the Mdewakantons who headed north to Canada, White Lodge's Sissetons preferred to stay on the Missouri River, and they never participated in the Battle of Wood Lake. While camped on the river, trader Charles E. Galpin discovered them on November 15, 1862.

The Indians fired at Galpin's boat, but an unidentified white woman raced to the shore and informed Galpin that captives were in the camp. Galpin convinced a group of Two Kettle Lakota men to go after the captives and ransom them. He gave them the goods necessary. Called the "Fool Soldiers" by their own people for taking on the task, they ultimately found White Lodge's camp near the mouth of Grand River. Here they offered a feast and began the bargaining.[70]

Sisseton men, including White Lodge, each claimed the two women who remained and six children. Accordingly, each captive had to be bargained for, offering food, clothing, or gunpowder, among other things. After being successful with the children and Mrs. Duley, all that remained was for White Lodge to surrender Mrs. Wright, which he refused to do. The "Fool Soldiers" took her by force and fled south toward Fort Randall, on the lower Missouri. It became a harrowing escape, as White Lodge pursued them for many miles. The weather then turned to snow and ice, and the women and children had only rags for coverings. The party finally reached Fort Randall and safety. Mrs. Duley went to bed for fifteen days, but she and the others survived.[71]

While the husbands of these two women came to get them, their lives thereafter were never the same. Along with Mrs. Cook, Duley and Wright pledged never to speak of their treatment by the Indians. "I never speak of my treatment while in captivity," Mrs. Cook, then in her eighties, later told Herbert Workman. "But the way Mrs. Duley and I were treated cannot be told, and from what Mrs. Wright told me afterwards, she fared no better." Once two of the women had passed on, Mrs. Duley then described the awful experience they had all suffered. Mrs. Wright, unfortunately, could not disguise her treatment. She became pregnant while in captivity. When she gave birth, and when her husband saw that the child was part Indian, he left her. Trying another marriage, a second husband ultimately deserted her as well.[72]

While the surviving narratives of the Dakota conflict offer a strong window into the world of Dakota captivity, some evidence of sexual abuse can simply be deduced even when the written accounts fail. There were a number of German women held as captives who left no narratives, one being Theresa Eisenreich. On the fateful day of August 18, her family home in Beaver Creek was attacked, and her husband, Balthasar, was promptly killed. According to oral history handed down in the family, Eisenreich, a rather large, strong lady, grabbed a tomahawk from a warrior and "defended herself and her three children." The warriors involved in the attack marveled at this courage, and they allowed her and her children to live.[73]

Yet seven to eight months after being released, Eisenreich gave birth to a child, the family's oral account stating it as, "a child born as a result of this captivity." Theresa remarried one Peter Dagen and had six more children; she was obviously a resilient woman. Her daughter by a Dakota man, however, died at a young age, perhaps at eighteen. A brief note on the back of her one surviving photograph explained: "It was said she went crazy." All that remains of this German-Dakota child is the picture, which distinctly shows her Indian heritage. The caption atop the picture reads as such: "Theresa's daughter while held captive by the Indians."[74] Theresa's story remains untold, as she left no narrative. Whether she was raped or found herself unable to prevent becoming a "wife"—perhaps as a result of the necessity of protecting her children—will never be known.

Despite the earnest attempt of Sarah Wakefield to convince the reading public in a narrative released soon after the war that there had been no abuse of white women captives, most of the evidence points in a different direction. Certainly, virtually all the young girls from twelve to twenty became wives, as did most of the middle-aged women. The exceptions included older and pregnant women, such as DeCamp, White, Earle, and Wakefield. Once arriving at Camp Release on September 26, Sibley had suspected that, at the very least, the "young girls" had been mistreated, but as the numbers grew and Sibley became more acquainted with the captives, he wrote his wife on October 1 that virtually all of the females had been treated "in a most beastly manner," being subject to "daily and nightly outrage." Stephen Riggs, who interviewed the women immediately after their release, later reached the same conclusion: "Some were middle-aged white women, such as Mrs. Earle and Mrs. White." They were not abused. "But quite a number of them were young women who suffered more than death." In the parlance of nineteenth-century language, when it was indecent to be more explicit, such words constituted a description of rape.[75]

Of course, Dakota warriors did not view the acquisition of wives as rape. They had watched as white traders and government employees had disgraced their women, often abandoning them with children. And as young Thomas Robertson noted, none of the white women had been "abused," which had not always been the case with the traders and their so-called Indian "wives." Two different cultural views suddenly came into collision. Young Mdewakanton warriors concluded that taking a wife into their tepee was in no way a crime. Many of these men had not found wives, because they were simply not available in their society. The conflict in fall 1862 provided many different opportunities—revenge for some, plunder for others, the chance to gain honors in warfare. For many Dakota young men, it offered the chance to obtain a wife.

Sibley had made a promise: warriors would not be punished as long as they had not killed a settler. But this rather lenient notion vanished when he saw the captive women come forward. The colonel grew more outraged with each passing day after the surrender at Camp Release. It became a matter of honor for him and others in his command: white men were protectors of their womenfolk and failing in that protection was disgraceful. There is no question that his growing intent to punish the Dakota people was elevated by his belief that all the white women and girls had been raped. However, few Dakota men understood that the growing evidence of the sexual abuse of white captive women enraged the general, his officers, and his army to a point where past promises were completely ignored. There would be retribution, and it would follow a course never suspected by the Dakota men who willingly surrendered to Sibley, a man they called Wapatanhanska, or the Tall Merchant, a man who many of them saw as a friend.

NINE

CAPTURE AND TRIALS

Colonel Sibley stayed in camp below the Yellow Medicine River for two days following the battle, fretting over the need to recapture the white women and children held by the Indians. He learned of the situation to the north of him by entertaining a number of friendly Indians, Anglo- and Franco-Dakota men, and Christian Indians from the missions who came and went, bringing letters and reports.[1] Finally, on September 26, Sibley marched north, bypassing Camp Release and reaching a point half a mile to its north. He did so to protect the captives from any retribution by the *akacita* warriors or to protect the friendly Indians from his own troops who had a difficult time accepting the argument that friendly Indians even existed. Returning, Sibley then went into Camp Release and ordered the Indians to turn over the captives. "To my in-expressible satisfaction," the colonel wrote to his wife, he "found most of the female captives [and] a few children safe therein."[2]

When Sibley entered the central council ground, a ceremony commenced as the protectors of those captives who had fled Little Crow's camp proudly handed them over. Mrs. White wrote that Stone Man and his wife brought seven forward. "Those [protectors] who had the largest number to deliver brought them forward in a haughty manner." Even so, White later admitted to a degree of affection for "her adopted parents."[3] Chaska brought forward Sarah Wakefield, though he "trembled in fear." She recalled that he pleaded with her to "talk good to your white people, or they will kill me."[4] Wakefield, aware that other captives had reported her supposed "marriage" to Chaska, defended him. This irritated Sibley, as he described Sarah as "a rather handsome woman" who had "become infatuated with the redskin who had taken her for a wife . . . [and] declared that were it not for her children, she would not leave her dusky paramour."[5] Sarah's defense of Chaska later proved fatal. Soldiers and Minnesota newspaper editors alike could not understand her outspokenness or Chaska's role as a savior.

The strong belief that the white women had been sexually abused convinced Sibley to assign Riggs with the initial task of interviewing them. The reverend was likely the only man capable of asking pointed questions relative to sensitive issues such as rape—and he too found the task difficult. He began the interviews on the afternoon of September 26, and they continued into the next week. A few women opened up to the missionary: "Poor Mattie Williams," Riggs wrote to his wife, "she had been horribly abused. She grieves much over it." Riggs's description surely confirms Cecelia Campbell Stay's relation of Williams's ordeal. While Riggs also interviewed Sarah Wakefield, he only concluded that hers was a "curious case," one that he refused to say anything about in a letter, even to his wife. The usually open Riggs said little about the investigation at the time, but it seems likely that his suspicions and whatever "evidence" he acquired was given privately to Sibley, so that the women would not have to testify. Riggs did identify Julia LaFramboise, who spoke openly. She confirmed that Wakefield had acted in camp as Chaska's wife.[6] As the trials of the Dakota men involved got underway later, the court recorder would conclude that Riggs became literally "the Grand Jury of the court," even though his evidence was never recorded. It was simply too sensitive, and with but a few exceptions, most of the women refused to testify.[7]

Sibley's careful march north convinced a significant number of Dakota men who had been involved in the fighting to return to Camp Release at night, pitching their tepees on the perimeter. The colonel's earlier promise to punish only those who had killed settlers seemed to work. The Indians who had turned over the captives had not been punished. But after Riggs's interviews on September 27, Sibley ordered that seven Indian men and the African American Joseph Godfrey be taken and held; most of the men were suspected of rape and murder. Also among the group was Chaska. Sarah Wakefield, who openly proclaimed his innocence, was livid. She confronted Sibley, telling him that "if her Indian, who is among those being seized, should be hung, she will shoot those of us who have been instrumental in bringing him to the scaffold." The next day, another nine Dakota men were detained.[8]

Sibley had written to Governor Ramsey on September 27 that when it came to rape, it was only the "young girls" who had been "retained as the wives of the young [Indian] men." Perhaps as many as seven or eight of these girls had been carried off when the Dakota warriors departed for the West, with some to be recaptured.[9] Sibley received just 94 "pure white captives" at Camp Release on September 26, but when those recovered later were added, the "pure white" captive list grew to 107 by October 3.[10] The treatment of the young girls led to more suspicion within the military camp that all the women had been abused. John Madison, a soldier in the Third Regiment, wrote his wife what most believed to be true: that women "like yourself and your friends" were "in the hands of savages who have *not the least restraint either moral or physical upon their conduct toward their victims.*"[11]

With prisoners in tow, Sibley ordered the formation of a military commission to try them on September 27. Working closely with Riggs, it heard its first case at 11:00 A.M. on the morning of September 28, hardly giving defendants the opportunity to learn of the charges let alone defend themselves in front of the judges or acquire legal counsel. Sibley selected just three officers for the court: Colonel William Crooks and Captains Hiram P. Grant of the Sixth Regiment and Lieutenant Colonel William R. Marshall of the Seventh Regiment. Such a small number, though, only constituted what the army called a court of inquiry, a body that collected evidence; it failed to meet the requirements for a commission. Somehow learning of this mistake—the colonel had no access to the army's "Articles of War"—the next day Sibley added in his Order No. 55 Captain Hiram Bailey of the Sixth Regiment and Lieutenant Rollin C. Olin of the Third Regiment as members of the commission. Lieutenant Isaac V. D. Heard, a lawyer by training, was ordered to serve as "recorder."[12]

Such commissions had been reinstituted by the army at the beginning of the Civil War, with General Henry Halleck first using them in Missouri in January 1862. Obviously, given that Halleck was Pope's commanding officer, this likely had much to do with both Sibley's determination to use one and Pope's approval of its use. But they were controversial, and a year later, in fall 1863, the judge advocate general later determined that Sibley lacked the legal right to organize such a commission in the field, given the level of prejudice. Sibley's actions violated Article 65 of the Articles of War; General Pope agreed even though by this time executions had occurred. But the Civil War distracted everyone in Washington, D.C., including the judge advocate general. A second question involved the local courts; normally, military commissions were used only when local law and order had broken down—and it had not in Minnesota. While questions prevailed in Sibley's own mind regarding his authority, this seemed to vanish when he was promoted to general in the Union Army a few days after his victory at Lone Tree Lake. As for the role of the commissioners, much would ride on the way they performed their duty.[13]

Military commissions had been used for the first time in Mexico in 1847, where General Winfield Scott defined them in Order No. 20. Because there is nothing in the Constitution to affirm their use, the only legal standing that they have, even today, comes from the "customs of war"; given this, the judge advocate general in Washington, D.C., followed Scott's outline virtually to the letter during the Civil War.[14] They provided military justice—the army could not try civilians by court martial—when martial law was needed to restore order.[15] Scott, a lawyer by training, insisted that the commissions he created be a combination of American civil law (such as existed in any given county in the United States) and court martial justice as defined in the Articles of War.[16]

While the commission had to consist of between five and thirteen officers, the "judge advocate" of the court had the largest responsibility. He was, according to Scott, the "official prosecutor of the Unites States . . . the legal advisor of the Court . . . the Recorder of the Court . . . and the Counsel for the Prisoner."[17] Defendants in any case tried by a commission had the same legal rights as a citizen in an American courtroom. They had right to legal counsel, even though the judge advocate also had the responsibility to defend the accused. While the counsel had no right to object to testimony, the judge advocate did have the duty of refusing to allow "leading questions," or questions asked "which might tend to criminate himself [the defendant]."[18] In other words, the judge advocate was both the person to rule on the legality of the questions asked—theoretically, he would ask most of them, along with legal counsel for the defendant—and to cross-examine witnesses. While no regulation prohibited hearsay evidence, it could be objected to, especially when of a vague nature. Finally, the defendant and the judge advocate had the ability to challenge any member of the court and to remove that person for prejudice.[19]

The next procedure was for the judge advocate to write "a concise state-ment of his [the defendant's] defense, and observations on the general im-port of evidence." This was countered by a written list of questions from the court, written down so that the defense knew the witnesses and questions to be asked; this is generally called discovery. Usually, in American courts this constituted an arraignment, whereby the judge advocate listed both the charges against the defendant and gave the defendant an opportunity to enter a plea and mount a defense.[20] Thereafter, usually a few days later, the examination of witnesses could begin. The defense counsel as well as the judge advocate had the ability to cross-examine a witness. After the presentation of evidence, the commission retired to vote on guilt or inno-cence. It took a vote of two-thirds of the commission members to convict a defendant in capital cases, but only the president of the United States could authorize an execution. The president did so only after a careful review of the testimony, and after trial records were examined by the judge advocate general, who advised the president.[21]

Sibley realized that he lacked the legal expertise necessary to conduct trials. He had briefly studied the law, but he had never practiced it. The men he selected to form the commission save Heard had little military and no legal experience. Despite this, Sibley readily informed General Pope that, if found guilty by his commission, he intended to have the accused Indians "immediately executed"; Sibley seemed to be totally unaware that only the president could issue such an order. While Sibley admitted that he was "somewhat in doubt whether my authority extends quite so far," he thought such action "imperatively necessary."[22] While Pope applauded the war department's decision to elevate Sibley to the rank of brigadier gen-eral, he must have been aware that Sibley lacked the authority to issue such an order. But those being tried were Indians, not white soldiers. Virtually all due process was ignored.[23]

Pope's only criticism of Sibley's actions involved his failure to disarm the growing number of Indian men who he had under his control—those who were quietly moving back into Camp Release. Instead, Sibley cast a wide perimeter guard around the camp, which soon held some 250 Dakota men. Pope thought all of them were guilty of the terrible atroci-ties; how could any of these men, the general argued, be innocent? While Pope expressed approval of Sibley's actions and policies, only reinforcing Sibley's sense of his own "authority," the letter likely brought the new gen-eral to the realization that most people back east were demanding severe retribution for all Dakota men. How could there be innocent men in this camp?[24]

Many Mdewakanton men had been reluctant to flee out onto the plains primarily because they had hunted in the woodlands all their lives. Plains people, like the majority of Sissetons, depended upon the buffalo, an animal that seemed ever more difficult to find by the 1860s. But after Pope's letter arrived, Sibley became increasingly aware that he needed to act quickly, and he sent a group of mixed-blood and full-blood messengers north on a scouting mission. The general knew that some fifty miles north of Camp Release, a number of Mdewakantons could still be found and perhaps convinced to surrender. Among the scouts were Gabriel Renville, Akipa, Joseph Kawanke, Red Iron, Solomon Two Stars, and John Otherday. They agreed to talk with some of the Indians who had fled to Big Stone Lake and beyond.[25]

Secondarily, to keep Pope at bay, Sibley quietly informed the department commander that "Indians are arrested daily on charges duly preferred by me, but as the proceedings are of course secret, it is impossible now to state how many will be executed."[26] In other words, those convicted by the commission—the first faced trial on September 28—knew nothing of their fate. By October 4, the number detained by Sibley had slowly grown to twenty-nine. Sibley did not want any of them to realize that they would face a commission that would determine whether they lived or died.[27]

The twenty-nine men came before the commission between September 28 and October 4. The trials were conducted in a tent, where Isaac Heard dutifully filled out the charges and specifications for each case on a piece of paper. In each trial, a copy of Sibley's Order No. 55 was included. It listed the five officers. The trial of Godfrey took the most time, likely a full day. He was charged with killing German settlers in the Milford settlement. Mary Schwandt, who noted his presence during the killing of Patoille, thought he was the Devil incarnate, but she never testified and he made a plausible case that his Indian relatives had coerced him to join them. Indeed, he spoke for many hours, giving details relative to the massacre of Germans, some of which were graphic, noting the severing of family members' heads.[28] It soon became obvious that Godfrey would be an excellent prosecution witness, and his sentence of death—which he was never informed of—was later commuted to a prison term.[29]

It took only a few minutes to convict the two men who clearly raped white women. One Who Forbids His House (Tihdoníća in Dakota; case

#2) and Laying Up Buffalo (Tazoo in Dakota; case #4) admitted their guilt, supposedly believing that taking white women as wives was simply not a crime. Unlike many prisoners, Laying Up Buffalo suddenly sensed that his conduct would lead to punishment, bringing into question why he surrendered to begin with. In a final statement, one tinged with a frequent reference to a "death wish," he told the court that he was prepared for the afterlife. He expected the road to be long: "It will probably take me a long time to reach the end of my journey." While the evidence against Laying Up Buffalo and One Who Forbids His House seemed indisputable, the trial of Chaska revealed the obvious bias of the court. Sarah Wakefield testified that he had on several occasions "saved my life" and that she had not suffered any sexual abuse. Angus Robertson, a brother to Thomas, stood up for Chaska as well, declaring that he was "a very good man." But the specter of an Indian man taking a white woman as "wife," despite its questionable truth, was too much for the court. The commission trial records show that Chaska was eventually sentenced to death and would later be executed, despite the fact that the president did not include him on the final list.[30]

During these early trials, many Dakota men incriminated themselves. There is no evidence that even the court recorder, Isaac Heard, who had legal training, tried to prevent this. Supposedly, the judge advocate, had there been one, would have prevented such testimony or at least informed the defendant that he need not answer questions. In Sibley's letter outlining Order No. 55, creating the commission, he did list the five officers, with Lieutenant Olin being the last one named. Under his name in an indented space was the term "judge advocate." Its placement suggests that it was added later, as Olin, if he ever recognized his role as "judge advocate," never so much as asked a question. And of course, he could not serve both as a military judge and the judge advocate.[31]

Other Indians who came before the court were simply asked to explain what they had done during the rebellion. His People or Nation (Oyatetawa in Dakota; case #5) admitted to killing Patoille even though Mattie Williams, who was there, could not identify him as the murderer. He too was later executed. Scarlet, or Red Shooter (Wahpeduta in Dakota; case #11), noted that he killed an old man. His only excuse must have pleased the court: "All the Dakota have killed whites," he said. "If the guilty are punished there will be none left."[32] There was no judge advocate there to explain that the he need not admit his guilt.

Other men soon joined Godfrey in testifying against various Indians. The most active was David Faribault Jr., who helped convict many men. At one point, Faribault exclaimed that Tainyanku (case #18) was simply "one of the worst" members of the soldiers' lodge. His reputation seemed to be the only evidence against him, and he too was sentenced to death. A similar fate was meted out to Running Rattling (Hdainyanka in Dakota; case #19), who was Wabasha's son-in-law. Paul Mazakutemani testified that he had refused to give up the white prisoners in the councils held in mid-September near Yellow Medicine. Faribault then claimed that he had "encouraged" the *akacita* soldiers to "kill white men." It is likely, however, that the court may have concluded that Running Rattling joined the group of young men at Wakute's house on the first evening of the war in their attack on the three white women, which may explain his verdict. Certainly, speaking out against surrendering the captives could hardly warrant execution.[33]

One case that took more time than most of the others was that of the Singer (Dowansa in Dakota; case #22). Godfrey testified against him, offering only hearsay evidence. While never near Swan Lake—east of the Minnesota River near the town of Nicollet—Singer supposedly committed murder. Godfrey claimed that Singer was "leading a young white woman away and her mother ran after her to take her away." He obviously wanted the elder woman's daughter for a wife. The Singer, so Godfrey claimed, supposedly shot the mother and wounded her daughter in the process. "One of the Indians," Godfrey claimed, "said she wasn't dead and he ran and pulled up her clothes and she jumped up and another Indian took his tomahawk and struck her." While Singer claimed to have killed no one, he too was later executed, based upon the hearsay evidence that Godfrey repeated.[34]

The trials that were completed by October 4 resulted in the conviction of twenty-one men, including Godfrey. Of those, twelve would later be executed, and eight would face the gallows but have their convictions commuted by the president. During these trials, the court concluded that just being at a battle and firing one's gun, such as in the trial of He Charges His Dwelling (Tiwanata in Dakota; case #27), led to a "not guilty" decision. In other words, the court initially believed that Dakota warriors who simply fought in battles were prisoners of war and innocent of any crime. The court was likely acting according to Sibley's promise: only those who supposedly killed white settlers would be punished.[35] This resulted in too few convictions, but this would soon change as a new batch of trials started some days later. General Sibley, pushed at times by his commanding officer, Pope, wanted more convictions.

While the court's actions would expand in the weeks to come to include convicting those Indians who had been participants in battles, so many rules of law were violated in these early trials that any sense of due process disappeared. The most blatant disregard for the letter of law obviously included a failure to disallow hearsay evidence and the use of pressure to acquire incriminating testimony from defendants. Perhaps worse, Sibley had stated that the groups still at large contained *akacita* warriors, who were far guiltier than the ones convicted. If so, what of the guilt of those who were being tried and convicted? The suspension of the trials on October 4 likely occurred because the general hoped to arrest more men who were supposedly guilty.

How the Indian prisoners viewed their trials is open to conjecture. Many pled not guilty when asked to enter a plea. After appearing in front of the court, most likely concluded that Sibley would live up to his bargain; the vast majority had not killed civilians, even though some had taken white wives, including the supposedly innocent Chaska. Yet another hope was held out for those who had been farmer Indians. Wabasha later argued that Sibley had assured the growing number of men at Camp Release that he "would not harm those who had adopted the customs of the whites." Left with their firearms intact and seeing only a loose, distant guard surrounding Camp Release, most of the Dakota men who surrendered after September 28 became increasing secure in their belief that Sibley would live up to his promise.[36] The general's private correspondence reveals a more sinister outlook, one perhaps emerging as more suspicions suggested that, with but a few exceptions, all the Mdewakanton men crowding into Camp Release were guilty, many of rape.[37]

Sibley's use of Dakota scouts who rode north and west after October 1 did lead to the surrender of more Dakota men and their families. Upon meeting with fleeing Indians who had participated in the battles, the scouts were to explain that the general only desired to punish those who had killed civilians. One of the notes that Sibley sent along offered the following promise: "I will see that no innocent person is injured who comes to me without delay." Just how these messengers explained the word "innocent" is impossible to determine.[38] Just four days after he had sent messengers north, on October 4, Sibley had Samuel Brown and others conduct a count of the Indians at Camp Release. The number of men had swollen to

286; Brown and others concluded that "just 46" were "above suspicion."[39] Plans were materializing to arrest virtually all of them, even many of the mixed-bloods who might have been involved in the killings.

Feeding all these people—the total number of people at Camp Release had reached some twelve hundred—had become a serious problem. Sibley hardly had enough food for his troops. When Agent Galbraith arrived on October 4, Sibley ordered Captain J. C. Whitney and a company of troops to move everyone, including most of the white captives, first to the Yellow Medicine Agency and then, later in mid-October, to the Lower Agency. Some ninety of the former white captives went; the remaining seventeen were, supposedly, to be used in court to testify against certain Indian men, if they surrendered. The former captives were sent on to Fort Ridgely and St. Peter. Destitute of clothing, they reached towns still packed with refugees. Captain A. K. Skaro, who commanded a defensive force at St. Peter, scurried to provide clothing. Governor Ramsey gave them some funds that he had on hand. While their ordeal was over, they had little to return to, as their farms and homes were destroyed, and for many, their husbands and children were dead.[40]

The twelve hundred Indians turned over to Galbraith were moved first to Yellow Medicine Agency, where a loose guard of soldiers surrounded their camp. Once at the agency, they dug potatoes and gathered corn at the various fields the government had opened. Most were relatively well fed; they received the same fare as Sibley's soldiers.[41] As for the Indians north of Camp Release who seemed willing to surrender, Sibley kept a close watch on them, getting hourly reports as to their movements. Despite his lack of mounted men, some thirty-seven lodges came in on October 7, and another scattered group of some twenty lodges were eight or nine miles above them, supposedly ready to surrender. "There are many desperate villains in both of these camps," Sibley reported to Pope. Some crept into Camp Release and set up their tepees at night. Sibley counseled with the ones who surrendered but let them remain at large "under his guns." After coaxing as many as possible down from the Big Stone Lake region, Sibley finally concluded that no more would willingly surrender.[42]

As the sun went down on October 11, the general ordered several hundred infantry troops to surround Camp Release and disarm the new group of four hundred men and women who had surrendered after October 4. There was no resistance, but Riggs, who witnessed the event, heard one Indian comment: "Why did you not come in daylight?" Most of the people in this camp, Riggs thought, were now "tired of war and long for peace." Riggs, who slept in the same tent as Sibley, knew that the general's plans did not include leniency. Despite the tempering facade that Sibley displayed, Riggs perceived that "the retribution intended will be terribly severe. The innocent will undoubtedly suffer with the guilty."[43]

General Sibley ordered Whitney and Galbraith to secure the Indian men at Yellow Medicine on the same day. Both officers recognized the difficulty involved: Whitney had only two companies of troops and the over two hundred Dakota men were armed. After recruiting Gabriel Renville, Samuel Brown, and many other reliable Anglo- and Franco-Dakota men, they designed a ruse, making it known in camp that the government annuity funds that were supposed to be distributed in June had finally arrived. Some indication of these men's vainness comes from Brown, who, in talking with many of them, found that they were "delighted to learn that they were at last to get their money." Using the walled structure that had been the large stone warehouse—its roof had been burned off—Brown and others lined up the men to supposedly create a roll. As they passed into the building, they were quickly disarmed and placed under the custody of soldiers. Brown took their tomahawks, knives, and guns and threw them into a barrel.[44]

Over the next few days, some 101 Mdewakanton Dakota men at Camp Release and another 236 at Yellow Medicine were chained together, with the right leg of one man connected to the left of another. The effort exhausted nearly all the "tree chains & suitable iron rods" that could be found. Rather miraculously, this had all been done without firing a shot. In all, Sibley had imprisoned over fifteen hundred Indians, virtually all of them Mdewakantons—nearly three-quarters of the band—including men, women, and children. The Dakota men in chains numbered 337, but only twenty-nine of this group had faced the military commission; a number of these had been released. Yet Sibley knew, based upon information from his scouts, that several smaller groups were still at large, including some near Big Stone Lake and others that fled to the Coteau des Prairies, some seventy miles to the west in Dakota Territory. While the general had scarce resources to work with, he put together an infantry force to scour Big Stone Lake and a number of mounted men to ride west into Dakota Territory. The general hoped to corral more Indians, using his promises as bait.[45]

Sibley placed Lieutenant Colonel Marshall in command of the mounted force, and Joseph R. Brown and Gabriel Renville went along as guides. Brown and Renville had operated a trade house on the north end of the

Coteau in the late 1830s and 1840s—apparently restocking it with stolen goods from the agencies' warehouses when Galbraith replaced Brown as agent in 1861—and both knew the region well. Despite their lack of horses, the infantry that marched north captured a band of twenty-two Dakota men and some women at Lac qui Parle. And when Marshall's force reached Ten Mile Lake, situated between the James and Big Sioux Rivers, he corralled another 150 Dakota men, women, and children. Although the men tried to run, they were all taken captive. The women, as scout William Quinn reported, "ran for cover and some of them began wailing the death song." As soldier George Bushnell put it, they came along "with considerable difficulty, knives being brandished at a great rate."[46] These patrols added over fifty men to those under confinement; a number of them, Sibley surmised, were heavily involved in the massacre.

Sibley sent men from the Third Regiment to ride with Marshall, mostly to get them out of camp; many had become unruly, and a number had been arrested for molesting Dakota women and stealing buffalo robes. The problems with discipline had reached such a level that Sibley asked Pope if he had authority under the Articles of War to form a general court martial. Apparently, the irony of the request never phased the general; Article 65 forbids an officer in the field from forming a court when serious questions existed regarding possible prejudice. The trials of the Indians fit this prohibition well; nevertheless, Sibley seemed to ignore it when it came to the Mdewakantons.[47] His concerns were warranted. Riggs called the Third "an unruly set of fellows." He had heard their talk of "killing Indians" without any trials.[48] Concerns regarding the lack of discipline even convinced Sibley to admonish Marshall, who he ordered to protect any Dakota woman he might capture.[49]

While Sibley hoped to launch a much broader campaign against the Indians who had fled, including White Lodge's band of Sissetons, this became impossible as the days turned cold and the air foreordained winter. All the general could do was send a threatening letter to the Charger and Standing Buffalo. While they had warned Little Crow to stay out of their territory, telling him to "go away," they could hardly understand Sibley's tone. The breach between the government and the Sisseton Indians would only grow into conflict over the next two years, even though they had not participated in the massacre.[50]

The Mdewakantons who had fled after the battle at Lone Tree Lake had obviously split up, making pursuit by the army more difficult. One group of a hundred lodges was camped over the winter just sixty miles north of the trading post at Fort Pierre, on the central Missouri River. While the nearest military post was well to the south at Fort Randall, the commander sent two companies of troops to Fort Pierre, actions that gradually led to the military occupation of the upper Missouri River over the next three years. General Pope also reinforced the small town of Sioux Falls, which had been briefly attacked. There could be little doubt that the Dakota war was expanding onto the plains, increasingly involving tribes such as the Hunkpapa, Yanktonai, and Yankton. The Hunkpapas, under rising chiefs such as Sitting Bull, later welcomed several Mdewakantons and Wahpekutes, including the indomitable Scarlet End (better known as Inkpaduta), who obviously did his best to taint the Americans as brutal invaders.[51]

Despite the growing tension in the West, the situation along the upper Minnesota River stabilized to some degree. Major General Pope received pressure to send various regiments east. Yet Ramsey worried; many of the volunteer troops had slowly withered away come October. Leonard Aldrich, who inspected volunteers at New Ulm, found that they had been given "guns of a foreign manufacture," and that the cartridges were "too small" for the caliber. They were tiring of being soldiers.[52] The usually capable Richard Strout at Hutchinson also could not keep his men in place; they had nothing to eat and tattered clothes. Even Captain Whitcomb at Forest City reported that his company of forty-five men "were tired of soldiering" and most had left for home.[53] While Pope initially agreed to send Minnesota's regulars east, he reversed himself in early November. Elements of various regiments were to remain in Minnesota. This included much of the Sixth, Seventh, Eighth, and Ninth as well as Twenty-Fifth Wisconsin.[54]

As defensive operations were being finalized, Sibley and Pope focused their attention on the remaining Indians in custody. Governor Ramsey recognized that some of these were "friendly," as did Sibley, but the governor made it clear that even those who had assisted the army, such as the Renvilles and Christian Indians, would have to be eventually removed from the state. The best way to proceed was to transport the Indians to Fort Snelling, where they could be shipped out by steamboat.[55] Sibley determined to first consolidate them at the Lower Agency. He ordered Whitney and Galbraith to move their captives to the new location on October 15. Major W. T. McSasen had proceeded to build a "log prison," some

30 x 150 feet, to house all the prisoners, including those recently captured. The location was quickly dubbed "Camp Sibley."[56] After Marshall returned from the Coteau, all those at Camp Release were moved to Yellow Medicine on October 24. This brought the total number of prisoners held by Sibley to 157. When added to those held by Whitney and Galbraith at the Lower Agency, the total ballooned to 393 men.[57]

The pitiful circumstances of the prisoners, as they were moved south to Camp Sibley, softened to some degree the general hatred that army troops had exhibited toward them. The four-mile-long column of infantry troops and prisoners made for quite a spectacle. The Dakota men, shackled together, were herded two at a time onto wagons, with ten being squeezed into each one. Riggs thought they "suffered very much."[58] Just before reaching Camp Sibley, the caravan encountered a number of Dakota women working in a field. As the men sat silently, rumbling on in the wagons, one reporter noticed that "the women began to weep and to set up a dismal wail."[59] When they reached the newly constructed prison at Camp Sibley, conditions improved as Major McSasen had built a large compound complete with a roof. Once inside, Dakota women brought the men food. One of the Native women also brought, as one soldier noted, "a sick girl that was dying." She had a father, a brother, and two cousins in the compound, all of whom reached out to greet her. The father grasped her hand, and then sat quietly on his haunches and "looked at her for half an hour without saying a word." Soldier John Kingsley Wood could not help but call it a "solemn event."[60]

Sibley hoped to try these men, sort out the guilty ones, and execute them, all before the winter set in. The commission, which began this monumental task at Camp Release, resumed its duties on October 16 at Yellow Medicine.[61] Four days later, some 109 men had faced the commission, or roughly 22 per day. After the march to Camp Sibley, the commission started up again on October 27. The last prisoner faced the commission on November 3. In other words, during the third and final sequence of trials, which covered just eight days, some 263 Indians came before the military commission, an average of thirty-three a day. The busiest day was November 2, when forty-three Dakota men stood trial. To expedite matters, some evidence suggests that as many as eight men were brought in front of the officers at one time, making it nearly impossible for anyone to receive justice.[62]

While the commission placed some emphasis on getting to the truth in the first twenty-nine trials, conducted in late September and early

October, a dramatic shift occurred thereafter. In earlier trials, the first charge included wording such as "Participation in murder," or simply murder. Accordingly, some Indians in this early group who pleaded not guilty were acquitted, even after they admitted to being at key battles. Thereafter, the first charge was modified to include "Murder, [and] Participation" in various murders and outrages. "Participation" was soon defined as simply fighting at the fort, New Ulm, Birch Coulee, or in the Big Woods. A second statement also added the following: "And thereupon the prisoner being asked what he had to say in answer to said charge made the following statement."[63] The commission had obviously institutionalized the use of incriminating evidence, demanding it from defendants. There was no judge advocate to speak for the Indians challenging such a format.

Just who ordered these changes is difficult to determine, but it must have been General Sibley. Virtually every record thereafter begins with a statement by the Indian being charged. Most Dakota defendants assumed that given Sibley's promise, they would be punished only if they had killed whites in the settlements. Most readily admitted to being at a battle. This quickly turned out not to be the case, and the majority of trials, which consisted of just one page of information, lasted only as long as it took for the defendant to declare that he had been at a battle and had fired a gun. Jared Daniels, who watched the entire process, noted that early on in October "there was such a strong feeling against the Indians" among the troops and commission members that their duties, as he put it, "were extended to include all that had participated in any battles." Daniels does not say who ordered the extension, but he does suggest that the change resulted in many being "condemned on general principles, which was more in harmony with the prejudices of the Whites, than justice."[64]

While the first twenty-nine Dakota men tried received some degree of justice, the trials that began on October 15 increasingly resembled a Star Chamber, combining arbitrary and harsh judgement that went well beyond the bounds of American common law. Of the 363 trials coming after October 4, some 157 cases were decided in a few minutes, perhaps even less, after the Indian charged was queried regarding his participation in the conflict and after he confessed to being at a battle. The confession led to a guilty verdict and death, even though not one witness was brought forward to speak against the defendant. In the remaining 206 cases, when the Indian defendant was asked if he had been at a battle, many simply said no. These trials took a bit longer because witnesses were then brought forward who could place them at a battle. At that point, they too were convicted and sentenced to death, often on hearsay evidence.

The case of Standing Lodge (Tinajinpi in Dakota; case #153) is typical. When asked to tell his story, he said simply "I was at the Fort, but had no gun. I was not at the battle of New Ulm. I was at Birch Coulee on the side of the timber. I fired one shot." While the trial record indicates that two witnesses were available, they never gave any testimony. It was not needed. By admitting to firing a shot at Birch Coulee, Standing Lodge was sentenced "to be hanged by the neck until dead."[65] In a few cases, when an Indian simply admitted to being at the fort but not shooting a gun (see trial of Hepan, which means literally "second son"; case #53), they were occasionally acquitted. But this too soon changed. When Eagle Plum (Wamdupidan in Dakota; case #171) faced the commission on October 28, he stated that he had "never been any wheres [sic]." David Faribault Jr. then came forward to testify that he had seen the defendant at the fort. Gabriel Renville then noted, "I heard the prisoner was out in the Big Woods [with Little Crow]." The defendant had openly denied participation and had apparently never fired a gun, but circumstantial and hearsay evidence led to him being sentenced "to death."[66]

In a few cases, Indian defendants tried artfully to dodge even the implication that they were participants. Walker Among Stones (Tunkaŋmani in Dakota; case #218) had been a member of Wakute's farmer band. He claimed that he was not at Fort Ridgely or New Ulm when the attacks went in, and while he was nearby when the Indians fired on the men at Birch Coulee, he had only a bow and arrow. No one was killed at Birch Coulee with an arrow. Given his unwillingness to incriminate himself, the commission then brought forward witnesses such as Thomas Robertson, who said he had never seen the Indian at any of the battles. Proving less than helpful, the commission then turned to Godfrey. He placed Walker Among Stones at a campfire of men who had returned from Birch Coulee. "He was with the other Indians when they made the attack," Godfrey suggested. For supposedly being with or nearby the war party, Walker Among Stones was sentenced to death by hanging.[67]

The commission used a battery of men, most all of whom were Anglo- and Franco-Dakota, as possible witnesses. Almost every trial had a list of one or two. Because so many Indians simply condemned themselves, the witnesses were often never called. While most history of the event suggests that the African American Godfrey was heavily used as a witness,

David Faribault Jr. actually offered to testify more than any other person, being involved in 139 trials. Godfrey does appear on 82 records, often giving what would be considered hearsay evidence in a normal courtroom. Others included Michael and Gabriel Renville, who had not been at any of the battles, and many other Renvilles and LaFramboises. They generally repeated what they had heard. In only a few cases did whites who had survived the fighting step forward, the exceptions being the two or three women who testified, David Carrothers, and two German boys who had survived. Ironically, most of the female captives never testified, even though a few were kept back for that purpose. In the final tally, 303 Indians were condemned to death by the commission, with 265 being convicted because they were at a battle. In other words, thirty-eight were convicted of being at a place where civilians were killed. A handful received prison terms, mostly for theft of property.[68]

Sibley's failure to identify a judge advocate and vest in that person the powers necessary to secure fair trials condemns the commission's work to nothing more than a travesty of justice. It would appear in many cases that members of the five-person commission asked questions, a clear violation of military law. Even President Lincoln realized this when he sent his message to Congress on November 11, 1862. He listed Olin as the fifth member of the commission without mentioning the existence of a judge advocate. He could easily see on the trial records, which he examined, that Olin was listed first as a member of the commission. Adding judge advocate below his name only muddled the records and brought serious questions regarding the commission's legitimacy.[69]

Perhaps the most disturbing element of all came in the time it took to try the Indians. In 90 percent of the trials, the entire event lasted only a minute or two; of the 392 trials, 352 contain one page or less of testimony, with often as little as two sentences. As soon as the charges were read and the testimony collected, the Indian defendant was dismissed.[70] As the defendant was ushered out, he had no idea that a verdict had been reached. Indeed, the trial records do not even suggest that the five commission members voted on innocence or guilt. The defendant had no time to acquire counsel, to mount a defense, or to even cross-examine witnesses. Indeed, cross-examination of witnesses never occurred. The Indians charged seldom spoke English, and it is unclear whether the testimony against a defendant was even translated into the Dakota language so that the defendant could answer to it.

Despite the massive increase in the numbers of men tried each day after October 16, Sibley remained steadfast in his convictions regarding the fairness of the trials, often justifying his actions in letters to his wife. He seemed uncertain of the number to be executed by October 19—over two hundred Dakota men would face the commission thereafter—but he assured his wife that "the number will be sufficiently great to satisfy the longings of the most bloodthirsty" citizen of the state. Eleven days later, on a day in which roughly forty men were tried, the general took a more defensive tone that sounded somewhat hollow: "We are trying the prisoners as rapidly as fair play and due regard to justice will admit."[71] Perhaps encouragement from Major General Pope helped. Pope received day-by-day reports and seemed totally committed to a large mass execution, one administered in front of the wives and children of the Dakota men as well as the nearby Winnebago Indians. Both men believed that some sort of spectacle needed to take place that would satisfy the Minnesota population at large.

These plans came to an abrupt halt on October 17, when a message from the president reached Pope by telegraph. Lincoln informed the major general that "no executions be made without his sanction." Pope dutifully sent the information along to Sibley, who received it four days later. The general then began planning to move the convicted men south; he still believed that Lincoln would sanction a mass execution. The prisoners, at first bound for St. Paul, were eventually sent to Mankato until Lincoln's wishes were known, and the women and children, along with those men considered to be above suspicion, were to be moved to Fort Snelling, making it possible to deport them in the spring.[72]

With more and more Indians being tried every day in order to finish before bad weather set in, a number of observers slowly began to question the legality of the entire process. Riggs, who was responsible for acquiring evidence that convicted scores of men, wrote his wife on October 15 that he "should not like to have my life set upon by this commission." Two days later, he lamented that "many will be punished on insufficient evidence."[73] Riggs's growing concerns finally boiled over on October 30: "I have just now protested with Mr. Heard the recorder of the commission on the point that they don't treat Indians [as fairly] as half breeds." The issue came up when the Franco-Dakota named the Swan (Magatanka in Dakota; case #236) faced the commission. He admitted to being in the fight against Strout's volunteers at Acton on September 3; several witnesses then placed him there. While he claimed never to have fired a gun—something one witness contradicted—the commission judged him not guilty. Riggs, in a confidential letter to his wife, noted that His Sacred Moccasin (Tahanpiwakan in Dakota; case #238), who was with the Swan, just two trials later, "has done the same thing . . . yet one [the Swan] is to be turned loose and the other [His Sacred Moccasin] put in irons." Despite such an obvious injustice, Riggs remained loyal to Sibley and came to believe that most of the men convicted were guilty.[74]

Yet another critic who mostly remained silent at the time was Doctor Jared Daniels. He thought it completely implausible that three hundred Indians "guilty of individual murders or the violation of white women" would simply surrender at Camp Release. He believed that most of the guilty Dakota men—perhaps two hundred—had fled west with Little Crow. Daniels knew that the vast majority of the convicted men had simply joined in the battles.[75] Thomas Hughes, a Minnesota lawyer who did extensive oral history and wrote extensively about the war in the latter part of the nineteenth century, also came to a similar conclusion: "The summary haste of the trials . . . and the fact that no Indian was given an opportunity to make a defense or even to know what he was accused of, made the proceedings of this tribunal a farce."[76]

While Riggs kept his criticism of the trials mostly to himself, this was not the case with his partner and co-missionary, Thomas S. Williamson. Initially, Williamson felt duty bound to praise Sibley for his cautious movement up the Minnesota River; it led to the retaking of the white captives and salvation for the innocent mixed-bloods and Christian Indians.[77] But once he heard that Robert Hopkins and Peter Tapetataŋka had been convicted and sentenced to death, he started asking questions. These two men were both devoted Christians who had belonged to his church. They had sat outside the door of his house at the mission above Yellow Medicine on August 19, guarding it from intruders and helping the missionary and his family flee to the east. Hopkins had even joined a war party that was looking for the missionaries to divert it from their trail. Williamson could not understand how they could be guilty of anything.[78]

Williamson enlisted his son John, who had briefly been a missionary among the Mdewakantons at the Lower Agency, to investigate these cases. John reached Camp Sibley when the commission's trials were finally concluding. His report on November 5 was forwarded directly to Seliah B. Treat, head of the American Board, in Boston. It only cemented what increasingly constituted growing skepticism of the trials in the East. "400 have been tried in less time than it generally takes in our courts with the trial of a single murderer," John Williamson began. "In very many of the cases a man's [*sic*] own testimony is the only evidence against him." Worse, if the defendant fails to incriminate himself, "he is cross examined with all the ingenuity of a modern lawyer to see if he cannot be detected in some error of statement." The fact that the defendants "were not allowed counsel . . . and are scarcely allowed a word of explanation themselves" seemed to John Williamson an utter disregard for justice.[79]

John Williamson's report only confirmed to many in Washington, D.C., suspicions that had been building ever since Lincoln's secretary, John Hay, had unveiled the corruption in the Indian business in the state earlier that year. At a cabinet meeting on October 14, Secretary of the Navy Gideon Welles put Pope's report of the atrocities on the table. Yet he noted the massive land speculation, corrupt officials who had pilfered Indian money, and the many provocations the Dakota people had endured. He openly asked how the president could sanction the execution of a large number of men without taking a careful look at all the circumstances?[80]

Perhaps aware of the growing lobbying effort to derail the executions, or at least limit them, General Pope hurriedly ordered Sibley to send down from Camp Sibley a list of the 303 condemned men—but not the trial records. Pope received it on November 6, and while it was many pages in length, he ordered it to be telegraphed to the president at the enormous cost of $400.[81] Given the severity of the commission's recommendations, someone in Washington—perhaps Welles himself or even Hay—leaked it to the press. In the *New York Times,* the headline read "MERCY TO THE SIOUX." Serious questions were being asked by the *Times*'s editors. "The large number of 'big injuns,'" an editorial began, "with all sorts of unpronounceable names, who have been condemned to the gallows, will be respited, and subjected to some punishment." What did this mean? Had Lincoln leaked to the press his intentions to punish a much smaller number of Dakota men, or was it Welles or others? The entire war, the *Times* continued, "seems to have been a burst of rage . . . incited by the atrocious injustice to which they [the Dakota] had been subjected." Perhaps worse, the *Times* concluded, "the Indians who had given themselves up to justice" had surrendered. They openly declared their innocence. It was really "a few bad men among them" who needed to be executed.[82] Whatever the source, this conclusion had to have come from a person in the government.

The *Times* article did little to deter either Pope or Sibley in their belief that the executions would proceed as planned. Accordingly, on November 7, preparations were made to move the prisoners to Mankato. Once again, the wagons were loaded, ten shackled men in each, and along with seventeen Dakota women, who would cook, and four friendly Indians, including Akipa, the caravan departed along the old New Ulm road. When just two miles north of New Ulm, however, a strange sight appeared. As Sibley described it, "I was met by two persons, one [of] whom representing himself as a major in the state militia, in full uniform." The major was Friederich (Fritz) Brandt. He presented Sibley with a note, presumably from Sheriff Roos of New Ulm, forbidding the caravan from passing through Brown County. Sibley put out skirmishers and told the two men that he was "a U. S. Officer in command of a U. S. Force," and he would proceed through "any part of the United States" that he wanted to. The men then stepped aside.[83]

Suspecting trouble, Sibley swung to the right, traveling a half mile west of the town. He ordered infantry troops to take positions on each side of the wagons and to load their muskets. Reaching a point abreast New Ulm, a massive mob suddenly appeared, "a crowd of excited people of all ages & sexes." They started throwing stones and bricks at the wagons, hitting a number of shackled Indians. Sibley thought "the women [from New Ulm] were particularly violent, blandishing knives & other weapons and endeavoring to penetrate through the guard." While Sibley dared not order his men to fire, he did have them "fix bayonets," and the Sixth Regiment soon cleared the way. At that point, several uniformed members of the state militia joined the women. Sibley arrested fifteen of them. As the New Ulm women were finally driven off—Sibley later called them "Dutch she devils!"—some fifteen Indians lay severely wounded in the wagons; two later died. Once southeast of New Ulm, Sibley turned the New Ulm militia men loose, forcing them to walk the twenty-five miles back to their town.[84]

Along the way south, Sibley's caravan crossed the Cottonwood River and entered the small village of South Bend. The caravan looked like a parade to at least one of the citizens. "General Sibley and his staff, in full uniform, and mounted, headed a strange procession," Sarah Purcell Montgomery reported. After them came the wagons full of Indians, "chained together and seated on the floor, five on a side." Then came the infantry, followed by more wagons carrying the Dakota women and supplies.[85] The calm at South Bend was appreciated by at least one infantryman: "It seems more like civilization to see the women come to the door and see us pass by" rather than throw stones and bricks.[86] By the evening of November 10, the entire party had reached a point selected ahead called Camp Lincoln, west of Mankato on the right side of the Blue Earth River. Another log enclosure had been erected here to house the Dakota prisoners.[87]

The women and children of the imprisoned men took a different route east, headed for Fort Snelling on November 9. Lieutenant Colonel Marshall and several companies of the Seventh Regiment guarded them, passing through the southernmost part of the Big Woods. The group contained 1,658 souls, including twenty-two Franco- and Anglo-Dakota men and their families, who had not been tried—the Franco-Dakota Renvilles, LaFramboises, and La Belles; the Anglo-Dakota Robertsons, Robinsons, and Moores; and even Sibley's old friend and hunting partner, Jack Frazier. Among the Christian and farmer Indians were Taopi, Wabasha, Joseph Kawanke, Paul Mazakutemani, Lorenzo Lawrence, and John Otherday. This caravan, which was nearly five miles in length, moved at a leisurely pace in the increasingly crisp fall weather.[88]

Two days out, the caravan approached Henderson. Here trouble erupted, as the town was packed with refugees. "We found the streets crowded with an angry and excited populace," Samuel Brown later wrote, "cursing, shouting and crying." Hundreds of them grabbed guns, sticks, clubs, and stones and attacked the caravan. Many reached the wagons before the soldiers could respond and "succeeded in pulling many of the old men and women, and even children" down to ground, grabbing them by their hair. One enraged woman rushed up to a wagon and grabbed a baby from the arms of her mother and dashed it on the ground. The soldiers finally drove them off, but not before a drunken citizen from the town leveled a gun at Charles Crawford. Colonel Marshall raced forward and struck the gun with his saber so forcefully that the man fell to the ground. The baby, however, died a few hours later and was buried in the crotch of a tree after a short ceremony.[89] Marshall's caravan finally reached Fort Snelling on November 14, where another camp had been erected for them.

The fate of the Mdewakanton Dakota people now lay in the hands of President Lincoln, who had a difficult decision to make. The Civil War had been going badly, as Union troops, often commanded by timid generals, wilted in the face of the Confederates. Worse, the midterm elections had turned ugly for the Republicans. Disappointment had led to Democratic victories in New York, New Jersey, and Iowa. Even Lincoln's friends urged him to act decisively, especially politicians in Minnesota who had voted for him and wanted him to punish the Dakota people.[90]

Minnesota newspaper editors soon joined the chorus of angry politicians who wanted revenge. "Nothing short of extermination" was acceptable, read a banner headline in the *St. Paul Press*. And as for the women and children, the paper recommended a "penal colony" be created on Isle Royale in Lake Superior.[91] The *St. Croix Monitor* waxed a bit more poetic: "Lo! The Poor Indian. Panthers and rattlesnakes are in the same manner a law unto themselves, but who for this reason will spare them?" The Indians' "refusal to be civilized, forces upon us the hard alternative of exterminating him." Never had an American frontier community been more closely aligned in supporting a policy approaching genocide than in Minnesota in the late fall of 1862.

COLONEL STEPHEN MILLER, later governor of the state, was in command
of the executions. Courtesy of Minnesota Historical Society.

ONE WHO FORBIDS HIS HOUSE (Tihdonića), a warrior executed at Mankato, December 26, 1862. Courtesy of Minnesota Historical Society.

WILLIAM DULEY, who left his family at Slaughter Slough, and later was given the honor of cutting the rope that dropped the scaffold at the executions. Courtesy of Elroy E. Ubl, original belonging to Gretchen M. Taflin.

"EXECUTION OF THE THIRTY-EIGHT DAKOTA MEN AT MANKATO, MINNESOTA, DECEMBER 26, 1862." Illustration by W. H. Childs from *Leslie's Illustrated Newspaper*, January 24, 1863. Courtesy Library of Congress.

"SCENE IN THE PRISON, MANKATO, MINNESOTA, where the Sioux murderers are confined, waiting the decision of the U.S. government. —From a sketch by W. H. Childs." From *Leslie's Illustrated Newspaper*, page 300, January 31, 1863. Courtesy of Minnesota Historical Society.

DAKOTA PRISON CAMP AT FORT SNELLING, November 13, 1862.
Photo by B. F. Upton. Courtesy of Minnesota Historical Society.

TEN

THE EXECUTIONS

As the days passed at Camp Lincoln on the Blue Earth River, Sibley expected to receive an order from the president to proceed with the executions. The names of the 303 condemned men had reached Lincoln's desk, and most Minnesotans assumed he would sanction their execution. A few newspaper editors were not so sure, hounding the president and even threatening him; one proclaimed that Minnesota would turn against Lincoln in the next election if he declined to act, or that an armed force would overrun the prison and slaughter the shackled Dakota men. Any failure to act, the *St. Paul Press* prophesied, would "fall like a thunderbolt of doom on every home in Minnesota."[1]

Sibley waited patiently for a few days for an order that never arrived, and in frustration, he turned the camp over to the very capable Colonel Steven Miller on November 15 and left for St. Paul. He had frequently sought a leave of absence and likely hoped to lend his weight to the lobbying effort in support of the executions. But day after day, no news arrived, bringing more concern at department headquarters, where Sibley and Pope communed. Could it be, they debated, that the president's views were expressed in the *New York Times* article: Lincoln would simply agree to execute a handful of supposedly "bad" men, making a token gesture to Minnesota?[2]

Steven Miller was a good man, a Republican friend of Ramsey who had joined Minnesota's First Regiment and fought in the East during the early Civil War battles. His likeability resulted in his election as Minnesota's fourth governor in 1863. But he assumed command at Camp Lincoln with some reluctance. The camp was hardly fit for human occupation, especially in mid-November, when temperatures occasionally dropped below freezing. A few rough-sawing carpenters had been hired before the arrival of the Indian caravan to build a shelter to hold the Indians. Thomas Williamson, upon visiting the place, described the new prison as being nothing more than "rough boards set on end," constructed in the form of a palisades in the shape of an "L." One leg was one hundred feet long, while the smaller one was only fifty. Because it was fifteen feet wide, the carpenters were able to put a leaky roof over the top. Into this building—if it could be called that—were crammed nearly four hundred Indians, with "a little straw being spread," as Williamson put it, to cover the frozen ground. The Indians literally lay side-by side, with little room to move; the only open spaces were several spots where fires were burning.[3]

While the prison offered some protection from the elements, Miller's troops had no such luxury. They pitched tents around the board enclosure; over two hundred soldiers then took turns guarding the prisoners, often marching without cold-weather gear and going to bed at night on the ground, with worn-out blankets. Miller, anticipating "the most intense suffering to my men," pleaded with Minnesota authorities for more blankets, clothing, and, obviously, better quarters. The Twenty-Fifth Wisconsin did commandeer a stone warehouse in Mankato, and Miller wondered why they could not be sent east and his troops occupy it.[4]

Miller did appreciate the men who Sibley sent to assist him. Being a hardware merchant before the war, he knew little about Indians. J. R. Brown, who knew them well, took charge of the prisoners, as superintendent. Given his knowledge of the language, he soon learned that some of the prisoners were plotting an escape. At one point, they even tried to burn the prison down; Brown put the fire out.[5] Several Renvilles were moved from Fort Snelling to assist. Akipa and Red Iron, both known medicine men, attended to the sick and brought some relief to prisoners, who were suffering from a variety of illnesses. But the handful of Dakota men and women who did the cooking for nearly four hundred Indians simply could not keep up with the demand. They lacked the necessary kettles and food that could be easily prepared.[6]

The food also left much to be desired, even that fed to the troops. "The blankets, sugar, and coffee, so-called, forwarded to this command are all unfit for use," Miller reported in utter disgust after surveying the situation on November 18. The sugar was "dark and dirty," even though the freezing troops consumed it.[7] The situation improved by late November when the Twenty-Fifth Wisconsin was ordered east. This freed up barracks in downtown Mankato. Yet the townspeople were increasingly agitated over the very existence of the Indians nearby and held meetings every evening regarding what to do about the situation.

Miller sensed the unrest in Mankato. Several junior officers visited the town and St. Peter and found dozens of men in saloons discussing virtual insurrection against the army. "I am informed that Mankato is in a blaze of excitement," the colonel declared. "The reports rapidly spread that Indians were about being taken below, and the citizens, as I am told, armed for the purpose of cutting loose the teams and killing the Indians."[8] At the "public meetings" in Mankato, several resolutions were considered; at least one offered a compromise: "Our motto shall be removal or extermination of every Indian from our State," the *Mankato Semi-Weekly Record* reported on November 15.[9] Other editorials promoted genocide. But it was not just Mankato; the colonel's scouts reported that "public meetings are being held upon the subject in all the villages and hamlets and secret associations are everywhere organized for the purpose of their [the Indians'] execution."[10]

Miller did visit with the Mankato townspeople a few days later, and he assured them that the Indians were not being moved. He implied that the executions would occur in Mankato, placating some of the more reasonable town leaders. Miller also surveyed the stone warehouse where the Wisconsin troops were housed and decided to build a much more permanent prison next door to it—the Wisconsin troops had agreed to leave on December 5. Miller reported to Sibley that while the Mankato residents seemed less hostile, he could "get the prisoners safely *into* town, but to get them *out* would require a small army."[11] The townspeople increasingly wanted to host the executions.

Meanwhile, Lincoln had surveyed the list of 303 condemned men, seeing little other than the number in front of their "unpronounceable" Dakota names. As the cabinet viewed the list—and leaked information regarding it to the press—several officials lent support to the concerns first voiced by Secretary Welles. Commissioner of Indian Affairs William P. Dole could hardly understand how "the indiscriminate punishment of men who have laid down their arms and surrendered themselves as prisoners partake more of the character of revenge than the inflection of deserved punishment." Dole, who had been to Minnesota and knew of the corruption at the heart of the Dakota conflict, pressed the president. It would be, he believed, "a stain on our National character" to execute them all. Secretary of the Interior Caleb Smith quickly concurred, urging Lincoln to acquire more information.[12] Lincoln, anguishing over the possibility of mass executions but also recognizing the political liability, penned a quick telegram to General Pope: "Please forward as soon as possible the full and complete record of their [the 303 Dakota men] conviction." If such a record did not exist—and at this time Lincoln knew nothing regarding the extent of the testimony—he then wanted Pope to have a "careful statement made" relative to the guiltiest of the men.[13]

Sitting down and revisiting every man's participation would take weeks. Accordingly, Pope had little choice but to send a message up the Minnesota River to have the trial records, which had remained with Colonel Miller, sent down. They were likely incomplete, with dates especially being suspect. And the term "judge advocate" likely was added quickly just below Olin's name. Pope knew, as did Sibley, that they would likely face criticism for the lack of evidence they revealed. Riggs carried the records to St. Paul, where they then began their long journey east; given the lateness of the season, they had to be sent to a railhead farther south.[14]

Sibley, Pope, and especially Governor Ramsey sensed that Lincoln's increasing interest in the issue might forestall the mass executions. The Civil War battles had gone better that fall, at least resulting in a stalemate or two, and winter brought a hiatus to combat. Nevertheless, Ramsey took up the charge of countering any criticism with a barrage of demands. In writing the president, he "hoped that every Sioux Indian condemned by the military court will be at once executed."[15] Ramsey had been one of the first western Republican governors to congratulate Lincoln on his election to the presidency in November 1860; politically, Lincoln needed to keep men like Ramsey in his corner if he were to be reelected in 1864. Other western states that had moved from the Democratic column to support Lincoln in 1860 were also interested in the Dakota trials. Among these were Minnesota's neighbors: Wisconsin, Illinois, and Iowa. Ramsey's letter reminded the president of the political realities.

General Pope did his best to support Ramsey, but he had to remain more cautious, given his position. Seeking to relieve Lincoln of his dilemma, on November 12 he telegraphed the president that if the federal government was unwilling to order the executions, then the "criminals be turned over to the state." This was certainly an option, because state officials had an argument regarding jurisdictional authority. Pope went on: "As to which of them murdered the most people or violated the most young girls . . . all of them are guilty more or less." More importantly, Pope continued, "I think it nearly impossible to prevent the indiscriminate massacre of all the Indians, old men, women and children," should the executions not go forward. The soldiers guarding both the sixteen hundred Dakota dependents at Fort Snelling as well as those in prison in Mankato were from Minnesota, and Pope believed that they might easily plot the mass murder of all those in custody.[16] Twelve days later, Pope pressed even further: he said the "organization of the inhabitants" continued in all the towns along the Minnesota River, with the "purpose of massacring the Indians . . . I trust that your decision and orders in the case will be transmitted as soon as practicable."[17]

Ironically, missionaries like Williamson nearly replicated the impatience of Ramsey and Pope while working for a different outcome. Williamson had first visited Camp Lincoln on November 13, being allowed into the prison compound by Sibley, who was still there. He nagged Sibley endlessly, finally being allowed to see some of the trial records just before they were sent to Washington. Sibley agreed to the request only if Williamson promised not to "publish, or print them." While he had little time to examine them all, Williamson went through as many cases as possible, focusing on the records of those Christian Indians who had been members of his church, especially Robert Hopkins and Peter Tapetataŋka.[18]

After reviewing this testimony and talking with many of the inmates, Williamson then penned a quick letter to a close friend in Washington, D.C., John C. Smith. As a prominent Presbyterian and a lawyer in what was still a small town, Smith knew Lincoln. While this relationship may have been slight, he did have very close ties with Commissioner of Indian Affairs Dole. Williamson took a legal approach in his letter to Smith: "I found them [the prisoners] ignorant of the specifications of the charges against them and of the testimony to support these charges as this testimony was given in a language they understood not." They were then "commanded" to tell the commission what they knew about the fighting, most frankly telling "everything which they had done which they supposed could be thought blamable." Smith got the letter to Dole, and the commissioner promptly made it official, recording it in the letters received file at the Indian bureau. Whether Lincoln saw it or not is not recorded, but certainly he knew of Williamson's efforts.[19] Two lobbying efforts were thus underway, one led by Williamson and the other by state and government

officials. The efforts came at an awkward time: given the better performance of the Union Army, Lincoln was considering an executive order to
free the slaves in the South, a heady decision in itself.

Williamson had gained access to the commissioner of Indian affairs,
and his letters to Seliah B. Treat at the American Board in Boston had also
brought some pressure on the administration, but his greatest adversary
at times seemed to be his old partner in the Dakota mission, Stephen
Return Riggs. He had been at the center of the trials and supported the
mass executions. Williamson worked on Riggs, urging him to convince
General Pope to reopen at least some of the trials. Williamson scoffed at
the testimony of David Faribault Jr., who, for some reason, had it out for
the Christians and helped bring about their condemnation. He then took
a new approach with Riggs: "I think we ought to pray and labor that these
Indians should have a new trial before unprejudiced judges who cannot be
found in Minnesota."[20]

Williamson's letters to Riggs were cautious and friendly, but after not
receiving a reply, he lashed out at Riggs in a letter to Treat at the American
Board. Riggs, he commented, seemed to completely accept as fact that
all the Indians, including the Christians, were guilty. Williamson could
hardly understand this given the fact that "members of my church saved
R. [Reverend] Riggs's family and my own and all traveling with us." The
missionaries seemed intent on saving their own converts, as most of the
Indians and mixed-bloods associated with Riggs's Hazelwood Republic
never even came to trial.[21]

The politics of this ongoing discussion soon involved the women
from the mission. Williamson's sister, Jane, wrote a long, detailed letter
to Mary Riggs, Riggs's wife, suggesting that both she and her husband
might not be "in possession" of all the facts. She blamed the conviction
of Peter Tapetataŋka on former agent and Indian trader J. R. Brown, who
had a trade house at the head of the Coteau des Prairies. Brown supposedly did brisk business in guns and gunpowder with both White Lodge's
and Inkpaduta's bands, those Indians who had first attacked Spirit Lake
in 1857 and then the settlers at Lake Shetek in 1862. Tapetataŋka's father,
chief Walking Runner, had supposedly blamed Brown for the violence at
Spirit Lake in 1857. Jane believed that Brown's meddling in Tapetataŋka's
trial was simple "revenge." While the trial records show no interference
from Brown, Jane obviously thought Mary's husband might intercede with
Sibley had he known these "facts."[22]

It took Stephen Riggs ten days to respond to Williamson, even though they were near each other. When he did on November 27, he stood his ground, acknowledging the hope that Williamson had in regard to his converts but recording his "strong doubts" regarding their innocence. When Robert Hopkins "confessed to being at Birch Coulee," Riggs wrote, even though he arrived after the battle had ended, "his fate was sealed before the commission." How Riggs could defend such a decision is rather baffling, as much of Faribault's testimony was faulty. Riggs ignored any influence that Brown might have had on the trials, telling Williamson only that Peter Tapetataŋka had joined a war party—despite his insistence that he did it to divert it from overtaking the Riggs and Willliamson party of sixty people who were fleeing east.[23]

Riggs may have been protecting his own role in the trials. He also had gone on record vetting his views in a letter to the president, dated November 17, the day he delivered the trial records to St. Paul and ten days before answering Williamson. "I feel that a great necessity is upon us to execute the *great majority* of those who have been condemned by the military commission," he wrote to the president. "This is required as a satisfaction to the demands of public justice." But then he backed off, knowing that Lincoln would eventually see the trial records. To execute so many, he mused, would certainly be "terrible," and that perhaps some deserved "clemency." Interestingly, nowhere does he admit that the vast majority of those convicted had only joined in a battle. Coming from a missionary who had worked with these Indians for twenty-five years, Riggs must have caused Lincoln to wonder about his motives; mass execution versus clemency was clearly contradictory.[24]

A week or more later, Riggs took his increasingly conflicting views to the press. In the November 29 edition of the *St. Pail Daily Press*, he asked for a "candid hearing." Many Indians were "doubtless guilty," he began, but others only took property—once again seemingly refusing to admit that many of the guilty Indians had only participated in battles. He then admitted that "forty men were tried in a day," and this did not lead to clear, concise decisions. Yet the demand of public justice "requires that the great majority . . . should be executed."[25] Bishop Henry Benjamin Whipple had been in the East visiting Minnesota troops. Upon his return, he quickly got up-to-date on the particulars regarding the trials. While talking to Minnesota troops in Virginia, however, he did spell out the causes for the conflict: "agents cheating them [the Indians] of their dues." Once back in Minnesota in mid-November, he eagerly read Riggs's letter and entered the fray. He first wrote Senator Henry Rice, suggesting that the country could not execute Indians who had surrendered. They were legitimate prisoners of war. While Rice vehemently disagreed, he sent Whipple's letter on to President Lincoln.[26]

Whipple had met briefly with Lincoln in late September while in the East, discussing the corruption in the Bureau of Indian Affairs and urging reform. At the time, the Dakota trials had not yet occurred. After returning to Minnesota, he set out to counter Riggs, specifically citing his letter in the *St. Paul Daily Press*. Whipple simply asked if vengeance was "something better than a savage thirst for blood?" God, he believed, "was not blind." He rejected the simple notion that "God has created any human being who is incapable of civilization." The Dakota conflict had erupted because of the massive corruption on the reservation; the government was as much at fault as the Indians. Lincoln had promised to address this cause after the Civil War had concluded.[27]

Even though Episcopal bishops could face a serious rebuke for making such public statements, Whipple continued his assault. The next day he penned a long letter to Henry Sibley. He challenged Riggs's assertions that the executions must go forward to serve "public justice," and he asserted that it was the "absence of law," the corruption—corruption that Sibley had readily participated in—that led to the disaster, not the depraved nature of Indians.[28] Sibley, a sympathetic Christian, responded to Whipple by defending his trials, describing them as being of "the character of a drumhead court martial." He explained that a military commission "cannot and is not expected to enter into details of a technical character which are judged necessary in ordinary criminal tribunals." This, of course, was untrue. Moreover, a drumhead court martial was permissible only when minor infractions occurred and could not be employed in capital cases. Sibley then took a different approach: if these Indians were not punished, there would be, "in my judgement, forthwith inaugurated a war of races which will extend along the whole frontier."[29]

While the debates went on in and out of the press, Colonel Miller and his troops still remained in temporary quarters in early December. Many of the companies of the Seventh Minnesota were stationed in the small towns around Mankato, where they received some cover from the elements. Miller had recruited spies to hang out in all the nearby towns. Disturbing news came from them on December 3: a large crowd of angry men came together in front of the court house at St. Peter. A newspaper later described them as having a rousing meeting in which they decided to exterminate the Dakota prisoners. They left with the intention of recruiting "sleighs and other vehicles" for a march on the prison. Once Miller got the news, he ordered companies from St. Peter and other surrounding towns to march to his defense. Most arrived the next afternoon, just in time.[30]

The vigilante party had formed by 8:00 P.M. on the evening of December 4 and headed along the road to Mankato. It took the crowd less than three hours to reach the town and march down Front Street (now Riverfront Drive) toward Camp Lincoln. One description placed over two hundred men in the mob, "principally Germans," although the *St. Peter Tribune* identified the organizers as Anglos, including Charles S. Bryant, a lawyer from St. Peter who later published an extensive account of the war using mainly captivity narratives.[31] Suddenly, to their left and right appeared large bodies of troops with fixed bayonets. Colonel Miller then rode to the front and ordered the crowd to drop its weapons or he would open fire. Quickly, the rioters abandoned their shotguns, hatchets, and even pitchforks. Miller then found a podium and addressed the rioters: "In a very decided manner, [he] expressed the contempt himself and his command felt for such a crowd composed, as it was, of men who ran from the foe leaving families to be butchered, or worse, to be taken prisoner." Miller recognized some of the men in the group as soldiers from his own regiment who had donned civilian dress. Having properly chastised them, Miller ordered the group back to St. Peter, with the loyal soldiers who had heeded his request for help marching behind them.[32] It was the second time that some Minnesota men had been accused of being cowards. (Lieutenant Sheehan offered the first indictment at Fort Ridgely.)

Miller realized that trouble still lay ahead. Although he heard of another mob organizing in Hastings, he most feared an attack from New Ulm, where a small force of the Seventh Regiment, under Captain William C. Williston, had been stationed. Militia Major Freiderich A. Brandt—the same man who had confronted Sibley on his march south with the prisoners on November 9—was organizing his own assault on the prison compound. Fortunately for Miller, Brandt set out on December 4 but turned back for whatever reason. Thereafter, Williston and his men became virtual prisoners in New Ulm. Miller sent urgent messages to both Pope and Sibley requesting a thousand men for reinforcements. This seemed unnecessary a few days later as over a hundred men who responded to the colonel's initial call stayed in Mankato. Sibley and Pope did urge Governor Ramsey to arrest Brandt, but Ramsey only issued a "proclamation" on December 6 condemning the effort to murder the prisoners. While this helped, Ramsey made it clear that if for some reason the president refused to act in regard to executions, he would urge state authorities to try, condemn, and execute the Indians.[33]

Miller's order on December 5 to retain over a hundred more troops in Mankato coincided with his ability to finally move his prisoners into their new compound next to the three-story Leech Building. The Leech Building became a makeshift headquarters and a warm barracks.[34] Uplifting as well was the fact that many of the troops under Miller's command began to praise his action. One soldier, Loren Collins, seemed to speak for a number of others when he wrote to a friend: "We felt that the Indians are our property and we shall protect them. If citizens want scalps, I can tell them of a place where they will find them!"[35]

Miller too seemed more certain of himself as the vast majority of his troops remained loyal in defense of the prisoners. In a somewhat jubilant mood, the colonel wrote regarding Major Brandt, "If Major Brandt approaches me . . . I shall send him to St. Paul in Irons, and if he resists, unless forbidden by General Sibley, I shall kill him upon the spot." He also laid down the law with the leading citizens of Mankato, who thereafter became increasingly cooperative. If they joined or encouraged any attempt to take the prisoners, he told them, "it will be necessary in self-defense to shell and burn a portion of the town." And after Williston at New Ulm managed to get several messages out regarding Brandt—mainly that he remained in a local saloon, increasingly unable to put together a force—he ordered the captain to arrest Brandt if he attempted to detain any more of his men.[36]

While laying down the law in Mankato, Miller then turned to reason on December 17. In Order No. 11, issued in Mankato, he urged leading citizens to think of the future of their town and state. Should she "suffer more fatally, in her prosperity and reputation, at the hands of our misguided, though deeply injured, fellow-citizens?" In other words, if executions occurred in Mankato, the country as a whole would be looking at the city and judging the actions of its founding fathers. Miller believed that the law, as laid down by the president, had to be obeyed to the letter at all costs.[37]

While the situation in Minnesota moderated, Lincoln remained seriously troubled by his new responsibility. Ramsey insisted that the entire group of 303 condemned men be executed. Lincoln had rejected such an argument, but he seemed uncertain about how to proceed. On December 1, he wrote the newly appointed judge advocate general of the army, Joseph Holt, asking for advice. "I wish your legal opinion," the president pondered, "whether if I should conclude to execute only a part of them [the 303 condemned men], I must myself designate which, or could I leave the designation to some officer on the ground?"[38] The *New York Times* article was correct in reporting that Lincoln wanted to select an arbitrary number of men to face the gallows. But was he thus thinking of offering Ramsey the authority, "on the ground," as he put it, to make the selections?

Holt quickly put a kibosh on the scheme. "I am quite sure that the power cannot be delegated," he wrote. It had simply never been done. Holt then offered some likely unwanted advice, suggesting that Lincoln should turn the trial records over to the attorney general "for the purpose of more satisfactory determining the question of their regularity."[39] The records had been in Washington for only a few days, but the meager evidence of guilt they offered was well known and regularity was far different from determining guilt. While it was standard procedure for the judge advocate general to review commission trial records—Holt had done so on many occasions when Civil War commissions were used—Holt obviously hoped to pin this responsibility on the attorney general. Lincoln obviously realized that "irregularities" might easily result in the trials being declared null and void; he decided to avoid both Holt and his attorney general.

Instead, Lincoln turned the trial records over to two trusted lawyers who worked for him in the White House. George C. Whiting had been associated with Know-Nothing politics in the 1850s, helping bring part of that group into the Republican fold, whereas the second lawyer, Francis H. Ruggles, was a sometimes state representative from Albany, New York. Neither had experience in doing the job that Lincoln asked of them, but they did know the law; they quickly recognized the total lack of due process that the trial records revealed. Lincoln did give them a directive on how to proceed. Whiting and Ruggles first had to identify any Indians who had committed rape, which was a crime punishable by death in most states. When it became obvious from the trial records that such a claim could be made in only two cases, Lincoln then directed the men to look at Indians who had joined parties in the countryside, even though there was seldom good evidence to convict them of murdering citizens. For sure, Lincoln's directives indicated that he intended to separate out those who had simply fought in battles, or were legitimate "prisoners of war," from those who might have killed civilians, or at least were in locations where civilians were killed.

What influence Whipple's argument had on the president was never recorded, but the great debate between officers of government, such as Ramsey and Sibley, and the missionaries had an obvious effect. On December 4, the two lawyers brought the president a list of forty Dakota men who they felt should face the gallows. This corresponds with the thirty-eight to forty men who could be placed at the scenes of some of the worst massacres. Whether Lincoln had suggested such a number as being politically acceptable in Minnesota or the two men simply arrived at that figure is unrecorded. Lincoln seemed extremely pleased with the list and promptly signed off on it.[40]

When word leaked that Lincoln had accepted an extremely short list, Minnesota senator Morton Smith Wilkinson from Mankato quickly took the floor at the Capitol in Washington on December 5. He gave one of the most vitriolic speeches in American history, an address dominated by misinformation and exaggeration. The substance of the diatribe was then sent to Lincoln in the form of a protest letter, signed as well by William Windom and Cyrus Aldrich. The letter noted that nearly ninety white women had been taken captive—literally dozens more than the actual number—and that their "testimony" demonstrated that they had been treated "by these Indians with a barbarity never known before," meaning that they had been raped. Actually, only two women testified in the trials that they had been raped. Even so, others would strongly imply abuse during the Sioux Commission testimony in 1863. One daughter of just thirteen, the letter continued, had her clothes "removed," and the Indians then "fashioned her upon her back on the ground." They repeatedly violated her to the point where she died. Another of just eighteen years "was taken, her arms were tied behind her, she was made fast to the ground, and ravished." The girl fortunately lived, Wilkinson claimed, "to testify against the wretches who had violated her." While no reliable testimony shows that a young girl died from rape and no evidence demonstrated that women had been tethered to the ground, the mistreatment of Mattie Williams and Mary Schwandt was well-known by this time. The Senate chamber, driven to a frazzle by the descriptions, quickly passed a resolution demanding that Lincoln turn over all "the evidence" that led to the conviction of the Indians.[41]

Lincoln seemed unmoved by the histrionics of Wilkinson and his two colleagues. He was dealing with a war in which thousands were dying.

His list of condemned men went off to General Pope on December 6, as the Senate debated the issue.[42] Yet Wilkinson had created such a stir that Lincoln decided to explain his actions to Congress in a long letter on December 11. "I caused a careful examination of the records of trials to be made," he began, noting that, unlike what Wilkinson had argued, just two records showed evidence of an Indian "violating females." This was of course true, as Lincoln was unaware of the circumstances involving the use of women captives as "wives" or of the terrible abuse suffered by the three women taken at Lake Shetek. He then informed the Senate that he had directed his lawyers to create a "classification of all who were proven to have participated in *massacres* as distinguished from participation in *battles*." Of this original group of forty men, one, Lincoln noted, had been recommended for a commutation of sentence to ten years in prison, leaving just thirty-nine on the list sent to Sibley. The one life saved was none other than Godfrey, the African American who had proved so useful in prosecuting other Indians.[43]

Lincoln fully understood the serious political implications of his decision; he might easily lose Minnesota in the next election. And he said nothing in his message to Congress about what he intended to do with the other 264 Dakota men who had been condemned to death. To smooth over relations with Minnesota, he sent then–assistant secretary of the Interior John Usher (soon to be secretary) to meet with Ramsey and Sibley. Back in Washington, Usher, after consulting with Lincoln, expressed the president's views in a letter to these men. Lincoln, he said, was in an awful position, as the trial records did not demonstrate the massive rape of women: "The evidence only discloses two instances in which it was done," Usher concluded. And the majority of men convicted had not killed civilians but only participated in battles. In an unusual and convoluted sentence, Usher then wrote the following to Sibley: "I do not understand from him [Lincoln] that he has determined not to approve of the finding of the court in more of the cases." In other words, he might authorize more executions. But Ramsey and Sibley needed to "explain to the people the difficulty in which the President is involved in this unlucky business." The political leaders of Minnesota must plead for calm, preserve order—allowing nothing like mob violence—and carry out Lincoln's initial order of December 6.[44]

Usher's plea may have persuaded Sibley to some degree, but the general continued to press for more executions and worried whether his troops could prevent a massacre of the Indian prisoners. This concern, whether real or exaggerated, was expressed in a final plea to Lincoln on December 15, in which Sibley described the "great excitement" in the state. He openly predicted "a collision between the US forces & the citizens." While Lincoln had initially set the execution date for December 19, Sibley, rather ironically, requested a delay of a week in the same letter. Part of the reason was the lack of preparations: Miller needed time to assemble a large concentration of troops in Mankato and he was having difficulty finding enough rope to accommodate thirty-nine men. He had informed Sibley that they might have to execute one man at a time unless more rope was provided. A second reason may have been the timing: a mass of unruly people was expected at the executions, and Sibley likely hoped that the numbers might be more manageable if the event were delayed into the Christmas holidays. Lincoln agreed and pushed the date back to December 26.[45]

As the particulars regarding the upcoming executions were made public, a huge debate broke out regarding the validity of the trials and, more importantly, what to do with the men Lincoln had temporarily spared. Isaac Heard, the trial recorder, started the affair on December 11, publishing a strong critique of Lincoln's message to Congress, claiming that in the battles "no quarter was given" and the condemned "should die." He then noted Riggs's role in providing the evidence.[46] The *St. Paul Pioneer* showed Heard's letter to Riggs, who wrote a rebuttal. For the first time, the Presbyterian minister broke with Sibley to some degree. He admitted that "the testimony *as recorded* was very meager in a good many cases." As for Sibley's military commission, he now noted that they were "good men," but they were biased: they "were trying Indians." "My sense of right," Riggs now lamented, "would lead me to give Indians as fair and full a trial as white men." Some men, he believed, deserved a new trial.[47]

Sibley likely simmered over Riggs's criticism as well as Usher's advice. In a long letter to Usher on December 19, he first thanked the administration for allowing a week delay, but he then reminded Usher of the terrible losses in Minnesota—six hundred settlers dead and $2 million in destroyed property. As for the military commission, which Riggs thought was biased, Sibley still openly defended it: the members "were instructed only to satisfy themselves of the voluntary participation of the individuals on trial, in the murders or massacres committed, either by his [the defendant's] voluntary confession or by other evidence." The "degree of guilt" was not an issue, he asserted; Sibley never explained what that meant. Nevertheless, like Riggs,

Sibley then relented a bit: "At least seven-eighths of these sentenced to be hung have been guilty of the most flagrant outrages," an obvious exaggeration. Given Lincoln's willingness to consider more executions, though, Sibley hoped to "obtain evidence" that would result in more executions.[48]

The news that Lincoln agreed to execute only thirty-nine men obviously seemed like a victory to Thomas Williamson. Riggs's admissions regarding the trials also encouraged him. Given the consensus for the removal of the survivors, however, Williamson turned to speculating about where these Indians might be placed. He did fear that much western land was incapable of agriculture; the Great Plains was still seen at this late date as a "Great American Desert." But if they were moved to a good place, his mission work might continue.[49] Whipple had similar thoughts, and he launched a newspaper campaign that not only called for resettlement but noted that there were many "friendly Indians" among the Mdewakantons, including those in Wabasha's and Wakute's bands, who had attended Hinman's church.[50] Lincoln's December 6 message offered a glimmer of hope for the future rebirth of the Dakota nation.

Another favorable trend surprisingly occurred among the vast majority of the prisoners in Mankato. Thomas Williamson had preached several times to the inmates in November and kept returning in December. He would preach for ten to fifteen minutes in one spot and then move to another, given the long length of the building and the problem with noise.[51] While he had lived among the Dakota people for twenty-seven years, he still struggled with the language. But he soon found willing listeners, men who seemed convinced that their traditional medicine men no longer had answers to serious questions regarding the future or even death. Williamson reiterated that the great God in heaven offered the only salvation. By December 1, Williamson reported to Treat that he had "never before preached" to such large audiences, "very seldom if ever audiences of any color who seemed to give such fixed attention."[52]

A few days later, Williamson's sister, Jane, showed up in Mankato and went out to the prison. She brought along writing material, and "many hands were outstretched" to receive it. J. R. Brown demanded that any letters leaving the compound be inspected. There was little need for the interference because the prisoners only wanted to address their relatives, who were encamped below Fort Snelling. Robert Hopkins and Peter Tapetaŋka helped men who had never written in the Dakota language before to form sentences.[53] Soon, dozens were doing it, and the mailbags leaving the prison grew ever larger. Most prisoners who wrote now professed a belief in Christianity. Wakute's son, who apparently had been involved in the mistreatment of Mary Schwandt and Mattie Williams, wrote: "If we live, I wish that all our wives and children may follow the law of the Great God." By late December, just before the executions, Williamson discovered that 137 Dakota men wished to be baptized.[54]

The religious revival at the Mankato stockade slowly caught on at the Fort Snelling camp. After the attack on the caravan near Hutchinson, Colonel Marshall became more cautious in moving the dependents to Fort Snelling, taking a circuitous route to avoid large concentrations of Minnesotans. Even so, along the route more stones and bricks were hurled at them, even from the doorways of isolated cabins.[55] After they arrived at the fort on November 14, they put up tepees in the river bottom, just above the Minnesota ferry. John Williamson held his first religious meeting three days later, attracting mostly women who were members of the various mission churches. Most of the Indians felt relatively safe because Marshall had organized a strong guard around the camp; no one came in or out without a pass. Williamson thought that Marshall was doing all in his power to protect the Indians under his charge, who, in a census dated December 1, numbered 1,601 persons (some had been allowed to leave).[56] Even so, when a young Dakota woman wandered too far from the camp to gather firewood, she was "seized by a number of soldiers and brutally outraged." It would be a hard winter for these people.[57]

Colonel Marshall ordered the construction of an "enclosure" to be built higher up the bank of the river, which the Indian dependents moved into on December 11. While it was safer, offering better air, it was also smaller, prompting Stephen Riggs, who visited the new stockade, to prophesize that it would lead to more illness and death—and it did. Measles broke out in December. While Williamson continued to preach, the most encouraging aspect of the entire experience was the growing exchange of letters with male family members at Mankato. A school even opened at the compound, albeit without much protection from the cold, teaching Indians to respond to the letters coming from loved ones in Mankato.[58]

Despite the debate over relocation and the Christian revival, by mid-December the attention of the state increasingly turned to Mankato and what everyone believed was going to be a spectacle. On December 20, The *Mankato Weekly Record* reprinted the Wilkinson, Aldrich, and Windom letter, helping to stir the fires of hatred that were already at a fever pitch. The editor, John Wise, speculated that Lincoln's decision to limit the number facing the gallows hinged on the possible recovery of white women and children still being held captive in the West. They needed to be ransomed from Little Crow's warriors, and a massive retribution would not help that cause. Yet the editor looked forward to the upcoming executions, publishing a garish poem that, following Sibley's aspirations, considered the upcoming event one of many to come: "Hemp on the throat of them. Hemp round the neck of them. Hemp under the ears of them, twisting and choking. Stormed at with shout and yell. Grandly they'll hang and well until the jaws of death until the mouth of hell takes the three hundred."[59]

Given such an atmosphere, Colonel Miller had his hands full in making preparations. A riot seemed in the offing as large numbers of ruffians arrived in town on December 18, expecting the event to occur the next day as originally planned. Miller sent out a call for more troops, explaining to Sibley that even though they would sleep outside, they were desperately needed. Officers from around Minnesota responded, and elements of the Sixth, Ninth, and Tenth Regiments soon arrived, increasing troop strength from three hundred men to over a thousand. Miller then ordered a grave to be dug. The grave would be seven feet deep, five feet wide, and thirty feet long. The bodies, when taken down from the scaffold, would be stacked in two layers. One location put it "on the low flat between Front Street and the river," which was a sandbar that had yet to freeze.[60]

The gallows posed a problem, however, as the colonel wanted all the men to be executed at once. The solution was a square donut, which was roughly twenty feet to a side, with a three-foot-wide platform around the perimeter. Eight large oak timbers, one at each corner and one in the center of each side, supported the gallows. Heavy oak hewn logs were placed along the top of these timbers, connecting them together. The ropes extended from them held the nooses. The gallows, a contraption that extended fourteen feet into the air, had another eight ropes attached to it, which came over the oak logs and converged on a ring attached to the very top of the center pole in the middle of the donut. Here, one blow from an axe to the rope holding up the ring brought the entire contraption down. Forty to fifty soldiers were marched out onto the platform to test its strength, and rather miraculously, it held.[61]

Seeing the massive display of troops and the preparation, the leading citizens of Mankato now offered Miller all their support, urging him to declare martial law. He did so, creating a group of "marshalls" in town who would preserve order. He also outlawed the sale or consumption of liquor within ten miles of the town.[62] Miller, a decent man with strong moral views, wanted to prevent any displays of inhumanity, either by the troops or the citizens who came to see the spectacle. In particular, there would be no drunkenness.

As the time fast approached for the fatal day Miller planned, a curious "blackrobe" came into town. Monsignor S. Ravoux approached Sibley, noting that the thirty-nine men needed to be separated from the other prisoners several days before the execution and offered a chance for redemption. Arriving on December 19, he had a note from Sibley asking Miller to provide reasonable assistance. Miller agreed and notified Williamson, Ravoux, and Riggs, who had just arrived, that on Monday, December 22, the designated men would be taken from the prison and housed in the Leech Building; the gallows would be completed by that day and located just in front of the building.[63]

Riggs had brought Lincoln's letter listing the men to be executed (believe it or not, Sibley thought he had misplaced it and hurriedly wrote Riggs, querying him regarding its whereabouts).[64] Riggs handed the letter over to Colonel Miller, who entered the prison compound and called out the names of thirty-nine men, all of whom seemingly stood up not knowing what for. Once at the Leech Building, Miller's adjutant, D. K. Arnold, then read to them the sentences of death, with Riggs doing the translations into Dakota. Newspaper reporters were allowed in. The occasion "was one of much solemnity to the persons present tho' very little emotion was mentioned by the Indians." One elderly Dakota man "knocked the ashes from his pipe and filled it a fresh," seemingly unconcerned.[65]

Colonel Miller then encouraged them to "turn their thoughts towards the Redeemer of the World." All were given a choice; they could pick Ravoux, a Catholic, or Williamson, a Protestant. Despite Williamson's devoted efforts in the months before, twenty-four selected Ravoux, and Brown inscribed their names for the priest, who would then spend considerable time with them over the next few days. Just twelve took Williamson, who ministered to them. On December 23, sufficient rope for nooses finally arrived from St. Paul, and the crowd of spectators slowly grew in number. Cavalry troops had also arrived, giving Miller an overwhelming force of 1,419 soldiers. There would be no rush on the prison, attempts at intimidation, or rocks thrown at the Indians when on the scaffold.[66]

Over the next few days, exchanges occurred between the condemned men and a variety of others who attended them. Akipa and Red Iron carried messages back and forth. At one point, Laying Up Buffalo (Tazoo in Dakota) whimsically told the two men that when they opposed the fighting during the war and called for the release of the captives, they faced many "taunts and threats." He now confessed: "We now see the wisdom of your words." While Laying Up Buffalo seemed complacent with facing death, others were far less so. Wabasha's son-in-law, Rattling Runner (Hdaiŋyaŋka in Dakota), remained bitter, writing his father-in-law that he had "deceived me" into thinking that if he surrendered, "all would be well." Now all he could do was ask that Wabasha take care of his wife and children, and that "when my children are grown up, let them know that their father died because he followed the advice of his chief."[67] Some of the news reaching the prisoners was good. Sibley's note of December 23 gave a reprieve to Round Wind (Tatemima in Dakota), the crier in Little Crow's village. Williamson had discovered that two young German boys had misidentified him as having killed their mother. After being removed from the list, the final count to face the gallows fell to thirty-eight.[68]

While Williamson worked to save innocent men, Riggs cunningly collected evidence that had a far different purpose. He interviewed the thirty-eight men, urging them to either admit their guilt or identify other guilty parties. Seventeen gave persuasive and believable statements proclaiming their innocence, while twelve seemed less able to defend themselves. Another nine joined groups who were either at Beaver Creek or Milford and were judged guilty by association. Sixteen men offered up the names of twenty-two Dakota Indians to Riggs, who they supposedly had witnessed killing white civilians. Of these newly identified men, Riggs concluded that eleven were in the prison compound, while the other eleven had escaped out onto the plains. Henry Millard, one of three mixed-bloods condemned, fingered Pine Tree (Waze in Dakota; case #75), indicating that Pine Tree had killed the woman that he, Millard, was to die for. Forbids His House (Tihdoniċa in Dakota; case #2), convicted for raping Margaret Cardinal, identified three men who joined him in killing members of the Cardinal family. One of them, Twin Baby Boy (Hokśidaŋnaŋpa in Dakota; case #55), remained in prison.[69] Somewhat later, Riggs turned all of this new information over to Sibley after he returned to St. Paul.

At 8:00 A.M. on December 26, Miller allowed the Dakota men facing death to have combs, paint, and even, for those who could procure them, feathers and beads. Despite the red paint and its meaning, the night before, some thirty-six had asked for baptism, and both Father Ravoux and Thomas Williamson administered the sacrament, even though Williamson questioned the validity of their convictions. While still shackled at the feet, they took great pride in preparing themselves. Virtually every man painted his face and hair bright red, a clear signal that they expected to soon start on the long, winding road that led to the Dakota Promised Land. But then, taking baptism with the Christians obviously had also occurred. What must have gone through the heads of these men? Did they simply think of covering all possibilities regarding the afterlife? But had their *Wicaśta Wakaŋs*, or medicine men, been right, they would soon face a Dakota woman, stationed in the middle of a river, and she would carefully look upon them. If they exhibited tattoos and red paint on their heads and body, with the paint coming from the iron oxide that they mined, they would pass over the river to paradise. If not, would the Christian God save them, as the missionaries had promised?[70] It was a conundrum that none spoke of.

Miller had also offered the best clothing that could be procured, and with the paint, feathers, and beads, they prepared for their death looking completely like Indians. And they acted the part, as not one of them broke down or exhibited weakness. They then shook hands with officials and reporters and had their elbows pinioned behind their backs, keeping their wrists and hands relatively free. Both ministers, Ravoux and Williamson, remained with them, offering brief payers and consolation. Finally, the shackles were taken off, and the men lined up, two at a time.[71]

The main door to the Leech Building opened, and they walked slowly to the steps of the gallows, covered on each side by a double line of sentries. Thousands of whites greeted them, most straining to see them. Some change of heart then hit a few of them. A soldier watched as they walked by: "They came out, some looking pale and sorrowful and some jumping and laughing," Eli Pickett began in a letter to his wife. "Some of them were striped with paint and some were painted entirely red, some were gaily smoking a pipe or cigar while others were seemingly deeply affected with the awful scene through which they were about to pass."[72] Close by were a thousand infantry that were stationed around the square gallows and nearly five hundred cavalry that kept moving around the outside perimeter. It all made for quite a spectacle.

As they mounted the gallows, the Dakota men began to sing. Laying Up Buffalo apparently started it, but then, as one newspaper observer put it, "all joined in shouting and singing . . . the tones seemed somewhat discordant and yet there was harmony in it." It seemed at times like song intermixed with dialogue. In a striking moment, as the men sang, their bodies swayed back and forth, somewhat in unison, not unlike the synchronized movements of the Medicine Dance that many of them had participated in numerous times. Some in the crowd thought it the "death song," commonly known to exist but seldom if ever heard by non-Indians. But a reporter from the *St. Paul Pioneer, Sunday Edition* spoke with men who knew the Dakota language, and they insisted that "no death songs" were chanted and that the singing "was only to sustain each other."[73] A few of the men shouted over the rest, explaining themselves to anyone who would listen. According to Dakota oral history—which may have been polished over time—one man proclaimed the following as he marched out onto the platform: "Today is not a day of defeat. It is indeed a day of victory. For we have made our peace with our creator and now go to be with him forever. Remember this day. Tell our children so they can tell their children that we are honorable men who die for an honorable cause."[74]

As they sang back and forth, eight soldiers—two on each side of the gallows—slowly adjusted the white caps that went down over the Indians' faces. Then the ropes were tightened around their necks. At that point, several men offered protests, one "exposing his person to the soldiers" and another spitting a cigar at them.[75] More songs emerged from the group, one likely the result of Thomas Williamson's sessions with them. Williamson had brought many hymnals into the prison, and hymns were sung often after the sermon. Dakota men and women loved to sing, and they frequently sung hymns in unison. Dakota oral history, as kept by Marcella R. Ryan Le Beau and several other Dakota Christian congregations in South Dakota today, asserts that at least some of the men broke into hymn number 141, the Dakota version of which had been memorized. The hymn was translated by Joseph Renville as early as 1842 and had apparently been sung many times at Christian services. It offered the following:

Great Spirit God, the things which are yours, are numerous and great. The heavens above you set in place, and earth received its form by your hands. The ocean depths respond to your will, for you can do all things.

That day you came to dwell on earth, bringing up all great joy. The Nations scattered over the world to them you gave the light of all life. O Jesus, O compassionate one, we offer praise to you.[76]

As the singing and the noise from the crowd of over three thousand people meshed together, the soldiers vacated the platform. At least two of the Dakota prisoners managed to clasp hands as they were so close together; others tried in desperation to do the same, with one grabbing the shirt of the man next to him. Joseph R. Brown then marched to the edge of the platform, carrying a large drum. He looked one more time at Colonel Miller and then beat out one note at sixteen minutes past 10:00 A.M. At this, William Duley, who assumed that his entire family had been killed at Lake Shetek, wielded the axe that severed the main rope. He swung once, but needed a second try; this time, the platform came crashing down. The Dakota men fell roughly two feet, snapping their necks. Thirty-six of the Indians died immediately, while the rope broke for Rattling Runner; soldiers hung him back up again. A final man, seemingly readjusting the noose, failed to have his neck broken, and his feet wrenched up and down for nearly twenty minutes as he agonizingly choked to death.[77]

For a moment, the crowd erupted in shouts of "huzza." Despite the awful scene, they could not, as one observer put it, "repress a shout of exultation." The soldiers, keeping their posts, joined in, raising their hats in jubilee. As one observer noted, a "boy soldier . . . his face pale and quivering . . . gave out a shout of righteous exultation." His entire family—mother, brothers, and sisters—had been killed by the Indians.[78] As the troops stayed at their posts, the crowd slowly dissipated, as most of the people had started the wagon trip home. There was little room to house anyone in Mankato, and given the fact that the spectacle had ended, a calm came over the town. Colonel Miller sent a message to officials in St. Paul—Sibley did not attend—that the "execution has been an entire success."[79] It was the largest mass execution in American history.

At the same hour, Miller ordered the bodies to be brought down and put in wagons. They were moved the hundred yards or so to the burial grave on the bank of the Minnesota River. There was still a question of trophies. Miller wondered if the ropes used to hang the Indians could be "sold" and the money donated to charities in Minnesota, in particular to hospitals. After ordering that each rope be brought to him, he was upset to discover that only thirty-seven showed up. As it turned out, his adjutant, Lieutenant Arnold, had secreted away the rope used on Chaska, Sarah Wakefield's defender. "I stole it," Arnold later proudly proclaimed. But Arnold ultimately relented, turning it over to Miller, who in the spring shipped it along with the axe that Duley had used to cut the rope to the Minnesota Historical

Society, where they remain today.[80] A search of many different archival collections has failed to reveal the existence of the thirty-seven other nooses.

After the sun went down, a number of men visited the grave site without being noticed by the soldiers. It was a cold night, and Miller never even thought of posting a guard over the mass grave. Because the grave was dug in sandy soil, it had yet to freeze. These men quietly began digging up the corpses. A doctor named Bootelier claimed a number of bodies. One was the inoffensive Chaska, the defender of Wakefield. A soldier, John Ford Meagher, wrote: "Among those resurrected was *Chaskadan* [Chaska]. We all felt keenly the injury he had done murdering our old friend Gleason in cold blood. I cut off the rope that bound his hands and feet and cut off one braid of his hair with the intention of sending them to Gleason's relatives." Gleason apparently had no relatives close by, and Meagher had the hair made into a "watch chain." Several bodies appeared in doctors' offices in a few days. The most celebrated of the lot taken, Cut Nose, ended up in Le Sueur, Minnesota, where Doctor William Mayo dissected his remains, sending parts to various places, including Michigan.[81]

The desecration continued into the wee hours of the morning and for at least another day. Upon hearing of the bodies, a doctor as far away as Chicago ordered three, offering to pay ten dollars apiece for them. Two more bodies ended up on top of the Blender Building in downtown St. Peter. They were left there to "dry out"; one was later placed prominently in Dr. Asa Daniels's office, which was on the ground floor of the same building. A soldier was finally sent to stop the grave robbing. He estimated that within a few days, only "a dozen remain" of the thirty-eight that had been buried. Colonel Miller, seemingly unconcerned but surprised by the invasion, finally placed a guard over the site.[82]

Four days after the executions, conditions had reached such a state of quiet that Miller no longer worried about the remaining prisoners; he even took the chains off of many of them. He asked for a thirty-day leave of absence, taking considerable pride in the fact that not one drunken citizen had been arrested during the ordeal and that oaths of retribution had been kept to a minimum.[83]

Arnold's admission of thievery in taking the noose that had killed Chaska did raise some questions. Wakefield's Chaska had not been on Lincoln's list. Wakefield exploded with rage when she heard that he had been executed. She suspected a conspiracy and had good reason to. After writing Riggs, who had been in the prison when the thirty-eight were identified, the missionary claimed that it was a simple mistake, that there were three men with the name Chaska, which led to confusion. Wakefield failed to accept the explanation, writing President Lincoln that "the mistake was intentional on the part of a certain 'officer' at Mankato, who has many children in the Sioux tribe." This could only be a reference to Joseph R. Brown, even though Riggs was more likely to blame. Lincoln apparently ignored the plea.[84] Thomas Robertson later claimed that yet another prisoner, a boy of sixteen who may have been white, was also executed by mistake. His name was White Man (Waśicuŋ in Dakota; case #318). The boy was "feeble of mind," according to Robertson and claimed to Riggs that he had killed no one.[85]

Sibley still remained upset over Lincoln's refusal to execute more Indians. He instructed Colonel Crooks, who had relieved Miller, to look for more evidence that could be used against those men still in the prison, even though they had already been tried once. Military law in the nineteenth century was different from civil law in that the Fifth Amendment to the Constitution, which protects against double jeopardy, mostly did not apply.[86] Sibley seemed somewhat exuberant when he received new evidence from both Riggs and Crooks. The general wrote Lincoln on January 7 that he would be able to send "additional evidence against a portion of the condemned men," but that there were still others in prison who were even more guilty.[87] Eleven of those identified by Riggs were in the prison compound and could be tried again. Wabasha and Taopi had been instrumental in collecting more evidence against them. The two chiefs could also be brought forward as witnesses.[88]

A serious challenge to Sibley's new plans emerged after Alexander Faribault, son of Jean Baptiste Faribault, one of the early leading citizens in Minnesota, hired a lawyer to defend his nephew, David Faribault Jr. David had testified against more Indians during the trials than any other witness, and then was convicted himself, saying only that he had been forced to go to the battles and fire a weapon.[89] Alexander had strong ties with Bishop Whipple, and the Bishop made sure that the argument against David's guilt went directly to President Lincoln. In his plea, David noted that he believed that "the object of the commission was merely to ascertain what parties should be held for a regular trial." In other words, Sibley's commission was simply an "inquiry." And further, that "there was no intimation to him that he was on trial for his life, or that there was any opportunity or occasion to make defense or to offer testimony or to have counsel."[90] The trial format was coming back to haunt Sibley. The failure to provide proper arraignment, the lack of time to provide for defense, the constant use of hearsay evidence, the refusal to allow counsel, and the massive use of self-incriminating evidence all seemed to be represented in David Faribault's trial. If David, a literate man, had no idea of what had transpired, what about all the others who were convicted. Most never even spoke English.

It was one thing for men of the cloth like Williamson and Whipple to call for clemency, but yet another for an articulate man who had faced the commission and been sentenced to death to condemn its procedures. The barrage of criticism still did not unnerve Sibley. He promptly wrote the president that "the actions of the military commission in the case of these prisoners has been fully justified." He conceded that "five or six" exceptions might exist, such as that of David Faribault Jr., who he named, yet he then proclaimed that "at least fifty more of those who are the most criminal, should be executed." The remainder could be sent to the federal prison at Alton, Illinois, to serve "life terms" at "hard labor."[91]

Ironically, even Sibley seemed to be vacillating, much like Riggs. He had once argued that four-fifths should be executed, but after Faribault's affidavit, he put the number at just fifty. He did scoff in letters to both the president and Whipple at the notion that there had been "so-called flags of truce," suggesting that the Dakota prisoners should be given rights as prisoners of war. Certainly, the Indians at Camp Release raised white flags and surrendered. Yet, Sibley responded in a decided manner: there was never an "intimation that the guilty whenever found, whether they delivered themselves up or were pursued and taken, would not receive punishment."[92]

In this atmosphere of argument and counterargument, Sibley moved forward with new arrests and new trials. But he organized the new military commission at St. Paul, where General Pope was still in command of the department. Pope, unlike Sibley, seemed increasingly uneasy about what new trials might do to his reputation unless they were properly conducted. Nevertheless, testimony began on April 15, 1863, in front of a new commission. It included charges against four men, with other trials supposedly planned in the future. The men were Ghost That Walks on Ice (Wayapamani in Dakota; case #361), His Own Tree Bud (Ciŋkpatawa in Dakota; case #261), His Red Weapons (Tawotawaduta in Dakota; case

#214), and His Own Thunder (Wakinyaṇtawa in Dakota; case #21). They were all on Riggs's list of men who had been implicated by those facing execution. Ironically, because the evidence against them came mostly from men who had been executed, it soon became problematic to present such evidence in court. The new commission, however, did allow several Indians to testify—this was generally not done in American courts at the time. The list included Wabasha, Taopi, four other Dakota men from the prison, and two Dakota women.[93]

Virtually all the testimony was hearsay, coming from people who were simply not at the locations where the crimes were supposedly committed. The Dakota wife of White Dog—the man who had distracted Marsh at the ferry and had been executed—spoke out against His Own Thunder, who had bravely saved George Spencer's life at the trade houses. She claimed that he killed the trader George Divoll, who was downstairs with Spencer when both were shot. While Spencer could have refuted the evidence, he did not need to. This time, defense counsel cross-examined the witness, and it was quickly pointed out that White Dog's wife believed that His Own Thunder had testified against her husband. The defense was also able to easily refute Wabasha's testimony because he could only suggest that he "had heard" that one of the defendants was in Milford and had killed a German settler.[94]

The trials took just four days, and the records were poorly kept. In the end, three of the men were acquitted, and while the fourth, Ghost That Walks on Ice, was found guilty, even Sibley by this time realized that Lincoln would not authorize the execution of one man when the testimony against him came from a woman named Hapan, whom the defense promptly pointed out had a grudge against the defendant.[95] This would not be the last attempt by General Sibley to try more Dakota Indians; other trials would occur in 1863 and 1865. But it was the last attempt to try the Indian men held in Mankato. The issue relative to the prisoners in Mankato and at Fort Snelling thereafter had little to do with guilt and increasingly more to do with where these Indians, the prisoners and their dependents, would end up.

While the trials were going on, most newspapers were focused on the bigger issue of deportation, only briefly mentioning the verdicts without giving much attention to the testimony.[96] As for the prisoners in Mankato, Lincoln slowly came to accept Sibley's views—that they could not be released. By spring, it appeared that the missionaries were only partially winning the debate over what to do with them. The trials at Fort Snelling, however, if they had accomplished anything, had demonstrated that it would be nearly impossible to get convictions for any of the others on Riggs's list. Given a fair trial, where the Dakota men did not incriminate themselves and counsel for defense could challenge witnesses, convictions were unlikely and perhaps impossible. The issue now was simply incarceration.

Worse, as summer dawned in 1863, fierce battles in the East seemed to foretell the nation's future. Conflict at Vicksburg and later Gettysburg took the eyes of Congress and the president far afield from Indian affairs in the West. Much of the burden for relocating the Dakota people fell to missionaries, local politicians, and even secretaries to the president. Those who sought to save the Dakota nation hoped to influence men like Sibley and Pope, who likely would make the final decision, one that might cast these Indians into the cauldron known as the Great Plains, where conflict with other tribes seemed inevitable, or save them by finding a hospitable home, where schools and churches might once again flourish from the ashes of war.

ELEVEN

DEPORTATION AND REBIRTH

As the celebrations over the executions subsided, Minnesota state officials turned their attention to the tragic circumstances surrounding the refugee problem in Minnesota. Thousands had still not returned to their farms and near famine was expected. Because Indians were legally wards of the federal government, considerable remuneration to pay for the destruction of the war was expected from Congress. And resettlement could occur only when security had been restored on the frontier. Any solution involved considerable troop deployment in the West over the winter and spring, and the state lacked the funds to support such an effort. Given the continued war effort in the East—and its immense cost—getting money from Congress would not be easy.

One issue seemed resolved. The Dakota people would have to be deported somewhere. While the Mdewakanton Dakota had started the war, the debate soon included others, especially the Winnebago Indians, who had a reservation south of Mankato, and the Anishinaabe, or Ojibwe, Indians who inhabited the northern reaches of the state. Ironically, little was said of the Sissetons and Wahpetons, who had held a reservation on the Minnesota River just to the northwest of the Mdewakantons. As for the Anishinaabes, they had sold much of their land to the United States in 1855 but had done nothing wrong during the rebellion. Fortunately, several of Lincoln's closest advisers had been in Minnesota just before the outbreak, and they knew that while corruption abounded when it came to handling all three tribes, at least two of them had remained loyal.

Trying to help the people of the state took precedence. Minnesota's congressional delegation hounded Congress for money to help fed the thousands of homeless and suffering people. The state borrowed $100,000 and distributed one quarter of it over the winter of 1862–63.[1] While such a stopgap measure did little to support people who were destitute, Ramsey's appeal for military financial aid proved more successful. Congress appropriated $250,000 to pay for salaries and food as well as teams and wagons that the army had confiscated. More money was added later, because Ramsey argued that the federal government was at least responsible for equipping and paying federal troops, several regiments of which stayed in Minnesota.[2]

An ambitious bill introduced by Cyrus Aldrich in the House on December 2, 1862, called for an appropriation of $1.5 million to help feed starving settlers and compensate them for lost farms and property. It never received a vote given the Christmas holidays. Aldrich brought up the bill again in February of 1863. Congress ignored him, focusing instead on confiscation of Indian lands; an act finally passed both houses on February 16 that "abrogated" all treaties made with all four Dakota bands, which, in effect, took away "all lands and right of occupancy" to the two reservations along the upper Minnesota River. It also invalidated "all annuities, and claims" of these Indians. The bill gave short shrift to the fact that the upper Indians, the Sissetons and Wahpetons, had not joined in the battles. In addition, Congress ignored the issue of corruption—perhaps because of the implications regarding colleagues.[3] Punishment of Minnesota Indians seemed to be the major focus of congressional debate.

In a curious twist, a few weeks later, on March 3, Congress appropriated $250,000 "for the suppression of Indians" in the future, funds theoretically designed to protect the state. The bill also noted that a handful of Indians had been involved in attempts to "save the lives of the whites in the late massacres." Such so-called "friendly Indians" were not identified, but supposedly they were men who had assisted Sibley and saved white settlers, such as John Otherday, Simon Anawaŋgmani, Peter Tapetataŋka, Paul Mazakutemani, Lorenzo Lawrence, and the Renvilles—mostly the Christian Indians from the Upper Agency. Whipple would soon add Taopi and Wakute.[4] Nevertheless, the most heated arguments in the Senate centered on compensation for lost property. Senators Henry M. Rice and Morton Wilkinson argued vehemently that people in the state needed $1.5 million to restart their farms and rebuild their homes; in essence, they advocated for Aldrich's failed legislation in the House. The Senate balked at this, offering a mere $100,000. When Wilkinson decried that this would be "an insult" to the state, the Senate finally agreed to set up the Sioux Commission to investigate claims, and it increased compensation to $200,000, the money coming from the 1862 and 1863 Dakota annuities.[5]

Once the commission set up shop at St. Peter in May 1863, it interviewed hundreds of people, including captive women who left narratives of their experiences, most of which were later published. The final report demonstrated that more money would be necessary to settle claims.[6] Unfortunately, as the early Minnesota historian William Watts Folwell notes, many of the claims for goods, farm equipment, cattle, and horses were the result of pillaging by organized gangs who invaded abandoned houses and spirited the goods to the east, selling them at considerable profit. The thievery was so bad that Thomas Galbraith dubbed the robbers "Algerines," a clear comparison to the pirates of Algiers. Thus, in 1864, Congress agreed to add another $1,170,374 to the settlement fund, bringing much needed cash to the Minnesota economy and helping many citizens return to their farms. In some cases, however, the money became a feast for lawyers and swindlers alike.[7]

While Congress sorted out claims, the revival at the Mankato prison swelled to include three quarters of the Dakota men who were incarcerated. The population included 326 men, 257 of whom were still condemned to death. The forty-nine who had been acquitted by Sibley's commission remained, but the guards had taken off their chains. Despite giving them a bit more room to walk and sleep, guard Daniel Densmore later wrote that when he opened the door to relieve the guard inside, "the stench nearly knocked me down." Facilities necessary for physical relief were not included in the prison, and inmates remained in the same clothes—or lack of them—that they had been captured in. At times, a few dozen were allowed outside. Those still in chains "came out hopping like a rabbit, [and] skipp [ed] across the yard." Part of the reason for the exercise was the growing fear of disease. Six men died of whooping cough in late January and February. The foul air in the prison was suspected as the culprit.[8]

Reverend Williamson seemed to ignore the stench, preaching to a growing crowd of willing listeners, sometimes several times a day. Some of those who listened could only recite the Lord's Prayer, but others, Williamson boasted, "prayed with such copiousness and fervency as to make it manifest that they are taught of God's spirit." All enjoyed the singing, and every worship had at least three, if not more, hymns. Some learned the hymns by rote. To better serve his growing flock, Williamson pressed his friends back east to send more hymnals. By January 20, Robert Hopkins had written down the names of some 230 Dakota men who were determined to "renounce heathenism" and be baptized as Christians, and the list grew thereafter. Yet Hopkins frankly confessed that likely only fifty fully understood what they were pledging.[9]

The revival suggested that the power of the traditional religious leaders had been broken. Even some members of the Medicine Society were selling their medicine sacks to eager entrepreneurs who resold them as souvenirs, some indication of the declining influence of the *Wicaśta Wakaŋs*. Yet Williamson remained cautious, especially when writing to Riggs. By January 27, Williamson was convinced that virtually every man in the prison, including some who had been baptized by the Catholic Father Ravoux, desired baptism, but he assured Riggs and Treat that he would move only when others had examined the level of faith in every man's heart. He had learned that Gideon Pond, who had remained interested in mission work, was coming to inspect the new converts. Williamson agreed to wait for his opinion before proceeding with baptisms.[10]

When Pond finally arrived in early February, he was astonished at the transformation among the Mdewakantons. In a few short weeks, most had learned how to write letters in their own language, often consisting of a simple phrase or two in Dakota, but many men rather triumphantly added, "I write this with my own hand." Pond also became convinced that most of the men asking for baptism were sincere. He even wrote a long letter, later published in the *New York Evangelist*, in which he stated that he had found at the prison "a manifestation of interest which is quite incredible." With help from Marcus Hicks, a local Presbyterian minister from Mankato, Pond and Williamson baptized 274 men on February 3. Williamson later confided to a friend that he had difficulty determining who among the group was completely earnest and who might simply be using religious conversion as a hedge against future execution. Yet he justified the effort by noting that in Biblical times, "the Apostles would have baptized them generally."[11]

Riggs decided to see for himself the level of commitment among the prisoners. Treat had written him for his views, knowing full well that Williamson would use the baptisms as a wedge for funds to continue mission work. "Can there be any sinister design in all this?" Treat suspiciously wrote to Riggs. "Do some hope, in this way, to escape hanging?"[12] Riggs reached the prison compound on March 23, and to his amazement he found Dakota men extremely attentive while at a service. Immediately afterwards, many turned to writing letters. Others practiced on slates while a few worked through Dakota grammar books. "I shall not be surprised if more Dakota learn to read and write this winter," he wrote to his wife, "than have learned before during the whole twenty seven or eight years of the ministry." Four hundred letters went out each week. Feeling a need to support the effort, Riggs helped officiate the first communion at the prison, which some 225 men took part in. Mrs. Hicks made the wine from dried currants.[13]

Riggs's enthusiasm had its limitations. Ever the suspicious Presbyterian, he spent several days quizzing men regarding the level of their commitment to Christianity. The usual problem with polygamy came up, as a number of older men had more than one wife. They hesitated when told that they could only have one.[14] In private correspondence with Treat, Riggs did express some concerns as some of the men told Riggs that they hoped "that the Lord would lose *that chain which was on his ankles.*" Riggs saw the conversions as *"mixed,"* as he put it, and that "deliverance from the chain has been one of the motives." The emotionally confused Riggs then concluded: "I think that no religious man can go there and spend a week in the prison, attend their meetings . . . and hear them sing and talk and pray and come away feeling that there is not a great deal of reality there."[15]

It had always been Dakota men who had resisted conversion, but now the letters they sent to their women and children at Fort Snelling often urged them to embrace the white man's God. Many dependents followed husbands and fathers and did turn to religion for help in surviving. By May, John Williamson, who entered the Fort Snelling compound every day to preach, had received some 140 into his church, most of whom were women and children. He often preached to crowds of over three hundred people, but there was competition. Episcopalian Samuel Hinman had entered the fray, well-fortified with hymn books in the Dakota language—those very books being first translated and published by Riggs and Williamson. Worse, Hinman apparently offered money to prospective converts, including the outspoken Paul Mazakutemani. Williamson asked his father in Mankato if Robert Hopkins might prepare a list of those Mdewakanton men who had been baptized. He intended to use it to influence their relatives at Fort Snelling.[16]

While life in Mankato was difficult, the dependents at Fort Snelling suffered even more from confinement. The new enclosure built for them was on roughly three to four acres of land, just over the bluff from the fort. In the enclosure some two hundred tepees were pitched; they were often so close together that one could not walk between them. A measles epidemic also swept through Minnesota in late December and January, killing mostly children, including many among the nearby white population. The Indians who survived the epidemic often caught what Riggs called "lung fever," a virus of some kind that on occasion proved fatal. The Indians at Fort Snelling suffered forty-two deaths by March 19, and according to the camp officer in command, Lieutenant William McKusick, some sixty more had died by the beginning of May—some 102 in all.[17]

To relieve congestion, McKusick allowed Bishop Whipple to take forty-two followers of Taopi to Faribault, resulting in considerable debate in the town. Another group of forty-two men, women, and children departed on February 2, being recruited by Gabriel Renville and Charles Crawford to inhabit a scout camp under Sibley's direction along the upper Minnesota River. They joined other mixed-bloods who had settled along the river. And a third group of mostly Franco- and Anglo-Dakota people, including the large families of Duncan and Scott Campbell, Joseph LaFramboise Jr., and several Renvilles, were allowed to move to Mendota, near Sibley's house. A few of the Christian Indians joined them, including Paul Mazakutemani, Simon Anawaŋgmani, and Joseph Kwanke. Most of these people spoke some English and dressed as whites, blending in with the local population. They remained in these locations for many years. These departures and the 102 deaths brought the total population at Fort Snelling to a mere 1,268 people by May, from an original figure of 1,601.[18]

The confinement of the Indians slowly produced some stability in the state. More importantly, while Pope sent the Third Minnesota back east to fight—they had always been troublemakers—he kept over three thousand men of the Sixth, Seventh, Eighth, and Ninth Minnesota Regiments in the state.[19] The only problem became finding billets for them during the difficult winter. Sibley had ordered that all towns along the frontier build stockades with bastions at two ends and provide barracks for soldiers.[20] The strategy included creating small garrisons stationed twenty miles apart. Fort Ridgely anchored the southern end of one line, extending east and north to Glencoe, thence north to Hutchinson, and beyond to Kingston, Forest City, Manannah, Paynesville, and, finally, Alexandria.[21]

From the last fort, a road had been opened to Fort Abercrombie, where Lieutenant Colonel Francois Peteler had built two large bastions "guarding the approach" to the fort, arming them with six-pound howitzers.[22]

When the troops designated to occupy these stations arrived, however, most of the towns had failed to build barracks. By late November, at Glencoe, Lieutenant Colonel John Thomas Averill sent some men home "from military necessity." As Averill put it, "Even cattle & horses standing rounded up in the storm are offering up prayers to be *relieved of Life.*" The story was much the same in Forest City, where Captain George F. Pettit wrote that half his men were in tents, "which seems rather severe at this season of the year." The problem with housing even existed at Fort Ridgely, where a company of troops slept in tents in December; as a result, over thirty became sick.[23] The situation near Alexandria was unique. The "barracks" at Chippewa Lake, according to its commander, was "not at all suitable—having no flouring but the ground; with roofs of mud and straw put loosely together which during the spring rains must certainly make them untenable."[24]

Conditions did improve at all these outposts come February. Even at far-off Alexandria, troopers completed a full stockade and built suitable barracks. The same was true in the other towns where lumber was plentiful and the troops pitched in to make a better place for themselves. Sauk Centre became the central command headquarters for the northern line of defense, as it housed the largest concentration of troops. It had billets for officers, a hospital, barracks for two complete companies, and a stable for two hundred horses.[25]

A second line of defense emerged south of the Minnesota River. While Fort Ridgely remained the cornerstone, soldiers occupied Madelia and built smaller posts on the Watonwan and Cottonwood Rivers. Some troops even occupied Tivoli, near the Winnebago Agency, and patrolled as far south as Jackson. New Ulm, finally brought under law and order by Sheriff Roos, organized its own town militia of thirty-three men. Roos had his men dig a ditch around the nine-block center of town and fortified the balance of it "with 12 log houses and a wall." The wall alone measured six thousand feet in circumference, likely being the most defensible position in all of Minnesota.[26] These fortifications, extending from Alexandria in the north to Jackson in the south, offered the sort of protection that newspaper editors and common citizens had been demanding for months. Slowly, come spring, farms were being reoccupied, although a report from Mankato indicated that a full half of them were still abandoned.[27]

Conditions for the troops might easily have been better than for many of the refugees, who were desperate by spring. A reporter for the *St. Paul Daily Union* noted that while there were "a great many poor people" living in the city, not far from the press building, "twenty-three" could be found in an afternoon "whose husbands had been killed by the Indians. They have in the aggregate, fifty-seven children, mostly small." There were "so many to be provided for here and elsewhere, that it is impossible to prevent suffering." Examples abounded, including "Mrs. Zimmerman, a blind woman" who lived hear Fort Ridgely. Her husband and two older sons were killed, but she and two small children survived. More names appeared, including a "Mrs. Dietrich," whose husband was killed when the Dakota attacked the recruiting party in Milford Township. Several, including Mrs. Castor, Mrs. Roebke, and Mrs. Sentzke, all lost their husbands in the battle for New Ulm. Worse, many of the children died during the measles epidemic that hit the city in December, a result of the cramped conditions in which they had to live. Mrs. Sentzke, who survived the measles outbreak, then lost her daughter six months later in yet another epidemic. She had a picture taken with the dead girl in her lap, an act commonly done in that day. Some aid arrived in late 1864 after Congress appropriated funds, but just two years later a terrible drought hit the state, devastating crops. There was starvation in many areas of the state, especially ones where recovery from the war had just begun.[28]

While the state went through a slow recovery, the issue of what to do with the Dakota prisoners finally came to a head in mid-February. Jonathan Nicolay, Lincoln's secretary, took on the task of finding some suitable location for relocation. He queried Sibley, who responded that as soon as navigation opened on the Mississippi River, steamboats could send the Indians down river, and then west. Upon being asked, Dakota Territorial Delegate J. B. S. Todd—a cousin to Mary Todd Lincoln—suggested Crow Creek on the upper Missouri River. Todd had never been there, but the spot had once sheltered an old trading post, suggesting the existence of plentiful wood for fire and ground to grow crops. Sibley had no objections to this. But as for the prisoners, he remained adamant: "I cannot suppose for a moment that the condemned men are to be released." Because it increasingly looked as though no more executions would occur, he proposed to send them to "confinement at hard labor" at some military prison.[29]

While Sibley had little knowledge of prisons, General Pope had been making inquiries. Governor Samuel J. Kirkwood of Iowa agreed to confine the Dakota men in Davenport, where four barracks remained unused. Some months after the Dakota men arrived, the Union would place five thousand Confederate prisoners of war nearby on Rock Island, in the Mississippi River, making it a center for incarceration.[30] Agreeing on locations, Secretary of Interior Usher asked for bids to remove the Indians by steamboat. The lowest bid came from Sibley's old partner in the fur trade, Pierre Chouteau Jr. of St. Louis. He offered to remove the Dakota at a rate of $25 per head. The numbers involved had been determined; the 277 males and 16 females at Mankato would be sent to Davenport. Another 1,318, mostly Dakota women and children, would be located at Crow Creek. Officials kept the removal secret for fear of citizen reprisals in Minnesota.[31]

On the morning of April 22, a company of infantry formed in a line leading from the door of the Mankato prison to the steamboat landing, two hundred yards to the north. The door opened and the 277 "condemned men," most still in chains, were quickly loaded on to the steamer *Favorite*. They huddled together near the boiler on the lower deck. While the forty-nine acquitted men also came on board, they had a free run of the upper deck.[32] Hardly anyone in Mankato noticed the departure, although several citizens confronted Colonel Miller after learning of it, nearly attacking him for allowing the Indians to leave.[33] A reporter who happened to know of the departure managed to stay on board. He was somewhat shocked when "the sober [*sic*] faces lit up with the red glare of the furnace fires" suddenly burst into song. They sang praises "to the white man's God in old Presbyterian tunes."[34]

As the *Favorite* approached Fort Snelling, a group of Dakota boys, fishing on the levee, saw the red blankets of their fathers and uncles as the steamboat pulled into the dock. Shouts of joy went up the bank as Dakota women and children poured out of the compound to catch a glimpse of their kindred. While Colonel Crooks, in command at the fort, allowed the women and children to leave the compound, he did order a company of troops to stand between the Indian prisoners and the dependents. Fearful of reprisals from whites nearby, the forty-nine innocent Indian men on board, including Wabasha, were very quickly unloaded, and the boat hurriedly left the dock. Many women on shore assumed that the boat was taking the men to their executions. The journalist from the *St. Paul Press* recorded the moment: "The scene was pitiable in the extreme, and defies description . . . the poor creatures [on shore] flung themselves on the ground, and pulled their hair, and beat their breasts with anguish."[35] As the *Favorite* disappeared down river, Colonel Crooks informed the crowd that the men were simply being moved to another prison. As the passion subsided, the women and children could hear their men sing a favorite hymn, a refrain of which went:

> Jehovah, have mercy upon me
> For they own mercy sake
> Thy loving kindness is very great
> Therefore place me in thy heart[36]

Camp McClellan at Davenport, named for the then-famous general, would be the home for most of these men for the next three years. The stockade "pen," as it was called, consisted of a square, some two hundred feet per side. Four buildings inside the enclosure served as barracks for the prisoners, a hospital, and quarters for guards. The compound was located on high ground, and it had good water. It was a major improvement over the prison in Mankato. John Williamson, who stopped to inspect it, was somewhat shocked to see that the government had selected a "delightful place," with ample room in the buildings for all.[37] Thomas Williamson convinced Lincoln to pardon forty inmates in April 1864, including Robert Hopkins and Peter Tapetataŋka. This left just 237 in the prison.[38]

With the departure of Hopkins and Tapetataŋka, the religious revival sputtered a bit. In June 1866, when it was finally decided to release these men—even General Ulysses S. Grant agreed that keeping them confined served no further purpose—Agent Jedediah Brown counted 182 men, forty women, and twenty-five children when they boarded the steamer *Cora*, on route into the west. This total included some forty men who had surrendered at Pembina in 1864. They were bound for Nebraska, where they were given new lands at a reservation that was later called Santee. Brown found his charges to be "much more intelligent" than he expected, as they could all now read and write in their own language. They regularly had religious services, and of the group some 157 still professed to be Christians. When the final group of 247 was shipped west, some ninety-five remained behind, buried somewhere along the banks of the Mississippi River. Death became common in military prison camps during the Civil War; hundreds of Confederate men died at Rock Island in just over a year.[39]

Plans to deport the remaining dependents, then located at Fort Snelling, had also been kept relatively secret. On May 5, 1863, when the steamer *Davenport* arrived at the levee at Fort Snelling, however, a hostile crowd gathered. They soon began throwing rocks at the Indians, despite the efforts of Colonel Crooks to drive them back. Worse, the *Davenport* had brought up some seventy-six so-called "contraband" people, forty of them men. They had agreed to serve General Sibley as teamsters in a western military campaign against Little Crow's band that coming summer; unfortunately, they brought smallpox with them. Despite the threat, the first contingent of 762 Indians boarded and were housed on the lower deck of the *Davenport*. Several women had been severely injured by rocks, but the men, including Wabasha, Wakute, Passing Hail, and Good Roads, remained unscathed. Reverend Hinman joined them as the boat slipped away from the dock. The next day, another 547 dependents boarded the *Northerner* and headed down the river.[40] Mary Riggs, Stephen's wife, watched from afar as the steamer went out of sight. "May God have mercy on them," she lamented, "for they can expect none from man."[41]

The two riverboats took different courses. The *Davenport* traveled down river to St. Louis and then pushed up the Missouri to Crow Creek. John Williamson, who joined the exodus on board the *Northerner*, soon discovered that they would transfer to a train at Hannibal, proceed on to St. Joseph, and then make the rest of the trip by steamboat. Once at St. Joseph, on the Missouri River, they waited patiently for the riverboat to take them farther up the river. By this time, there were no troops with them; there was not even an Indian agent or doctor. Williamson and Lorenzo Lawrence acted as agents and interpreters. Yet everyone behaved properly. Most of the women and children were quite relieved to have left Minnesota and the confines of the compound at Fort Snelling. Even so, on the final leg the boat was overcrowded. Williamson likened the experience to "the middle passage for the slaves," as many Indians became sick.[42]

By the time they arrived at Crow Creek, some twenty-four Dakota Indians had died, and the number was growing. Part of the problem included the same incompetence and corruption that had plagued the agencies before the war. Clark W. Thompson, as Indian superintendent, was in charge of bringing in food supplies and agricultural equipment. But his wagons started for Crow Creek only a week before the Indians arrived, and along the way, the steamboat *Isabella* hit a snag near Vermillion. Some $40,000 worth of food and farming equipment was off-loaded;

much of it apparently never reached the agency. While a herd of cattle had been purchased, only sixteen of the forty head found their way to Crow Creek. According to Thompson's own calculations, he intended to provide enough food to sustain the Indians through August, when other supplies would supposedly arrive. But the river was low, and the snows came in early, leading to half-rations by September and near starvation by October.[43]

Death rates at Crow Creek climbed appreciably by late summer, mainly from illness and malnutrition. By spring 1864, roughly two hundred had died, many of them children.[44] While the camp consisted originally of roughly 600 women, 600 children, and 116 men, literally two-thirds of the remaining people left Crow Creek by spring 1864. By this time, even Dakota Indians knew that crops could not easily be grown in the rocky soil, which dominated the landscape around Crow Creek. Worse, the early years of the 1860s had been dry on the Great Plains, leading to dust storms. John Williamson, who stayed at Crow Creek, thought that "the greater part of the river bottoms are so dried up that cattle would have a hard chance to make a living." Muddy water, heavily salted pork, a little dried corn, and half-rations were a prescription for disaster.[45]

Large numbers of these Mdewakanton Dakota people fled east to join the scout camp established by Gabriel Renville near Coteau des Prairies, while others migrated south to Fort Randall, where younger Dakota women prostituted themselves to the officers and men for food. Crow Creek had become a death camp with a mere five hundred occupants remaining from the original group of just over thirteen hundred that had been dropped at the location the year before. Thus, it took little prompting to convince the Dakota Indians, then spread out along the Missouri River, to move once again in spring 1866 to new lands at Santee, Nebraska. Here, the Mdewakanton band was finally reunited, as their men, released from Davenport, arrived first, with their dependents following. The location soon solved the supply problem, and within a few years, the Santee Indian Reservation had been surveyed, lands that these Indians live on today.[46]

The Mdewakantons who fled to the plains, including Little Crow, soon found it difficult to procure food for themselves, much like those at Crow Creek. While General Sibley tried to capture the elusive chief during a campaign in the summer of 1863, he only met and fought with Sissetons and Wahpetons at the so-called Battle of Big Mound. These Indians, close relatives of the Mdewakantons but people who had not participated in the

Minnesota war, saw Sibley as an invader. The engagement settled nothing. Even so, over the next two years, Gabriel Renville made contact with his Sisseton relatives and coaxed many of them to join his camp at the head of the Coteau des Prairies. His uncle, Scarlet Plume, became a staunch advocate of peace and led many of his people into the camp. In 1867 Renville, J. R. Brown, and others proceeded to Washington, D.C., where they negotiated a new treaty creating the Lake Traverse Indian Reservation in eastern Dakota Territory. The treaty also made allowances for other Sissetons and Wahpetons who had not joined Renville by giving them a reservation at Devils Lake, in northeastern Dakota Territory. Given their refusal to join Little Crow in August and September 1862, the government had no justifiable reason to punish them and no reason to take their lands in Minnesota, but it did anyway; the new reservations then became something of a reparation for the misappropriation of government power.[47]

The efforts of Renville and others to resettle the Sissetons and Wahpetons were hampered to some degree by Little Crow and his followers, who fled in September 1862. Various sketchy reports came in relative to their location and circumstances, with most suggesting that nearly two hundred Dakota warriors—many connected to the soldiers' lodge—had fled along with some of their women and children. They lingered near the Missouri River come fall, feasting on captured flour and pork. Little Crow had a plan: he wanted to unify all the plains tribes—the Yankton, Yanktonai, and even the Arikara—as well as the Sissetons and Wahpetons. Little Crow's four wives were Sissetons, and they had stayed with him. The chief's first efforts to affect an alliance, however, failed, as he and a number of his men approached the Arikara village just up from the great bend of the Missouri shortly before Christmas. The Dakota warriors shouted and waved robes in the air, seeking a council, and the Arikara responded with gunfire, killing eight of Little Crow's followers.[48]

Failing with the Arikara, Little Crow turned east to Devils Lake. He had spoken with Standing Buffalo and other Sisseton leaders, including Gabriel Renville's uncle Scarlet Plume, shortly after fleeing from the Minnesota River valley. Neither Sisseton leader had given him any encouragement. By late fall, the refusal was even more pronounced, with Standing Buffalo bluntly stating: "You have already made much trouble for my people. Go to Canada or where you please, but go away from me and off the lands of my people."[49] The suggestion of going to Canada had been brought up during the war, as many Dakota men recalled that they had once been allies and brothers to the British during the War of 1812. Accordingly, several Mdewakanton *akacita* warriors, accompanied by a few Sissetons, journeyed north to see the Canadians.

This small party reached the quaint little Métis community of St. Joseph first, located along the border some fifty miles west of Pembina. St. Joseph, a community increasingly specializing in the buffalo hide trade, possessed little semblance of law and order; the traders in town did brisk business with the Dakota Indians in goods taken in Minnesota.[50] The Dakotas set up a base camp north of St. Joseph, as some of their group visited St. Norbert, Winnipeg, and Fort Garry, all in Manitoba. While the part-French and part-Cree Métis wanted little to do with these Dakota Indians, British officers at the fort feared what they might do if all the Sioux bands united in a war. Bishop Alexandre-Antonin Taché at St. Boniface thus welcomed the Dakota delegation into his church, and Governor Alexander Grant Dallas explained that the Queen's government wanted peace and would offer them some food.[51]

Meanwhile, more Dakota Indians showed up at St. Joseph, feasting on food that the community could ill afford to share. These families had consumed all the plundered goods taken from Minnesota, and many of their horses had died during the difficult winter. Father A. André, the locale Catholic priest, thought they would soon "consume the little food we have—the stomack [*sic*] and mouths of the Sioux are more to be feared than their axes and arrows."[52] Canadian traders, including Norman Kittson, who was closely associated with Sibley, met the Mdewakantons and Sissetons in council. The Indians made it clear that "they had been driven from their old homes by the Americans and that they intended to keep the country around Devils Lake."[53]

Governor Dallas of the Hudson's Bay Company, at Fort Garry, certainly had the right to fear a Dakota invasion, especially if some two thousand Sissetons and Wahpetons joined in the effort. But this seemed unlikely given that, through a St. Joseph trader named John Dease, Standing Buffalo sent a strongly worded message to Dallas that he and his people were never involved in the Dakota War, and that they had no intention of joining Little Crow. To make matters worse, Scarlet Plume, Renville's Sisseton uncle, and Sweet Corn were lobbying for peace among the Yanktons and Yanktonais, the former tribe having a treaty with the United States that provided annuities.[54] Any hope of a Plains Indian alliance was fast fading.

Even so, Little Crow decided to play the Canadian card. He needed ammunition and food for his people. He gathered a band of sixty warriors and twenty women together and headed north to speak with Governor Dallas. Arriving at Fort Garry on May 29, 1863, several councils occurred. Little Crow and his men wore George III medals given to Dakota chiefs during the War of 1812, and they even displayed British flags. But Dallas, now convinced that the chief had a dwindling following and realizing that many of his Métis constituents might provoke a war, refused requests for assistance. In the end, Little Crow was left with only one minor concession: he asked Dallas to write General Sibley to see if any terms existed for creating peace. Dallas did write, informing the general about the council and explaining how he had refused to help the Dakotas. The failed diplomacy had an immediate impact on Little Crow; within a few weeks, the number of his followers dwindled to less than two dozen. While no record exists of his thoughts, he seemingly sank into a state of depression, believing that his people had now forsaken him.[55]

Returning south in mid-June, Little Crow gathered a handful of supporters to make one final raid into Minnesota, taking along his seventeen-year-old son Wowinape. In later testimony, the boy claimed that the intent of the raid was to steal horses—many had been lost during the winter. Yet a second motive seems likely. In the previous fall, as the fighting at Fort Ridgely and New Ulm failed to produce victory, Little Crow had a frank talk with Susan Brown. He knew her husband, Agent J. R. Brown, well, and he was distantly related to Susan. He noted that the war had not gone well and that he would be blamed for its failures. He sensed that his only recourse was to return to the Big Woods for one final foray "and kill as many whites as possible," and that "if he should get killed himself it would be all right."[56] It was better to die in the Big Woods, a place he loved, than to be captured and hanged by Sibley.

The saving of face and the will to sacrifice one's life when the cause seemed hopeless was common among Plains Indians. The fact that Little Crow had reached that point where death was preferable to escape farther out onto the plains, or even attempting to live in Canada, seemed even more obvious when he approached his son and asked him to "carry his [medicine] bundles."[57] When Dakota warriors reached old age, making it impossible to use their medicine effectively in war or in the hunt, they often gave such sacks, or bundles, to the eldest son. To some extent, the passing symbolized the transition from one generation to another, but it also foreordained death. Whether the purpose was to steal horses, kill more whites, or die in the effort was never clear. All that is certain is that sixteen men followed the chief south—one was likely his brother, White Spider, who surrendered the next year—all that remained of his following. Virtually all of them, except Little Crow and his son Wowinape, decided to head back north after they attacked and massacred the family of Amos Dustin near Howard Lake. This was some twenty miles north of Hutchinson. Little Crow and Wowinape proceeded on by themselves.[58]

They camped several miles north of Hutchinson, where the berries had ripened to the point where the two men spent several hours picking fruit. Toward evening on July 3, a shot suddenly rang out, striking Little Crow in the groin; he returned fire. A second shot then glanced off his rifle and lodged in his chest. Wowinape, hiding in the dense underbrush adjacent to the raspberry patch, quickly came to his father's aid, but there was little he could do other than give him some water. Little Crow died within a few minutes, and Wowinape prepared him as best as possible in the time-honored ceremony that a Dakota person needed for the trip into the afterlife. He dressed his father in new moccasins, set his body as upright as possible, and wrapped it in a blanket.[59]

Wowinape then took the two guns that Little Crow carried and left for Devils Lake, hoping to find his mother there. Instead, a patrol from Sibley's summer expedition captured him. Sibley created yet another military commission to try the young boy.[60] While the officers found him guilty, General Pope overruled their sentence of death, claiming that under Article 65 of the Articles of War, Sibley had no right to organize a commission while in the field, due to the prejudice of the officers, an ironic conclusion that rankled Sibley because it brought his use of a military commission to try the 392 Dakota men the previous fall into question. Wowinape joined the Dakota prisoners at Davenport, Iowa, and was deported to the Santee Reservation two years later.[61]

In death, Little Crow suffered a humiliating fate. His body was dragged into Hutchinson, where Nathan and Chauncey Lamson were honored as heroes for killing an Indian. They received five hundred dollars from the state legislature once it was recognized that they had killed Little Crow.[62] The corpse looked somewhat like Little Crow, but such an identification was not confirmed at first. On July 4, kids put firecrackers in the chief's nostrils and other orifices. One bashed in his skull with a rock. Ultimately, they tired of the fun, and the body, after its head was severed, was dragged to a refuse pit. Here, a week or two later, still curious as to the identity of the Indian, Captain James H. Bond of the Minnesota volunteers examined the corpse. This quickly revealed the broken arm bones that Little Crow had lived with since 1846, when his half-brothers tried to kill him. Knowing that it was indeed the famous chief, Bond took the scalp that had been taken off his head on the first day, the skull, and the forearms and donated them to the Minnesota Historical Society.[63] They remained on display until 1919, when their ghoulish nature led to their being put in storage. Embarrassed, the society shipped his remains to South Dakota for burial in 1971.[64]

As more Mdewakantons fled north to Canada to escape the military campaigns that hounded them, the total reached roughly five hundred people. Many had congregated near Long Lake, just over the border from St. Joseph.[65] Canadians soon tired of their presence and worked with American officials to rid themselves of at least some of these intruders. Ninety-five, including at least one of Little Crow's wives and his brother, White Spider, surrendered to Major Edwin Hatch in January 1864. Hatch had occupied Pembina the year before. Canadians then drugged and kidnapped Little Six and Medicine Bottle, both of whom were tried in St. Paul the next year and executed. With these final actions, punishment came to a close. It had been devastating for both sides.[66]

For many decades, Little Crow became the symbolic "devil incarnate" in Minnesota history books, an enigma whose actions seemed incomprehensible to most learned men and women.[67] He was viewed as the man who agreed to the treaty of 1851 that opened up Minnesota as well as the leader of the most brutal and destructive ethnic war in American history. Yet he had always been a leader who sought compromise and accommodation with the invading white man. Rather than a symbol of butchery—there is no evidence that Little Crow ever killed anyone—he was the ultimate example of the tragic nature of the Minnesota-Dakota War. While there were others—Little Six, Red Middle Voice, and Cut Nose—who would have contended against the civilization movement that Brown finally brought to the reservations, had Little Crow been supported by the government, had fair treaties been negotiated, had food and money annuities been fairly distributed, the civil chiefs who Little Crow spoke for could have maintained order. Unfair treaties and corruption led to the creation of the soldiers' lodge and its leaders, such as Cut Nose, who usurped the power of the civil chiefs.

Those responsible for the treaties and the corruption that led to the conflict were never punished. Some, such as Sibley and Pope, went on to become honored generals, while others like Ramsey and Miller served as governors; Ramsey later served in the U.S. Senate and as a cabinet official. They need to be viewed as coconspirators in this corruption, along with many officials of the Bureau of Indian Affairs, including agents, superintendents of Indian affairs, commissioners of Indian affairs, interior secretaries, and even congressmen and senators. They openly knew of the corruption; were told of it by missionaries, clergymen, and numerous Indian leaders; and did nothing to correct the abuse. Many of these men later had buildings and counties named after them.

Those who suffered the most were innocent settlers, who experienced horrible deaths at the hands of violent men who had reasons to be upset, but not so many that they can be pardoned for hacking women and children to death with tomahawks. And a large number of the thousands of mostly poor settlers who survived received little compensation from the money authorized by the government for claims. And what is certainly as excruciating, a civilized government, led supposedly by Christian men, seemingly wrought with a desire to do little to save over a thousand Mdewakanton women and children, sent them to a desolate place called Crow Creek where many perished, some literally from starvation.

Most citizens of the state today hardly know the history behind the few monuments that were put up to honor those who fought on both sides; one marks the spot where the hangings of the thirty-eight Dakota men occurred, another honors just a handful of Indians who remained "loyal" to the state, a third was erected in a desolate spot where fourteen settlers at Lake Shetek perished in a slough, a fourth was put up in 1910 near where the misnamed Wood Lake battle occurred, and, finally, a fifth, a simple caricature of Little Crow, recently appeared in downtown Minneapolis. In many ways, the war defines the state's early history, but people in the state, both Indians and whites, have been unable to find consensus regarding what the war means and who was responsible for it. Perhaps such consensus is impossible, which is also a tragedy. For we all know, those who do not know their history—and the mistakes that came with it—are doomed to make similar errors in the future.

And let us finally remember that accounts that are designed to vilify or honor the actions of men and women who are undeserving of either only compound the problem associated with facing our past. Both history and biography are often a complex mixture of factual assessment and supposition, but if written objectively, it can never be part of a political agenda. And the struggle for that objectivity has always been with us and always will be. Remember, indeed memorize, the Greek historian Polybius, who wrote in about 150 BC: "If we make deliberate misstatements in the interest of our country or of friends or for favor, what difference is there between us and those who gain their living by their pens . . . readers should carefully look out for this fault and authors themselves be on the guard against it."

NOTES

ABBREVIATIONS

AAG   Assistant Adjutant General

ABCFM   American Board of Commissioners for Foreign Missions Papers

AGO   Adjutant General's Office

CWS-A   Center for Western Studies, Augustana College, Sioux Falls, S.Dak.

DRNRUT   Documents Relating to the Negotiation of Ratified and Unratified Treaties

DWWD   Department of the West and Western Department

LR   Letters Received

LS   Letters Sent

MHSA   Minnesota Historical Society Archives

MS   Minnesota Superintendency

NARG   National Archives and Records Administration, Record Group

OIA   Office of Indian Affairs

SPA   St. Peter's Agency

WHS   Wisconsin Historical Society

CHAPTER ONE

1. See the description of Taoyateduta in Gary Clayton Anderson, *Little Crow, Spokesman for the Sioux* (St. Paul: Minnesota Historical Society, 1986).

2. Genealogy Appendix, ibid.; Thomas Hughes, *Indian Chiefs of Southern Minnesota* (Mankato, Minn.: Free Press Company, 1927), 53.

3. Stephen Return Riggs, in "History of the Dakotas, James W. Lynd's Manuscript," *Minnesota Historical Society Collections* 2, part 2 (1860–67): 147–48; Asa W. Daniels, "Reminiscences of Little Crow," ibid. 12 (1908): 514.

4. Anderson, *Little Crow*, 71–73; E. Dudley Parson to Editor of *Minneapolis Journal*, c. 1938, in Allan Woolworth Papers, MHSA.

5. Elizabeth Wiŋyaŋ to Mary Collins, 1885, Collins Collection, CWS-A.

6. See Henry Rowe Schoolcraft, *Narrative Journals of Travels from Detroit Northwest through the Great Chain of American Lakes to the Sources of the Mississippi River in 1820* (Albany, N.Y.: E. E. Hosford, 1821), 298.

7. Henry Sibley gave a somewhat different description, taken from the mixed-blood Jack Frazier. It suggested that the person seeking the afterlife would have to cross a body of water larger than a river, perhaps even an ocean—but Frazier had never seen an ocean. See Sibley, *Iron Face: The Adventures of Jack Frazer, Frontier Warrior, Scout, and Hunter* (Chicago: Caxton Club, 1950), 203.

8. Gary Clayton Anderson, *Kinsmen of Another Kind: Dakota-White Relations on the Upper Mississippi River, 1650–1862* (Lincoln: University of Nebraska Press, 1984), 124–26.

9. John Nairn Narrative, MHSA.

10. Anderson, *Kinsmen of Another Kind*, 77–101.

11. Samuel W. Pond, "The Dakota or Sioux in Minnesota as They Were in 1834," *Collections of the Minnesota Historical Society* 12 (St. Paul: Published by the Society, 1908): 322–23; reprinted in Pond, *The Dakota or Sioux in Minnesota as They Were in 1834*, intro. Gary Clayton Anderson (St. Paul: Minnesota Historical Society Press, 1988), 6–10 (hereafter cited as Pond, *Dakota as They Were in 1834*). On population, see Taliaferro to T. Hartley Crawford, September 30, 1839, NARG 75, LR, SPA.

12. Philander Prescott, *The Recollections of Philander Prescott: Frontiersmen of the Old Northwest, 1819–1862*, ed. Donald Dean Parker (Lincoln: University of Nebraska Press, 1966), 58–61.

13. Ibid., 61.

14. Pond, *Dakota as They Were in 1834*, 13–16, 68–69. Taliaferro concluded that village "hereditary chiefs" were nearly gone by 1839, concluding that villages were ruled by "little kings, many of whom possess but little influence with their people." See Taliaferro to Crawford, September 30, 1839, NARG 75, LR, SPA.

15. Population numbers vary. See, for example, ibid.; Thomas S. Williamson to Amos Bruce, September 30, 1840; Amos Bruce to Superintendent John Chambers, June 15, 1841; and Statistical Report, September 1, 1846, all in NARG 75, LR, SPA.

16. Anderson, *Kinsmen of Another Kind*, 236.

17. Pond, *Dakota as They Were in 1834*, 139.

18. A detailed description is given in Sibley, *Iron Face*, 17–19; Pond, *Dakota as They Were in 1834*, 60–65.

19. See Prescott, *The Recollections of Philander Prescott*, 78–79.

20. Pond, *Dakota as They Were in 1834*, 126–29.

21. See Bertha L. Heilbron, ed., *With Pen and Pencil on the Frontier in 1851: The Diary and Sketches of Frank B. Mayer* (St. Paul: Minnesota Historical Society, 1932), 163; (St. Paul) *Minnesota Pioneer*, January 2, 1851; Pond, *Dakota as They Were in 1834*, 120–21.

22. Pond was extremely critical of the Scalp Dance because of the "illicit intercourse" that it encouraged. See Pond, *Dakota as They Were in 1834*, 122. See also Stephen R. Riggs to David Greene, October n.d., 1838, ABCFM, MHSA.

23. Taliaferro Journal, July 14, 1830, MHSA; E. D. Neill, "Battle of Lake Pokeguma," 1841, *Collections of the Minnesota Historical Society* 1 (repr., 1902): 142–45; Pond, *Dakota as They Were in 1834*, 132–33; Prescott, *Recollections of Philander Prescott*, 79–80.

24. Anderson, *Kinsmen of Another Kind*, 124–26; Strong Earth's Speech, May 30, 1827, Josiah Snelling Diary, MHSA.

25. William Aitkin to E. R. Williams, February 5, 1833; Lyman M. Warren to Henry Schoolcraft, March 8, 1833; Taliaferro to Elbert Herring, June 6, 1833; Taliaferro to William Clark, June 12, 1833; and Lieutenant Jefferson Vail to Clark, March 4, 1833, NARG 75, LR, SPA.

26. Pond, *Dakota as They Were in 1834*, 28–29; Sibley, *Iron Face*, 56. See also Fur Returns as compiled by Taliaferro, St. Louis Superintendency, William Clark Papers, Kansas State Historical Society. The numbers reported represent only hides turned over to the traders. One estimate suggested that half, or more, of the deer hides taken were used domestically by the villagers. Such numbers still are small in comparison to the number of deer taken in recent decades from both Minnesota and Wisconsin, numbers that range into the hundreds of thousands.

27. Pond, *Dakota as They Were in 1834*, 28–29.

28. Ibid., 45–46. An excellent example of a "soldiers' kill" is in Sibley, *Iron Face*, 98–100.

29. Edmund C. and Martha C. Bray, eds., *Joseph Nicollet on the Plains and Prairie: The Expeditions of 1838–1839 with Journals, Letters, and Notes on the Dakota Indians* (St. Paul: Minnesota Historical Society Press, 1976), 108, 279–80; Taliaferro Journal, October 18, 1835, MHSA; Stephen Return Riggs, "Dakota Portraits," *Minnesota History Bulletin* 2 (1918): 536–37. Stephen Return Riggs, *Mary and I: Forty Years with the Sioux* (Boston: Congregational Sunday-School and Publishing Society, 1880), 109. For the concern of the army, see Major John Bliss to General Henry Atkinson, May 3, 1834, NARG 94, LR, AGO.

30. Pond, *Dakota as They Were in 1834*, 97.

31. Heilbron, *With Pen and Pencil on the Frontier in 1851*, 202; George Featherstonhaugh, *A Canoe Voyage Up the Minnay Sotor; with an Account of the Lead and Copper Deposits in Wisconsin; of the Gold Region in the Cherokee Country; and Sketches of the Popular Manners* (London: Richard Bentley, 1847; repr. St. Paul: Minnesota Historical Society Press, 1970), 378–79.

32. Elizabeth Winyaŋ to Mary Collins, 1885, Collins Collection.

33. Pond, *Dakota as They Were in 1834*, 86–89.

34. For information on the Medicine Dance, see the many references in Pond, *Dakota as They Were in 1834*; Sibley, *Iron Face*; and Amos E. Oneroad and Alanson B. Skinner, *Being Dakota: Tales & Traditions of the Sisseton and Wahpeton*, ed. Laura L. Anderson (St. Paul: Minnesota Historical Society, 203), 188–90.

35. Prescott's article in Henry R. Schoolcraft, ed., *Information Respecting the History, Condition, and Prospects of the Indian Tribes of the United States* (Philadelphia: J. B. Lippincott, 1865), 2:195.

CHAPTER TWO

1. Ramsey to John Speel, June 5, 1849, Alexander Ramsey Papers, MHSA.

2. See Charlotte Ouisconsin Van Cleve, *Three Score Years and Ten: Life-Long Memories of Fort Snelling, Minnesota, and Other Parts of the West* (Minneapolis: Harrison and Smith, 1888), 11, 18–19.

3. Historian William Watts Folwell wrote of Taliaferro that he was "cordially hated by all who could neither bribe nor frighten him to connive at lawbreaking to the harm of the Indians." Nevertheless, a careful reading of Taliaferro's journals demonstrates that he often had a greater sense of his importance than was warranted. See Taliaferro Journals, 1819–39, MHSA; William Watts Folwell, *A History of Minnesota* (St. Paul: Minnesota Historical Society, 1921–30), 1:141–42.

4. See Charles Eastman's letters of September 8 and 27, 1930, to H. M. Hitchock, Edward Ayer Collection, Newberry Library, Chicago, Illinois.

5. Captain W. J. Jouett to the Secretary of War, August 3, 1832, NARG 94, LR, AGO; Taliaferro to Clark, August 15, 1833, NARG 75, LR, SPA; Taliaferro Journal, July 27, 1835, MHSA; Elbert Herring to Alexis Bailly, September 1, 1835, NARG 75, LS, OIA.

6. See Sibley, *Iron Face*, 70–76; Anderson, *Little Crow*, 36–38.

7. Rhoda R. Gilman, *Henry Hastings Sibley: Divided Heart* (St. Paul: Minnesota Historical Society, 2004), 34–46; Sibley to McLeod, January 27 and April 27, 1848, McLeod Papers, MHSA. A few of the older traders, such as Alexander Faribault, remained independent after Sibley arrived, but they took their goods and sold their furs to the American Fur Company.

8. Ibid.; Anderson, *Kinsmen of Another Kind*, 100–104.

9. In the 1830s, Taliaferro hired Philander Prescott and Gideon Pond to break some land with a plow near Lake Calhoun, very likely the first productive agriculture in Minnesota.

10. Anthony F. C. Wallace, *The Long Bitter Trail: Andrew Jackson and the Indians* (New York: Hill and Wang, 1993).

11. For the treaty negotiation, see Chauncey Bush Journal, Treaty Council Notes, September 25, 1837, Bentley Historical Library, Ann Arbor, Michigan.

12. Anderson, *Kinsmen of Another Kind*, 158–59. A census of the Mdewakanton mixed-bloods gave 143 men. They received payments of from $400 to $1,500. See ibid., 160.

13. Stephen Return Riggs, *Grammar and Dictionary of the Dakota Language* (Washington, D.C.: Smithsonian Institution, 1852). The volume was later reprinted by the Minnesota Historical Society (see repr. St. Paul: Minnesota Historical Society, 1992).

14. For descriptions of the missionaries, see Linda M. Clemmons, *Conflicted Mission: Faith, Disputes, and Deception on the Dakota Frontier* (St. Paul: Minnesota Historical Society Press, 2014), 29, 61–64. See Williamson Sermon, "Planting of the Gospel in Minnesota and among the Dakotas," ABCFM; Mary Riggs to mother, September 9, 1837, Riggs Papers, MHSA.

15. Riggs to Treat, March 7, 1848, ABCFM.

16. Anderson, *Kinsmen of Another Kind*, 177–80.

17. The law is discussed in Folwell, *A History of Minnesota*, 1:272–73.

18. Sibley made it clear to Ramsey how difficult it would be to convince the Indians and their mixed-blood relatives to sell under such circumstances. See Orlando Brown to Commissioners Ramsey and John Chambers, August 25, 1849, *House Executive Document* 5, 31st Congress, 1st Session, at 979–80. See also Sibley to Ramsey, September 15, 1849, Ramsey Papers, MHSA.

19. Riggs to Sibley, September 7, 1849, Sibley Papers, MHSA; Riggs to Ramsey, October 13, 1849, NARG 75, LR, MS; Anderson, *Kinsmen of Another Kind*, 177–80.

20. For quotes, see Alexander D. Campbell to Martin McLeod, January 3, 1849, McLeod Papers, MHSA; McLeod to Sibley, January 3, 1850, and January 28, 1851, Sibley Papers, MHSA; Riggs to Treat, January 12, 1850, ABCFM; Ramsey to Brown, February 22, 1850, and Brown to Ramsey, March 22, 1850, NARG 75, LR, MS.

21. Anderson, *Little Crow*, 55–60.

22. Fred Sibley to Joseph LaFramboise, March 10, 1852, Sibley Papers (letterbook), MHSA.

23. McLeod to Sibley, March 25, 1846, Sibley Papers, MHSA. See also Gilman, *Henry Hastings Sibley*, 118. The ball game is described in Gwen Westerman and Bruce White, eds., *Mini Sota Makoce: The Land of the Dakota* (St. Paul: Minnesota Historical Society, 2012), 111–19.

24. Anderson, *Kinsmen of Another Kind*, 185. A good description of the council grounds and the vast array of people who gathered at Traverse des Sioux is found in Gilman, *Henry Hastings Sibley*, 122–24.

25. Anderson, *Little Crow*, 59–60.

26. See Traverse County, Minnesota, Oral History Project, located in Wheaton, Minnesota.

27. Anderson, *Kinsmen of Another Kind*, 185–87.

28. Anderson, *Little Crow*, 55.

29. Ibid., 61–62.

30. Ibid., 62–63.

31. "Journal of the Joint Commission," August 5, 1851, NARG 75, DRNRUT.

32. Ibid.

33. Ibid.; Charles Kappler, ed., *Indian Affairs: Laws and Treaties* (Washington, D.C.: Government Printing Office, 1904), 2:588–90; William E. Lass, *The Treaty of Traverse des Sioux* (St. Peter, Minn.: Nicollet County Historical Society, 2011).

34. Anderson, *Little Crow*, 58–64.

35. McLeod to Luke Lea (CIA), December 13, 1851, NARG 75, LR, MS; Sibley to Dousman, November 13, 1851 and February 14, 1852, Dousman Papers, WHS.

36. Quotation in Sibley to Ramsey, May 15, 1852, Ramsey Papers, MHSA. See also McLean to Lea, August 19, 1851, NARG 75, SPA; McLean to Ramsey, January 15, 1852, NARG 75, LR, MS.

37. The interview is found in the *Minnesota Pioneer*, May 27, 1852.

38. Gilman, *Henry Hastings Sibley*, 110–19.

39. The best example of this comes in the negotiations over the 1858 treaty, when the delegation, led by Little Crow, was stunned to discover that they owned no lands in Minnesota. See Anderson, *Little Crow*, 103–5.

40. The quote is found in Riggs to Treat, July 31, 1852, ABCFM. See Prescott's account in Prescott, *Recollections of Philander Prescott*, 188.

41. Kappler, *Indian Affairs: Laws and Treaties*, 2:588–92.

42. The receipts signed by the Indians are found in various places, including Power of Attorney for Ramsey, September 8, 1852, NARG 75, LR, SPA; and Wahpekute Power of Attorney, November 8, 1852, Ramsey Papers, MHSA.

43. Sibley had a torrid exchange of letters with Hercules Dousman over the money. See Sibley to Dousman, October 16 and 31, November 12 and 13, and December 29, 1851, and February 2, 5, 14, and 24, and March 4, 1852; and Rice to Dousman, February 23, 1852, Dousman Papers, WHS. See also testimony in *Senate Executive Document* 61, 33d Congress, 1st Session, at 124–288.

44. See "Mdewakanton Claims," NARG 75, LR, SPA; Ramsey Crooks to Sibley, December 30, 1852, and "Amount Received for Account of American Fur Company," December 1852, Sibley Papers, MHSA.

45. Dousman Account Records, 1852, Green Bay and Prairie du Chien papers, WHS.

46. Ibid. The figure of $144,984.40 was calculated during the Ramsey investigation. See Folwel, *History of Minnesota*, 1:283.

47. Fred Sibley to Pierre Chouteau, July 16, 1850, and August 26, 1850, Sibley Papers (letterbook), MHSA; Fred Sibley to Henry Sibley, July 16, 1850; September 26, 1850; and July 17, 1851, Sibley Papers, ibid.; Sibley Credit Book, March 1851–April 1852, ibid.; Sibley to Dousman, May 24, 1854, Dousman Papers, MHSA.

48. Sibley to Dousman, May 14, 1854, Dousman Papers, MHSA. The debt from the 1820s and 1830s is documented in the Green Bay and Prairie de Chien Papers, WHS.

49. In one final act, Ramsey had the audacity to demand $5,000 of Sibley and Dousman to cover his expenses at the investigation, because he was protecting their interests. See *Senate Executive Document* 61, 33d Congress, 1st Session; Folwell, *History of Minnesota*, 1:281–82; Anderson, *Kinsmen of Another Kind*, 193–97; and Prescott to Ramsey, May 11, 1852, NARG 75, LR, MS.

50. See Newton H. Winchell, *The Aborigines of Minnesota* (St. Paul: The Pioneer Co., 1911), 554.

CHAPTER THREE

1. See petitions from "Residents of Wabasha," 1852; Petition of "Whites from Shakopee," June 13, 1853; and Agent Robert G. Murphy to Willis Gorman, February 16, 1854, NARG 75, LR, MS.

2. Gorman to CIA, September 6 and 8, 1853, NARG 75, LR, MS; Williamson to Treat, July 18, 1853, ABCFM; Riggs to Treat, December 5, 1853 and January 30, 1854, ABCFM.

3. Quotation in Bailly to Gorman, October 27, 1853, NARG 75, LR, MS; Gorman to George Manypenny, June 1, 1853, Gorman to Faribault, June 18, 1853, and J. W. Hancock to Gorman, July 1, 1853, ibid. See also Hancock to S. B. Treat, June 14, 1853, ABCFM.

4. See Gary Clayton Anderson, *Ethnic Cleansing and the Indian: The Crime That Should Haunt America* (Norman: University of Oklahoma Press, 2014).

5. Bailly to Murphy, October 9, 1853, NARG 75, LR, MS; Lee to Acting Governor J. Travis Rosser, April 20, 1854, and Lee to Major F. N. Page, April 23, 1854, NARG 393, LR, DWWD, 1853–61.

6. Pond to Treat, November n.d., 1853, ABCFM.

7. Daniels, "Reminiscences of Little Crow," *Minnesota Historical Society Collections* 12 (1908): 520–22.

8. Gorman to the CIA, January 9, 1854, and Murphy to Gorman, March 4, 1854, NARG 75, LR, MS.

9. The five-year term was apparently proposed by Secretary of Interior Alexander H. Stuart in October 1852, but it was never acted on. Ramsey had been much more optimistic, telling the Indians that they could stay for a longer period. The issue finally reached the president's desk when it became obvious that any investment in buildings at the new reservation would be foolish unless the Indians were to be kept there. See Stuart to the CIA, October 2, 1852, and Secretary of Interior to the President, April 5, 1854, with note from the President, April 13, 1854, NARG 48, LS, Indian Division of the Secretary of Interior.

10. Lee to Page, July 8, 1854, NARG 393, LR, DWWD, 1853–61.

11. Lucius F. Hubbard and Return I. Holcombe, *Minnesota in Three Centuries* (St. Paul: The Publishing Society of Minnesota, 1908), 3:273.

12. Memoir of John H. Case, *Hastings Gazette*, July 1, 1921; Philander Prescott to Ramsey, May 11, 1852, NARG 75, LR, MS; Daniels, Reminiscences, MHSA.

13. Hubbard and Holcombe, *Minnesota in Three Centuries*, 3:270–71.

14. See G. A. McLeod to Martin McLeod, May 18, 1853, McLeod Papers, MHSA; Testimony of William Quinn, Antoine J. Campbell, and George Spencer, 1885, NARG 75, Special File 274.

15. See *North-west Democrat* (St. Anthony), March 22, 1856. For the corrupt nature of the system, see Williamson to Treat, February 22, 1858, ABCFM; Daniels, Reminiscences, MHSA; Anderson, *Kinsmen of Another Kind*, 205–7.

16. See Manypenny's treaties in Kappler, *Indian Affairs: Laws and Treaties*, volume 2.

17. Riggs letters in *Minnesota Pioneer,* May 26 and June 9, 1853; Riggs, *Mary and I,* 132–33; Riggs to Treat, August 26, 1854, and February 19, 1855, ABCFM.

18. See Hughes, *Indian Chiefs of Southern Minnesota,* 103–10; Stephen Return Riggs, "Dakota Portraits," *Minnesota History Bulletin* 2 (November 1918): 504–5.

19. See "Claims of Henoc Maȟpiyahdinape and Eli Wakiyehdi for potatoes lost," June 3, 1856, NARG 75, SPA; Riggs to Treat, January 21 and June 12, 1858, ABCFM.

20. Manypenny to Gorman, May 8, 1855, NARG 75, LS, MS; Murphy to Gorman, May 17, 1855, and Gorman to Murphy, May 30, 1855, NARG 75, LR, MS.

21. Prescott to Murphy, September 3, 1856, *Senate Document* No. 5, 34th Congress, 3d Session, at 606–11.

22. Manypenny to Francis Huebschmann, November 20, 1856, *Senate Document* No. 5, 34th Congress, 3d Session, at 612. Manypenny later published an account of his experiences as commissioner titled *Our Indian Wards* (1880; repr., New York: Decapo, 1972).

23. Huebschmann to Manypenny, July 19, 1856, NARG 75, LR, SPA.

24. Murphy to Manypenny, September 28, 1855, Manypenny to Secretary of Interior, April 8, 1856, Huebschmann to Manypenny, December 24, 1856, ibid.; Murphy to Gorman, July 5, 1855, NARG 75, LR, MS; Williamson to Treat, June 13, 1855, ABCFM.

25. Anderson, *Kinsmen of Another Kind*, 212–15. The Little Crow quotation is in Francis Huebschmann to George Manypenny, June 28, 1856, NARG 75, LR, NS.

26. Day to Agent Murphy, October 19, 1854, and Day to AAG, January 26, 1855, NARG 393, Letterbook, Fort Ridgely, June 1854–November 1858.

27. See Nairn's Narrative, MHSA; Hayden to Lieutenant A. F. Bond, November 18, 1854, NARG 393, LR, Fort Ridgely, 1853–59.

28. *Daily Minnesota Pioneer,* June 1, 1854; *St. Paul Minnesota Times,* August 3, 1854; Murphy to Lee, July 1, 1854, NARG 393, LR, Fort Ridgely; Lee to Page, July 8, 1854, NARG 393, LR, DWWD; Moses Adams to Manypenny, August 3, 1854, NARG 75, LR, SPA.

29. The 1858 Constitution of the State of Minnesota included Article 7, which indicated that any Indian who "made progress" toward civilization could qualify to vote.

30. Letter of "J. H." in *St. Peter Tribune,* July 10, 1861; "Application of Sioux Indians," found in *Record,* ABCFM, June 21, 1861.

31. Riggs to Treat, July 31, 1856, ABCFM; *Henderson Democrat,* August 14, 1856; *Daily Pioneer & Democrat,* August 18, 1856.

32. Riggs to Treat, January 30, 1855, May 23, 1855, March 21, 1859, and April 11, 1859, and Riggs to Williamson, June 20, 1857, ABCFM.

33. Riggs to Treat, May 23, 1855, ABCFM; Riggs to Lucy Drake, February 20, 1857, and Mary Riggs to Mrs. Drake, February 20, 1857, Riggs Papers, CWS-A; *Daily Pioneer and Democrat,* August 18, 1856.

34. Timothy Sheehan's Diary, July 6, 1862, MHSA; Victor Renville, "A Sketch of the Minnesota Massacre," *North Dakota Collections* 5 (1923): 258. See also "Murphy Organizes Civilized Band," *Daily Pioneer & Democrat,* August 18, 1856; "Civilized Band," *Henderson Democrat,* August 14, 1856; Williamson to Treat, November 18, 1859, ABCFM; Samuel Brown to J. R. Brown, September 25, 1858, *Senate Executive Documents No. 1, 35th Congress, 2nd Session, Serial* 974, at 401–13.

35. Charles E. Flandrau, *History of Minnesota and Tales of the Frontier* (St. Paul: E. W. Porter, 1900), 64–68; Charles L. Emerson, *Rise and Progress of Minnesota Territory; Including a Statement of the Business Prosperity of Saint Paul; and Information in Regard to the Different Counties, Cities, Towns, and Villages in the Territory, etc.* (St. Paul: C. L. Emerson, 1855), 35–37; Henry Poehler Memoir, MHSA.

36. Alexander Berghold noted that early German settlers "were free to occupy their comfortable places of bark [Indian houses] without paying a high rent." See Berghold, *The Indians Revenge; or, Days of Horror, Some Appalling Events in the History of the Sioux* (San Francisco: P. J. Thomas, 1891), 26–27.

37. Obituary of Frederick Beinhorn, 1900, Brown County Historical Society; "Pioneers Invited to Honor Feast of Anniversary," *New Ulm Review,* no day, 1925; Scrapbook in Charles Roos Papers, MHSA; "Brown County," *St. Peter Courier,* June 21, 1855; Petition of Farmers from New Ulm, August 1855, NARG 75, LR, MS; Edward Frederick Reminiscence, 1854–55, MHSA.

38. Captain Theodore Potter, "Captain Potter's Recollections of Minnesota Experiences," *Minnesota History Bulletin* 1, no. 8 (November 1916): 423; Emery Johnson, "Memoir of New Sweden," Johnson Papers, Gustavas Adolphus College Library; Newton Southworth to Captain Seth Freeman, November 3, 1856, Southworth Papers, MHSA.

39. Petition of Farmers from New Ulm, August 1855, NARG 75, LR, MS.

40. Steele to Day, August 8, 1855, Lieutenant Robert Hunter to Lieutenant Jonathan Hawkins, March 7, 1856, and Petition of William Forsyth and Fifty-One Others, April 23, 1855, NARG 393, LR, Fort Ridgely, 1853–59; *Daily Minnesota Pioneer,* July 28, 1855.

41. Murphy to Gorman, October 25 and 26, 1855, NARG 75, LR, MS; Gorman to Manypenny, June 28, 1856, NARG 75, LS, MS.

42. Antoine Frenier addresses the corruption in *St. Paul Press,* December 14, 1862. Frenier claims that the corruption went all the way into the halls of the Secretary of Interior.

43. Potter, "Captain Potter's Recollections of Minnesota Experience," 424.

44. Contract, W. S. Gorman, Nathan Hill, with Frandrau, May 27, 1854, Flandrau Papers, MHSA.

45. Ibid.; Receipts from Purchases of Indian Food, February 1857, ibid.

46. General accounts of the attack are in F. I. Herriott, "The Origins of the Indian Massacre Between the Okabojis, March 8, 1857," *Annals of Iowa* 18 (July 1932): 323–82; Hubbard and Holcombe, *Minnesota in Three Centuries,* 3:217–21; Thomas Teakle, *The Spirit Lake Massacre* (Iowa City: Iowa State Historical Society, 1918). More recent interest has focused on biographies of Inkpaduta. See Mary Bakeman, *Legends, Letters, and Lies: Reading About Inkpaduta and the Spirit Lake Massacre* (Roseville, Minn.: Park Genealogy Books,

2001); and Paul Beck, *Inkpaduta: Dakota Leader* (Norman: University of Oklahoma Press, 2008).

47. See Testimony of Ta-te-yah-he, or Shifting Wind, 1857, and Alexander Faribault Affidavit on Inkpaduta Band, February 19, 1860, NARG 75, LR, SPA; Thomas Hughes, "Causes and Results of the Inkpaduta Massacre," *Minnesota Historical Society Collections* 12 (1905–8): 264–65; McLean to Ramsey, February 26, 1853, NARG 75, LR, MS. Flandrau denied the Wahpekutes' annuities. See Flandrau letter to *Pioneer and Democrat,* April 11, 1857, in *Senate Documents* No. 11, 35th Congress, 1st Session, at 357–59.

48. Major Samuel Woods Diary of Survey Work in Iowa, October 23, 1849, and Lieutenant Colonel G. Loomis to Major D. C. Buell, October 23, 1849, Sibley Papers, MHSA.

49. Woods to Gorman, February 4, 1854, and Gorman to CIA, March 2, 1854, NARG 75, LR, Upper Missouri Agency.

50. Martin McLeod discusses the raids, tying in the Sissetons, who he knew well. See M. McLeod letter, March 12, 1855, McLeod Papers, MHSA.

51. "The wife's [Inkpauta's son's] Story of the Massacre at Spirit Lake," 1857, in Daniels, Reminiscences, MHSA. See also "Minutes of the Examination of the Wife of Ta-te-yah-he (Shifting Wind), One of the Slain by the Party of the Expedition of Sioux in Search of Inkaputa," NARG 75, Miscellaneous LR, NS.

52. Ibid.

53. Beck, *Iŋkpaduta,* 30–74. See also L. P. Lee, *History of the Spirit Lake Massacre! 8th March 1857, and of Miss Abigail Gardiner's Three Month's Captivity among the Indians* (1857; repr., Iowa City: State Historical Society, 1971), 5–47.

54. See Hughes, "Causes and Results of the Inkapaduta Massacre," *Minnesota Historical Society Collections,* 12:280.

55. Huebschmann to J. W. Denver, May 8, 1857, NARG 75, LR, SPA. See also Gorman to General William B. Dodd, April 18, 1857, Dodd Papers, MHSA; A. J. Campbell Affidavit, 1857, Claims of Andrew J. Myrick, 1857, and Claims of Amos W. Huggins, NARG 75, Special File 132; Thomas Cowan to Assistant Adjutant General, April 18, 1857, NARG 393, LR, Fort Ridgely.

56. Alexander to AAG, March 23, May 13, and May 15, 1857, NARG 393, Fort Ridgely, Letterbook; Report of Captain Bernard E. Bee to Lieutenant H. E. Maynadier, April 9, 1857, *Senate Document* No. 11, 35th Congress, 1st Session, at 351–52; Captain H. W. George Report, 1857, NARG 75, LR, Special File 132.

57. An well-written account of the fate of these women is Abbie Gardner Sharp, *History of the Spirit Lake Massacre and Captivity of Miss Abbie Gardner* (Des Moines: Iowa Printing Company, 1902).

58. Riggs, *Mary and I,* 138–42; Captain Barnard Bee to AAG, June 18, 1857, NARG 393, Fort Ridgely, Letterbook.

59. Bee to AAG, June 18, 1857, NARG 393, LR, DWWD.

60. Cullen Annual Report, September 28, 1857, *Senate Document* No. 11, 35th Congress, 1st Session, at 336–38.

61. Riggs to Flandrau, July 1, 1857, Flandrau Papers, MHSA. Hubbard and Holcombe, *Minnesota in Three Centuries,* 3:2255–56, gives Roaring Cloud as Mahpiyahotomani.

62. Daniels, Reminiscences, MHSA.

63. See "Final Report" of Kintzing Pritchette, October 5, 1857, NARG 75, LR, SPA.

64. Daniels, Reminiscences, MHSA; *Henderson Democrat,* July 7, 1857; Sherman to Abercrombie, July 16, 1857, and Bee to Abercrombie, July 12, 1857, NARG 393, LR, Fort Ridgely.

65. Daniels, Reminiscences, MHSA; Memoir of A. Jeremiah Chester, July 1861, MHSA.

66. Much of the party is identified in Hubbard and Holcombe, *Minnesota in Three Centuries,* 3:263. See also Sherman to AAG, July 22, 1857, NARG 393, LR, Fort Ridgely.

67. Cullen to J. W. Denver, July 20, 1857, and Denver to Cullen, July 20, 1857, *Senate Document* No. 11, 35th Congress, 1st Session, Serial 919, at 362–63; Cullen to Denver, July 26, 1857, NARG 75, LR, SPA; Sherman to Abercrombie, July 16 and 30, 1857, NARG 393, LR, Fort Ridgely.

68. Pratt to Abercrombie, September 15, 1857, NARG 393, LR, Fort Ridgely.

69. Flandrau to Cullen, August 7, 1857, and Pritchette Report, October 15, 1857, NARG 75, LR, SPA.

CHAPTER FOUR

1. *Henderson Democrat,* May 29 and June 5, 1856.

2. Williamson to Treat, January 18, 1858, ABCFM.

3. George Featherstonhaugh, *A Canoe Voyage up the Minnay Sotor; with an Account of the Lead and Copper Deposits in Wisconsin; of the Gold Region in the Cherokee Country; and Sketches of the Popular Manners* (St. Paul: Minnesota Historical Society, 1970), 1:253–54, 312–14.

4. George Allanson, "A Pioneer Romance," n.p. Paper in possession of Guy Mackner, Sisseton, S.Dak.; John Williamson to his father, September 13, 1864, Williamson Papers, MHSA; Riggs to Thomas Williamson, May 30, 1865, Riggs Papers, CWS-A.

5. Thomas Robertson's Reminisces, MHSA; Renville, "A Sketch of the Minnesota Massacre," 258; Anderson, *Kinsmen of Another Kind,* 215.

6. Anderson, *Kinsmen of Another Kind,* 228.

7. Thomas Robertson's Reminiscences, MHSA; Williamson to Treat, February 22 and March 18, 1858, ABCFM; Upper Agency Annuity Rolls, 1859, NARG 75, LR, SPA.

8. Big Eagle's account is found in Gary Clayton Anderson and Alan R. Woolworth, eds., *Through Dakota Eyes: Narrative Accounts of the Minnesota Indian War of 1862* (St. Paul: Minnesota Historical Society Press, 1988), 21–26, 35–36, 93, 147–52, 234–37.

9. Thomas Robertson's Reminiscences, MHSA; "Return of the Sioux Chiefs from Washington City," *The Daily Minnesotan,* July 7, 1858.

10. *The Washington Union,* March 20, 28, and 29, 1858; Anderson, *Little Crow,* 105; Riggs to Treat, March 21, 1859, ABCFM. See also Barbara T. Newcombe, "The Sioux Sign a Treaty in 1858," in *North Star State: A Minnesota History Reader,* ed. Anne Aby (St. Paul: Minnesota Historical Society Press, 2002), 68.

11. Riggs to Treat, March 21, 1859, ABCFM; Newcombe, "The Sioux Sign a Treaty in 1858," 67–78; Thomas Robertson's Reminiscences, MHSA.

12. Minutes of the Council, March 15–June 21, 1858, in NARG 75, DRNRUT.

13. Ibid.

14. Ibid.

15. Anderson, *Kinsmen of Another Kind,* 230–31.

16. See Kappler, *Indian Affairs, Laws and Treaties,* 2:781–85; Newcombe, "The Sioux Sign a Treaty in 1858," 78; Cullen to Greenwood, February 25, 1861, NARG 75, LR, SPA; See In the Court of Claims of the United States, Mdewakanton and Wahpakoota Bands of Sioux Indians, Otherwise Known as Santee Sioux Indians, PLAINTIFFS vs. The United States, No. 33728 (filed in June 1922).

17. Abercrombie to AAG, June 18 and June 24, 1858, NARG 393, LR, DWWD.

18. Thomas Robertson's Reminiscences, MHSA; Cullen to Mix, August 23, 1858, NARG 75, LR, SPA.

19. The lake today is known as Cattail-Kettle Lake. Cullen to Mix, August 23, 1858, NARG 75, LR, SPA; Brown to Cullen, September 17, 1858, NARG 75, LR, NS; Mix to Jacob Thompson, April 20, 1859, and AAG to Abercrombie, May 3, 1859, NARG 393, LR, Fort Ridgely.

20. Abercrombie to Cullen, June 21, 1859, and Cullen to A. B. Greenwood, June 24, 1859, NARG 75, LR, SPA; Cullen to Abercrombie, June 22, 1859, Abercrombie to AAG, June

23, 1859, Sherman to AAG, June 25, 1859, Sherman to Captain D. Davidson, June 29, 1859, and Sherman to Abercrombie, June 28, July 21, and August 5, 1859, NARG 393, LR, Fort Ridgely.

21. Cullen to Greenwood, August 15, 1859, NARG 75, LR, SPA.

22. Ibid.; Description of Standing Buffalo is in Jeremiah C. Donahower Papers, July 1861, MHSA.

23. Brown to Cullen, August 21, 1859, NARG 75, SPA.

24. Brown to Cullen, August 30 and September 1, 1858, and March 28, 1859, Cullen to Mix, July 5, 1858 and September 18, 1859, and Cullen to Greenwood, August 13, 1859, NARG 75, SPA; Brown Report, September 30, 1858, *Senate Executive Document* No. 1, 35th Congress, 2nd Session, at 401–2; Brown Report, October 25, 1860, *Senate Executive Document* No. 1, 36th Congress, 2nd Session, at 278–84.

25. Cullen to Greenwood, August 13, 1859, NARG 75, LR, SPA; Riggs to Treat, August 24 and November 27, 1859, and Williamson to Treat, November 18, 1859, ABCFM. Brown hired Frederick P. Leavenworth to begin surveying the eighty-acre parcels. See his diary, 1859–60, Leavenworth Papers, MHSA.

26. Report in *St. Paul Pioneer Press*, August 28, 1858; Williamson to Treat, November 18, 1859, ABCFM.

27. Pond, *Dakota as They Were in 1834*, 13.

28. Ibid.; *St. Paul Pioneer and Democrat*, August 15 and 28, 1859; Lieutenant Colonel J. George to Colonel H. P. Van Cleve, August 29, 1861, and Williamson to Thomas Galbraith, June 5, 1862, Governors Papers, MHSA; Thomas Robertson's Reminiscences, MHSA; Williamson to Treat, November 18, 1859, ABCFM; Anderson, *Kinsmen of Another Kind*, 254.

29. Williamson to Treat, October 7 and November 18, 1859, ABCFM.

30. Interview with Lawrence, *St. Peter Minnesota Tribune,* October 2, 1862; "Whipple's Notes on the Dakota," 1890?, Whipple Papers, MHSA.

31. Brown to Culllen, February 3 and 6, March 3, May 17, and July 7, 1860, NARG 75, LR, SPA. See Thomas Hughes on White Lodge, in *Indian Chiefs*, 107.

32. Brown reported on the strife suggesting that it likely meant the breakup of the Hazelwood Republic. See Brown to Cullen, May 17, 1860, NARG 75, LR, SPA.

33. Riggs to Treat, August 2, 1859, ABCFM; Riggs to Captain G. A. DeRussy, February 1, 1860, Cullen to Major W. W. Morris, June 15, 1860, Brown to DeRussy, August 10, 1860, Captain A. A. Gibson to Lieutenant J. J. Dana, July 5, 1860, DuRussy to AAG, August 10 and 11, 1860, NARG 393, LR, Fort Ridgely; Morris to AAG, August 14, 1860, NARG 393, LR, DWWD; Jacob Thompson to Greenwood, March 1, 1860, Brown to Cullen, July 7 and August 11, 1860, NARG 75, LR, SPA.

34. Soldier Testimony to Morris, June 21, 1860, Governors Papers, MHSA; Cullen to Morris, June 8 and 25, 1859, 1860, NARG 393, LR, Fort Ridgely; Jared Daniels, Reminiscence, MHSA; Thomas Galbraith to Clark Thompson, July 24, 1861, NARG 75, LR, SPA; Lieutenant Caleb Smith to Major Irwin McDowell, November 1, 1860, NARG 393, LR, DWWD.

35. Brown to Morris, February 27, 1860, Petition from Residences of New Ulm, on behalf of Jacob Pfenninger, March 1, 1860, J. C. Rudolph to Morris, January 11, 1960, Sherman to Lieutenant G. H. Weeks, March 1, 1860, and Hartman to Morris, September 10, 1860, NARG 393, LR, Fort Ridgely; William G. Orkney to Morris, September 17, 1860, Governors Papers, MHSA; *New Ulm Post*, December 24, 1859, translated by Darla Gebhard, Brown County Historical Society.

36. John P. Williamson to Lucy Drake, January 21, 1861, Riggs Papers, CWS-A; Whipple's letter, June 22, 1860, later published in the *Morton Enterprise,* November 8, 1884, and found in the Samuel Hinman Papers, MHSA. Anderson, *Kinsmen of Another Kind*, 247.

37. *Henderson Democrat*, June 15, 1859, and *St. Paul Pioneer and Democrat*, August 15, 1859.

38. Federal Census of 1860.

39. Morris to AAG, March 7, 1860, NARG 393, LR, DWWD. "Settler sovereignty" is discussed in Lisa Ford, *Settler Sovereignty: Jurisdictional and Indigenous People in America and Australia, 1788–1836* (Cambridge, Mass.: Harvard University Press, 2010), 1–6; Lorenzo Veracini, *Settler Colonialism: A Theoretical Overview* (New York: Palgrave Macmillian, 2010), 305. For George Washington's views regarding settler sovereignty, see James Belich, *Replenishing the Earth: The Settler Revolution and the Rise of the Anglo World, 1783–1939* (New York: Oxford University Press, 2009), 146–47.

40. Lieutenant George Ruggles to Major G. W. Patten, January 22, 1858, Cullen to Morris, June 22, 1860, Brown to Morris, February 27, 1860, Cullen to Greenwood, January 28, 1860, and Major W. Wilson to the CIA, January 20, 1860, NARG 393, LR, Fort Ridgely; Brown to Cullen, July 7, 1860, NARG 75, LR, SPA; Thomas Hughes, *History of Blue Earth County and Biographies of Its Leading Citizens* (Chicago: Middle West Publishing, 1909), 104.

41. Roger G. Kennedy, "In Search of the Joseph R. Brown House," *Minnesota History* 13 (Fall 1965): 272–77; Edith Washell, "Exhaustive Biography of Joseph R. Brown," 1938, original in possession of Guy Mackner, Sisseton, S.Dak., 6; Allanson, "Stirring Adventures of J. R. Brown," MHSA; List of Employees at the Dakota Agencies, December 1860, Governors Papers, MHSA.

42. Thomas Hughes, "Collection of Statements," manuscript in MHSA; Brown Memoir, undated (written after 1862), Brown Papers, MHSA.

43. Galbraith to Thompson, January 31, 1862, Thompson Papers, MHSA. Henry Benjamin Whipple brought the corruption to the attention of the new Republican Secretary of Interior Caleb B. Smith, who summarily dismissed it. It was "useless to dwell upon the wrongs," he noted, and Smith assured Whipple that the "whole system of trading with the Indians shall be broken up." See Smith to Whipple, March 3 and June 12, 1862, Whipple Papers, MHSA. To his credit, Smith followed up the Whipple letter with a recommendation to Chairman of the Committee on Indian Affairs in the Senate J. R. Doolittle. See Smith to Doolittle, March 31, 1862, NARG 48, LS, Indian Division of the Department of Interior.

44. Charley Mix Jr.'s relationship with the Browns is revealed in the Brown papers at MHSA. Reminiscence of Edith Waschell, paper in possession of Guy Mackner, Sisseton, S.Dak.

45. Brown's Accounting of Money, 1860, and Brown to Mix, May 1861, Brown Papers, MHSA; Brown to Mix, September 23, 1861, Madison Cults (Comptroller of the Treasury) to William P. Dole, November 11, 1861, and Galbraith to Clark Thompson, January 1, 1862, NARG 75, LR, SPA. Riggs openly charged Brown with corruption in a private letter, the agent answering him with a confusing assessment of money spent, which included the overall figure of $280,566. Brown argued that he had spent $102,667 to pay employees, even though they vigorously claimed that they had not been paid when he left office. See Brown's reply to Riggs (edited by Brown), 1861, Brown Papers, MHSA.

46. Galbraith to Whipple, May 31, 1862, and Hinman to Whipple, June 19, 1862, Whipple Papers, MHSA.

47. Hay to Lincoln, January 1, 1862, Lincoln Papers, Library of Congress.

48. See Galbraith to Thompson, July 31, 1861, and J. W. Ray, "Relative to Claim of Carothers and Co.," August 1861, NARG 75, LR, SPA. It was common for citizens to send claims directly to congressmen and senators, who then became their advocates, for a fee. See Aldrich to William P. Dole, May 29, 1862, ibid. Whipple wrote Aldrich regarding the corruption, and he responded that the charges were nothing more than "general allegations and undefined charges." See Aldrich to Whipple, June 12, 1862, Whipple Papers, MHSA. Antoine Frenier claimed that a claim for $5,000 was paid to a Mr. Brugier in 1859, with

Brugier agreeing to pay two-thirds of the money to Washington officials. See *St. Paul Press,* December 14, 1862.

49. See Pierson to Thompson, January 30, 1862, and February 1 and 7, 1862, Galbraith to Thompson, February 28, 1862, and A. B. Munch to Thompson, March 12, 1862, Thompson Papers, MHSA. Riggs called Pierson's actions "a perfect outrage" in Riggs to Jonas Pettyjohn, March 6, 1862, Riggs Papers, MHSA.

50. Pierson to Thompson, February 1 and 7, 1862, and Galbraith to Thompson, February 28, 1862, Thompson Papers, MHSA.

51. Galbraith to Thompson, January 31, 1862, Thompson Papers, MHSA. The purchases are listed in Galbraith to Thompson, January 27, 1863, *House Executive Document* No. 1, 28th Congress, 1st Session, Serial 1182, at 384–85.

52. Galbraith urged Thompson to bring as much gold as possible, with the agent utterly refusing to accept paper. See C. B. Hensley to Thompson, May 20, 1862, and Galbraith to Thompson, July 19, 1862, NARG 75, LR, SPA; Testimony of Thomas Galbraith, no date, NARG 75, Special File 274. The "rumor" regarding payment in greenbacks reached merchants in New Ulm. See Benjamin Armstrong, *Early Life among the Indians: Reminiscences from the Life of Benj. G. Armstrong. Treaties of 1835, 1837, 1842, and 1854. Habits and Customs, of the Red Men of the Forest. Indians, Biographical Sketches, Battles, Etc. Dictated to and Written by Thos. P. Wentworth* (Ashland, Wis.: Press of A. W. Brown, 1892), 75–76. John Williamson reported the exchange rate. See Winifred Williamson Barton, *John P. Williamson: A Brother to the Sioux* (New York: Fleming H. Revell Co., 1919), 47.

53. Riggs to Treat, August 24, 1859, ABCFM; "Statement of George Quinn," taken by R. I. Holcombe, in Holcombe Papers, MHSA; Red Owl's entire speech is in "A Week on the Frontier," (Minneapolis) *State Atlas,* June 22, 1861; reprinted in *The Thoreau Society Bulletin* 57 (Fall 1956): 1–4. "Local Affairs: A Trip to Redwood, and a Day Among the Indians," *Pioneer and Democrat,* June 28, 1861.

54. Traveling Hail joined the rebellion in August 1862. His son was later killed at the battle of Birch Coulee. He survived the war as a prisoner at Davenport, dying there in 1866. See "Statement of George Quinn," taken by R. I. Holcombe, MHSA; Anderson and Woolworth, eds., *Through Dakota Eyes,* 163.

55. Missionary Samuel Pond has a good description of Little Six. Less is known about Red Middle Voice. See Pond, *Dakota as They Were in 1834,* 13–14. Little Crow's church visits are reported in the *St. Paul Pioneer Press,* October 24, 1897.

56. Jane Williamson to family, December 31, 1861, and January 9, 1862, ABCFM.

57. Mrs. N. D. White, "Captivity among the Sioux, August 18 to September 26, 1862," *Minnesota Historical Society Collections* 9 (1898–1900): 396–97; Sarah F. Wakefield, *Six Weeks in Little Crow's Camp: A Narrative of Indian Captivity* (Shakopee, Minn.: Argus Book and Job Printing Office, 1864), 9–10; Mrs. J. E. DeCamp-Sweet, "Narrative of Her Captivity in the Sioux Outbreak of 1862," in *Minnesota Historical Society Collections* 6 (1894): 356. Several settler's wives mention selling cattle to Little Crow, including White and Mrs. E. M. Earle. See Earle, *Reminiscences of the Sioux Massacre of 1862* (Fairfax, Minn.: Renville County Pioneers Society, 1907): n.p.

58. Galbraith exaggerated in his official report, stating that the Indians took one hundred sacks. Sheehan puts the number at just twenty. See Sheehan, Court of Claims Testimony, No. 22524, August 4, 1862, at 272–78; Sheehan Diary, August 4–8, 1862, MHSA; Riggs, "The Dakota Bread Riot," *St. Paul Daily Pioneer,* August 13, 1862; Narrative of Orlando McFall, August 4–13, 1862, MHSA.

59. Sheehan, Court of Claims Testimony, August 6, 1862; Sheehan Diary, August 6, 1862, MHSA.

60. See Barton, *John P. Williamson,* 49. Riggs later noted that Galbraith was dependent upon the traders because he had little food left in the warehouses. See Riggs, *Mary and I,* 150–52.

61. The meeting with Marsh is described in R. I. Hubbard, "Narrative of the Fifth Regiment," found in The Board of Commissioners, *Minnesota in the Civil and Indian Wars, 1861–1865*, 2nd ed. (St. Paul, Minn.: Pioneer Press, 1891), 1:245. For the role of the soldiers' lodge within Lakota bands, see Clark Wissler, *Societies and Ceremonial Associations in the Oglala Division of the Teton-Dakota*, in *Anthropological Papers of the American Museum of Natural History*, XI, Part 1 (Washington, D.C.: Order of the Trustees, 1912), 1–99.

62. See Andrew Myrick to Nathaniel Myrick, May 18, 1862, NARG 75, Special File 274.

63. Quote in Thomas Gere Memoir, June 28, 1862, MHSA; Folwell, *History of Minnesota*, 2:398–99; Testimony of A. J. Campbell and Samuel Hinman, NARG 75, Special File 274.

64. Andrew Myrick to Nathaniel Myrick, May 18, 1862, NARG 75, Special File 274. How this letter survived in government files is a mystery.

65. Ibid.

66. The insult is mentioned dozens of times, apparently originating at the Lower Agency. See Testimony of Hinman, Noah Sinks, Galbraith, and Maȟpiyawakoŋza, ibid.; Testimony of Robert Hakewaśte, Court of Claims Testimony, No. 22524. On Marsh's refusal, see Isaac V. D. Heard, *History of the Sioux War and Massacre of 1862 and 1863* (New York: Harper, 1865), 49.

67. Testimony of Noah Sinks (Myrick's clerk), August 6, 1862, NARG 75, Special File 274. Sheehan later testified that Galbraith "told Little Crow and his men that they would immediately issue rations to the lower Indians . . . I know that they were not [issued]." See Sheehan Testimony, August 7–8, 1862, Court of Claims, No. 22524. Galbraith describes the Sisseton soldiers' lodge in Galbraith to Thompson, July 30, 1861, NARG 75, SPA.

68. While some accounts put the figure at $80,000, which was a little less than what was supposed to be shipped, the freight bill lists the total amount at $71,000. See American Express Company Freight Charge, August 18, 1862, NARG 75, LR, SPA.

69. Galbraith to Thompson, January 27, 1863, *House Executive Document* 1, 38th Congress, 1st Session, Serial 1182, at 390; Thomas Hughes's Statements, August 1862, MHSA.

70. See Testimony of Naȟpidinźa, no date, NARG 75, Special File 274; Hinman to Whipple, August 5, 1862, Whipple Papers, MHSA.

71. DeCamp Sweet, "Narrative of Her Captivity," 355; Thompson to Ramsey, September 12, 1861, NARG 75, LR, SPA. Thomas Robertson mentions the discussions regarding the Civil War that went on in the soldiers' lodge. See Thomas Robertson's Reminiscences, MHSA.

72. Sam E. Adams spoke with a woman named Bryant who lived hear Acton. She knew the young men and their attachment to Cut Nose, whose Dakota name was rendered as Maḣpiyaokenaźiŋ. Adams to Ramsey, August 25, 1862, Governors Papers, MHSA.

73. The Acton affair is well researched in the R. I. Holcombe papers. See Holcombe to Satterlee, April n.d., 1915, MHSA. Another account is in "Big Eagle's Account," in Anderson and Woolworth, *Through Dakota Eyes*, 35–36. One with poetic license was given to the poet Hanford L. Gordon by Wowinape, Little Crow's son. It is reproduced in ibid., 40. The neighbor who reveals Jones's business with the Indians is Irene Persons. See her "Memoir," ms., MHSA.

74. The death of "Old Shakopee" was announced in the *St. Paul Pioneer and Democrat*, October 16, 1860. See also Thomas Robertson's Reminiscences, MHSA.

75. Marion P. A. Satterlee, *A Detailed Account of the Massacre by the Dakota Indians of Minnesota in 1862* (Minneapolis: Marion P. Satterlee, 1923), 8–10; Return I. Holcombe, "Notes on Acton," (August 17, 1862), Holcombe Papers, MHSA. On Snelling's actions, see Anderson, *Kinsmen of Another Kind*, 124–25; Thomas Robertson's Reminiscences, August 17, 1862, MHSA. Pond, *Dakota as They Were in 1834*, 6–9. Robinson made the connection between Little Six and his uncle. See Doane Robinson, *A History of the Dakota or Sioux Indians* (Pierre: South Dakota State Historical Society, 1904), 127.

76. On council issues, see Thomas Robertson's Reminiscence and Jared Daniels's Reminiscence, MHSA.

77. "Little Crow's Speech," recorded by Gordon, in Anderson and Woolworth, *Through Dakota Eyes*, 40–42; "Taoyateduta is not a Coward," *Minnesota History* 38 (September 1962): 115. Others include White Spider's Interview, *St. Paul Pioneer Press*, October 24, 1897; Heard, *A History of the Sioux War*, 59–60; Riggs, *Mary and I*, 153.

1. Marion P. Satterlee, "Massacre at the Redwood Indian Agency," ms. in the MHSA. Waŋmditaŋka, or Big Eagle, later claimed that he spoke out for peace at the council, but if so, he quickly converted to the argument for war. See "Big Eagle's Account," in Anderson and Woolworth, *Through Dakota Eyes*, 36.

2. A riveting account is "Cecelia Campbell Stay's Account," in Anderson and Woolworth, *Through Dakota Eyes*, 44–52. Marion P. Satterlee reports the statement by Tawasuota in *A Detailed Account of the Massacre by the Dakota Indians of Minnesota in 1862* (Minneapolis: Marion P. Satterlee, 1925), 14. See also Stephen Return Riggs, "Memoir of Hon. Jas. W. Lynd," *Minnesota Historical Society Collections* 3 (1880): 107–14; R. I. Homcombe, *Sketches Historical and Descriptive of the Monuments and Tablets Erected by the Minnesota Valley Historical Society in Renville and Redwood Counties* (Morton, Minn.: Minnesota Valley Historical Society, 1902), 42. Mary LaCroix's grandmother was the woman hiding behind the door. See her interview in the Brown County Historical Society. Hippolite Campbell was later implicated in the murder of civilians and executed at Mankato on December 26, 1862.

3. Bouratt was one of the first from the agency to reach St. Paul and gave an account regarding the opening attack. See *St. Paul Pioneer & Democrat*, August 26, 1862.

4. Spencer's account of the attack is reproduced in Harriet E. Bishop, *Dakota War Whoop: or, Indian Massacres and War of 1862–3* (St. Paul: published by author, 1864; repr., Minneapolis: Ross and Haines, 1970), 33–37.

5. Satterlee, "Massacre at the Redwood Agency," MHSA; Satterlee, *A Detailed Account*, 14–15. Cecelia Campbell Stay reported that Myrick's mouth was "stuffed full of green grass." See Stay interview, (Madison, Minnesota) *Independent Press*, May 18, 1906. Big Eagle, or Wamŋditanka, confirmed the story in "Big Eagle's Account," in Anderson and Woolworth, *Through Dakota Eyes*, 56.

6. Satterlee, *A Detailed Account*, 14–16.

7. Satterlee, "The Massacre at the Redwood Agency," MHSA.

8. See Joseph Connors, "The Elusive Hero of Redwood Ferry," *Minnesota History* 34 (Summer 1955): 233–38.

9. *Missionary Papers. By the Bishop Seabury Mission. Number Twenty-Three* (Faribault, Minnesota: Alex. Johnston, Book and Job Printer, *Statesman* Office, 1862), no pages. Issac V. D. Heard interviewed Hinman, who gave the same story. See Heard, *History of the Sioux War and Massacres of 1862 and 1863* (New York: Harper & Brothers, publishers, 1864), 61–71. Satterlee collected the information on White Dog's role in saving West but then charges him with being principally responsible for killing others along the road to Fort Ridgely. See Satterlee Notes, Satterlee Papers, MHSA. See also "Statement of Valencia J. Reynolds," Charles S. Bryant and Abel Murch, *A History of the Great Massacre of the Sioux Indians, in Minnesota, including the Personal Narratives of Many Who Escaped* (Cincinnati: Richy & Carrol. 1864; repr., New York: Kraus Reprint Co., 1977), 404–10.

10. Satterlee, "The Massacre at the Redwood Indian Agency," MHSA; John Ames Humphrey, "Boyhood Reminiscences of Life Among the Dakota and the Massacre of 1862," *Minnesota Historical Society Collections* 15 (1909–14): 339–46.

11. Most newspaper accounts later emphasize scalping and mutilation of whites at the agencies, but other sources suggest that few victims were mutilated. See Jared Daniels Reminiscences, MHSA; DeCamp Sweet, "Mrs. J. E. DeCamp Sweet's Narrative of Her Captivity

in the Sioux Outbreak of 1862," *Minnesota Historical Society Collections* 6 (1894): 365; Moses Adams's letter in *St. Paul Weekly Press,* September 11, 1862.

12. De Camp, "Mrs. DeCamp Sweet's Captivity," MHSA 6:358–62.

13. Ibid.

14. Reminiscences of Thomas Robertson, MHSA.

15. Ibid. See also "An Account of the Redwood and Yellow Medicine Indian Agencies by John H. Case, Pioneer of Nininger, Minnesota, 1856," *Hastings Gazette,* July 1, 1891.

16. Benedict Juni, *Held in Captivity* [a pamphlet] (New Ulm, Minn.: Liesch-Walter Printing, 1926), 1–5.

17. Katpantpanu was later tried, convicted, and sentenced to be hung. See Trial Record 63, NARG 46, Senate Records 37A-F2, National Archives. A recent publication of the records is John Isch, *The Dakota Trials: Including the Complete Transcripts and Explanatory Notes on the Military Commission Trials in Minnesota* (New Ulm, Minn.: Brown County Historical Society, 2012), 209.

18. Ibid.; Mrs. N. A. Door to Marion P. Satterlee, January 2, 1891, Satterlee Papers, MHSA.

19. Several narratives appeared in 1863, being the byproduct of a Sioux Commission, which met in Minnesota to gather information regarding the conflict. See "Narrative of Jonathan W. Earle–Narrative of Mrs. Helen Carrothers," in Bryant and Murch, *A History of the Great Massacre,* 275–323.

20. The problem of sorting through the various narratives is best exemplified by a second account written forty years later by Mrs. Helen Carrothers (who had divorced her husband and married a man named Tarble). It is filled with exaggerated claims. See Mrs. Helen Tarble, *The Story of My Capture and Escape During the Minnesota Indian Massacre of 1862: with Historical Notes, Descriptions of Pioneer Life, and Sketches and Incidents of the Great Outbreak of the Sioux or Dakota Indians as I Saw them* (St. Paul, Minn.: Abbott Printing Company, 1904). It was reprinted in *The Garland Library of Narratives of North American Indian Captivity,* ed. Wilcomb E. Washburn, Vol. 105 (New York: Garland Publishing, 1975).

21. See Ezmon W. Earle, Reminiscences, MHSA.

22. Ibid.; Mrs. White, who left a valuable narrative, concludes that of the party of twenty-seven, nine were killed, eleven were taken captive, and seven escaped. See Mrs. N. D. White, "Captivity Among the Sioux, August 18 to September 26, 1862," *Minnesota Historical Society Collections* 9 (1901): 400.

23. David Carrothers to Ramsey, August 18, 1862, Governors Papers, MHSA.

24. *The Pioneer and Democrat,* August 21, 1862.

25. See "Narrative of Mrs. Helen Carrothers, of Beaver Creek," in Bryant and Murch, *A History of the Great Massacre,* 286.

26. Mrs. Helen [Carrothers] Tarble, *The Story of My Capture and Escape during the Minnesota Indian Massacre of 1862* (St. Paul: The Abbott Printing Company, 1904), 29.

27. "Narrative of Justina Boelter," in Bryant and Murch, *A History of the Great Massacre of the Sioux Indians,* 324–35. A similar story occurred just north of the Boelter home, where the family of Joha Koorhendorfer was killed. This occurred at around 10:00 A.M., documenting the movement of the Indians northward. See Joha Koorhendorfer [Kochendorfer is another spelling] to Satterlee, n. d., Satterlee Papers, MHSA.

28. Minnie Buce Carrigan, *Captured by Indians: Reminiscences of Pioneer Life in Minnesota* (Buffalo Lake, Minn.: Buffalo Lake News, 1903), 6–16; reprinted as Carrigan, *Captured by the Indians: Reminiscences of Pioneer Life in Minnesota* (Forest City, S.Dak.: Forest City Press, 1907). Carrigan was seven years old when captured, but she waited until 1903 to give her narrative to the newspaper, leaving suspicions regarding its accuracy.

29. Curtis Dahlin has spent nearly a lifetime collecting evidence from graveyards and primary documents on how many settlers died at the hands of Dakota warriors. His figures can be reviewed in *Dakota Uprising Victims: Gravestones and Stories* (Edina, Minn.:

Beaver's Pond Press, 2007). A map is found in Dahlin, *A History of the Dakota Uprising* (Edina, Minn.: Self-Published, n. d.), 67. See also "Mrs. DeCamp Sweet's Narrative," 362.

30. Tarble, *The Story of My Capture*, 20. See oral history account of Mrs. Boelter at www.dakotavictims1862.com/ Flora Township.

31. First quotation is found in George C. Allanson, "Stirring Adventures of the Joseph R. Brown Family," in *The Garland Library of Narratives of North American Indian Captivity*, ed. Wilcombe E. Washburn, Vol. 103 (New York: Garland Publishing, 1976), n.p. Allanson was the son of Ellen Brown, J. R. Brown's daughter, and wrote the narrative in the 1910s. The second is in Samuel J. Brown's narrative, "In Captivity: The Experiences, Privations and Dangers of Samuel J. Brown, and Others, while Prisoners of the Hostile Sioux, during the Massacre and War of 1862," *Mankato Weekly Record*, April 6, 13, 20, 27, May 4, 11, 1897; reprinted in Anderson and Woolworth, *Through Dakota Eyes*, 77.

32. Interview with Margareta Holl Hahn, n. d., MHSA; Caroline Smith, "Observations by Caroline Ester Thomas Concerning Her Experiences in the Sioux Outbreak," n.d., MHSA.

33. Hugo Roos, "Reminiscences of Early Days," *Mankato Semi-Weekly Record*, October 25, 1862.

34. Roos to Ramsey, August 21, 1862, *The Pioneer and Democrat*, August 22, 1862. See also Godfrey's biography, Walt Bachman, *Northern Slave Black Dakota* (Bloomington, Minn.: Pond Dakota Press, 2013), xv–xix, 63–86.

35. "Fascinating Story Gives Experiences in Pioneer Days," *New Ulm Review*, June 19, 1929.

36. Ibid. A published version of the attack is Alexander Berghold, *The Indians' Revenge; or Days of Horror. Some Appalling Events in the History of the Sioux* (San Francisco: P. J. Thomas, 1891), 106. For the first victims, see "Statistics Concerning the Sioux Massacre: Collected by Town Assessors," MHSA; L. A. Fritsche, *History of Brown County Minnesota: Its People, Industries, and Institutions* (Indianapolis: B. F. Bowen, 1916; repr. University of Minnesota, Digitized, 2014), 163. A few days later, the *St. Paul Pioneer & Democrat* published an embellished version of the killing of the Henle children, enclosed in a letter from "E. J. H.," likely E. J. Hatch. It stated that Mrs. Henle saw "before her eyes" the murder of her children. See *St. Paul Pioneer & Democrat*, August 27, 1862.

37. Roos, "History of Early Days," MHSA.

38. "Story of Caecilie Schilling," *New Ulm Review*, February 17, 1929.

39. Ibid.

40. "Narrative of Mary Schwandt," in Bryant and Murch, *A History of the Great Massacre by the Sioux Indians*, 335–37.

41. Ibid.

42. Report of John Porter, *The Pioneer and Democrat*, August 22, 1862; *Mankato Semi-Weekly Record*, August 22, 1862.

43. Roos to Ramsey, August 18, 1862, Ramsey Papers, MHSA; "Statistics Concerning the Sioux Massacre: Collected by Town Assessors," ms., MHSA. The final number of fifty-three was used when the Milford Monument was erected.

44. Satterlee, "Massacre at the Redwood Indian Agency," 7–8; Lieutenant John F. Bishop "Battle of Redwood," in Board of Commissioners, *Minnesota in the Civil and Indian Wars*, 2:166–70.

45. Historians have speculated regarding Marsh's lack of caution. He had been wounded at Bull Run and, after facing such a ferocious onslaught, likely underestimated the abilities of the Dakota Indians to wage war upon a company of troops. Another more intriguing suggestion is that he may have impregnated a Dakota woman from the agency and wished to protect the mother. Such a suggestion is very speculative, given the fact that Marsh had only been at Fort Ridgely for roughly four months. Board of Commissioners, *Minnesota in the Civil and Indian Wars*, 1:244. On Marsh's possible liaison, see "Army Officers and Dakota Women on the Minnesota Frontier," Part 5, a Blog by Carie Zeman

@ athrillingnarrative.com; John Marsh Military Papers, especially W. R. Marsh to R. B. Dunsworth, January 4, 1960, MHSA.

46. The trial records give his name as Shoon-ka-ska. See Sioux Trials, Senate Records, NARG 46, 37A-F2.

47. A good discussion of Śuŋkaska's role is found in Isch, *The Dakota Trials*, 83–85. Although White Dog bitterly protested his innocence while awaiting execution in December 1862, most sources contradict his pleadings. Ezmon W. Earle, who survived the massacre on Beaver Creek, met one of the returning soldiers from Marsh's command, who said "An Indian in citizens dress appeared on the other side [of the river] and told the Captain there were no Indians there." See Earle Reminiscences, MHSA. Historian William Watts Folwell concluded: "White Dog at length gave the signal for concerted action." See Folwell, *History of Minnesota*, 2:113. Nancy Huggan later wrote, "White Dog did the talking and it was agreed that when he gave the order the concealed Indians were to fire." See Huggan to Holcombe, June 14, 1894, Holcombe Papers, MHSA; Holcombe, *Sketches Historical and Descriptive*, 21–23.

48. The "Narrative of Orlando McFall," ms., MHSA, offers some insight into the retreat of Marsh's men.

49. This description of the nailing of children to fences or trees is repeated over and over again in the Minnesota press. It comes from the "Narrative of Justina Kreiger," in Bryant and Murch, *A History of the Great Massacre by the Sioux Indians*, 300–301. A second more reputable source is Harper Workman, who interviewed Louis Kitzman early in the twentieth century. He gave an identical description, which is likely an embellishment. See Workman Papers, MHSA. Burial details never confirmed finding such a child. See Mary Schwandt's interview with Marion P. Satterlee, Satterlee Papers, MHSA.

50. Ibid. The statement comes from the Charles Schrepel "Narrative," MHSA.

51. "Narrative of Justina Kreiger," in Bryant and Murch, *A History of the Great Massacre by the Sioux Indians*, 302–3.

52. Ibid. A narrative left by six-year-old Fred Lammers suggests that some of the children fled to a slough, while he, his brother Charles, and his mother agreed to surrender. See Interview with Fred Lammers, Survivor of the Indian Massacre, Now Residing at Fairfax, Minnesota, at the Age of 74, Fort Ridgely State Park and Historical Society, 1930, MHSA.

53. The victims are all identified in Dahlin, *A History of the Dakota Uprising*, 57.

54. Sarah F. Wakefield, *Six Weeks in the Sioux Tepees: A Narrative of Indian Captivity* (Shakopee, Minn.: Argus Book & Job Printing, 1864), 112–14; repr., Wakefield, *Six Weeks in the Sioux Tepees: A Narrative of Indian Captivity,* ed., June Namias (Norman: University of Oklahoma Press, 1997).

55. Brown, "Samuel J. Brown's Recollections," in Anderson and Woolworth, *Through Dakota Eyes*, 71–74. George Allanson, taking oral history from his mother, Ellen, who was there, gives a more colorful account in "Stirring Adventures of the Joseph R. Brown Family." Allanson gives special attention to Cut Nose, who "took particular delight in describing the slaughter" of the settlers.

56. All three of these men would later be executed.

57. "Samuel J. Brown Recollections," in Anderson and Woolworth, *Through Dakota Eyes*, 74–75. Brown likely exaggerated the remark regarding Little Crow, as there is little evidence that he advocated killing civilians, and Brown wrote his memoir well after Little Crow had become the scapegoat, considered the leader of the conflict.

58. Ibid., 76.

59. Otherday became a hero when he reached St. Paul. One report called him "a lion in our streets." He spoke at Ingersoll's Hall, and the crowd collected $41 and gave it to him. See Otherday Interview, *St. Paul Daily Press,* August 28, 1862; "Statement of Otherday," undated, Whipple Papers, MHSA; Folwell, *A History of Minnesota*, 2:117–18; report, *St. Paul Pioneer & Democrat*, August 24 and 27, 1862.

60. The ordeal of the missionaries is best described in Thomas Alfred Riggs, *Sunset to Sunset: A Lifetime with My Brothers, the Dakotas,* as told to Margaret Kellogg Howard (Pierre: South Dakota State Historical Society Press, 1997), 24–30; "The Riggs Mission Party," in Satterlee Papers, MHSA.

61. The so-called "Leavenworth Expedition" was not encouraged by Sheriff Roos, who was concerned that it would weaken the defenses at New Ulm. See "Brave Defenders From Leavenworth," *New Ulm Review,* October 24, 1912. A new history of New Ulm that outlines the defense of the city is Darla Cordes Gebhard and John Isch, *Eight Days in August: The Accounts of the Casualties and Survivors in Brown County during the US-Dakota War of 1862* (New Ulm, Minn.: Brown County Historical Society, 2012).

62. See George W. Doud Diary, August 22, 1862, MHSA. Dr. J. W. Daniels and R. B. Henton had some seventy victims buried in both Milford and Leavenworth, and they found one person mutilated and another scalped. See Daniels to Holcombe, October 21, 1894, Holcombe Papers, MHSA.

63. Ibid.; Hugo Roos, "Reminiscences of Early Days," *New Ulm Review,* August 14, 1912. Gary Wiltscheck, *The Leavenworth Rescue Expedition Revisited* (New Ulm, Minn.: Brown County Historical Society, 2011), 6–55.

64. Fritsche, *A History of New Ulm,* 165–71; "Brave Defenders From Leavenworth," *New Ulm Review,* October 24, 1912; Ross, "Reminiscences of Early Days," *New Ulm Review,* August 19, 1862.

65. See Workman Papers, MHSA; Statement of Thomas Ireland and Statement of Aaron Meyers, Currie Papers, MHSA; H. J. Hibschman, "The Lake Shetek Pioneers and the Indians," in *The Garland Library of Narratives of North American Indian Captivities,* ed. Wilcomb Washburn, Vol. 104 (New York: Garland Publishing, 1976), 8–26. Aaron Meyers identifies Smith and Rhodes as draft dodgers, and the group certainly included Hatch.

66. "Statement of Mrs. Andreas Koch" and "Statement of Aaron Meyers," in Currie Papers, MHSA.

67. Eastlick left two narratives. See Reminiscences of Lavina Eastlick, MHSA; and Eastlick, *Thrilling Adventures in the Indians War of 1862: Being, a Personal Narrative of the Outrages and Horrors Witnessed by Mrs. L. Eastlick in Minnesota* (Minneapolis: Atlas Steam Printing Co., 1864).

68. Reminiscences of Lavina Eastlick, MHSA.

69. Duley's role in the affair has often been questioned. Workman later wrote: "Everett, Hatch, and Mrs. Kock [Cook] say Duley was a coward, that he was running when they entered the slough, and never stopped." Duley's son, Jefferson, later defended his father, saying he fought until there was no use in continuing. See Workman Papers, MHSA.

70. Reminiscences of Lavina Eastlick, MHSA.

71. Ibid. On the cowardice of Hatch and Bentley, see Hughes, *A History of Blue Earth County,* 118.

72. C. C. Nelson, "History of the Early Pioneers of the Neighborhood in the Western Parts of New Sweden, Nicollet County, Minnesota, and of the Indian Massacre in this Neighborhood in 1862," ms., MHSA; also found in the Nicollet County Historical Society, St. Peter, Minn. An excellent account of the murders in Nicollet County is provided in Karl Jakob Skarstein, *The War with the Sioux: Norwegians against the Indians, 1862–1863,* trans. Melissa Gjellstad and Danielle Skjelver (Grand Forks: The Digital Press of the University of North Dakota, 2015).

73. Erick Johnson to his brother-in-law, March 3, 1863, Nicollet County Historical Society, St. Peter, Minn.; Reminiscences of Ingar [Johnson] Holquist, 1920, MHSA.

74. Ibid.; Dahlin, *A History of the Dakota Uprising,* 67; Franklin Clinton Griswold Letter, August 25, 1862, MHSA.

75. Skarstein, *The War with the Sioux,* 61–86.

76. Dahlin, *A History of the Dakota Uprising*, 31, 67; Hughes, *A History of Blue Earth County*, 119–23. The attack at Norway Lake is described in Lena Lundborg, "Testimony," and in Petition of Governor Ramsey, August 21, 1862, Governors Papers, MHSA.

77. Reminiscences of Aaron Meyers, MHSA.

78. Zierke interview, *Mankato Semi-Weekly*, September 20, 1862.

79. Workman Papers, MHSA.

80. "Reminiscences of Mrs. Robert Thul," *St. Paul Pioneer Press*, August 16, 1925.

81. George W. Doud Diary, August–September 1862, MHSA. For Dane's military experience, see Hughes, *A History of Blue Earth County*, 118.

82. Lavina Eastlick, "Thrilling Incidents of the War (Indian) 1862: A Personal Narrative of the Outrages and Horrors," MHSA.

83. The information from Henton and Asa Daniels is found in a letter from Jared W. Daniels to Holcombe, October 21, 1894, Holcombe Papers, MHSA.

84. Ibid.; Donnelly's letter, *St. Paul Journal*, August 28, 1862.

85. Examples of commentary far from the scenes of the murder include Sarah Purcell Montgomery, "Some Recollections of the Indian Outbreak of 1862," MHSA; A. J. Ebell letter, *St. Paul Press,* September 3, 1862 (Ebell escaped with the missionaries at Yellow Medicine and never saw a dead body); Rosanna Sturgis to her husband, October 8, 1862, MHSA.

86. Dahlin, *A History of the Dakota Uprising*, 61. Another comparative destructive massacre that had an ethnic origin is Nat Turner's rebellion of 1831. Most scholars agree that just sixty whites were killed by Turner and his supporters. Some fifty African Americans were later executed, and another sixty or one hundred more were lynched in the aftermath of the rebellion. See John Hope Franklin, *From Slavery to Freedom: A History of Negro Americans* (New York: Alfred Knopf, 1956), 212–13; and Stephen B. Oates, *The Fires of Jubilee: Nat Turner's Fierce Rebellion* (New York: Harper Perennial, 2014), 126.

CHAPTER SIX

1. Gilman, *Henry Hastings Sibley*, 172–78.

2. Fort Ridgely had become a school for artillerymen, and they left manuals behind. Twice each week, artillery drills were conducted, and Ordinance Sergeant John Jones had been left behind to continue training. See Major W. W. Morris to Lieutenant Colonel L. Thomas, May 1, 1860, NARG 393, LR, DWWD.

3. General L. F. Hubbard, "Narrative of the Fifth Regiment," in Board of Commissioners, *Minnesota in the Civil and Indian Wars*, 1:243–44.

4. Quotation in Abercrombie to Captain S. Williams, May 20, 1861, NARG 393, LR, DWWD. See also Major H. Day to the AAG, August 21, 1860, ibid.

5. City Officials of Stillwater, "The Draft," August 11, 1862 Circular, NARG 393, LR, DWWD. See other circulars in Governors Papers, MHSA.

6. Sibley to Ramsey, August 20, 1862, in Board of Commissioners, *Minnesota in the Civil and Indian Wars*, 2:165; Ramsey to Sibley, August 25, 1862, Marshall Papers, MHSA; Ramsey to Sibley, August 22, 1862, NARG 393, LR, Department of the Northwest, Unentered Files.

7. Sibley to Ramsey, August 20, 1862, in Board of Commissioners, *Minnesota in the Civil and Indian Wars*, 2:165; Reminiscences of Edwin Bell, MHSA. Both the Union and Confederate armies bought Augustin musket/rifles; the Union took 226,000 of them.

8. The first quote is in the *St. Paul Pioneer & Democrat*, August 28, 1862, and second, in Aaron M. Sidwell, "Selected Extracts from the Soldier's Gazette," ms., MHSA. R. K. Boyd noted the refusal of officers to advance in Boyd, "What a Boy Saw at Fort Ridgely," in Fort Ridgely State Park and Historical Association Papers, MHSA.

9. Sibley to Ramsey, August 22, 1862, in Board of Commissioners, *Minnesota in the Civil and Indian Wars*, 2:196.

10. Reminiscences of Edwin Bell, MHSA; Sidwell, "Extracts from the Soldier's Gazette," ms., MHSA.

11. See "Samuel J. Brown's Recollections," in Anderson and Woolworth, *Through Dakota Eyes*, 130.

12. "Nancy McClure Faribault Huggan's Account," in Anderson and Woolworth, *Through Dakota Eyes*, 139.

13. Antoine J. Campbell interview in Holcombe, *Sketches Historical and Descriptive*, 18; A. J. Campbell Interview, *St. Paul Press*, October 24, 1897. An excellent description of the Campbell family and its origins near Fort Snelling is found in Annette Atkins, *Creating Minnesota: A History from Inside Out* (St. Paul: Minnesota Historical Society Press, 2007).

14. Ibid.

15. Antoine J. Campbell interview in Holcombe, *Sketches Historical and Descriptive*, 18.

16. Kenneth Carley, ed., "Lightning Blanket's Story," *Minnesota History* 38 (September 1962): 144.

17. "Official Reports and Correspondence," in Board of Commissioners, *Minnesota in the Civil and Indian Wars*, 2:181–82. Gere was awarded the Medal of Honor on February 22, 1865, after being wounded at Nashville. See ibid., 1:282. Gere left two memoirs, one titled "Life in Uncle Sam's Army" and a "Journal," covering events at Fort Ridgely, both found in MHSA. Sergeant J. G. McGrew later wrote of Gere: "There is probably not another instance in the history of the country where an officer so young had such grave responsibilities so suddenly thrust upon him." See McGrew to Holcombe, July 25, 1895, Holcombe Papers, MHSA. For a description of the chaos at the fort, see Lucy Leavenworth Wilder Morris, ed., *Old Rail and Fence Corners: Frontier Tales Told by Minnesota Pioneers* (St. Paul: Minnesota Historical Society Press, 1976), 146–52, 300–301.

18. Interview with Col. T. J. Sheehan, Holcombe Papers, MHSA; "Official Reports and Correspondence," in Board of Commissioners, *Minnesota in the Civil and Indian Wars*, 2:181–82.

19. Narrative of Orlando McFall, August 17 and 19, 1862, MHSA; Deposition of Timothy J. Sheehan, Sheehan Papers, MHSA. Thomas Scantlebury from New Auburn gives the time of 3:00 A.M. as when Sheehan arrived in town. See Thomas Scantlebury, "Wanderings in Minnesota During the Indian Troubles in that State in the Autumn of 1862. By a Minnesotan," ms., MHSA.

20. On the cannon, see Interview with August Rieke, Survivor of the Battle of Fort Ridgely Now Living at Fairfax at the Age of 86 Years [1925], Fort Ridgely State Park and Historical Association Papers, MHSA.

21. "Statement of George Quinn," Holcombe Papers, MHSA. Some Dakota scouts sent to observe the fort had fallen asleep, only to be awakened by Jack Frazier. Frazier said, "If he did not know our fathers and mothers so well," he would have shot us.

22. "Narrative of Helen Carrothers," in Bryant and Murch, *A History of the Great Massacre of the Sioux Indians*, 291; Wakefield, *Six Weeks in a Sioux Tepee*, 71.

23. Isaac Heard suggests that about 120 warriors stayed with Little Crow below the fort, and that two hundred went on to New Ulm, although nothing close to that number appeared on the tableland north of the town. William Hayden, who was there, put the number of warriors at thirty to forty. See Heard, *History of the Sioux War*, 79–80; *St. Paul Pioneer & Democrat*, August 26, 1862; Account of William Hayden, August 19, 1862, ms., MHSA. Gebhard and Isch, *Eight Days in August*, 17.

24. For the arming of the civilians, see Ezmon W. Earle, Reminiscences, MHSA. Some reports put the number of civilian men at eighty. But the official roster includes only sixty-six men. Skarstein found the names of six Norwegians who claimed to have participated but whose names are not on the roster. The roster obviously did not include all who made up the civilian corps, including young Ezmon Earle, who left a wonderful account of the battles. See Skarstein, *The War with the Sioux*, 57.

25. It apparently took the Renville Rangers twelve hours to reach the fort, putting them there about the time of the rainstorm, or 6:00 P.M. See B. H. Goodell, "Personal Recollections of the Sioux Massacre of 1862," MHSA; Ezmon W. Earle, Reminiscences, MHSA; J. G. McGrew to Holcombe, July 22, Holcombe Papers, MHSA.

26. See "Testimony of Antoine J. Campbell," in *Sisseton and Wahpeton Court of Claims* No. 22524; "Testimony of Timothy J. Sheehan," ibid.

27. "Testimony of Timothy J. Sheehan," ibid.; McGrew to Holcombe, July 23, 1895, Holcombe Papers, MHSA; "Battle of Fort Ridgely," by General L. F. Hubbard in Board of Commissioners, *Minnesota in the Civil and Indian Wars*, 2:183–85.

28. "Testimony of Timothy J. Sheehan," *Sisseton and Wahpeton Court of Claims* No. 22524.

29. There is no way to confirm the losses suffered by the Indians, Curtis Dahlin suggesting that sixty to seventy may be a fair number, although that seems extremely high. Dahlin, *A History of the Dakota Uprising*, 82. McGrew later testified that one of his shells fell "in the midst of them," another in an Indian camp of mostly women. See McGrew to Holcombe, July 22, 1895, Holcombe Papers, MHSA. Heard suggested that "several" Indians were killed, and A. J. Campbell also offered a small number. Thomas Robertson counted only four dead who were carried back to Little Crow's village, but he did not see those in other camps. Lightening Blanket listed four Indians killed on the north side of the fort. He admitted to knowing nothing about the other groups who also faced the canons. See Heard, *History of the Sioux War*, 82–83; "Testimony of Antoine J. Campbell," *Sisseton and Wahpeton Court of Claims* No. 22524; Reminiscences of Thomas Robertson, MHSA; "Lightening Blanket's Account," in Anderson and Woolworth, *Through Dakota Eyes*, 155–57.

30. Orlando McFall, an enlisted man in Company C, noted that "about 30 citizens in the fort had done good effective work and fought bravely. All the rest were a curse and a hindrance." See "Narrative of Orlando McFall," ms., MHSA.

31. Earle, Reminiscences of the Sioux Massacre, ms., MHSA.

32. "Colonel T. J. Sheehan," in Holcombe Papers, ms., MHSA. Gere later wrote in his journal: "The country awoke to the fact that the Sioux were destroying Minnesota and troops in numbers came to our relief. I shall never forget those days at Fort Ridgely—May we some day see a truthful history of them," Gere, "Journal," MHSA.

33. "Samuel J. Brown's Recollections," in Anderson and Woolworth, *Through Dakota Eyes*, 133–34. See also Mark Diedrich, *Old Betsey: The Life and Times of A Famous Dakota Woman and Her Family* (Rochester, Minn.: Coyote Books, 1995), 61.

34. There is no indication that the Sisseton and Wahpeton chiefs from the upper Minnesota River joined this war party. Heard makes the argument for Little Six as being the recruiter. See Heard, *History of the Sioux War*, 83.

35. Reminiscences of Ezmon W. Earle, ms., MHSA.

36. "Testimony of Timothy J. Sheehan," *Sisseton and Wahpeton Court of Claims* No. 22524. Good Thunder apparently counted the warriors who left, giving a figure of eight hundred. See "Big Eagle's Account" in Anderson and Woolworth, *Through Dakota Eyes,* 148.

37. One report has Little Crow lying beside the road on his back after the ball struck him, an incident that obviously had a demoralizing impact on the charge. See Holcombe, *Minnesota in Three Centuries*, 3:337. Another, recorded by Samuel Brown, has the chief laying on his back on a rock when a cannonball came over his head, and while ducking, he hit his head on a rock. Regardless, Little Crow was suffering thereafter from intense headaches, which likely affected his actions. See Brown, "Samuel J. Brown's Recollections," in Anderson and Woolworth, *Through Dakota Eyes*, 173.

38. "Testimony of Timothy J. Sheehan," ibid.; "Battle of Fort Ridgely," in Board of Commissioners, *Minnesota in the Civil and Indian Wars*, 2:185–87; Heard, *History of the Sioux War*, 83–84. A young Dakota woman, Snana, or Tinkling, who was at Little Crow's village, reported the impact of the casualties at the fort and the killing of the two unnamed

captives. See "Snana's Story," in Anderson and Woolworth, *Through Dakota Eyes*, 141. "Big Eagles Account," in ibid., 148–49.

39. Van Vorhes's account is in the *St. Paul Pioneer & Democrat,* August 24, 1862. The offer of surrender is in "Narrative of Orlando McFall," ms., MHSA.

40. A. A. Mix to Governor Ramsey, August 21, 1862, Governors Papers, MHSA; Sibley to his wife, August 21, 1862, Sibley Papers, MHSA.

41. Missionary Gideon H. Pond expressed the exact concern of an "ambuscade" in an urgent letter to the governor. Pond had lived with the Dakota for nearly thirty years and knew them well. See Pond to Ramsey, August 24, 1862, Governors Papers, MHSA.

42. Sibley to Ramsey, August 24 and 26, 1862, Governors Papers, MHSA; Ramsey to Sibley, August 23, 1862, NARG 393, Department of the Northwest, Unentered File.

43. Ramsey to Sibley, August 25, 1862, NARG 393, LR, Department of the Northwest.

44. Troxel wrote an account of the situation at Henderson in an appeal to Sibley for financial assistance. See Troxel to Sibley, April 28, 1881, Sibley Papers, MHSA.

45. Cullen to Ramsey, August 22 and 23, 1862, Governors Papers, MHSA.

46. Reminiscences of Julia E. Farnsworth Lobdell, ms., MHSA.

47. John Steins to Ramsey, August 21 and 22, 1862, Petition from Forest City, August 22, 1862, Petition from Paynesville, August 22, 1862, and W. G. Butler to Ramsey, August 22, 1862, Governors Ppers, MHSA; "Fort Skedaddle" at Glencoe, from letter of Henry Wadsworth, McLeod County Historical Museum, Hutchinson, Minn.

48. "Statistics Concerning the Sioux Massacre: Collected by Town Assessors," ms., MHSA; Diary of Rebecca MacAlmond, August 20, 1862, ms., MHSA; "Recollections of Elizabeth Whitcomb," ms., MHSA.

49. Reminiscences of Mary Ann Marston Hallock, ms., MHSA; Diary of Kate Marston, August 20–25, 1862, McLeod County Historical Museum, Hutchinson, Minn.; Hughes, *A History of Blue Earth County*, 114–15.

50. Reminiscences of Mary Ann Marston Hallock, ms., MHSA; Hughes, *A History of Blue Earth County*, 114–15.

51. *St. Paul Pioneer & Democrat*, August 24, 1862.

52. Ibid.

53. Louisa Scantlebury, "Flight from New Auburn, Minnesota, during the Indian Uprising in Minnesota, August 1862," ms,, MHSA.

54. Thomas Scantlebury, "Wanderings in Minnesota during the Indian Troubles in that State in the Autumn of 1862. By a Minnesotan," ms., MHSA.

55. Reminiscence of Dick E. Blanchard, ms., MHSA.

56. Captain William Tattersall to Ramsey, August 23, 1862, Governors Papers, MHSA.

57. Ramsey Proclamation, August 22, 1862, Governors Papers, MHSA.

58. *St. Paul Pioneer & Democrat,* August 22, 1862.

59. A good description of Flandrau and his career is in Russell W. Fridley, "Charles E. Flandrau, Attorney at Law," *Minnesota History* 43 (September 1962): 117.

60. Sibley to Flandrau, August 22, 1862, in Board of Commissioners, *Minnesota in the Civil and Indian Wars,* 2:197.

61. Jared Daniels, who joined the force, counted 150 men originally, but Flandrau reports that only ninety reached New Ulm. Flandrau to Ramsey, August 20, 1862, in Board of Commissioners, *Minnesota in the Civil and Indian Wars*, 2:165–66; Reminiscences of Jared Daniels, ms., MHSA; Interview with Richard Pfefferle [Pfeiffer], Fort Ridgely State Park and Historical Association Papers, "Clippings," 1926, MHSA.

62. Frandrau to Sibley, August 20, 1862, in Board of Commissioners, *Minnesota in the Civil and Indian Wars*, 2:165–66; Reminiscences of Jared Daniels, ms., MHSA. Bierbauer's efforts are recorded in Gebhard and Isch, *Eight Days in August*, 22. The figure of thirty rifles comes from Flandrau, *The History of Minnesota and Tales of the Frontier*, 151–56.

63. Flandrau to Sibley, August 22, 1862, in Board of Commissioners, *Minnesota in the Civil and Indian Wars*, 2:197–98; Flandrau, "The Indian War of 1862," in ibid., 2:197–98; Hughes, *History of Blue Earth County*, 112–14.

64. The quotation from Anna Schmitz as well as the description of Mary Schmitz Ryan comes from Terry Sveine, *The Lady with the Gunpowder: A Luxembourger's Tale of Courage in the U. S. Dakota War of 1862* (New Ulm: Privately printed, 2015), no pages.

65. Some of the leading men in town had a premonition about an attack, petitioning Governor Ramsey on August 14, 1862. The men said that the Indians would soon "commit outrages," and that "families would be massacred." See Petition of Francis Erd, John Rudolph, John Manderfield, Adolph Strecker, and others, Governors Papers, MHSA. Some missionaries believed that these same men, some of whom were in the liquor business, added to the general animosity that the Dakota held toward the Germans, because of the wide distribution of whiskey. On the liquor issue, see Jonas Pettijohn, *Autobiography, Family History and Various Reminiscences of the Life of Jonas Pettijohn among the Sioux or Dakota Indians. His Escape during the Massacre of August, 1862. Causes That Led to the Massacre* (Clay Center, Kans.: Dispatch Printing House, 1890), 82–83. Flandrau to Sibley, August 22, 1862, in Board of Commissioners, *Minnesota in the Civil and Indian Wars*, 2:197–98.

66. Jacob Nix, *The Sioux Uprising in Minnesota, 1862: Jacob Nix's Eyewitness Account*, ed. Don Heinrich Tolzmann (Indianapolis: Indiana German Heritage Society, Inc., 1994), 109.

67. The evacuation issue is discussed in Nix's account in ibid., 120.

68. Friend's narrative is in Thomas Hughes, "Collection of Statements," ms., MHSA; Flandrau, "Battle of New Ulm," August 27, 1862, newspaper clipping from *The St. Paul Pioneer & Democrat*, Riggs Papers, MHSA. This is essentially the same report as Flandrau, "The Battle of New Ulm, August 23, 1861," in Board of Commissioners, *Minnesota in the Civil and Indian Wars*, 2:203–7. I cite the newspaper account only because it was the first printing.

69. Frandrau, "The Battle of New Ulm," August 27, 1862, clipping from *St. Paul Pioneer & Democrat*, Riggs Papers, MHSA.

70. Daniels noted that while volunteers arrived in town before the battle, some "left for their homes the day before the fight," and those who fled to the cellars were simply "cowards." See Reminiscences of Jared Daniels, MHSA.

71. Frandrau, "the Battle of New Ulm," August 27, 1862, clipping from *St. Paul Pioneer & Democrat*, Riggs Papers, MHSA. Another good description of the battle is Jared Daniels's Reminiscences, ms., MHSA.

72. Ibid. Diary, kept by William Dodd's wife, Dodd Papers, MHSA. See also Curtis Dahlin, "Outside the Barricades: The August 23, 1862 Battle of New Ulm," *Minnesota's Heritage* 2 (July 2010): 24–39.

73. Sibley knew of Cox's vulnerability, and he ordered him to be cautious. In reaching the Minnesota River below New Ulm. If he was unable to cross safely, he was to "strengthen your position and wait reinforcements." See Sibley to Cox, August 24, 1862, NARG 393, LR, Department of the Northwest.

74. The estimate of damages comes from the *Minnesota Staats-Zeitung* (New Ulm), September 10, 1862. The total reported of all losses, including goods, was $260,000.

75. Folwell gives a figure of twenty-six killed, while the monument at New Ulm lists twenty-four. The latter number conforms with the list in Board of Commissioners, *Minnesota in the Civil and Indian Wars*, 1:818. Some certainly died of wounds in the days that followed. See Folwell, *History of Minnesota*, 2:142. Descriptions of the town in the aftermath are found in Reminiscences of Aaron Myers, ms., MHSA; and Franklin Clinton Griswold letter, August 28, 1862, ms., MHSA.

76. For an extended discussion of the forces available on both sides, see Gebhard and Isch, *Eight Days in August*, 23–24.

77. Nix, *The Sioux Uprising*, 103.

78. Flandrau to Ramsey, August 27, 1862, in Board of Commissioners, *Minnesota in the Civil and Indian Wars*, 2:203–7.

79. Flandrau to Ramsey, August 27, 1862, ibid., 2:206–7. This letter was later published in the *St. Paul Pioneer & Democrat*, August 30, 1862. The use of strychnine became a hotly contested issue, as Flandrau's son wrote about it in the newspapers in 1917. Given the World War, editors from New Ulm newspapers denied it and called it "German bashing." Nevertheless, the story was reinforced by a departing volunteer and published in the *St. Paul Pioneer & Democrat*, August 28, 1862. See the denial in "Heartless Story is Denied," *New Ulm Review,* September 4, 1917, Roos Papers, MHSA.

80. Knight to his wife, August 27, 1862, Governors Papers, MHSA.

81. Sibley to Ramsey, August 26, 1862, and Lincoln to Ramsey, August 27, 1862, in Board of Commissioners, *Minnesota in the Civil and Indian Wars*, 2:199–200, 2:201; Hughes, *History of Blue Earth County*, 118; Flandrau to Ramsey, August 31, 1862, Governors Papers, MHSA.

82. Gebhard and Isch, *Eight Days in August*, 26–27.

83. The history of exchanges during the Civil War is itself interesting, as large numbers of men on both sides were sent back to their homes in 1862. However, the practice ended the next year as prison camps were established to house them.

84. M. M. Pomeroy to Ramsey, August 27, 1862, O. Densmore to Ramsey, August 27, 1862, and L. McDonald to Ramsey, August 28, 1862, Governors Papers, MHSA; Riggs to Treat, August 29, 1862, ABCFM.

85. Report on Minnesota Home Guard, August 27, 1862, NARG 94, LR, AGO; Sibley to Ramsey, August 26, 1862, Governors Papers, MHSA; Boyd, "What a Boy Saw at Fort Ridgely," in Fort Ridgely State Park and Historical Association Papers, MHSA; McPhail to Ramsey, August 31, 1862, Governors Papers, MHSA.

86. Sibley to his wife, August 28 and August 29, 1862, Sibley Papers, MHSA.

87. *St. Paul Pioneer & Democrat*, August 26, 1862.

88. See "order" in *St. Paul Pioneer & Democrat*, August 22, 1862; H. J. Mitchell to Ramsey, August 28, 1862, Governors Papers, MHSA. Nelson soon resigned, apparently being upset about serving under the "civilian" Sibley. See Charles H. Johnson, "Narrative of the Sixth Regiment," in Board of Commissioners, *Minnesota in the Civil and Indian Wars,* 1:302–3.

89. Redfield to Ramsey, September 4, 1862, and Roos to Ramsey, September 4, 1862, Governors Papers, MHSA. Hughes notes that troops of the Ninth Regiment, sent to Mankato to restore order, had orders to impress whatever they needed, including food and clothing. See Hughes, *History of Blue Earth County*, 115–16.

90. Swift to Ramsey, August 29, 1862, and Wakefield to Ramsey, August 27, 1862, Governors Papers, MHSA.

91. Dane in *Mankato Independent,* August 29, 1862.

92. *Mankato Independent,* August 29, 1862.

93. Flandrau letter with "Petition from Mankato," August 31, 1862, and Captain Jerome Dane to Ramsey, August 27, 1862, Governors Papers, MHSA.

94. J. Coward to Ramsey, August 28, 1862, George M. Green to Ramsey, August 29, 1862, and Whipple to Ramsey, September 1, 1862, ibid.

95. Eliza to her sister Laura Guigg Swett, August 29, 1862, ms., MHSA.

96. Flandrau has a good description of the town stockades in "The Indian War of 1862," in Board of Commissioners, *Minnesota in the Civil and Indian Wars,* 1:739. See also Rosters of militia units, ibid.; 1:761–63. Captain J. Hall to Ramsey, August 23, 1862, Wilt Pendergast to Ramsey, August 24, 1862, and Lewis Harrington to Ramsey, August 27, 1862, Governors Papers, MHSA; "Remarks of A. H. DeLong on Dedication of the Acton Monument," Satterlee Papers, MHSA.

97. *St. Cloud Democrat,* August 28, 1862; William P. Dole to Ramsey, August 25 and 30, 1862, Governors Papers, MHSA; Folwell, *History of Minnesota*, 2:375–77.

98. Mitchell's aunt, Jane Grey Swisshelm, a rather famous abolitionist, started the newspaper in St. Cloud. See Mitchell to Ramsey, August 28, 1862, Governors Papers, MHSA. All of the rosters for the various city militias are found in Board of Commissioners, *Minnesota in the Civil and Indian Wars*, 1:754–818.

99. Chairman, Vigilante Committee, St. Cloud, to Ramsey, August 28, 1862, Governors Papers, MHSA.

100. Sally S. Wood to her brother, August 26, 1862, Bentley Historical Library, University of Michigan, Ann Arbor, Michigan.

CHAPTER SEVEN

1. See Ramsey's rebuke of Stanton in Ramsey to Lincoln, August 26, 1862, in Board of Commissioners, *Minnesota in the Civil and Indian Wars*, 2:200.

2. Lincoln to Ramsey, August 27, 1862, ibid., 2:201.

3. Nicolay to Stanton, August 27, 1862, ibid., 2:202.

4. Folwell, *History of Minnesota*, 2:186–87.

5. *St. Paul Journal*, August 28, 1862; *Mankato Independent*, August 29, 1862; *Mankato Weekly Record*, August 30, 1862; and *St. Paul Press*, August 30, 1862.

6. Sibley to his wife, August 28, 1862, Sibley Papers, MHSA; Sibley to Ramsey, August 26, 1862, in Board of Commissioners, *Minnesota in the Civil and Indian Wars*, 2:199.

7. Sibley to his wife, August 28, 1862, Sibley Papers, MHSA; Brandt, Nix, Roos, and Vayen to Ramsey, August 28, 1862, Governors Papers, MHSA.

8. "Samuel J. Brown Recollections," in Anderson and Woolworth, *Through Dakota Eyes*, 134–35. Jared Daniels places Little Crow at the Battle for New Ulm on August 23, but he apparently did not participate in the fighting. See the Daniels Papers, MHSA.

9. Mrs. N. D. White, "Captivity Among the Sioux," *Minnesota Historical Society Collections* 9 (April 1902): 411–12.

10. Wakefield, *Six Weeks in the Sioux Tepees*, 32–33. Wakefield's narrative is reproduced as *Six Weeks in the Sioux Tepees: A Narrative of Indian Captivity*, ed. June Namias (Norman: University of Oklahoma Press, 1997).

11. Gabriel Renville, "A Sioux Narrative of the Outbreak of 1862, and of Sibley's Expedition of 1863," in Anderson and Woolworth, *Through Dakota Eyes*, 104, 186.

12. Ibid., 187; Testimony of Charles R. Crawford, *Sisseton and Wahpeton Court of Claims* No. 22524.

13. Ibid.

14. Ibid.

15. "Samuel J. Brown's Recollections," in Anderson and Woolworth, *Through Dakota Eyes*, 170.

16. Flandrau recorded the speeches. See "The Indian War of 1862–1864, and Following Campaigns in Minnesota," and "The Indian War of 1862," in Board of Commissioners, *Minnesota in the Civil and Indian Wars*, 1:742, 2:472. Flandrau's reports, although mostly accurate, combine the three different councils of August 29, September 6, and September 15 into one long dialogue. He recognizes that the various speeches came at different times. Thomas Robertson also offers a version of it in his Reminiscences, MHSA. Iron Gourd was later tried, convicted, and then pardoned in 1866. See Case No. 82, NARG 46, Dakota Trial Records, Senate Records, 37A-F2.

17. Flandrau, "The Indian War of 1862," in Board of Commissioners, *Minnesota in the Civil and Indian Wars*, 2:472. Mary Butler Renville apparently wrote a letter that Paul Mazakutemani wanted sent to Governor Ramsey, dated September 2. It noted the two councils held, but it is unclear whether the letter was actually written at the time. For certain, it was never delivered. See Mary Butler Renville, *A Thrilling Narrative of Indian Captivity* (Minneapolis: Atlas Company, 1863); reprinted as *A Thrilling Narrative of Indian Captivity: Dispatches From*

the Dakota War, ed. Carrie Reber Zeman and Kathrny Zabelle Derounian-Stoba (Lincoln: University of Nebraska Press, 2012), 154–55.

18. Renville, "A Sioux Narrative of the Outbreak of 1862, and of Sibley's Expedition of 1863," 601–2.

19. Interview with A. J. Campbell, in Hubbard and Holcombe, *Minnesota in Three Centuries,* 3:343–63.

20. Ibid.

21. Holcombe, *Sketches Historical and Descriptive,* 31–32.

22. Sibley's report on the organization of the company does not mention who was in command. See Official Report to Adjutant General O. Malmros, September 1, 1862, Sibley Papers, MHSA. Captain Anderson believed that Brown was always in command. See Anne C. Anderson to J. W. Daniels, 1894, Anderson Papers, MHSA.

23. See Daniels, entry for August 31, 1862, Reminiscences, MHSA.

24. Hiram P. Grant, "Report" in Board of Commissioners, *Minnesota in the Civil and Indian Wars,* 2:215–19.

25. "Narrative of Justina Kreiger," in Bryant and Murch, *A History of the Great Massacre of the Sioux Indians,* 319–20.

26. Grant, "Report," in Board of Commissioners, *Minnesota in the Civil and Indian Wars,* 2:219. Quotation in Anderson to Daniels, 1894, Anderson Papers, MHSA.

27. Brown to Sibley, September 6, 1862, Governors Papers, MHSA; Hubbard and Holcombe, *Minnesota in Three Centuries,* 3:348–49.

28. Report of Joseph Anderson and Report of James J. Egan, in Board of Commissioners, *Minnesota in the Civil and Indian Wars,* 2:212–13, 2:219–23; Brown to Sibley, September 6, 1862, Governors Papers, MHSA; Reminiscences of Jared Daniels, MHSA; Reminiscences of Ezmon Earle, MHSA. Sibley apparently heard of Grant's behavior, and when Grant came to address him, handing in his report of the action, Sibley "coolly" told him to report to his commanding officer, Brown. See Report of Captain Grant, in Board of Commissioners, *Minnesota in the Civil and Indian Wars,* 2:217–18.

29. Hubbard and Holcombe, *Minnesota in Three Centuries,* 3:348–51.

30. McPhail Report, September 5, 1862, and Sheehan to Ramsey, September 5, 1862, Governors Papers, MHSA; Sheehan, Reminiscence, Holcombe Papers, MHSA.

31. Sibley to his wife, September 4, 1862, Sibley Papers, MHSA. See also James Ramer Diary, September 2–3, 1862, MHSA; Grant's Report, in Board of Commissioners, *Minnesota in the Civil and Indian Wars,* 2:217–18.

32. Sibley to his wife, September 7, 1862, Sibley Papers, MHSA.

33. Hubbard and Holcombe, *Minnesota in Three Centuries,* 3:358–59. Heard reports the story of the letters, which were never sent. See Heard, *History of the Sioux War,* 144. See also Campbell interview, Holcombe Papers, MHSA.

34. Flandrau's commission came somewhat later than Stevens's. He received it in the field on September 4, 1862. See Flandrau to Ramsey, September 4, 1862, Governors Papers, MHSA.

35. Hubbard and Holcombe, *Minnesota in Three Centuries,* 3:358–59; Stevens to Ramsey, August 31, 1862, Governors Papers, MHSA. Marion P. Satterlee published an account of the conflict as *The Story of Capt. Richard Strout and Company, Who Fought the Sioux Indians at the Battle of Kelly's Bluff, at Acton, Minn., on Wednesday, September 3rd, 1862* (Minneapolis: Marion P. Satterlee, 1909), 1–9.

36. Hubbard and Holcombe, *Minnesota in Three Centuries,* 3:357; Darryl Sannes, "The U.S.-Dakota War of 1862 and the Battle of Acton," tricountynews.mn/2012/09/28/the-u-s-dakota-war-of-1862-and-the-battle-of-acton. Whitcomb was viewed by some men in Forest City as a petty dictator, forcing all men in the town to join his company of fifty men. See A. C. Smith to Ramsey, August 30, 1862, Governors Papers, MHSA.

37. The quotation comes from Sannes, "The U.S.–Dakota War of 1862 and the Battle of Acton."

38. While the story of Little Crow's bowing from the fence might be apocryphal, it is recorded in two separate narratives. Campbell told Hubbard, however, that the Indian was actually White Spider, Little Crow's brother. See Reminiscences of Mrs. Peter Rodange, MHSA; and Hubbard and Holcombe, *Minnesota in Three Centuries*, 3:361.

39. Hubbard and Holcombe, *Minnesota in Three Centuries*, 3:349–61. Strout was among those wounded, literally losing an arm in the fight. He later asked Congress for a disability pension. See *Senate Report No. 1101*, 54th Congress, 1st Session, June 2, 1896.

40. Stevens to Ramsey, September 3, 1862, Lieutenant Jason Weiman to Stevens, September 5, 1862, and James M. Harvey to Ramsey, September 7, 1862, Governors Papers, MHSA; Madison Bowler to Lizzie, September 5, 1862, and "Statistics Concerning the Sioux Massacre by Town Assessors," both in MHSA; Skarstein, *The War with the Sioux*, 125–26.

41. For the battle, see Hubbard, "Narrative of the Fifth Regiment," in Board of Commissioners, *Minnesota in the Civil and Indian Wars*, 1: 255–57; Hubbard and Holcombe, *Minnesota in Three Centuries*, 3:385–88.

42. Ibid.; James A. Shotwell to son James, September 14, 1862, and Reminiscences of John H. McKenzie, August–September 1862, MHSA.

43. Donahue to Ramsey, September 6, 1862, and Wilson to Ramsey, September 6, 1862, Governors Papers, MHSA; Wood to her brother, September 5, 1862, Wood Family Papers, Bentley Library, University of Michigan.

44. Mary Crowell letter, September 14, 1862, MHSA.

45. *The Winona Daily Republican,* September 6, 1862.

46. Swishelm to Ramsey, September 5, 1862, Governors Papers, MHSA.

47. Wakefield to Ramsey, September 3, 1862, ibid.; *Mankato Independent,* September 4, 1862. The town of St. Peter had even cast two small cannons, one for each fortress. See Skaro to Sibley, September 12, 1862, NARG 393, LR, Department of the Northwest.

48. J. A. Van Duzee to Ramsey, September 3, 1862, Governors Papers, MHSA.

49. *Hastings Independent,* September 4, 1862; *Faribault Central Republican,* September 10, 1862. The references to Sibley's Indian child can be found in many places. One, written by Horace Austin, a Ramsey supporter, says Sibley, "who has more children among them than white, should be appointed by you to conduct a campaign against them . . . staggers us all!" Austin to Ramsey, September 9, 1862, Governors Papers, MHSA.

50. Chatfield to Sibley, September 2, 1862, NARG 393, LR, Department of the Northwest; Sibley to Malmros, September 4, 1862, Sibley Papers, MHSA.

51. See Flandrau to Ramsey, September 4, 1862, Governors Papers, MHSA; and Riggs to Ramsey, September 8, 1862, in Board of Commissioners, *Minnesota in the Civil and Indian Wars,* 2:226–27.

52. Sibley to Little Crow, September 3, 1862, Sibley Papers, MHSA. Charles Crawford discovered the letter after Susan Brown had asked him to return to the scene of the Birch Coulee battle to see if her husband had been hurt. Renville, "A Sioux Narrative of the Outbreak of 1862, and of Sibley's Expedition in 1863," in Anderson and Woolworth, *Through Dakota Eyes,* 188–89. On Sibley's early relationship with Little Crow, see Sibley, *Iron Face: The Adventures of Jack Frazer.*

53. Sibley to Adjutant General Malmros, September 8, 1862, Sibley Papers, MHSA.

54. Reminiscences of Thomas Robertson, MHSA.

55. Renville, "A Sioux Narrative of the Outbreak of 1862, and of Sibley's Expedition of 1863," in Anderson and Woolworth, *Through Dakota Eyes,* 187–202; Samuel Brown's Recollections, in ibid., 171. Victor Renville, who was Gabriel's young fourteen-year-old son, noted that the increase in the friendly camp went from a mere fifty tents to one hundred in the two days following September 7. Renville, "A Sketch of the Minnesota Massacre," 264–65.

56. There are different accounts of the various councils at both camps, some combining events into one narrative. See, for example, "Testimony of Joseph La Framboise," *Sisseton and Wahpeton Court of Claims* No. 22524.

57. Paul Mazakutemani gave the account to missionaries after the war. See "Declaration of Paul Mazakutemani," ABCFM. During the war trials following the conflict, Rattling Runner was found guilty, primarily because he opposed handing over the captives. He was later executed, while Blue Thunder escaped the gallows. See Isch, *The Dakota Trials*, 62–63, 63–64.

58. "Lorenzo Lawrence's Story," in Anderson and Woolworth, *Through Dakota Eyes*, 205–15; John P. Williamson, "Simon Anawaŋgmani," in *The Word Carrier* (called Iapi Oaye in Dakota; published in both English and Dakota) 20 (December 1891): n.p.; Renville, "A Thrilling Narrative of Indian Captivity," 23–26; Sibley to Ramsey, September 11, 1862, in Board of Commissioners, *Minnesota in the Civil and Indian Wars*, 2:227–28.

59. Sibley to Adjutant General Malmros, September 8, 1862, and Sibley to his wife, September 8 and 10, 1862, Sibley Papers, MHSA.

60. "Gabriel Renville's Memoir," in Anderson and Woolworth, *Through Dakota Eyes*, 190–91.

61. "Gabriel Renville's Memoir," ibid., 196–202, 230–34; "Declaration of Paul Mazakutemani," Whipple Papers, MHSA.

62. "Gabriel Renville's Memoir," in Anderson and Woolworth, *Through Dakota Eyes*, 199–202, 230–34.

63. Little Crow letter, September 10, 1862, Sibley Papers, MHSA.

64. Reminiscences of Thomas Robertson, MHSA; Andrew Good Thunder Statement, Simeon P. Folsom papers, Henry E. Huntington Library, San Marino, California; Riggs to his wife, September 13, 1862, Sibley Papers, MHSA.

65. Sibley message to Little Crow, September 12, 1862, Sibley Papers, MHSA; Sibley to "The Half-Breed Sioux and Sioux Indians Who Have Not Been Concerned in the Murders," September 13 [12?], 1862, and Sibley to Captain A. K. Skaro, September 12, 1862, NARG 393, LS, Sibley's Indian Campaign.

66. See "Big Eagle's Account," in Anderson and Woolworth, *Through Dakota Eyes*, 235.

67. Sibley to his wife, September 13, 1862, Sibley Papers, MHSA; Sibley to Adjutant General Malmros, September 13, 1862, NARG 393, LS, Sibley Indian Campaign.

68. Sibley to Ramsey, September 14, Sibley to Flandrau, September 15, and Sibley to Captain Skaro, September 16, 1862, all in NARG 393, LR, District of Iowa (this is Sibley's official "letterbook" for the expedition; the correspondence begins on September 14, 1862, suggesting that the first half has been lost).

69. Stanton to Pope, September 6, 1862, in Board of Commissioners, *Minnesota in the Civil and Indian Wars*, 2:225. See also Ramsey to Lincoln, September 6, 1862, Lincoln Papers, Library of Congress.

70. See Pope to Sibley, September 17, 1862, and Sibley to Pope, September 19, 1862, in Board of Commissioners, *Minnesota in the Civil And Indian Wars*, 2:233–34, 2:234–36. For the next two weeks, Pope continued to lobby Washington generals on the seriousness of the conflict in Minnesota, with little or no success. See Richard N. Ellis, *General Pope and U.S. Indian Policy* (Albuquerque: University of New Mexico Press, 1970), 8–10.

71. The date of this council is confusing. The initial conclusion that Alan Woolworth and I came to placed it on September 6. Standing Buffalo was at the camp near Yellow Medicine on that day, but not the Charger. Even though Samuel Brown did not attend the council, he correctly dates it on September 15. See Brown, "Samuel Brown's Recollections," in Anderson and Woolworth, *Through Dakota Eyes*, 175.

72. See "Ecetukiya's Testimony" and "Little Face's Testimony," in Anderson and Woolworth, *Through Dakota Eyes*, 200 and 205.

73. There are four reports of Standing Buffalo's speech. See Flandrau, "The Indian War of 1862–1864, and Following Campaigns in Minnesota," in Board of Commissioners, *Minnesota in the Civil and Indian Wars*, 1:743; "Testimony of Antoine Joe Campbell," 1902, *Sisseton and Wahpeton Court of Claims* No. 22524, at 259; Brown, "Samuel Brown's Recollections" and "Ecetukiya's Testimony," in Anderson and Woolworth, *Through Dakota Eyes*, 174, 200.

74. "Narrative of the Seventh Regiment," in Board of Commissioners, *Minnesota in the Civil and Indian Wars*, 1:351.

75. Pope to Sibley, September 17, 1862, NARG 393, LS, Department of the Northwest.

76. *Mankato Weekly Record*, September 20, 1862. The *Mankato Independent*, on September 20, 1862, said much the same: Pope "proposes immediate and invigorous [*sic*] measures for the extermination of the Sioux race."

77. Pope to Halleck, September 23, 1862, in Board of Commissioners, *Minnesota in the Civil and Indian Wars*, 2:238.

78. Samuel Brown believed the rumors as did Sarah Wakefield. See "Samuel J. Brown's Recollections," in Anderson and Woolworth, *Through Dakota Eyes*, 176; and Wakefield, *Six Weeks in the Sioux Tepees*, 45. Campbell's denial is in several places, including Holcombe, *Sketches Historical and Descriptive*, 19.

79. The council of September 22 is best reported in Renville, "A Sioux Narrative of the Outbreak of 1862, and of Sibley's Expedition of 1863," in Anderson and Woolworth, *Through Dakota Eyes*, 230–32. See also Robinson, *A History of the Dakota or Sioux Indians*, 294. Two other versions have similar accounts. See "Solomon Two Stars's Testimony," in Anderson and Woolworth, *Through Dakota Eyes*, 243. This is derived from "Wicaŋhpinoŋpi's Testimony," in *Sisseton and Wahpeton Court of Claims* No. 22524.

80. Renville, "A Sioux Narrative of the Outbreak of 1862, and of Sibley's Expedition of 1863," in Anderson and Woolworth, *Through Dakota Eyes*, 231.

81. Ibid.; "Solomon Two Stars's Testimony," in Anderson and Woolworth, *Through Dakota Eyes*, 243.

82. Sibley later heard of Little Crow's plan of attack from A. J. Renville. See Sibley to Ramsey, September 23, 1862, Governors Papers, MHSA.

83. General C. C. Andrews, "Narrative of the Third Regiment," in Board of Commissioners, *Minnesota in the Civil and Indian Wars*, 1:159. See also Stephen E. Osman, "Audacity, Skill, and Firepower: The Third Minnesota's Skirmishers at the Battle of Wood Lake," *Minnesota's Heritage* 3 (January 2011): 24–40.

84. Ibid.

85. Ezra T. Champlin, "Recollections of the Wood Lake Battle," in Board of Commissioners, *Minnesota in the Civil and Indian Wars*, 2:244–46.

86. Ibid.; "Statement of George Quinn," Holcombe Papers, MHSA; James T. Ramer, "Narrative of the Seventh Regiment," *Minnesota in the Civil and Indian Wars*, 1:351; Sibley to Ramsey, September 23, 1862, NARG 393, LR, District of Iowa; Holcombe, *Sketches Historical and Descriptive*, 61.

87. Holcombe, *Sketches Historical and Descriptive*, 39; Report of Col. Marshall, 7th Regiment, to Sibley, September 23, 1862, Adjutant Generals Papers (Minnesota), MHSA; Sibley to Ramsey, September 23, 1862, Governors Papers, MHSA.

88. While early reports put the number of dead at just four, a commission that studied the battle later reported Sibley's casualties as seven dead and forty-four wounded. See "Report of the Battle of Wood Lake," Minnesota Commission, MHSA. The figure for thirty Indians killed comes from Campbell. See Sibley to Ramsey, September 23, 1862, NARG 393, LS, Department of the Northwest.

89. Riggs mentions with disgust the actions of the troops. As the Third had initially retreated, some of their dead were mutilated, perhaps prompting the actions of the

Americans. See Riggs to his wife, September 23, 1862, Riggs Papers, Chippewa County Historical Society.

90. Sibley to Ramsey, September 23, 1862, NARG 393, LS, Department of the Northwest; Sibley to his wife, September 23, 1862, Sibley Papers, MHSA; Sibley to the "Hostile Camp," September 23, 1862, NARG 393, LR, District of Iowa. Celia Campbell Stay, who was 13 years old at the time, identified two of the others with her father as Joseph LaFramboise and Joseph Rooyer. See "Cecelia Campbell Stay's Account," in Anderson and Woolworth, *Through Dakota Eyes*, 250.

91. Robinson, *History of the Dakota or Sioux Indians*, 296–97.

92. See "Cecelia Campbell Stay's Account," in Anderson and Woolworth, *Through Dakota Eyes*, 253. The original is titled "Massacre at the Lower Sioux Agency," August 18, 1862, typescript, 1882, Provincial Archives of Manitoba, Winnipeg, MB. See also Celia M. Campbell Stay, "Memoir," July 6, 1925, MHSA.

93. See Campbell's interview in the *St. Paul Pioneer Press*, October 24, 1897.

94. Sibley to Standing Buffalo, September 24, 1862, NARG 393, LR, District of Iowa.

95. Sibley to Paul Mazakutemani, Taopi, and Walking Spirit, September 24, 1862, ibid.

96. Brown, "Samuel J. Brown's Recollections," in Anderson and Woolworth, *Through Dakota Eyes*, 224; Wakefield, "Six Weeks in the Sioux Tepees," 50–55.

97. Sibley to Pope, September 27, 1862, in Board of Commissioners, *Minnesota in the Civil and Indian Wars*, 254–56.

98. Ibid., 256.

99. Wakefield, *Six Weeks in the Sioux Tepees*, 55.

100. Ramsey letter, *St. Paul Weekly Press,* September 11, 1862. While local newspapers wrote comparative assessments of the violence, the governor's voice carried much more weight. The level of violence received "national" recognition when photographer Adrian J. Ebell published "The Indian Massacre and War of 1862" in *Harpers New Monthly* 27, no. 157 (June 1863): 1–24. Ebell, who never witnessed any of the killings, wrote that after tomahawking eleven children, warriors held the mother "before this agonizing spectacle" and then "chopped off her arms and legs." His account is pure fabrication.

101. Jared Daniels Reminiscences, MHSA.

CHAPTER EIGHT

1. Cecelia Campbell Stay noted that Taoyateduta had urged his men to free the captives. See Cecelia Campbell Stay Reminiscences, MHSA.

2. Cecelia Campbell Stay told this story several times. Good accounts are found in Stay Reminiscence, MHSA, and in another interview, found in "Committee Selecting Historical Data from New Ulm, Minnesota," August 5–6, 1924, Fort Ridgely State Park and Historical Association Papers, MHSA; see also Nancy Huggan to Holcombe, May 30, 1894, Holcombe Papers, MHSA.

3. Cecelia Campbell Stay Reminiscence, MHSA; Nancy McClure Huggan to Holcombe, May 30, 1894, Holcombe Papers, MHSA.

4. "Nancy McClure Faribault Huggan's Account," in Anderson and Woolworth, *Through Dakota Eyes*, 247.

5. A recent study of the women who left narratives that focuses on both their ordeals and the process of recovery—memory history—is Emily Rankin Wardrop, "'All the Women … were Violated in this Way': Rhetoric, Rape, and Memory in the Dakota War" (PhD Diss., University of Oklahoma, 2015).

6. Sibley to his wife, September 17, 1862, Sibley Papers, MHSA; Riggs to his wife, September 17, 1862, Riggs Papers, Chippewa County Historical Society. The number thirty-four comes from comparing the various references to captives found in NARG 75, LR, Northern Superintendency, and Sibley and Brown Papers, MHSA.

7. Riggs to his wife, September 17, 1862, Riggs Papers, Chippewa County Historical Society.

8. Heard, *History of the Sioux War*, 186.

9. Folwell, *History of Minnesota*, 2:185.

10. See, for example, Kenneth Carley, *The Sioux Uprising of 1862* (St. Paul: Minnesota Historical Society, 1976); Duane Schultz, *Over the Earth I Came: The Great Sioux Uprising of 1862* (New York: St. Martin's Press, 1992); and Michael Clodfelter, *The Dakota War: The United States Army versus the Sioux, 1862–1865* (Jefferson, N.C.: McFarland, 2006).

11. See Wakefield, *Six Weeks in the Sioux Tepees*, 40, 60, 123; Kathryn Zabelle Derounian-Stodola, *The War of Words: Reading the Dakota Conflict through the Captivity Literature* (Lincoln: University of Nebraska Press, 2009), 37, 108, 130, 138, 143, and 172–73.

12. See Darakay Cohen, "Explaining Rape during Civil War: Cross-National Evidence, 1980–2009," *American Political Science Review* 107 (August 2013): 461–77; Robert Hayden, "Rape and Rape Avoidance in Ethno-National Conflicts: Sexual Violence in Liminalized States," *American Anthropologist* 102 (No. 1): 27–41.

13. See Paul Kirby, "How is Rape a Weapon of War? Feminist International Relations, Modes of Critical Explanation and the Study of Wartime Sexual Violence," *European Journal of International Reparations* 19, no. 4 (2013): 797–821.

14. There is an important distinction here, as many studies of colonial conflict in eastern North America involved Indians who were matrilineal.

15. Ibid.; Janine Natalya Clark, "Making Sense of Wartime Rape: A Multi-Causal and Multi-Level Analysis," *Ethnopolitics* 13, no. 5 (2014): 461–82; Zoe Mark, "Sexual Violence in Sierra Leone's Civil War: Virgination, Rape and Marriage," *African Affairs* 113 (2014): 67–87; Elissa Helms, "Rejecting Angelina: Bosnian War Rape Survivors and the Ambiguities of Sex in War," *Slavic Review* 73 (Fall 2014): 612–34.

16. See Schoolcraft, *Information Respecting the History, Condition, and Prospects of the Indian Tribes*, 4:63. Recent work employing this argument includes Sharon Block, *Rape & Sexual Power in Early America* (Chapel Hill: University of North Carolina Press, 2006), 221–25; Estelle B. Freedman, *Redefining Rape: Sexual Violence in the Era of Suffrage and Segregation* (Cambridge, Mass.: Harvard University Press, 2013), 18–20. See also James Axtel, *The European and the Indian: Essays in the Ethnohistory of Colonial North America* (New York: Oxford University Press, 1981), 176–216.

17. See Janet Dean, "Nameless Outrages: Narrative Authority, Rape Rhetoric, and the Dakota Conflict of 1862," *American Literature* 77 (March 2005): 93–112. A similar argument is found in Stanley B. Kimball, "The Captivity Narrative on the Mormon Trail, 1846–1865," *Dialogue: A Journal of Mormon Thought* 18 (1985): 81–88.

18. See Kirsten Fischer, *Suspect Relations: Sex, Race, and Resistance in Early North Carolina* (Ithaca, N.Y.: Cornell University Press, 2001).

19. Susan Brownmiller, *Against Our Will: Men, Women and Rape* (New York: Open Road, 1975; repr., New York: Fawcett Columbine, 1993), 140–53.

20. Richard Trexler has argued that rape and sexual servitude was prevalent in both Native and Spanish groups in the Southwest, being practices used upon "vanquished enemies." See Trexler, *Sexual Conquest: Gendered Violence, Political Order, and the European Conquest of the Americas* (Ithaca, N.Y.: Cornell University Press, 1995).

21. See David T. Haberly, "Women and Indians: The Last of the Mohicans and the Captivity Tradition," *American Quarterly* 28 (Autumn 1976): 431–44.

22. Freedman, *Redefining Rape*, 3–7.

23. Ibid., 18.

24. Riggs to Treat, February 22, 1861, ABCFM.

25. Sheehan's Report, July 13, 1862, Sheehan Papers, MHSA.

26. There is some confusion over Myrick's multiple wives; Henry Belland is the source for three. Cecelia Campbell Stay mentions just two, but she confirms the three children.

See Mrs. Celia Stay interview, in *Madison Minnesota Independent Press*, May 18, 1906; Henry Belland letter, *Madison Minnesota Independent Press*, April 20, 1906. In an interview given by ninety- year-old Mary Myrick Hinman LaCroix in 1980, she indicates that her grandmother was married to Myrick, and that she and her mother, then a baby, escaped the carnage at the agencies on August 18. They were later moved to Crow Creek, S.Dak. Mary's mother later married Reverend Samuel Dutton Hinman, who returned to Morton to practice his ministry. See La Croix's narrative, "An Overview of the Life of Reverend Samuel Dutton Hinman," Brown County Historical Society, New Ulm, Minn.

27. Ibid.; Edwin Hatch to his wife, February 24, 1864, Hatch Papers, MHSA; Hatch to Sibley, January 2, 1864, NARG 393, LR, Department of the Northwest; *Nor'wester* (Winnipeg), February 5, 1864.

28. The basis for this demographic assessment is the annuity roles for the late 1850s and early 1860s, found in NARG 75, LR, SPA.

29. *Minnesota Times,* March 11, 1857.

30. Berghold, *The Indians' Revenge,* 77.

31. The genealogy of the Dakota "Mixed Bloods" was compiled in 1855 by a commission sent to determine who among them deserved receiving "Land Scrip" in exchange for a "Mixed Blood Reservation," set aside for them in 1830. While a thousand such mixedbloods applied for the land, only about seven hundred were determined to be legitimate. See "Mixed Blood Reserve Papers," NARG 75, Special Files (a copy on microfilm is available at the Minnesota Historical Society).

32. The best description of marriage is left by Samuel Pond. See Pond, *Dakota as They Were in 1834,* 137–39.

33. Ibid., 148–50. Another report of the feast is found at "The Sioux Maiden Feast," in *Minnesota Historical Society Collections* 9 (1901): 218.

34. Daniels, Reminiscences, 1857, MHSA. There is a mention of a "Maiden's Feast" in the Whipple Papers, written apparently in the 1890s, but it is impossible to determine where it was performed and even if Whipple witnessed it firsthand. Whipple notes that a "large company" of girls came forward to "touch the stone" that attested to their virtue. But when a young man then challenged one of the girls, "a friend of the girl replied in angry words . . . [and] in a moment amid loud cries & shouts, the air was filled with sticks." A riot apparently ensued. See Whipple, "Notes on the Dakota," Whipple Papers, MHSA.

35. Ibid.

36. "Narrative of Justina Kreiger," in Bryant and Murch, *A History of the Great Massacre by the Sioux Indians,* 306–7. Kreiger survived the shotgun blast to her back and the siege at Birch Coulee.

37. "Narrative of Helen Carrothers," in ibid., 286.

38. Ibid., 289–90.

39. Ibid., 289–90.

40. Ibid., 292.

41. Satterlee, "Massacre at the Redwood Indian Agency," 5, MHSA.

42. List of Captives Delivered at Camp Release, NARG 75, LR, Northern Superintendency Files, Miscellaneous.

43. "Nancy McClure Faribault Huggan's Account," in Anderson and Woolworth, *Through Dakota Eyes,* 82.

44. "Samuel J. Brown's Recollections," in Anderson and Woolworth, *Through Dakota Eyes,* 73–75.

45. Ibid., 76.

46. Ibid.

47. Ibid.

48. Ibid.; 78.

49. "Mrs. J. E. De Camp Sweet's Narrative of Her Captivity in the Sioux Outbreak of 1862," in *Minnesota Historical Society Collections* 6 (1894): 363.

50. See "Narrative of Mary Schwandt," in Bryant and Murch, *A History of the Great Massacre of the Sioux Indians*, 339–40, as well as later narratives found in MHSA. One of these is published as "Captivity Among the Sioux: The Story of Mary Schwandt," in *Minnesota Historical Society Collections* 6 (1894): 461–74. The report of the gang rape of Mary Schwandt is found in a letter signed by "H," which was undoubtedly Isaac V. D. Heard, who later wrote *History of the Sioux War and Massacre of 1862 and 1863*. It seems logical that Heard got the story while working as clerk during the Sioux trials. See the letter in *St. Paul Pioneer,* November 12, 1862.

51. "Mrs. J. E. De Camp Sweet's Narrative of Her Captivity in the Sioux Outbreak of 1862," in *Minnesota Historical Society Collections* 6 (1894): 365.

52. The identity of Mattie Williams's captor, Laying Up Buffalo, is confirmed by Alexander Seifert, who interviewed Cecelia Stay for the Committee Selecting Historical Data for New Ulm on August 24–25, 1924. Seifert's account included the statement that Williams offered Laying Up Buffalo gold, if he would only kill her. This powerful plea is indicative of the serious way that frontier families took the phrase "the fate worse than death." Williams obviously believed that she would be better off dead. See Reminiscences of Alexander Seifert, MHSA. Seifert served as a state senator from Minnesota and took careful notes from Stay.

53. Cecelia Campbell Stay interview in "Committee Selecting Historical Data From New Ulm, Minnesota," Fort Ridgely State Park and Historical Association papers, MHSA.

54. Testimony in Case No. 4, Tazoo, Senate Records, 37A-F2. Isch believes that Tazoo was a nickname; the man's real name was Red Otter (Ptanduta in Dakota). See Isch, *Dakota Trials,* 42–43.

55. Ibid., trial number 2, One Who Forbids His House (Tihdonića in Dakota). See also Isch, *Dakota Trials,* 37. Good Thunder, in a statement published in a newspaper, commented that shortly after being forced to leave Wakute's house, "the teacher was at once given up to the young bucks." This may be reflective of the other Indian who One Who Forbids His House mentions as having slept with Margaret Cardinal. See "Good Thunder's Wife," Clipping in the Holcombe Papers, MHSA.

56. Interview with Thomas Robertson, contained in a letter of A. J. Ebell, *St. Paul Daily Press,* September 11, 1862.

57. Thomas A. Robertson to Satterlee, March 30, 1923, and Satterlee to Robertson, March 26, 1923, Satterlee Papers, MHSA.

58. Mary Schwandt Schmidt Narrative #2, Schwandt Papers, MHSA.

59. See the various "Narratives" in the Schwandt Papers, MHSA; "The Story of Mary Schwandt: Her Captivity During the Sioux 'Outbreak'—1862," in *Minnesota Historical Society Collections* 6 (1894): 461–74; "Narrative of a Friendly Sioux, by Snana, the Rescue of Mary Schwandt," in *Minnesota Historical Society Collections* 9 (1901): 427–32; "Recollections of the Indian Massacre of 1862 in Minnesota," by Mrs. Mary E. [Schwandt] Schmidt, October 25, 1915, before the Colonial Dames of America, MHSA.

60. Wakefield, *Six Weeks in the Sioux Tepees,* 14–16.

61. Ibid., 27–28.

62. Ibid., 37–47.

63. See Campbell's interview, *St. Peter Minnesota Tribune,* October 10, 1862; Mrs. N. D. White, "Captivity Among the Sioux, August 18 to September 26, 1862," in *Minnesota Historical Society Collections* 9 (1901): 404.

64. Testimony in Sioux Trial #279, Wind Comes Home, or Tataydhedon, in Isch, *The Dakota Trials,* 308.

65. Interview with Mrs. Huggins, Riggs Papers, CWS-A. A long newspaper clipping outlining Huggins's captivity is also in this collection. See also Riggs, *Sunset to Sunset,* 32–33.

66. Eastlick, "Thrilling Incidents of the War (Indian) of 1862," ms., MHSA. Both a printed and handwritten copy of the narrative have survived.

67. Testimony of Mrs. William Duley, given to Herbert Workman, Workman Papers, MHSA.

68. Joseph H. Michalski argues that ritualistic rape represents "a way of dealing with grievances, or as a form of punishment or social control." See Michalski, "Ritualistic Rape in Sociological Perspective," *Cross-Cultural Research* 50, no. 1 (2016): 3–33.

69. Ibid.; *Mankato Semi-Weekly Record*, October 18, 1862.

70. Mrs. Cook offered most of this information while at Camp Release. See *Mankato Semi-Weekly Record*, October 18, 1862. The rescue is covered in Robinson, *A History of the Dakota or Sioux Indians*, 305–9.

71. Robinson, *A History of the Dakota or Sioux Indians*, 310–13; Notes on Getting the Lake Shetek Captives, 1902?, Brown Papers, MHSA. The two Ireland girls, Rosanna and Ellen, were also rescued. Their fate is difficult to determine, as Mrs. Cook later indicated that both "were abused." See "Incidents of the Indian Massacre as Told by Mrs. Kock [Cook]," in Currie Papers, MHSA. The story of the rescue by the Lakota Sioux "Fool Soldiers" is often retold in South Dakota. See Jim Nelson, "Fool Soldiers' Story Told Many Ways," *Minnesota's Heritage* 4 (July 2011): 20–35.

72. Mrs. Duley later tried to interest a publisher in her story, which may suggest some exaggeration on her part. See William Duley to Mr. Arnold, July 27, 1885, ms., MHSA. Nevertheless, Workman learned of her son, who worked as a policeman in Tacoma, Wash. While only seven years old when taken captive, he was tied to a stake, and he later described the attack on the two women, albeit from a distance. See the Workman Papers, MHSA.

73. Oral history for the Eisenreich Family, Brown County Historical Society, New Ulm, Minn.

74. Ibid.

75. See "A List of the White Prisoners and Half Breeds Delivered at Camp Release—October 1862," NARG 75, LR, Northern Superintendency. Compare the language in Sibley to Pope, September 27, 1862, NARG 393, LR, District of Iowa, with Sibley to his Wife, October 1, 1862, Sibley Papers, MHSA. Riggs's comments came years later. His description is found in *The Dakota Word Carrier*, May 1873, a newspaper published at the Presbyterian Mission at Santee, Neb.

CHAPTER NINE

1. The messengers brought letters from the Indians controlling Camp Release, including Paul Mazakutemani, Akipa, Red Iron, Taopi, and others. A number, some of which may not have been delivered, are in Renville, *A Thrilling Narrative*, 37–42.

2. Sibley to his wife, September 27, 1862, Sibley Papers, MHSA.

3. White," "Captivity Among the Sioux," 420–21.

4. Wakefield, "Six Weeks in Little Crow's Tepee," 50.

5. Sibley to his wife, September 27, 1862, and Sibley to General Pope, September 27, 1862, NARG 393, LS, Sibley's Indian Campaign.

6. Riggs to daughter Martha, September 27, 1862, Riggs Papers, MHSA.

7. Heard, *History of the Sioux War*, 251. Riggs continued to pry information from Indians well into February 1863, resulting in a second group of trials that will be discussed later.

8. Sibley to his wife, September 28, 1862, Sibley Papers, MHSA. Wakefield's statement was widely reported in the press. See, for example, the *Mankato Semi-Weekly*, October 4, 1862.

9. Sibley to Ramsey, September 27, 1862, NARG 393, LR, District of Iowa.

10. Sibley to Flandrau, September 28, 1862, ibid.; Sibley to Pope, October 3, 1862, NARG 393, LS, Department of the Northwest. The role of Renville and La Framboise Jr.

in retaking captives is reported in Brown, "Samuel J. Brown's Recollections," in Anderson and Woolworth, *Through Dakota Eyes*, 223.

11. John Madison Bowlee to Lizzie, September 27, 1862, ms., MHSA.

12. Flandrau, a lawyer and judge, defended the trials and the officers who conducted them. See Flandrau, "The Indian War of 1862–1864, and Following Campaigns in Minnesota," in Board of Commissioners, *Minnesota in the Civil and Indian Wars*, 1:747. Carol Chomsky addresses the legal issues involved in "The United States-Dakota War Trials: A Study in Military Justice," *Stanford Law Review* 43 (November 1990): 13–98.

13. See *The 1863 Laws of War: Articles of War General Orders No. 100 Army Regulations* (Washington, D.C.: War Department, 1863; repr., Stackpole Books, 2006), Article 65. The adjutant general would conclude after the Civil War that such "commissions" could not be used to try American Indians even at the headquarters of a department, as a "State of War"— the Civil War—no longer existed. This decision came after the U.S. Supreme Court ruled in *Ex Parte Milligan* (71 U.S. [4 Wall] 2 [1866]) that commissions could not be used when local courts functioned. Also, in 1874, the War Department held 101 Comanche and Kiowa prisoners in Oklahoma. Rather than face a military tribunal, the Indians were deported to Florida. See Anderson, *Ethnic Cleansing and the Indian*, 284–85.

14. Lee's correspondence shows that many commission decisions were rejected in the early months of the Civil War. See Lee's correspondence, NARG 153, LS.

15. Sibley did face the legal question of whether martial law, and thus the need for commissions, was necessary on Minnesota's frontier. He had mostly ignored it until September 18, when Lieutenant M. A. Merrell at Henderson asked permission to employ martial law. Sibley responded: "It may be well to allow the proper civil authorities to resume their functions." This raises the question whether Sibley had an obligation to bring the Indians into a civil court. See Sibley to Merrell, September 18, 1862, NARG 393, LR, District of Iowa. Sibley again addressed Pope regarding his "authority" when it came to creating a court martial for his troops in Sibley to Pope, October 15, 1862, ibid.

16. The best description of the creation of commission justice is found in Erika Myers, "Conquering Peace: Military Commissions as a Lawforce Strategy in the Mexican War" *American Journal of Criminal Law* 35, no. 2 (2008): 201–40. See also Louis Fisher, *Military Tribunals and Presidential Power* (Lawrence: University of Kansas Press, 2005), and Maeve Herbert, "Explaining the Sioux Military Commission of 1862," *Columbia Human Rights Law Review* 40 (2009): 743–98. For a discussion regarding commissions in modern times, see Joshua E. Kastenberg, *Shaping US Military Law: Governing a Constitutional Military* (New York: Routledge, 2014). Kastenberg argues that up until the 1950s, the civil courts did not meddle with military law, and there is no evidence that the civil courts in Minnesota tried to intervene in the Dakota trials.

17. Myers notes the importance of the judge advocate. See Myers, "Conquering Peace," 217.

18. See Article 69 in *The 1863 Laws of War*. Chomsky notes that while the issue of legal counsel never really came up during the Dakota trials, when the agent for the Winnebago Indians, who were tried in November 1862, did bring it up, Sibley refused to allow such counsel, a violation of due process. See Chomsky, "The United States-Dakota War Trials," 53.

19. Myers, "Conquering Peace," 219.

20. Ibid., 218.

21. Ibid., 217–20.

22. Sibley to Pope, September 28, 1862, NARG 393, LR, District of Iowa; Sibley Commission, September 29, 1862, Sibley Papers, MHSA; Chomsky, "The Unites States-Dakota War Trials," 13–87.

23. Pope to Sibley, October 2, 1862, NARG 94, LR, AGO.

24. Ibid. There is some question about whether Pope's letter had an impact on Sibley's growing determination to punish large numbers of Dakota men. The letter did arrive after

Sibley had apparently agreed, or ordered, that men could be declared guilty and executed if they participated in any of the battles.

25. Renville and Joseph Kawanke had originally gone south with the Indians sent to Yellow Medicine on October 4, but Sibley ordered their return "to act as messengers for me in any intercourse with the upper country." Riggs noted that the Christian members of his church also joined the group. See Sibley to Whitney, October 9 and 12, 1862, NARG 393, LS, Sibley's Indian Expedition; Sibley to Whitney, October 10, 1862, NARG 393, LR, District of Iowa; and Riggs to Treat, October 11, 1862, ABCFM; Renville, "Sioux Narrative of the Outbreak of 1962," *Minnesota Historical Society Collections* 10 (1905, Part 2): 610.

26. Sibley to Pope, September 30, 1862, NARG 393, LR, District of Iowa.

27. Sibley to Pope, October 4, 1862, NARG 393, LR, Sibley's Indian Expedition. The convictions and penalties in each case were never revealed to the Indians. See Chomsky, "The United States-Dakota War Trials," 52.

28. See Heard, *History of the Sioux War*, 191–201.

29. Isch notes that while some writers have been sympathetic with Godfrey's role in the massacre, Dakota Indians viewed him as a Judas. See Isch, *The Dakota Trials*, 34–35. Godfrey even testified against his father-in-law. See Case No.11, Wapayduta, in NARG 46, Dakota Trial Records, Senate Records 37A-F2, National Archives (hereafter Senate Records, 37A-F2).

30. NARG 46, Senate Records, 37A-F2. Isch, in *The Dakota Trials,* carefully researched the names of each defendant, and I am indebted to him for this incredibly important research.

31. Sibley's letter identifying the court was exactly the same, placed at the front of every trial record. See NARG 46, Senate Records, 37A-F2.

32. Ibid.

33. Ibid.

34. Ibid.

35. Ibid.

36. Wabasha's testimony, in *Proceedings of the Great Sioux Commission*, ed. Vine V. Deloria and Raymond J. DeMallie (Washington, D.C.: Institute for the Development of American Law, 1975), 127.

37. Sibley to his wife, October 1, 1862, Sibley Papers, MHSA.

38. Sibley message, October 3, 1862, NARG 75, LR, District of Iowa.

39. Brown, "Samuel J. Brown's Recollections," in Anderson and Woolworth, *Through Dakota Eyes*, 225. Brown also lists a large number of cattle, horses, wagons, and so on that were also turned over to the army.

40. Annual Report of the State Auditor, September 29, 1862, MHSA; and Skaro to Sibley, October 8, 1862, NARG 393, LR, Sibley's Indian Expedition. The funds distributed included thirty-seven checks ranging from $150 to $400, roughly equal to the number of family units that were rescued.

41. Brown, "Samuel J. Brown's Recollections," in Anderson and Woolworth, *Through Dakota Eyes*, 225.

42. Sibley to Pope, October 5, 7, 8, and 10, 1862, NARG 393, LR, District of Iowa; Sibley to Pope, October 11, 1862, NARG 393, LS, Department of the Northwest.

43. Riggs to Treat, October 11, 1862, ABCFM.

44. Brown, "Samuel J. Brown's Recollections," in Anderson and Woolworth, *Through Dakota Eyes*, 226.

45. Sibley to Pope, October 13, 1862, NARG 393, Sibley's Indian Expedition; Sibley to Whitney, October 14, 1862, and Sibley to Pope, October 15, 1862, NARG 393, LS, Department of the Northwest.

46. Quotations in George W. Bushnell's Journal, October 16–17, 1862, Henry E. Huntington Library, San Marino, Calif. See also William Quinn, "Quinn the Scout," recorded

by Return I. Holcombe in *Pioneer Press,* April 29, 1894; General C. C. Andrews, "Narrative of the Third Regiment," in Board of Commissioners, *Minnesota in the Civil and Indian Wars,* 1:160–61.

47. For Sibley's concerns, see Sibley to Pope, October 10 and 13, 1862, NARG 393, LR, District of Iowa.

48. Riggs to his wife, October 9, 1862, Riggs Papers, Chippewa County Historical Society; Riggs to Treat, October 11, 1862, ABCFM.

49. Sibley to Marshall, October 13, 1862, NARG 393, LR, District of Iowa.

50. The letter was carried by Paul Mazakutemani. See Sibley to The Charger and Standing Buffalo, October 3, 1862, NARG 393, LR, Sibley's Indian Expedition of 1862; Testimony of "Little Paul, or Wa-hna-xki-ya," Paul Mazakutemani's son, in Sisseton/Wahpeton Claims Case No. 22524.

51. Sibley to Pope, October 4, 1862, NARG 393, LS, Department of the Northwest; Sibley to Pope, October 5, 1862, NARG 393, LR, District of Iowa; Major John Pattee to Pope, September 10, 1862, Sibley to Pope, October 10, 1862 and Charles Primeau and W. G. Guilberth to Major John Pattee, November 5, 1862, NARG 393, LR, Department of the Northwest.

52. Leonard Aldrich to Ramsey, September 9, 1862, Governors Papers, MHSA.

53. T. C. Jewett to the AAG, October 11, 1862, NARG 393, LR, Department of the Northwest; Richard Strout to Ramsey, September 24, 1862, in Board of Commissioners, *Minnesota in the Civil and Indian Wars,* 2:250–51.

54. Ramsey to Pope, November 5, 1862, and Pope to Ramsey, November 6, 1862, Governors Papers, MHSA. Some Minnesota officers protested leaving the state to fight in the south; one stated that it would be "disastrous to the interests of the state to let a single company leave." Some likely realized that garrisoning Minnesota would be less stressful than fighting against the Confederacy. See Captain Joseph C. Whiting to Ramsey, November 6, 1862, ibid.

55. Ramsey to Sibley, October 3, 1862, NARG 393, LR, Fort Ridgely.

56. Sibley to McSasen, October 20, 1862, NARG 393, LR, District of Iowa.

57. Of these 393, only 392 were eventually tried (one trial record is missing). The discrepancy cannot be account for. See Sibley to Pope, October 7 and 11, 1862, Sibley to Galbraith, October 14, 1862, Sibley to Whitney, October 14, 1862, Sibley to Pope, October 20 and 21, 1862, NARG 393, LR, District of Iowa; Pope to Sibley, October 10, 1862, NARG 94, LR, AGO; Sibley to his wife, October 22 and 25, 1862, Sibley Papers, MHSA. Sibley offers a complete breakdown of the Indian men he held on October 17: 123 were at Camp Release, another 236 at Yellow Medicine, and 68 were considered "friendly." See Sibley to Pope, October 17, 1862, NARG 393, LS, Sibley's Indian Expedition. Two accounts of the movements of troops and prisoners are James T. Ramer, "Narrative of the Seventh Regiment," in Board of Commissioners, *Minnesota in the Civil and Indian Wars,* 1:353; and Hubert N. Eggleston Diary, October 6–December 26, 1862, MHSA.

58. Riggs to his wife, October 25, 1862, Riggs Papers, Chippewa County Historical Society.

59. *St. Paul Pioneer,* November 4, 1862.

60. John Kingsley Wood Diary, November 3, 1862, MHSA.

61. The commission trial records give "Camp Sibley, Lower Agency" as the location for all trials conducted after October 16. More than likely, this citation was added at the end of the trial period when it was learned that the records would be scrutinized in Washington. The dates on the records are also suspect, as some were clearly added later. See NARG 46, Senate Records, 37A-F2.

62. See NARG 46, Senate Records, 37A-F2, for November 3, 1862.

63. John Isch, in *The Dakota Trials,* has meticulously reproduced the records, including much information on each individual tried. He notes the change on page 485.

64. Jared Daniels Reminiscences, MHSA.

65. Isch, *The Dakota Trials*, 158.

66. Ibid., 100–101, 216–17.

67. Ibid., 255.

68. Senate Records, 37A-F2.

69. See Sibley to Pope, September 27, 1862, NARG 393, LR, District of Iowa; and Sibley's Order, September 28, 1862, Sibley Papers, MHSA. Sibley's initial order included just "two field officers [Crooks and Marshall] and the captain of the 6th Reg." He consistently failed to identify a judge advocate in his correspondence or even suggest that one was needed. Judge Advocate General John F. Lee outlined proper procedures for a commission trial in October 1861. See Judge Advocate General's papers, October 1861, NARG 153, LS, Book 1.

70. When giving a fifty-minute address in 2012 at Gustavus Adophus College, I suggested that all of the trials had a page or less of testimony. I was giving an overview of the trials that offered little time for explanation, and the statement was an exaggeration, but not by much. After taking an exact count, using the original records in the National Archives, I came to a number of 352 for those trials where testimony consisted of one page or less, or in fully 90 percent of the trials.

71. Sibley to his wife, October 30, 1862, Sibley Papers, MHSA.

72. Pope to Sibley, October 17, 1862, NARG 94, LR, AGO; Sibley to Pope, October 19 and 20, 1862, NARG 393, LR, District of Iowa; Ramsey to Sibley, September 1, 1862, NARG 393, LR, Sibley's Indian Expedition of 1862; Sibley to Pope, October 21, 1862, NARG 393, LS, Sibley's Indian Expedition of 1862; Sibley to his wife, November 3, 1862, Sibley Papers, MHSA.

73. Riggs to his wife, October 15 and 17, 1862, Riggs Papers, Chippewa County Historical Society.

74. Riggs to his wife, October 30, 1862, ibid. Somewhat later in life, Riggs wrote: "In the majority of instances, the trial was so brief and hurried that the facts could not possibly be ascertained. It is to be remembered that forty cases were finished in one day, and there were other days when over thirty were disposed of." See Riggs, *Tah-koo-Wah-kan; or, The Gospel Among the Dakota* (Boston: Congregational Publishing Society, 1880), 333–34.

75. See Jared Daniels Reminiscences, MHSA. At one point, Colonel Crooks, who was president of the commission, came into the tent where Riggs and Sibley slept and suggested that rather than execute so many men, perhaps a better punishment would be to cut all their hair off and whip them. Sibley disagreed. See Riggs to his wife, October 17, 1862, Riggs Papers, Chippewa County Historical Society.

76. Hughes, *A History of Blue Earth County*, 126.

77. Williamson to Riggs, October 25, 1862, Riggs Papers, MHSA.

78. Williamson gives Hopkins the Indian name of Chaska. See Williamson to Riggs, October 25, 1862, ibid.

79. John Williamson to Treat, November 5, 1862, ABCFM.

80. Welles's diary, October 14, 1862, as quoted in David A. Nichols, *Lincoln and the Indians: Civil War Policy and Politics* (Urbana: University of Illinois Press, 1978), 96.

81. *St. Paul Pioneer Press,* November 23, 1862.

82. *New York Times,* November 6, 1862. In my lecture at Gustavus Adophus College in 2012, I did say that Lincoln had decided to condemn an "arbitrary" number of Indians, suggesting 30, 40, or 50. My argument stems from the *Times* article, where it is stated that the government seemed convinced that only "a few bad men" on the list of 303 deserved severe punishment.

83. Sibley to Pope, November 11, 1862, Governors Papers, MHSA. Major Brandt later wrote Ramsey that he "could not prevent the stoning," and apparently Ramsey agreed, allowing Brandt and several other New Ulm militia men to enlist in regular Minnesota regiments. Pope urged Ramsey to arrest both Brandt and Sheriff Roos. See Brandt to Ramsey, November 9, 1862, and Pope to Ramsey, November 14, 1862, Governors Papers,

MHSA. See also Lois A. Glewwe, "Journey of the Prisoners: Convoy to South Bend," in Mary H. Bakeman and Antona M. Richardson, eds., *Trails of Tears: Minnesota's Dakota Indian Exile Begins* (Roseville, Minn.: Park Genealogical Books, 2008), 98.

84. Ibid. See also Sibley to his wife, November 12, 1862, Sibley Papers, MHSA.

85. Sarah Purcell Montgomery, "Some Recollections of the Indian Outbreak," MHSA.

86. James Ramer Diary, November 10, 1862, MHSA.

87. See William E. Lass, "Rediscovering Camp Lincoln," *Minnesota's Heritage* 20, no. 6 (July 1212): 20–37. Lieutenant George McLeod had been sent to Mankato to erect the log prison, selecting a point just southwest of what was then-designated as Sibley's Mound; it is now known as Sibley Park. For a description, see *Mankato Semi-Weekly Record,* November 2, 1862.

88. See "List of Loyal Indians & Mixed Bloods," 1862, NARG 393, Department of Dakota, Campaign Scouts & Dakota Indians.

89. Brown, "Samuel J. Brown's Recollections," in Anderson and Woolworth, *Through Dakota Eyes,* 227.

90. Francis Springer to Hawkins Taylor, October 19, 1862, and Oliver S. Halstad to John G. Nicolay, November 7, 1862, Lincoln Papers, Library of Congress.

91. *St. Paul Press,* October 22 and 24, 1862.

CHAPTER TEN

1. *St. Paul Press,* November 9, 1862. See also *St. Peter Tribune,* November 15, 1862, *Mankato Semi-Weekly Record,* November 15, 1862, and the *St. Paul Daily Press,* November 22, 1862.

2. The list of men reached Lincoln by telegraph on November 6. Six days later, Sibley wrote his wife: "I am hourly expecting a decision of President Lincoln involving the fate of the latter." See Sibley to his wife, November 12, 1862, and Sibley General Order #78, Sibley Order Book, Sibley Papers, MHSA.

3. Williamson to Treat, November 21, 1862, ABCFM.

4. Miller to Olin, November 19 and 29, 1862, NARG 393, LR, District of Minnesota.

5. Brown's quick actions are reported in Miller to Olin, December 3, 1862, NARG 393, LR, District of Minnesota. See also George Bushwell Journal, November 11–15, 1862, Henry E. Huntington Library, San Marino, Calif.

6. See "List of Employees," December 1862, Brown Papers, MHSA. Williamson reports that the prisoners were fed beef and hard bread, which constipated them. Many were sick with coughs, and some had measles. While they could have been fed cheaply with corn and potatoes, the lack of kettles made that difficult. See Williamson to Treat, December 1, 1862, ABCFM.

7. Miller to Sibley, November 18, 1862, NARG 393, "Unentered LR," Department of the Northwest.

8. Miller to Sibley, November 22, 1862, NARG 393, LR, District of Minnesota.

9. *Mankato Semi-Weekly Record,* November 15, 1862.

10. Miller to Olin, November 28, 1862, NARG 393, LR, District of Minnesota.

11. Ibid.; Miller to Sibley, November 23, 1862. and Miller to Olin, December 1, 1862, ibid.

12. See Dole to Smith, November 10, 1862, Lincoln Papers, Library of Congress; Smith to Lincoln, November 11, 1862, NARG 48, LS, Indian Division of the Department of Interior. The argument that the Indians were "prisoners of war," likely originated with John Beeson, who is considered the first serious Indian reformer in the country, publishing *A Plea for the Indian: with Facts and Features of the Late War in Oregon* (New York: n.p., 1857). Beeson wrote Lincoln on November 18, 1862, arguing that the Dakota had "surrendered" and deserved "amnesty." See Beeson to Lincoln, November 18, 1862, NARG 48, LR, Indian Division of the Department of Interior.

13. Lincoln to Pope, November 10, 1862, in Board of Commissioners, *Minnesota in the Civil and Indian Wars,* 2:289.

14. Riggs to Lincoln, November 17, 1862, Lincoln Papers, Library of Congress.

15. Ramsey to Lincoln, November 10, 1862, in Board of Commissioners, *Minnesota in the Civil and Indian Wars,* 2:289.

16. Pope to Lincoln, November 12, 1862, Lincoln Papers, Library of Congress.

17. Pope to Lincoln, November 24, 1862, ibid.

18. Williamson to John C. Smith, November 15, 1862, NARG 75, LR. SPA.

19. Ibid.

20. Williamson to Riggs, November 17, 1862, Riggs Papers, MHSA.

21. Williamson to Treat, November 21, 1862, ABCFM.

22. Jane Williamson to Mary Riggs, November 23, 1862, Riggs Papers, MHSA.

23. Riggs to Williamson, November 27, 1862, Riggs Papers, CWS-A.

24. Riggs to Lincoln, November 17, 1862, Lincoln Papers, Library of Congress.

25. *St. Paul Pioneer Press,* November 29, 1862.

26. Gustav Niebuhr, *Lincoln's Bishop: A President, a Priest, and the Fate of the 300 Dakota Sioux Warriors* (New York: Harpercollins, 2014), 152–53.

27. Whipple letter, Faribault *Central Republican,* December 3, 1862.

28. Whipple to Sibley, December 4, 1862, Sibley Papers, MHSA.

29. Sibley to Whipple, December 7, 1862, Whipple Papers, MHSA. On the validity of a drumhead court martial, see Chomsky, "The United States-Dakota War Trials," 54.

30. Miller to Olin, December 5, 1862, NARG 393, LR, District of Minnesota; *St. Peter Tribune,* December 8, 1862.

31. See Bryant and Murch, *A History of the Great Massacre by the Sioux Indians in Minnesota, Including the Personal Narratives of Many Who Escaped.*

32. Miller's comments are found in Loren W. Collins to a Friend, December 7, 1862, Collins ms., MHSA. See also George W. Bushwell Journal, Huntington Museum and Library, San Marino, Calif. Judge Lorin Cray offers a different description in Morris, *Old Rail Fence Corners,* 176–77.

33. Captain W. C. Williston to Miller, December 5, 1862, and Sibley to Ramsey, December 6 and 8, 1862, Governors Papers, MHSA; Miller to Olin, December 9, 1862, NARG 393, LR, Department of the Northwest, "Two or More Names File." Ramsey's "Proclamation," December 6, 1862, Digital Collection of the American Antiquarian Society.

34. Miller to Olin, December 5, 1862, NARG 393, LR, District of Minnesota. William E. Lass of Minnesota State University, Mankato, helped identify buildings. Lass to Anderson, private correspondence, November 15, 2016.

35. Collins to a friend, December 7, 1862, Collins Papers, ms., MHSA.

36. Miller to Olin, December 6, 1862, NARG 393, LR, Department of the Northwest, Unentered Files.

37. Special Order No. 11, by Colonel Stephen Miller, December 17, 1762, Picket Papers, ms., MHSA.

38. Lincoln to Holt, December 1, 1862, Lincoln Papers, Library of Congress.

39. Holt to Lincoln, December 1, 1862, ibid.

40. See Lincoln's explanation to Congress and the report of Whiting and Ruggles in "Message of the President," December 11, 1862, in 37th *Congress,* 3d *Session, Executive Document* 7, Exhibit E.

41. The resolution explains why the original trial records are today located in NARG 46, Senate Records, 37A-F2, the National Archives. See also J. W. Forney (Secretary of the Senate) "Resolved," December 5, 1862, Lincoln Papers, Library of Congress. See also Wilkinson, Cyrus Aldrich, and William Windom's letter to Lincoln, December ? (likely the 5th), 1862, 37th *Congress,* 3d *Session, Senate Executive Document* #7, Exhibit E. The letter was apparently telegraphed to the *St. Paul Press,* which published it.

42. Lincoln to Sibley, December 6, 1862, NARG 94, LR, AGO. Another list is found in the Sibley Papers, MHSA.

43. "Message of the president," December 11, 1862, in 37th *Congress,* 3rd *Session, Senate Executive Document #7.* There is little question that the Dakota men should have been treated as "prisoners of war," those committing crimes against civilians being tried. Members of Lincoln's administration obviously thought the same, as did Henry Benjamin Whipple, who argued the issue with then Senator Henry Rice.

44. Usher to Sibley, December 10, 1862, NARG 48, LS, Indian Division of Department of Interior.

45. Sibley to Lincoln, December 15, 1862, Lincoln Papers, Library of Congress. Lincoln responded by telegram, Lincoln to Sibley, December 16, 1862, Sibley Papers, MHSA. Miller explained the rope issue in a note attached to the original Lincoln message of December 6, later given back to Sibley and found in the Sibley Papers.

46. Letter of "H," later identified as Heard, *St. Paul Pioneer,* December 11, 1862.

47. Riggs' Letter, *St. Paul Pioneer,* December 11, 1862.

48. Sibley to Usher, December 19, 1862, NARG 94, LR, AGO.

49. Thomas Williamson to Treat, December 1, 1862, ABCFM. The argument regarding early views of the Great Plains is found in W. Eugene Hollon, *The Great American Desert* (New York: Oxford University Press, 1966).

50. Whipple letter, *St. Paul Press,* December 17, 1862.

51. Thomas Williamson to Riggs, November 17, 1862, Riggs Papers, MHSA; Thomas Williamson to Treat, November 21, 1862, ABCFM.

52. Thomas Williamson to Treat, December 1, 1862, ABCFM.

53. Jane Williamson to the Riggs family, December 5, 1862, Riggs Papers, MHSA.

54. Quotation in Capaduta letter, December 25, 1862, ABCFM. See also "Letters of Dakota Prisoners" and "Translation of Correspondence," all forwarded by Williamson to Treat, December 25, 1862, ibid.

55. John Williamson to Treat, November 28, 1862, ABCFM.

56. John Williamson to his father, November 17, 1862, Williamson Papers, MHSA; *St. Paul Pioneer,* November 14, 1862; William McKusick "census," December 2, 1862, NARG 393, LR, Department of the Northwest, Unentered files.

57. *St. Paul Daily Union,* November 22, 1862.

58. Riggs to Thomas Williamson, December 10, 1862, Riggs Papers, CWS-A; John Williamson to Treat, November 28, 1862, Riggs to Treat, December 1, 1862, and Treat to John Williamson, December 19, 1862, ABCFM.

59. *Mankato Weekly Record,* December 13, 1862. For the argument promoting the executions of the other 265 men, see the paper for December 20, 1862.

60. Miller to Sibley, December 17, 1862, and Miller to Olin, December 18, 1862, LR, District of Minnesota. The new troops came from all over, 220 came under command of Colonel Wilkins at St. Peter, 100 from Glencoe, 100 from Baker, 50 from New Ulm, 40 from Madelia, 50 from Tivoli, 40 from Garden City, 40 from Jackson, and 100 from Winnebago City. Eli Picket described the grave in Picket to his wife, December 16, 1862, Picket Papers, MHSA. William E. Lass, professor of history emeritus at Minnesota State University, Mankato, believes that the grave was on a large sandbar. Lass to Anderson, November 15, 2016. The location is described in *Mankato Weekly Record–Supplement,* December 26, 1862.

61. Hughes, *A History of Blue Earth County,* 132.

62. The "Order" is found in Hughes, *A History of Blue Earth County,* 130.

63. Ravoux to Sibley, December 17, 1862, NARG 75, LR, AGO; Ravoux, *Reminiscences, Memoirs, and Lectures* (St. Paul, Minn.: Brown, Treacy & Co., 1890), 72–73.

64. Sibley to Riggs, December 15, 1862, Sibley Papers, MHSA.

65. "Indian Hanging Recalled in Book of Parker Pierce," in *New Ulm Review,* December 31, 1924, clipping in Charles Roos Papers, MHSA.

66. Ravoux, *Reminiscences,* 73; *Mankato Weekly Record—Supplement,* December 26, 1862.

67. Oral history recorded in Hughes, *A History of Blue Earth County*, 131.

68. Sibley to Miller, December 23, 1862, NARG 94, LR, AGO; Charles E. McColley Reminiscences, December 1862, MHSA.

69. Riggs, "Copy of Revelations Made by Indians Who Were Executed," January 1863, NARG 393, LR, District of Minnesota; Riggs, "List of Those Implicated by the Revelations of the Executed." NARG 393, LR, Department of the Northwest, Unentered Files; *Mankato Weekly Record—Supplement*, December 26, 1862; Riggs to his wife, December 23–25, 1862, Riggs Papers, Chippewa County Historical Society. Pine Tree was pardoned in 1866.

70. This rare description of the journey after death comes from Elizabeth Wiŋyaŋ to Mary Collins, 1885, Collins Collection, Western History Center, Augustana College, Sioux Falls, S.Dak.

71. *Mankato Weekly Record—Supplement*, December 26, 1862; Eli Picket to his wife, December 26, 1862, Picket Papers, MHSA; "38 Indians Die on the Gallows for Massacre Roles," repr. from Mankato newspapers, *Minneapolis Star,* August 16, 1962; *St. Paul Pioneer,* December 28, 1862.

72. Picket to his wife, December 26, 1862, copy of a letter found at Fort Ridgely, now in the Nicollet County Historical Society, St. Peter, Minn.

73. Various accounts of the singing can be found in Edward H. Wood to his wife, December 26, 1862, Wood Papers, MHSA; *Mankato Weekly Record—Supplement*, December 26, 1862; Memoir of Julius Owen, December 26, 1862, MHSA. The *St. Paul Pioneer Sunday,* December 28, 1862, edition reports that the songs were "nothing defiant."

74. Oral history account, given to the author by Sidney H. Byrd and Marcella R. Ryan Le Beau while attending a conference in Sioux Falls, S.Dak., in 1993.

75. Edward H. Wood to his wife, December 26, 1862, Wood Papers, MHSA; *St. Peter Tribune*, December 27, 1862.

76. Marcella R. Ryan Le Beau to the author, with translations from Sidney H. Byrd, 1993. This hymn is traditionally sung after the doxology at Episcopalian services in South Dakota in remembrance of the thirty-eight men.

77. Eli Picket to his wife, December 26, 1862, Picket Papers, MHSA; Edward H. Wood to his wife, December 26, 1862, Wood Papers, MHSA; Hughes, *A History of Blue Earth County*, 132–34. Hughes identifies the Indian who had his rope break as Cut Nose.

78. See "Mankato Hanging Vividly Pictured," newspaper clipping from the Sleepy Eye *Herald Dispatch,* no date, Nicollet County Historical Society, St. Peter, Minn.

79. Miller to Olin, December 26, 1862, NARG 393, LR, District of Minnesota.

80. Arnold to "Fletch," note in General Correspondence Files, MHSA; Miller to Ramsey, May 28, 1863, and Ramsey to Miller, June 6, 1863, Governors Papers, MHSA.

81. John Ford Meagher letter, December 26, 1862, MHSA. Description of the repatriation of Cut Nose in *Lubbock Avalanche Journal,* July 17, 2000, on the Internet at lubbockonline. com. For the bodies on display in Mankato, see Daniel Buck, *Indian Outbreak* (1904; repr., Minneapolis: Ross and Haines, 1956), 270.

82. Loren Warren Collins to a Friend, January 4, 1863, Collins Papers, MHSA; *Mankato Independent,* January 2, 1863; Miller to Olin, December 28, 1862, NARG 393, LR, District of Minnesota. The story regarding the moving of bodies to St. Peter is found in Howard M. Nelson, "The Transition of Traverse des Sioux and St. Peter Areas from Indian to Pioneer Community" (Master's thesis, Mankato State College, 1956), 119. William E. Lass suspects that what remains existed in the riverbank were swept away by the many terrible floods that inundated the region in the nineteenth and twentieth centuries. Personal correspondence, Lass to Anderson, November 16, 2016.

83. Miller to Olin, December 28, 1862, NARG 393, LR, District of Minnesota; Miller to Olin, December 30, 1862, NARG 393, LR, Department of the Northwest, "Two or More Name File."

84. Wakefield to Lincoln, March 23, 1863, Lincoln Papers, Library of Congress.

85. Thomas Robertson Reminiscences, December 26, 1862, MHSA. See also Isch, *The Dakota Trials*, 338.

86. Double jeopardy does apply today in military law, with the issue being revised in the Articles of War just before World War I. See *War Powers and Military Justice* (Ann Arbor, Mich.: J.A.G.S. Text No. 4, Judge Advocate General School, 1943), 21–22. The issue was first raised in *Grafton vs. U.S.* (206 U.S. 333). The entire article is pages 1–177.

87. Sibley to Lincoln, January 7, 1863, Lincoln Papers, Library of Congress.

88. Crooks to Sibley, January 2, 1863, NARG 393, Department of the Northwest, Unentered Files.

89. See David Faribault Jr., Case No. 134, in Isch, *The Dakota Trials*, 174–76.

90. In a strange twist, Major S. H. Fowler, from Sibley's staff, apparently helped Faribault with the affidavit. See "Affidavit of David and Alexander Faribault, January 16, 1863," NARG 46, Senate Records, 37A-F2, National Archives.

91. Sibley to Lincoln, February 16, 1863, Lincoln Papers, Library of Congress.

92. Sibley to Whipple, March 11, 1863, Whipple Papers, MHSA.

93. "Military Commission Records," April 15–19, 1863, NARG 393, LR, Department of the Northwest, Unentered Files.

94. Ibid.

95. Ibid.

96. See the *St. Paul Press*, April 30, 1863, and *St. Paul Daily Press*, April 30, 1863.

CHAPTER ELEVEN

1. Stephen Riggs helped distribute this money. Some 101 claims were accepted for an average of $160 per claim. See Compensation Paid Out for Claims, December 1–January 30, 1862–1863, Governors Papers, MHSA; Folwell, *A History of Minnesota*, 2:244. While Folwell argues that most of the money went to homeless people in St. Paul, Riggs actually traveled to Hutchinson and Glencoe to help settlers.

2. Folwell, *A History of Minnesota*, 2:245.

3. February 16, 1863, Statutes at Large, 12:652–54. For the later litigation, see *The Sisseton and Wahpeton Court of Claims* No. 22524.

4. March 3, 1863, Statues at Large, 12:819–20.

5. Folwell, *History of Minnesota*, 2:247–48. The first session of the commission convened on April 1, 1863, and later moved on to St. Cloud, New Ulm, and St. Paul. See (Chaska) *Valley Herald*, March 14, 1863.

6. Claims evidence is being assembled at the Brown County Historical Society, New Ulm, Minn.

7. Sibley's first attempt at warning the population is found in Sibley to Skaro, September 16, 1862, in Board of Commissioners, *Minnesota in the Civil and Indian Wars*, 2:233. Galbraith's comments are in Folwell, *History of Minnesota*, 2:247–48.

8. Daniel Densmore to a friend, January 5, 1863, Densmore Papers, MHSA; Miller to Olin, February 15, 1863, NARG 393, LR, Department of the Northwest, "Two or More Names File."

9. Thomas Williamson to Treat, January 20, 1863, ABCFM.

10. Thomas Williamson to Riggs, January 27, 1863, ibid.

11. Pond in *New York Evangelist*, February 9, 1863, and Thomas Williamson to Walter Griffith, April 10, 1863, ibid.; Riggs to his wife, March 18, 1863, Riggs Papers, CWS-A.

12. Treat to Riggs, March 12, 1863, ABCFM.

13. Riggs to his wife, March 18, 1863, Riggs Papers, CWS-A.

14. Riggs to his wife, March 20, 1863, ibid.

15. Riggs to Treat, March 26, 1863, ABCFM.

16. Riggs to Treat, March 10, 1863, and John Williamson to Treat, May 7, 1863, ABCFM; John Williamson to his Father Thomas, April 6, 1863, Williamson Papers, MHSA.

17. The figure of 102 deaths is derived from McKusick's records, filed as "Morning Reports" for each month. A complete breakdown of Dakota people at Fort Snelling is found in McKusick to William Crooks, May 20, 1863, NARG 94, Entry 173, Indian Prisoners, National Archives. For the epidemic, see Riggs to Treat, January 21, 1863, ABCFM. For a good description of the camp, see George Biscoe to Ellen, March 2, 1863, Biscoe Papers, MHSA.

18. There is some confusion in the literature over just how many Indians died at Fort Snelling. Corinne L. Monjeau-Marz concluded that at least 102 Indians died, but she is unsure of the numbers beyond that. See Monjeau-Marz, *The Dakota Internment at Fort Snelling, 1862–1864* (St. Paul, Minn.: Prairie Smoke Press, 2005), 57. McKusick indicates that 230 people were allowed to leave the compound. When subtracted from the 1,601 original occupants, this left just 1,371 people. Of these, 102 died, leaving 1,269, to which 49 men from Mankato, who had not been convicted of any crimes, would be added in late April, making in total 1,318 dependents. This last figure is the number who would be deported out of the state by steamboat. See McKusick to Crooks, May 20, 1863, NARG 94, Entry 173, Indian Prisoners, National Archives. Sibley incorrectly reported some 130 deaths from the measles. He may have been including some who later died at the scout camps and even those at Mankato. See Sibley to J. P. Usher, March 14, 1863, NARG 75, SPA; John Williamson to his mother, May 13, 1863, Williamson Papers, MHSA. At least one inmate at Fort Snelling went unaccounted for—an unidentified Indian woman "ran away" with Joseph Coursoule. McKusick wanted her back, but he never reported her return. See McKusick to Sibley, March 13, 1863, NARG 393, LR, District of Minnesota.

19. Pope to Ramsey, November 6, 1862. It was even published in the *New York Times*, November 15, 1862.

20. Sibley's order in Captain H. C. Rogers, November 11, 1862, NARG 393, LR, Fort Ridgely.

21. These posts were occupied by companies from the Sixth, Eighth, and Ninth Regiments. See the various narratives in Board of Commissioners, *Minnesota in the Civil and Indian Wars,* 1:300–454. A good general discussion of the defenses is John R. Howard, "The Sioux War Stockades," *Minnesota History* 12 (September 1931): 301–3.

22. Peteler to Sibley, February 28, 1863, NARG 393, LR, District of Minnesota.

23. Averill to Sibley, November 15 and 27, 1862 and Pettit to Sibley, December 12, 1862, NARG 393, LR, District of Minnesota; W. S. Lefft to Ramsey, December 8, 1862, Governors Papers, MHSA.

24. Captain William S. Rockwood to Sibley, January 1, 1863, NARG 393, LR, District of Minnesota.

25. Averill to Olin, February 16 and 17, 1863, Captain William S. Rockwell to Olin, March 26, 1863, Major George Camp to Olin, April 24, 1863, and Lieutenant William Larned to Sibley, April 11, 1863, ibid.

26. Roos to Sibley, January 17, 1863, and Ross to Aldrich, January 19, 1863, Roos Papers, MHSA.

27. *Mankato Weekly Record*, March 7, 1863.

28. See *St. Paul Daily Union*, December 22, 1862. While the majority of these widows were from Milford and New Ulm, several others were from Beaver Creek and Middle Creek. The plight of settlers was so severe by spring 1867 that county boards were set up to distribute "relief" across the state. See G. K. Cleveland to William Marshall, April 8, 1867, and Sam McPhail to Marshall, April 30, 1867, Marshall Papers, MHSA. Mary Bakeman has used the mounds of testimony taken after the war for "claims," showing how massive the refugee problem became. See Bakeman, "Forgotten Victims: Terror, Refuge, and Recovery," *Minnesota's Heritage* 7 (January 2013): 84–107.

29. Sibley to Usher, March 14, 1863, NARG 75, LR, SPA; Usher to Clark W. Thompson, April 20, 1863, NARG 48, LS, Indian Division of the Department of Interior.

30. Pope to Kirkwood, March 13, 1863, NARG 48, LS, Indian Division of Department of Interior.

31. A second bid came from Robert Campbell and Company, at $28–$30 a head. Chouteau received over $40,000 for the removal. The Winnebago were removed under similar circumstances. See Usher to Ramsey, April 6, 1863, NARG 48, LS, Indian Division of the Department of Interior; Chouteau to Usher, April 6, 1863, and Charles Mix to Commissioner of Indian Affairs, May 18, 1863, NARG 75, LR, Northern Superintendency; Captain B. M. Little receipt (at Davenport), April 25, 1863, NARG 393, LR, District of Minnesota.

32. Sibley had wanted to send the forty-nine acquitted men into confinement with the others, but Riggs protested and the general relented, agreeing to drop the forty-nine men off at Fort Snelling. See Riggs to Treat, April 21, 1863, ABCFM.

33. Riggs to his wife, May 2, 1863, Riggs Papers, CWS-A; *St. Paul Press*, April 24, 1863.

34. *St. Paul Press*, April 24, 1863.

35. Ibid.

36. The hymn is reported in Thomas Hughes, *A History of Blue Earth County*, 136.

37. John Williamson to Riggs, May 9, 1863, Riggs Papers, MHSA; *Davenport Daily Democrat*, April 27, 1863.

38. Williamson to Lincoln, April 24, 1864, and Lincoln's Pardons, April 30, 1864, Lincoln Papers, Library of Congress; Williamson to Riggs, April 7, 1864, and John Williamson to Riggs, July 5, 1864, Riggs Papers, MHSA.

39. Among the new Indians added to the Davenport prison in 1864 was Wowinape, Little Crow's son. See E. Kirkpatrick to D. N. Cooley, May 19, 1863, and Jedediah Brown to the Secretary of Interior, June 30, 1866, report entitled "Removal of Santee Sioux Prisoners from Davenport, Iowa, 1866," NARG 75, Special File 235, National Archives; Williamson to Lincoln, Aprill 27, 1864, Lincoln Papers, Library of Congress; Winifred Williamson Barton, *John P. Williamson: A Brother to the Sioux* (London: Fleming H. Revell Company, 1919; repr., Nabu Public Domain Reprints, no date), 110.

40. Mary Riggs to her daughter, May 5–9, 1863, Riggs Papers, CWS-A; Charles Mix to Commissioner of Indian Affairs, May 18, 1863, NARG 75, LR, Northern Superintendency; *St. Paul Daily Press*, May 5 and 6, 1863.

41. Mary Riggs to her daughter, May 5–8, 1863, Riggs Papers, CWS-A.

42. John Williamson to his father, May 9, 1863, and John Williamson to his mother, May 13, 1863, Williamson Papers, MHSA.

43. Clark W. Thompson to Dole, April 17 and June 1, 1863, NARG 75, LR, Northern Superintendency; Williamson testimony to A. W. Hubbard, September 11, 1865, NARG 75, LR, Dakota Superintendency.

44. John Williamson testimony to A. W. Hubbard, September 11, 1865, NARG 75, LR, Dakota Superintendency; John Williamson to his father, June 3 and 5, and July 7, 1863, Williamson Papers, MHSA.

45. John Williamson to his father, June 3, 1863, Williamson Papers, MHSA; Hinman to Whipple, June 8, 1863, Whipple Papers, MHSA.

46. Samuel Brown to J. R. Brown, January 6, 1864, Brown Papers, MHSA; Samuel Hinman to Whipple, February 8, 1864, Whipple Papers, MHSA.

47. Robinson, *History of the Dakota or Sioux Indians*, 388–90; Meyers, *History of the Santee Sioux*, 247–88.

48. The best account of this encounter comes from young John Euni, a seventeen-year-old captive who witnessed the brief fight. See Euni narrative in *Winona Daily Republican*, September 23, 1863. See also Joseph R. Brown statement in the Satterlee Papers, MHSA; Brown, "Samuel J. Brown's Recollections," in Anderson and Woolworth, *Through Dakota Eyes*, 272; *St. Paul Pioneer*, February 12, 1863.

49. Standing Buffalo's statement is in Robertson, Reminiscences, MHSA.

50. Anderson, *Little Crow,* 172–73.

51. See Father Mester, "Relation of the Visit of the Sioux to St. Boniface," and Father André to Bishop Taché, March 4, 1863, Belleau Collection, Assumpton Abby Archives, Richardton, N.Dak.; William Mactavish to Thomas Fraser, January 9, 1863, Winnipeg Correspondence, Letterbooks, 1861–64, Hudson's Bay Company Archives, Winnipeg, MB.

52. See the *Nor'Wester,* February 9, 1863.

53. James M. Petridge to Henry M. Rice, November 23, 1862, NARG 75, LR, Northern Superintendency.

54. *Nor'Wester,* March 17, 1863; *St. Paul Daily Press,* May 26, 1863.

55. The councils are reported in several sources including Alexander Grant Dallas, "Private Journals," and Dallas to Viscount Monck, June 3, 1863, Hudson's Bay Company Archives; Dallas to Sibley, June 3, 1863, NARG 75, LR, SPA; *Nor'Wester,* June 2, 1863. See also William E. Lass, *Minnesota's Boundary with Canada: Its Evolution since 1783* (St. Paul: Minnesota Historical Society Press, 1980), 76–78.

56. Brown, "Samuel J. Brown's Recollections," in Anderson and Woolworth, *Through Dakota Eyes,* 174.

57. Testimony of William L. Quinn and Joseph DeMarais Sr., August 24, 1863, in "Proceedings of a Military Commission Which Convened at Fort Abercrombie D. T. by Virtue of the Following Special Order," cited hereafter as "The Trial of Wowinape," ms., MHSA.

58. Testimony of Wowinape, August 24, 1863, in "Trial of Wowinape," MHSA.

59. Anderson, *Little Crow,* 178. The first interview with Wowinape after his capture is found in Major M. Cook to Colonel Miller, August 3, 1863, NARG 393, Supplement to LR, Department of the Northwest. A second interview was published in *St. Paul Pioneer Press,* August 13, 1863.

60. The organization of the commission is found at R. C. Olin to General Sibley, August 22, 1863, in "Trial of Wowinape," MHSA.

61. Pope's "disapproval" of the proceedings is in J. F. Meline for General Pope, November 13, 1863, in "Trial of Wowinape," MHSA. After learning that the judge advocate general of the army had argued that Sibley had no authority to form a military commission while in the field, Sibley wrote him a scathing letter, defending his trials. See Sibley to Judge Advocate General, December 7, 1862, Sibley Papers, MHSA.

62. Anderson, *Little Crow,* 167.

63. Bond's statement, August 20, 1863, *St. Paul Pioneer.* Other similar descriptions are found in "Little Crow, or Not Little Crow, That is the Question," *St. Paul Daily Press,* August 21, 1863.

64. Personal conversation between Alan R. Woolworth and the author, 1984. Woolworth organized the shipment of the remains and the burial.

65. This number is reported in the *Nor'Wester,* February 5, 1864.

66. On the surrender, see *Nor'Wester,* February 5, 1864; Hatch to Wife, February 24, 1864, Hatch Papers, MHSA; Hatch to Sibley, January 2, 1864, NARG 393, LR, Department of the Northwest. For the capture of Little Six, or Śakpedaŋ, and Medicine Bottle, see Folwell, *A History of Minnesota,* 2:443–50.

67. The most comprehensive Minnesota historian, William Watts Folwell, found Little Crow's life difficult to write about. In 1916, he wrote, "Deceived by white men, discredited by his own people, he has been given an unjust character in history which should be corrected. When the bitterness of the survivors of the days of 1862 shall have died out, this will probably be done." Yet he then added: "His ignoble end was not unfit." Quotation from Folwell to Jane Williams, June 22, 1916, Folwell Papers, MHSA.

ENGLISH-DAKOTA NAME GLOSSARY

MDEWAKANTONS

Andrew Good Thunder (Wakinyanwaste): Mdewakanton Christian and farmer. He worked to help captives. Good Thunder returned to Minnesota in the 1880s and helped create the Lower Sioux Community.

Big Eagle (Waŋmditaŋka): Left Little Crow's band to form his own small village. He was a strong supporter of the soldiers' lodge after the war began. He left the best narrative of events, later published from the point of view of the Dakota soldiers. He died in 1906.

Cut Nose (Maḣpiyaokenaźin): Often considered the leader of the Mdewakanton soldiers' lodge. He was executed at Mankato December 26, 1862.

Laying Up Buffalo (Tazoo or Taźu): One of the leaders of the soldiers' lodge from Red Middle Voice's village. He was executed on December 26, 1862.

Little Crow (Taoyateduta, or His Red Nation): Chief of the Kaposia band and considered the leader of the rebellion. He was killed on July 3, 1863, near Hutchinson.

Little Six (Śakpedaŋ): Son of Shakopee. He was kidnapped in Canada and executed in 1865 at Fort Snelling.

Mankato (Maḣkato): Chief of a small band that joined the rebellion. He was killed in the war.

Rattling Runner (Hdaiŋyaŋka): Son-in-law to Wabasha and strong supporter of the soldiers' lodge. He was executed on December 26, 1862.

Red Middle Voice (Hocokayaduta): Brother to Shakopee. He formed his own village at Rice Creek, where most of the plotting occurs for the war. He fled to Canada after the war.

Red Owl (Hiŋhaŋduta): Briefly served as the "speaker" who replaced Little Crow. He died in 1861.

Refuge (Wowinape): Little Crow's son. He later takes the name Thomas Wakeman.

Shakopee (Śakpe): Chief of the village named for him along the Minnesota River. He died of natural causes in 1860.

Wabasha (Wapaśa): Chief of the Wabasha band, many of whom became "farmer" Indians. Wabasha III, as he was known, died of natural causes at Santee, Nebraska in 1876.

Wakute (Wakute, or Shooter): Chief of a small band of Mdewakantons often called Red Wing's Band. Wakute apparently died at Santee, Nebraska, in 1880.

White Spider (Uŋktomiska): Little Crow's half-brother. He worked in a trader's store before the war. He joined the rebellion after his brother agreed to lead it. He later surrendered at Pembina in 1864. He survived two years as a prisoner and later assumed the name John C. Wakeman.

Wound (Taopi, or Wound): A farmer in Wabasha's band just before the war. He was strongly attached to the Episcopalian mission led by Samuel Hinman. He died at Faribault, Minnesota in 1868.

WAHPEKUTES

The Cane (Tasagya): Chief of the Wahpekute band. He was killed by the Sac and Fox in 1844.

Red All Over (Sintomniduta): Succeeding The Cane, Red All Over was murdered by Thomas Lott in 1856, allowing Scarlet End, or Inkpaduta, to become chief.

Scarlet End (Inkpaduta): Led the infamous massacre at Spirit Lake in 1857. Fleeing west, he joined Sitting Bull's Hunkpapa Lakota band in the West and fought at Little Big Horn in 1876.

LOWER SISSETONS

Limping Devil (Itewakiŋyaŋ): Chief of a Sisseton band that by the 1850s is led by his son, White Lodge. Involved in the attack on Lake Shetek in 1862, the band moved north with the Plains Sissetons, later settling at Devils Lake.

Sleepy Eyes (Ištahba): Chief of a small Sisseton band located originally near present-day Mankato. After his death in 1860, his people generally joined with White Lodge's Sissetons, who roamed from camp to camp southwest of the Minnesota River, often living near Lake Shetek.

Walking Runner (Iŋyaŋgmani). Chief of a Sisseton/Wahpeton band located just south of Lac qui Parle along the Minnesota River. He was Little Crow's father-in-law.

White Lodge (Waŋkaska): Leader of a strong contingent of Sissetons who refused to settle on the reservation and resisted government acculturation programs. White Lodge was the uncle of the later Dakota scholar Amos E. Oneroad, who wrote an extremely important ethnography of the Sisseton people. See Amos Oneroad, *Being Dakota: Tales and Traditions of the Sissetons and Wahpetons,* ed. Laura L. Anderson (St. Paul: Minnesota Historical Society Press, 2003).

UPPER OR PLAINS SISSETONS

The Charger (Waanata): Chief of a combined Yanktonai/Sisseton band that frequented Lake Traverse. With Standing Buffalo, he tried to prevent Little Crow from fleeing out onto the plains.

Standing Buffalo (Tataŋkanaźin): Major chief of the Plains Sissetons, who often camped at Big Stone Lake. He opposed the war and mostly prevented his people from joining it. He was killed by Assiniboine Indians in 1870.

Scarlet Plume (Waŋmdiupiduta). Gabriel Renville's uncle. He was a chief who camped with Standing Buffalo and Sweet Corn near Big Stone Lake and lobbied against the war, helping to keep the Yankton Sioux out of it.

Sweet Corn (Wamnahezaskuya): Chief of the Big Stone Lake band. Gabriel Renville was born in his village in 1825.

WAHPETONS

Extended Tail Feathers (Upiyahdayeya): He was a Wahpeton Chief who frequented Big Stone Lake.

Red Iron (Mazaduta): Chief of the village fifteen miles north of the Yellow Medicine, or Upper, Sioux Agency. His brothers were Akipa and Walking Iron.

Walking Iron (Mazamani): Brother to Red Iron and Akipa. He was a chief of a small Sisseton band.

Walking Spirit (Wakaŋmani): He was the chief of a Sisseton village just south of Big Stone Lake.

CHRISTIAN INDIANS

Akipa (Meeting): He was stepfather to Gabriel Renville and the husband of Winona Crawford.

Simon Anawaŋgmani (Walking Galloping): He saved several white captives and died of natural causes at Sisseton, South Dakota, in 1891.

John Aŋpetutokeea (Other Day): He was also known as John Otherday. Otherday brought sixty-one whites to St. Paul, saving their lives.

Amos Etetukiya: He was the brother of Solomon Two Stars.

Enos Ecetukiya (Brings About): He joined Camp Release. He opposed the war.

Robert Hopkins: He was a full-blood convert who led the revival at Camp Lincoln.

Joseph Kwanke (Struck Down): Joseph worked as a scout for General Sibley.

Lorenzo Lawrence (Toŋwaŋitetoŋ): He saved several white settlers and worked as a scout for Sibley.

Henoch Maĥpiyahdinape (Appearing Cloud): He was the "secretary of state" of the Hazelwood Republic. He fled to Canada with relatives, although he took no part in the conflict. He later returned to Sisseton, South Dakota.

Paul Mazakutemani (Walks Shooting Iron): He served as governor of the Hazelwood Republic and primary speaker for the friendly camp during the war.

Peter Tapetataŋka: He was the son of Walking Runner (Iŋyaŋgmani) and brother-in-law to Little Crow.

Solomon Wicaŋĥpinoŋpi (Two Stars): He worked with General Sibley to defeat the Mdewakantons.

FRANCO- AND ANGLO-DAKOTA MIXED-BLOODS

Samuel Brown: Seventeen-year-old son of Joseph R. Brown. He left the best written account of the captivity of both white women and children and various mixed-bloods.

Antoine J. Campbell: Son of Scott Campbell, Anglo-Dakota interpreter at Fort Snelling. Scott's father, Colin Campbell, married a woman from Little Crow's village, and the chief called Campbell his "cousin." Little Crow often spoke with Antoine Campbell about the war and what to do with the captives.

Charles Crawford: He was the Sisseton son of Akipa and Winona Crawford (Victor Renville's widowed wife). He helped form Camp Release.

Susan Frenier Brown: She was the wife of Indian agent Joseph R. Brown and the daughter of Winona Crawford.

Gabriel Renville: Sisseton/French son of Victor Renville, who died in 1834. He was raised by Akipa, his stepfather. Renville was leader of the friendly soldiers' lodge.

John B. Renville: Son of Joseph Renville and Gabriel Renville's cousin. John later became a minister.

BIBLIOGRAPHY

ARCHIVAL SOURCES

Assumption Abbey Archives, Belleau Collection, Richardton, N.Dak.
 Father Mester and Father André Collections

Bentley Historical Library, Ann Arbor, Mich.
 Bush, Chauncey. Journal of 1837
 Wood, Sally S. Letters 1862

Brown County Historical Society, New Ulm, Minn.
 Beinhorn, Frederick. Obituary 1900
 Eisenreich Family. Papers
 Mary LaCroix Interview

Center for Western Studies, Augustana College, Sioux Falls, S.Dak.
 Collins, Mary. Collection
 Riggs, Stephen Return, and Family. Papers

Chippewa County Historical Society
 Riggs, Stephen Return. Miscellaneous Letters

Gustavus Adolphus College Library, St. Peter, Minn.
 Johnson, Emory. "Memoir of New Sweden"

Henry E. Huntington Library, San Marino, Calif.
 Bushnell, George W. Journal
 Folsom, Simeon P. Papers

Kansas Historical Society
 Clark, William. Papers

Library of Congress
 Lincoln, Abraham. Papers

Macker, Guy. Papers. Private Collections in the hands of the author.
 Sisseton, South Dakota

McLeod County Historical Museum
 Marston, Kate. Diary
 Wadsworth, Henry. Letter

Minnesota Historical Society Archives
  Adjutant Generals Papers (Minnesota)
  American Board of Commissioners for Foreign Missions. Transcripts of Papers.
    (ABCFM)
  Anderson, Joseph. Papers
  Annual Report of the State Auditor
  Bell, Edward. Reminiscences
  Blanchard, Dick E. Reminiscences
  Bowlee, John Madison. Letter
  Briscoe, George. Papers
  Brown, Joseph R. Papers
  Champlin, Ezra T. Recollections
  Chester, Jeremiah. Memoir
  Collins, Loren W. Papers
  Crowell, Mary. Letter
  Currie, Neil. Papers
  Daniels, Jared W. Reminiscences and Papers
  Dodd, William B. Diary and Papers
  Donahower, Jeremiah C. Papers
  Earle, Ezmon W. Reminiscences
  Eastlick, Lavina. Reminiscences and "Thrilling Incidents"
  Eggleston, Hubert N. Diary
  Flandrau, Charles. Papers
  Fort Ridgely State Park and Historical Association. Papers
  Gere, Thomas. Memoir and Journal
  Goodell, B. H. "Personal Recollections"
  Governors Papers
  Griswold, Franklin Clinton. Letters
  Hahn, Margareta Hall. Interview
  Hallock, Mary Ann Marston. Reminiscences
  Hatch, Edwin. Papers
  Hayden, William. Account
  Holcombe, R. I. Papers
  Holquist, Ingar [Johnson]. Reminiscences
  Hughes, Thomas. Papers
  Kramer, Edward Frederick. Reminiscences
  Leavenworth, Frederick P. Papers
  Lobdell, Julia E. Farnsworth. Reminiscences
  MacAlmond, Rebecca. Diary
  Marshall, William. Papers
  McFall, Orlando. Narrative
  McColley, Charles E. Reminiscences
  McKenzie, John H. Reminiscences

McLeod, Martin. Papers

Meagher, John Ford. Letter

Meyers, Aaron. Reminiscences

Minnesota Commission. "Report on the Battle of Wood Lake"

Montgomery, Sarah Purcell. "Some Recollections"

Myers, Aaron. Reminiscences

Nairn, John. Narrative

Nelson, C. C. "History of Early Pioneers," Narrative

Person, Irene. Memoir

Picket, Eli. Papers

Poehler, Henry. Memoir

Pond, Gideon H., and Samuel W. Pond. Papers

"Proceedings of a Military Commission which convened at Fort Abercrombie, D. T."

Ramer, James. Diary

Ramsey, Alexander. Papers

Riggs, Stephen Return and Family. Papers

Robertson, Thomas. Reminiscences

Rodange, Mrs. Peter. Reminiscences

Roos, Charles. Papers and Scrapbook, including "History of Early Days"

Satterlee, Marion P. Papers

Scantlebury, Thomas. "Wanderings in Minnesota During the Indian Troubles"

Schrepel, Charles. Narrative

Schwandt, Mary. Papers

Seifert, Alexander. Reminiscences

Sheehan, Timothy J. Papers and Diary

Sibley, Henry Hastings. Papers

Sidwell, Aaron M. "Selected Extracts from the Soldier's Gazette"

Smith, Caroline. "Observations by Caroline Ester Thomas Concerning her Experiences in the Sioux Outbreak"

Snelling, Josiah. Diary

Southworth, Newton. Papers

"Statistics Concerning the Sioux Massacre: Collected by Town Assessors"

Stay, Cecelia Campbell. Reminiscences

Sturgis, Rosanna. Letter

Taliaferro, Lawrence. Journals

Thompson, Clark W. Papers

Whipple, Henry Benjamin. Papers

Whitcomb, Elizabeth. Recollections

Wood, Edward S. Letter to his wife

Wood, John Kingsley. Diary

Woolworth, Alan W. Papers

Workman, Harper. Papers

National Archives and Records Administration, Washington, D.C.

Record Group 46, 37A-F2, Senate Records of the Dakota Trials

Record Group 48, Letters Sent, Indian Division of the Secretary of Interior

Record Group 75, Letters Received, St. Peter's Agency (SPA)

Record Group 75, Letters Sent, Office of Indian Affairs (OIA)

Record Group 75, Letters Received, Dakota Superintendency (DS)

Record Group 75, Letters Sent and Received, Minnesota Superintendency (MS)

Record Group 75, Letters Received, Northern Superintendency (NS)

Record Group 75, Miscellaneous Letters Received, Northern Superintendency

Record Group 75, Letters Received, Upper Missouri Agency

Record Group 75, Documents Relating to the Negotiation of Ratified and Unratified Treaties

Record Group, 75, Special File 132

Record Group, 75, Special File 235, Brown Report

Record Group, 75, Special File 274

Record Group 75, Special Files, "Mixed Blood Reserve" Papers

Record Group 94, Letters Received, Adjutant General's Office (AGO)

Record Group 94, Entry 173, Indian Prisoners

Record Group 153, Records of the Judge Advocate General of the Army

Record Group 393, Letters Received, Department of the West and Western Department, 1853–1861 (DWWD)

Record Group 393, Letterbook, Fort Ridgely

Record Group 393, Letters Received, Fort Ridgely, 1853–59

Record Group 393, Letters Sent, Sibley's Indian Campaign

Record Group 393, Letters Received, District of Iowa (General Sibley's Official Letterbook of his campaign)

Record Group 393, Department of Dakota, Campaign Scouts & Dakota Indians

Record Group 393, Department of the Northwest (including "unentered files")

Newberry Library, Chicago, Ill.

Ayer, Edward. Collection

Nicollet County Historical Society, St. Peter, Minn.

LaBatte, John. Newspaper Files

Picket, Eli. Letters

Johnson, Erick. Letters

Provincial Archives, Winnipeg, Manitoba, Canada

Dallas, Alexander Grant. "Private Journals." Hudson's Bay Company Archives

Hudson Bay Company Archives, Winnipeg Correspondence, Letterbooks, 1861–1864

Stay, Cecelia Campbell. "Massacre at the Lower Sioux Agency"

Traverse County Historical Society, Wheaton, Minn.

Oral History Project

Wisconsin Historical Society, Madison, Wis.
  Dousman, Hercules L. Papers
  Green Bay and Prairie du Chien Papers

**MISCELLANEOUS DOCUMENTS FROM
GOVERNMENT AND INTERNET SOURCES**
American Antiquarian Society, Digital Collection, Internet.
Le Beau, Marcella R. Oral Accounts, translated by Sidney H. Byrd, given to the
    author, 1993.
Serial Set for Senate and House of Representatives.
Sisseton and Wahpeton Bands of Dakotas or Sioux Indians v. United States, 1901–1907,
    *U.S. Court of Claims No. 22524.*d
Zeman, Carie. Blog @athrillingnarrative.com.

NEWSPAPERS
Clippings that deal specifically with the Dakota War from various newspapers below can
be found in the John LaBatte Collection at the Nicollet County Historical Society. Other
cited newspapers come from microfilm at the Minnesota Historical Society.

(Chaska) *Valley Herald*
Daily Minnesotan
Davenport Daily Democrat
Faribault Central Republican
Hastings Gazette
Hastings Independent
Henderson Democrat
Iapi Oaye (The Word Carrier)
Lubbock Avalanche Journal, at lubbockonline
Madison Minnesota Independent Press
Mankato Independent
Mankato Weekly Record
Mankato Semi-Weekly Record
Minneapolis Star
(Minneapolis) *State Atlas*
Minnesota Times
New York Times
(New Ulm) *Minnesota Staats-Zeitung*
New Ulm Post (translations from the German by Darla Gebhard)
New Ulm Review
(Sleepy Eye, Minn.) *Herald Dispatch*
(St. Anthony) *North-West Democrat*
St. Cloud Democrat
St. Paul Daily and Pioneer
(St. Paul) *Daily Pioneer & Democrat*
(St. Paul) *Daily Minnesota Pioneer*

St. Paul Journal
St. Paul Minnesota Pioneer
St. Paul Pioneer and Democrat
St. Paul Pioneer Press
St. Paul Press
St. Paul Weekly Press
St. Peter Courier
St. Peter Minnesota Tribune
St. Peter Tribune
(Winnipeg) *Nor'wester*
Winona Daily Republican

PUBLISHED PRIMARY SOURCES

Allanson, George. "Stirring Adventures of J. R Brown Family: Their Captivity during the Indian Uprising of 1862 and Description of Their Old Home, Destroyed by the Indians." Wheaton, Minn.: Wheaton Gazette, 1947. Copy in MHSA.

Armstrong, Benjamin. *Early Life Among the Indians: Reminiscences from the Life of Benj. G. Armstrong. Treaties of 1835, 1837, 1842, and 1854. Habits and Customs, of the Red Men of the Forest. Indians, Biographical Sketches, Battles, Etc., Dictated to the Written by Thos. P. Wentworth.* Ashland, Wis.: Press of A. W. Brown, 1892.

Barton, Winifred Williamson. *John P. Williamson: A Brother to the Sioux.* New York: Fleming H. Revell Co., 1919.

Beeson, John. *A Plea for the Indian: With Facts and Features of the Late War in Oregon.* New York: n. p., 1857.

Berghold, Alexander. *The Indians Revenge: or, Days of Horror, Some Appalling Events in the History of the Sioux.* San Francisco: P. J. Thomas, 1891.

Bishop, Harriet E. *Dakota War Whoop: or, Indian Massacres and War of 1862-3.* St. Paul: Published "for the author," 1864. Reprint, Minneapolis: Ross and Haines, 1970.

Board of Commissioners. *Minnesota in the Civil and Indian Wars.* 2 vols. St. Paul, Minn.: *Pioneer Press*, 1891.

Boelter, Justina. Oral History Account. www.dakotavictims1862.com/FloraTownship.

Bray, Edmund C., and Martha C. Bray, eds. *Joseph Nicollet on the Plains and Prairie: The Expeditions of 1838-1839 with Journals, Letters, and Notes on the Dakota Indians.* St. Paul: Minnesota Historical Society Press, 1976.

Bryant, Charles L. and Abel Murch. *A History of the Great Massacre of the Sioux Indians, in Minnesota, including the Personal Narratives of Many Who Escaped.* Cincinnati, Ohio: Richy & Carrol, 1864. Reprint, New York: Kraus Reprint Co., 1977.

Buck, Daniel. *Indian Outbreak.* 1904. Reprint, Minneapolis: Ross and Haines, 1956.

Carley, Kenneth. Ed. "Lightning Blanket's Story." *Minnesota History* 38 (September 1962): 126-45.

Carrigan, Minnie Buce. *Captured by Indians: Reminiscences of Pioneer Life in Minnesota.* Buffalo Lake, Minn.: Buffalo Lake News, 1903. Reprint, Forest City, S.Dak.: Forest City Press, 1907.

Daniels, Asa. "Reminiscences of Little Crow." *Minnesota Historical Society Collections* 12 (1908): 513–30.

De Camp-Sweet, Mrs. J. E. "Narrative of Her Captivity in the Sioux Outbreak of 1862." *Minnesota Historical Society Collections* 6 (1894): 354–96.

Deloria, Vine V., and Raymond J. DeMallie, eds. *Proceedings of the Great Sioux Commission.* Washington, D.C.: Institute for the Development of American Law, 1975.

Earle, Mrs. E. M. *Reminiscences of the Sioux Massacre of 1862.* Fairfax, Minn.: Renville County Pioneers Society, 1907.

Eastlick, Lavina. *Thrilling Adventures in the Indian War of 1862: Being, a Personal Narrative of the Outrages and Horrors Witnessed by Mrs. L. Eastlick in Minnesota.* Minneapolis: Atlas Steam Printing Company, 1864.

Ebel, Adrian J. "The Indian Massacre and War of 1862." *Harpers New Monthly* 27, no. 157 (June 1863): 1–24.

The 1863 Laws of War: Articles of War General Orders No. 100 Army Regulations. Washington, D.C.: War Department, 1863. Reprint, Mechanicsburg, Pa.: Stackpole Books, 2006.

Emerson, Charles L. *Rise and Progress of Minnesota Territory: Including a Statement of the Business Prosperity of Saint Paul; and Information in Regard to the Different Counties, Cities, Towns and Villages in the Territory, etc.* St. Paul, Minn.: D. L. Emerson, 1855.

Featherstonhaugh, George. *A Canoe Voyage Up the Minnay Sotor: with an Account of the Lead and Copper Deposits in Wisconsin; of the Gold Region in the Cherokee Country; and Sketches of the Popular Manners.* Reprint, St. Paul: Minnesota Historical Society Press, 1970.

Fitsche, L. A. *History of Brown County, Minnesota: Its People, Industries, and Institutions.* Indianapolis, Ind.: B. F. Bowen & Company, 1916. Reprint, Minneapolis: University of Minnesota, Digitized, 2014.

Flanagan, John T. "Thoreau in Minnesota." A paper read at the Minnesota Historical Society, January 21, 1935. Minnesota Historical Society Archives.

Flandrau, Charles E. *History of Minnesota and Tales of the Frontier.* St. Paul, Minn.: E. W. Porter, 1900.

Heard, Isaac V. D. *History of the Sioux War and Massacre of 1862 and 1863.* New York: Harper, 1865.

Heilbron, Bertha L., ed. *With Pen and Pencil on the Frontier in 1851: The Diary and Sketches of Frank B. Mayer.* St. Paul: Minnesota Historical Society Press, 1932.

Hibschman, H. J. "The Lake Shetek Pioneers and the Indians." In *Garland Library of Narratives of North American Indian Captivities*, edited by Wilcomb Washburn, Vol. 104. New York: Garland Publishing, 1976.

Humphrey, John Ames. "Boyhood Reminiscences of Life Among the Dakota and the Massacre of 1862." *Minnesota Historical Society Collections* 15 (1909–1914): 337–48.

Juni, Benedict. *Held in Captivity.* Pamphlet. New Ulm, Minn.: Liesch-Walter Printing, 1926.

Kappler, Charles J., ed. *Indian Affairs: Laws and Treaties.* 2 vols. Washington D.C.: Government Printing Office, 1904.

Lee, L. P. *History of the Spirit Lake Massacre! 8th March 1857, and of Miss Abigail Gard-ner's Three Months Captivity Among the Indians.* New Britain, Conn.: 1857. Reprint, Iowa City, Iowa: State Historical Society, 1971.

Manypenny, George. *Our Indian Wards.* 1880. Reprint, New York: DeCapo, 1972.

Marsh, John. Military Papers. http://www2.mnhs.org/library/findaids/01166/pdfa /01166-00145.pdf.

Missionary Papers. By the Bishop Seabury Mission. Number Twenty-Three. Faribault, Minn.: Alex. Johnson, Book and Job Printer, *Statesman* Office, 1862.

Morris, Lucy Leavenworth Wilder, ed. *Old Rail Fence Corners: Frontier Tales Told by Minnesota Pioneers.* St. Paul: Minnesota Historical Society, 1976.

Neill, E. D. "Battle of Lake Pokegama," 1841. *Minnesota Historical Society Collections* 1 (1901): 142–45.

Niebuhr, Gustav. *Lincoln's Bishop: A President, a Priest, and the Fate of the 300 Dakota Sioux Warriors.* New York: Harpercollins, 2014.

Nix, Jacob. *The Sioux Uprising in Minnesota, 1862. Jacob Nix's Eyewitness Account.* Edited by Don Heinrich Tolzman. Indianapolis: Indiana German Heritage Society, Inc., 1994.

Pond, Samuel W. "The Dakota or Sioux in Minnesota as They Were in 1834." *Collections of the Minnesota Historical Society* 12 (1908): 319–501.

———. *The Dakota or Sioux in Minnesota as They Were in 1834.* Introduction by Gary Clayton Anderson. St. Paul: Minnesota Historical Society Press, 1988.

Potter, Captain Theodore. "Captain Potter's Recollections of Minnesota Experiences." *Minnesota History Bulletin* 1, no. 8 (November 1916): 419–521.

Prescott, Philander. *The Recollections of Philander Prescott: Frontiersmen of the Old Northwest, 1819–1862.* Edited by Donald Dean Parker. Lincoln: University of Ne-braska Press, 1966.

Renville, Mary Butler. *A Thrilling Narrative of Indian Captivity.* Minneapolis: Atlas Company, 1863.

———. *A Thrilling Narrative of Indian Captivity: Dispatches From the Dakota War.* Edited by Carrie Reber Zeman and Kathryn Zabelle Derouniam Stodola. Lincoln: University of Nebraska Press, 2012.

Renville, Victor. "A Sketch of the Minnesota Massacre." *Collections of the North Dakota State Historical Society* 5 (1923): 251–72.

Riggs, Stephen Return. "History of the Dakotas, James W. Lynd's Manuscript." *Minnesota Historical Society Collections,* 2, Part 2 (1860–1867): 143–75.

———. "Dakota Portraits." *Minnesota History Bulletin* 2 (November 1918): 481–568.

———. *Mary and I: Forty Years with the Sioux.* Boston: Congregational Sunday-School and Publishing Society, 1880.

———. *Grammar and Dictionary of the Dakota Language.* Washington, D.C.: Smithso-nian Institution, 1852.

———. *Tah-koo-wah-kan; or, Gospel Among the Dakota.* Boston: Congregational Pub-lishing Society, 1880.

———. "Memoir of Hon. Jas. W. Lynd." *Minnesota Historical Society Collections* 3 (1889): 107–14.

Riggs, Thomas Alfred. "Sunset to Sunset: A Lifetime with My Brothers, The Dakota." *South Dakota Historical Collections* 19 (1958): 87–306. Reprint, Pierre: South Dakota Historical Society, 1997.

Robinson, Doane. *A History of the Dakota or Sioux Indians.* Pierre: South Dakota State Historical Society, 1904. Reprint, Minneapolis: Ross and Haines, 1974.

Schoolcraft, Henry R. *Information Respecting the History, Conditions, and Prospects of the Indian Tribes of the United States.* 6 vols. Philadelphia: J. P. Lippincott, 1865.

Sharp, Abbie Gardner. *History of the Spirit Lake Massacre and Captivity of Miss Abbie Gardner.* Des Moines: Iowa Printing Company, 1902.

Sibley, Henry Hastings, ed. *The Adventures of Jack Frazer, Frontier Warrior, Scout, and Hunter.* Chicago: Caxton Club, 1950.

"The Sioux Maiden Feast." *Minnesota Historical Society Collections* 9 (1898–1900): 218.

Sisseton Court of Claims Case No. 22524. Bound Testimony, 1901. Minnesota Historical Society Archives.

"Taoyateduta is not a Coward." *Minnesota History* 38 (September 1962): 115.

Tarble, Mrs. Helen [Carrothers]. *The Story of My Capture and Escape during the Minnesota Indian Massacre of 1862: With Historical Notes, Descriptions of Pioneer Life, and Sketches and Incidents of the Great Outbreak of the Sioux or Dakota Indians as I Saw Them.* St. Paul, Minn.: Abbott Printing Company, 1904.

Van Cleve, Charlotte Ouisconsin. *"Three Score Years and Ten," Life-Long Memories of Fort Snelling, Minnesota, and Other Parts of the West.* Minneapolis: Harrison and Smith, 1888.

Wakefield, Sarah F. *Six Weeks in Little Crow's Camp: A Narrative of Indian Captivity.* Shakopee, Minn.: Argus Book and Job Printing Office, 1864. Reprint, Sarah F. Wakefield. *Six Weeks in the Sioux Tepees: A Narrative of Sioux Captivity.* Edited, annotated, and with an introduction by June Namias. Norman: University of Oklahoma Press, 1997.

White, Mrs. N. D. "Captivity Among the Sioux, August 18 to September 26, 1862." *Minnesota Historical Society Collections* 9 (1898–1900): 395–422.

BOOKS AND ARTICLES

Anderson, Gary Clayton. *Little Crow, Spokesman for the Sioux.* St. Paul: Minnesota Historical Society, 1986.

———. *Kinsmen of Another Kind: Dakota-White Relations on the Upper Mississippi River.* Lincoln: University of Nebraska Press, 1984.

———. *Ethnic Cleansing and the Indian: The Crime That Should Haunt America.* Norman: University of Oklahoma Press, 2014.

———. *Gabriel Renville: From the Dakota War to the Creation of the Sisseton-Wahpeton Reservation, 1825–1892.* Pierre: South Dakota Historical Society Press, 2018.

——— and Alan R. Woolworth, eds. *Through Dakota Eyes: Narrative Accounts of the Minnesota Indian War of 1862.* St. Paul: Minnesota Historical Society, 1988.

Anderson, Julie A. "Reconciling Memory: Landscape, Commemoration and Enduring Conflicts of the U.S.-Dakota War of 1862." PhD diss., Georgia State University, 2011.

Atkins, Annette. *Creating Minnesota: A History from Inside Out*. St. Paul: Minnesota Historical Society Press, 2007.

Bachman, Walt. *Northern Slave Black Dakota*. Bloomington, Minn.: Pond Dakota Press, 2013.

Bakeman, Mary. *Legends, Letter, and Lies: Reading About Inkpaduta and the Spirit Lake Massacre*. Roseville, Minn.: Park Genealogy Books, 2001.

———. "Forgotten Victims: Terror, Refuge, and Recovery." *Minnesota's Heritage* 7 (January 2013): 84–107.

Barton, Wilifred Williamson. *John P. Williamson: A Brother to the Sioux*. London: Fleming H. Revell Company, 1919. Reprint, Nabu Public Domain Reprints, n.d.

Beck, Paul. *Inkpaduta: Dakota Leader*. Norman: University of Oklahoma Press, 2008.

Belich, James. *Replenishing the Earth: The Settler Revolution and the Rise of the Anglo World, 1783–1939*. New York: Oxford University Press, 2009.

Block, Sharon. *Rape & Sexual Power in Early America*. Chapel Hill: University of North Carolina Press, 2006.

Brownmiller, Susan. *Against Our Will: Men, Women and Rape*. New York: Faucett Columbine, 1993.

Carley, Kenneth. *The Sioux Uprising of 1862*. St. Paul: Minnesota Historical Society, 1976.

Chomsky, Carol. "The United States-Dakota War Trials: A Study in Military Justice." *Stanford Law Review* 43 (November 1990): 13–98.

Clark, Janine Natalya. "Making Sense of Wartime Rape: A Multi-Causal and Multi-Level Analysis." *Ethnopolitics* 13, no. 5 (2014): 461–82.

Clodfelter, Michael. *The Dakota War: The United States Army Versus the Sioux, 1862–1865*. Jefferson, N.C.: McFarland and Co., 2006.

Cohen, Darakay. "Explaining Rape during Civil War: Cross-National Evidence, 1980–2009." *American Political Science Review* 107 (August 2013): 461–77.

Connor, Joseph. "The Elusive Hero of Redwood Ferry." *Minnesota History* 34 (Summer 1955): 233–38.

Dahlin, Curtis. *Dakota Uprising Victims: Gravestones and Stories*. Edina, Minn.: Beaver's Pond Press, 2007.

———. *A History of the Dakota Uprising*. Edina, Minn.: Self-Published, n. d.

———. "Outside the Barricades: The August 23, 1862 Battle of New Ulm." *Minnesota's Heritage* 2 (July 2010): 24–39.

Dean, Janet. "Nameless Outrages: Narrative Authority, Rape Rhetoric, and the Dakota Conflict of 1862." *American Literature* 77 (March 2005): 93–112.

Derounian-Stodola, Kathryn Zabelle. *The War of Words: Reading the Dakota Conflict through the Captivity Literature*. Lincoln: University of Nebraska Press, 2009.

Ellis, Richard N. *General Pope and U. S. Indian Policy*. Albuquerque: University of New Mexico Press, 1970.

Fisher, Kirsten. *Suspect Relations: Sex, Race, and Resistance in Early North Carolina*. Ithaca, N.Y.: Cornell University Press, 2001.

Fisher, Louis. *Military Tribunals and Presidential Power*. Lawrence: University of Kansas Press, 2005.

Folwell, William Watts. *A History of Minnesota*. 4 vols. St. Paul: Minnesota Historical Society Press, 1921–1930.

Ford, Lisa. *Settler Sovereignty: Jurisdictional and Indigenous People in America and Australia, 1788–1836*. Cambridge, Mass.: Harvard University Press, 2010.

Franklin, John Hope. *From Slavery to Freedom: A History of Negro America*. New York: Alfred Knopf, 1956.

Freedman, Estelle B. *Redefining Rape: Sexual Violence in the Era of Suffrage and Segregation*. Cambridge, Mass.: Harvard University Press, 2013.

Fridley, Russell W. "Charles E. Flandrau, Attorney at Law." *Minnesota History* 43 (September 1962): 116–25.

Gebhard, Darla, and John Isch. *Eight Days in August: The Accounts of the Casualties and Survivors in Brown County During the US-Dakota War of 1862*. New Ulm, Minn.: Brown County Historical Society, 2012.

Gilman, Rhoda R. *Henry Hastings Sibley: Divided Heart*. St. Paul: Minnesota Historical Society Press, 2004.

Glewwe, Lois A. "Journey of the Prisoners: Convey to South Bend." In *Trail or Tears: Minnesota's Dakota Indian Exile Begins*, edited by Mary H. Bakeman and Antona M. Richarson, 79–106. Roseville, Minn.: Park Genealogical Books, 2008.

Haberly, David T. "Women and Indians: The Last of the Mohicans and the Captivity Tradition." *American Quarterly* 28 (Autumn 1976): 431–44.

Hayden, Robert. "Rape and Rape Avoidance in Ethno-National Conflicts: Sexual Violence in Liminalized States." *American Anthropologist* 102, no. 1 (2008): 27–41.

Helms, Elissa. "Rejecting Angelina: Bosnian War Rape Survivors and the Ambiguities of Sex in War." *Slavic Review* 73 (Fall 2014): 612–34.

Herbert, Maeve. "Explaining the Sioux Military Commission of 1862." *Columbia Human Rights Law Review* 40 (April 2009): 743–47.

Herriott, F. I. "The Origins of the Indian Massacre Between the Okabojis, March 8, 1957." *Annals of Iowa* 18 (July 1932): 323–82.

Holcombe, R. I. *Sketches Historical and Descriptive of the Monuments and Tablets Erected by the Minnesota Valley Historical Society in Renville and Redwood Counties*. Morton, Minn.: Minnesota Valley Historical Society, 1902.

Hollon, W. Eugene. *The Great American Desert*. New York: Oxford University Press, 1966.

Howard. John R. "The Sioux War Stockades." *Minnesota History* 12 (September 1931): 301–3.

Hubbard, Lucius F., Return I. Holcombe, Frank R. Holmes, et al. *Minnesota in Three Centuries*. 3 vols. New York: The Publishing Society of Minnesota, 1908.

Hughes, Thomas. *Indian Chiefs of Southern Minnesota*. Mankato: Free Press Company, 1927.

———. "Causes and Results of the Inkpaduta Massacre." *Minnesota Historical Society Collections* 12 (1905–1908): 263–82.

———. *History of Blue Earth County and Biographies of its Leading Citizens*. Chicago: Middle West Publishing, 1909.

Isch, John. *The Dakota Trials: Including the Complete Transcripts and Explanatory Notes on the Military Commission Trials, 1862–1864*. New Ulm: Brown County Historical Society, 2012.

Kastenberg, Joshua E. *Shaping U. S. Military Law: Governing a Constitutional Military*. New York: Routledge, 2014.

Kennedy, Roger G. "In Search of the Joseph R. Brown House." *Minnesota History* 39 (Fall 1965): 272–77.

Kimball, Stanley B. "The Captivity Narrative on the Mormon Trail, 1846–1865." *Dialogue: A Journal of Mormon Thought* 18 (1985): 81–88.

Kirby, Paul. "How is Rape a Weapon of War? Feminist International Relations, Modes of Critical Explanation and the Study of Wartime Sexual Violence." *European Journal of International Reparations* 19, no. 4 (2013): 797–821.

Lawrence, Elden. *The Peace Seekers: Indian Christians and the Dakota Conflict*. Sioux Falls, S.Dak.: Pine Hill Press, 2005.

Lass, William E. *The Treaty of Traverse des Sioux*. St. Peter, Minn.: Nicollet County Historical Society, 2011.

———. "The Removal From Minnesota of the Sioux and Winnebago Indians." *Minnesota History* 38 (December 1963): 353–64.

———. "Rediscovering Camp Lincoln." *Minnesota's Heritage* 87 (July 2012): 20–37.

———. *Minnesota's Boundary with Canada: Its Evolution since 1783*. St. Paul: Minnesota Historical Society, 1980.

Mark, Zoe. "Sexual Violence in Sierra Leone's Civil War: Virgination, Rape and Marriage." *African Affairs* 113 (2014): 67–87.

Meyers, Erica. "Conquering Peace: Military Commissions as a Lawfare Strategy in the Mexican War." *American Journal of Criminal Law* 35, no. 2 (2008): 201–40.

Meyer, Roy. *History of the Santee Sioux: United States Indian Policy on Trail*. Lincoln: University of Nebraska Press, 1967.

Michalski, Joseph H. "Ritualistic Rape in Sociological Perspective." *Cross-Cultural Research* 50, no. 1 (2016): 3–33.

Nelson, Howard M. "The Transition of Traverse des Sioux and St. Peter Areas from Indian to Pioneer Community." Master's thesis, Mankato State College, 1956.

Nelson, Jim. "Fool Soldiers' Story Told Many Ways." *Minnesota's Heritage* 4 (July 2011): 20–35.

Newcombe, Barbara T. "The Sioux Sign a Treaty in 1858." *Minnesota History* 45, no. 3 (Fall 1976): 82–96.

Nichols, David A. *Lincoln and the Indians: Civil War Policy and Politics*. Urbana: University of Illinois Press, 1978.

Niebuhr, Gustav. *Lincoln's Bishop: A President, a Priest, and the Fate of 300 Dakota Sioux Warriors*. New York: HarperOne, 2014.

Oates, Stephen B. *The Fires of Jubilee: Nat Turner's Fierce Rebellion*. New York: Harper Perennial, 2014.

Oneroad, Amos. *Being Dakota: Tales and Traditions of the Sissetons and Wahpetons*. Edited by Laura L. Anderson. St. Paul: Minnesota Historical Society Press, 2003.

Osman, Stephen E. "Audacity, Skill, and Firepower: The Third Minnesota's Skirmishers at The Battle of Wood Lake." *Minnesota's Heritage* 3 (January 2011): 24–40

Ravoux, Monsignor S. *Reminiscences, Memoirs, and Lectures.* St. Paul, Minn.: Brown, Treacy & Co., 1890.

Sannes, Darryl. "The U. S.-Dakota War of 1862 and the Battle of Acton." http://www.usdakotawar.org/events/community/2047.

Satterlee, Marion P. A. *A Detailed Account of the Massacre by the Dakota Indians of Minnesota in 1862.* Minneapolis: Marion P. Satterlee, 1923.

———. *The Story of Capt. Richard Strout and Company, Who Fought the Sioux Indians at the Battle of Kelly's Bluff, at Acton, Minn., on Wednesday, September 3rd, 1862.* Minneapolis: Marion P. Satterlee, 1909.

Schultz, Duane. *Over The Earth I Come: The Great Sioux Uprising of 1862.* New York: St. Martin's Press, 1992.

Skarstein, Karl Jakob. *The War with the Sioux: Norwegians Against the Indians, 1862–1863.* Translated from the Norwegian by Melissa Gjellstad and Danielle Skelver. Grand Forks: The Digital Press of the University of North Dakota, 2015.

Smith, Corinne Hosfeld. "What A Difference A Year Can Make: Henry David Thoreau and the Grand Excursion of 1861." *Minnesota's Heritage* 4 (July 2011): 76–89.

Snyder, Rebecca, ed. *The 1851 Treaty of Mendota: A Collection of Primary Documents Pertaining to the Treaty.* South St. Paul: Dakota County Historical Society, 2002.

Teakle, Thomas. *The Spirit Lake Massacre.* Iowa City: Iowa State Historical Society, 1918.

Trexler, Richard. *Sexual Conquest: Gendered Violence, Political Order, and the European Conquest of the Americas.* Ithaca, N.Y.: Cornell University Press, 1995.

Veracini, Lorenzo. *Settler Colonialism: A Theoretical Overview.* New York: Palgrave Macmillian, 2010.

Wallace, Anthony F. C. *The Long Bitter Trail: Andrew Jackson and the Indians.* New York: Hill and Wang, 1993.

Wardrop, Emily Rankin. "'All the Women . . . Were Violated in this Way': Rhetoric, Rape, and Memory in the Dakota War." PhD Diss., University of Oklahoma, 2015.

War Powers and Military Justice. Ann Arbor, Mich.: Judge Advocate General School, 1943.

Waziyatawin. *What Does Justice Look Like? The Struggle for Liberation in Dakota Homeland.* St. Paul: Living Justice Press, 2008.

Westerman, Gwen, and Bruce White, eds. *Mini Sota Makoce: The Land of the Dakota.* St. Paul: Minnesota Historical Society, 2012.

Wilson, Raymond. "Forty Years of Justice." *Minnesota History* 57 (Fall 1998): 284–91.

Wiltscheck, Gary. *The Leavenworth Rescue Expedition Revisited.* New Ulm, Minn.: Brown County Historical Society, 2011.

Winchell, Newton H. *The Aborigines of Minnesota: A Report on the Collections of Jacob V. Brower and on the Field Surveys and Notes of J. Hill and Theodore H. Lewis.* St. Paul: Pioneer Company, 1911.

Wingerd, Mary Lethert. *North Country: The Making of Minnesota.* Minneapolis: University of Minnesota Press, 2010.

INDEX

Aborigines of Minnesota, The (Winchell), 33

Abercrombie, John, 55, 67, 136

Acton, Minn., 78, 81, 135, 170; battle of, 172–73, 181, 184

akacita (soldier's lodge; head warrior), 6, 11, 13, 27, 49, 51, 53, 61, 65, 69, 79, 81–83, 100, 137–38, 140–41, 153, 163, 165, 167, 170, 173, 175, 182, 186, 189–90, 197–99, 205, 210, 213, 281

Akipa (Joseph Renville), 54, 64–65, 78, 101, 122, 163–64, 183, 217, 242, 259, 269

Aldrich, Cyrus, 73, 75, 256, 269–70; corruption of, 297n48

Aldrich, Leonard, 224

Alexander, E. B., 58

Alexandria, Minn., 111, 273–74

American Board of Commissioners for Foreign Missions (ABCFM), 22, 230

American Fur Company, 18, 26

American House (hotel), 22

Anawaŋgmani, Simon (Walks Galloping), 25, 54, 78, 102, 114, 164, 177, 183, 185, 190–91, 269, 273

Anderson, Joseph, 167–69

Anderson, Mary, 96, 200–201

Anishinaabes (Ojibwes; Chippewas), 6–15, 18, 32, 53–54, 72–74, 81, 159, 161, 194, 204, 268

Anoka, Minn., 173

Antelope (steamer), 148–49

Arikaras, 280

Arnold, D. K., 258, 262–63

Ash Hallow, 59

Astor, John Jacob, 18

Averill, John, 274

Bailey, Hiram, 214

Bailly, Alexis, 18

ball game (*takapsićapi*), 24

Beaver Creek, 78, 87, 89, 91–93, 99, 107, 142, 146, 167–68, 197, 206, 209, 259

Bee, Bernard, 59

Begging Dance, 70

Beinhorn, Fred, 55

Bell, Edwin, 137

Belland, Joseph, 84

Belle Plaine, Minn., 55

Bentley (survivor), 105, 108

Bierbauer, William, 151

Big Eagle (Wamditaŋka), 65, 69, 78, 82–83, 119, 138, 141, 143–44, 166–67, 179, 180, 195

Big Fire, Peter (aka Tapetataŋka), 25, 54

Big Stone Lake, 8–9, 20, 31, 58, 67, 78, 103, 165, 180, 196–97, 217, 221–22

Big Woods, 6, 8, 12–13, 20, 47, 71, 81, 159, 167, 170, 172, 180–81, 226–27, 233, 282 bilinear marriage rules, 7

Birch Coulee, 87–89, 92–93, 100; battle of, 167–70, 174–75, 183, 202, 226–27, 247

Bishop, John R., 139

Black Dog (Mdewakanton), 7, 9; village of, 20

Blair, Charles, 199–200

Blanchard, Dick, 149

Blows on Iron (Mazabomdu), 203–4

Blue Earth, Minn., 47

Blue Earth County, Minn. 71, 107, 158

Blue Earth River, 8, 49, 233, 241

Blue Thunder (Wakiŋyaŋto), 166, 176

Boelter, Justina, 91–93

Bond, James H., 284

Bootelier, 263

Bouratt, William, 84

Boyer, Peter, 169

Brandt, Friederich (also Fritz), 232, 249–50

Branham, Jesse, 171

Brobergs (Norwegian family), 107

Brown, Ellen, 73–74, 101–2, 143

Brown, Jedediah, 277

Brown, Joseph R., 18, 24, 28, 54, 64–65, 67–70, 72–74, 76, 94, 102, 108, 136, 143, 164, 167–70, 187, 222–23, 242, 246, 255, 258, 262, 264, 280, 282; and corruption as agent, 297n45

Brown, Orlando, 22

Brown, Samuel, 73, 93, 101–2, 108, 143, 163, 176, 187, 199–200, 220, 221–22, 233

Brown, Susan Frenier, 64, 72, 101–2, 108, 143, 163, 199, 282

Brown County, Minn., 71, 107, 109, 158, 232

Brownmiller, Susan, 192

Brownsville, 174

Bryant, Charles S., 249

Buce (also Busse), Gottfried, 92

Buce (also Busse), Minnie, 92

Buchanan, James, 74

Buffalo Creek, 78

Bull Run, 75, 97, 161, 179

Bushnell, George, 223

Campbell, Antoine J., 60, 80, 84, 137–38, 167, 170, 175, 178, 182–83, 185–86, 189–91, 195, 201–2, 205

Campbell, Baptiste, 60, 80

Campbell, Hippolite, 84

Campbell, Mrs. Antoine, 202

Campbell, Scott, 138, 273

Camp Lexington, 70, 77

Camp Lincoln, 233, 241–42, 245, 249

Camp McClellan, 277

Camp Release, 78, 187, 189, 198, 202, 207, 211–14, 216, 220–22, 225, 230, 265

Camp Sibley, 225

Canada, 32, 166, 180–81, 208, 280–82

Cane (Tasagya), 56

Cannon River, 20

Cardinal, Margaret, 202, 259

Carrier, Electra, 110

Carrothers, David, 89–90, 140, 168, 197, 228

Carrothers, Helen, 91, 134, 140, 198

Carrothers, John, 91, 140, 197

Carver, Minn., 148

Castor, Mrs., 275

Catlin, George, 86

Cedar Mills, Minn., 167

Charger, the (Waanata; Sisseton/ Yanktonai), 9–10, 25, 65, 78, 180, 223

Chaska (also Ćaske; First Born Son), 101, 204–6, 212–13, 218, 220, 262–63, 264

Chatfield, A. G., 174

Child, W. H., 238–39

Chippewa Lake, 274

Chippewa River, 78

Chippewas (Ojibwes; Anishinaabes), 6, 88, 99

Chouteau, Pierre, Jr. 18, 32, 276

citizenship: and Dakota Indians, 53; and Minnesota state constitution, 292n29

civil chiefs, 9–10, 13, 69, 82

civilian militia (volunteers) at Fort Ridgely, 141–44, 306n24, 307n30, 309n70

Civil War (American), 80; and impact on Dakota war, 299n71

Clear Lake, 146

Clinton Falls, Minn., 158

Cloud Man (Maḣpiyawićaṡta), 25, 28, 78

Collins, Loren, 250

Columbia Fur Company, 8

Cook, Mariah, 105

Cook (also Koch), Andreas, 104

Cook (also Koch), Mrs., 207–9

Cooper, James Fenimore, 73, 87

Cora (steamer), 277

corruption (by government officials): during reservation period, 50–52, 72–77; after Treaty of 1851, 29–32

Coteau des Prairies, 222–23, 225, 245, 279–80

Cottonwood County, Minn., 71

Cottonwood River, 25, 51, 55, 58, 61, 78, 102–3, 108, 109, 152–53, 155, 178, 232, 274

coup (Indian victory), 10

Cox, Eugene St. Julien, 150, 154

Crane, Ichabod (Stephen Riggs) 21

Crawford, Charles, 65, 163–64, 233, 273

Crawford, Thomas, 164

Crook, Ramsey, 18, 32

Crooks, William, 136, 214, 264, 276–77

Crowell, Mary, 173

Cross River, 208

Crow Creek, 194, 275–76, 278, 279, 285

Crow River, 78

Crow Wing River valley, 12

Cullen, William J., 59–61, 67–68, 74, 146

Cullen Mounted Guard, 167

Custer, George Armstrong, 144

Cut Nose (Maḣpiyaokennaźin), 81, 93, 101–2, 141, 199–200, 263, 284

Dacotah House (hotel), 102, 151, 154

Dagen, Peter, 210

Dahlin, Curtis, and census of conflict's victims, 301n29

Dakota Casualties in the Fight at Fort Ridgely, 307n29

Dallas, Alexander Grant, 281–82

Dane, E. Jerome, 108–9, 155, 157, 158

Daniels, Asa, 48–49, 59, 61, 71, 109–10, 151, 153, 188, 196–97, 263

Daniels, Jared: on lack of mutilation, 168–69, 230, 304n62

Davenport, Iowa, 276, 279

Davenport (steamer), 278

Davis, L., 96

Day, Henry, 52

DeCamp, Captain, 144

DeCamp, Jannette E., 86–87, 92, 96, 123, 177, 190–91, 200–201, 205

Democratic Party, 18, 33, 55, 63, 72, 74, 244

Densmore, Daniel, 270

Denver, J. W., 59

deportation of Dakota people from Minnesota, 276–80

Des Moines River, 3, 6, 31, 51, 56, 107

Devils Lake, 31, 280–81, 283

Dickinson, J. C., 85

Dickinson, Lathrop, 85

Dietrich, Mrs., 275

Divoll, George W., 84, 266

Dodd, William B., 120, 153–54

Dole, William P., 161, 243, 245

Donahue, Matthew, 173

Donnelly, Ignatius, 109–10

Doud, George W., 108

Dousman, Hercules, 18, 31–32; Dousman papers, 32

Drexler, Benedict, 94

Duley, Emma, 126

Duley, Jefferson, 126

Duley, Laura Terry, 105, 126, 130, 207–9

Duley, William J., 104–5, 237, 262; and possible cowardice, 304n69

Dustin, Amos, 283

Eagle Plum (Waŋmdiupidaŋ), 227

Earle, Ezmon, 142, 197

Earle, Mrs. J. W., 205–6, 210

Earle family, 89–91, 140, 190, 197–98

Eastlick, Frank, 105

Eastlick, Freddie, 105

Eastlick, John, 104–5, 109

Eastlick, Lavina, 105, 108, 109, 207

Eastlick, Merton, 106

Eastman, Seth, 24

Ebel, Adrian J., fabricated account of conflict, 316n100

Eden Prairie, Minn., 110

Eisenreich, Balthasar, 209

Eisenreich, Liasa, 128

Eisenreich, Theresa, 127, 209

Erd House (hotel), 102–3, 151–52

Everett, Lillian, 126

Everett, William, 104–5, 108

Ewing, George, 31

Excelsior (steamer), 24

executions at Mankato, 254–63; and Dakota men's preparations for gallows, 260–61; Lincoln and the selection of the condemned men, 251–53; singing on gallows, 261

executive order for occupation of the reservations, 49

Extended Tail Feathers (Upiyahdayeya), 24, 78

"extermination" as contemplated policy, 159–60, 188, 315n76

eyaśića (bad language), 93

Faribault, Alexander, 32, 264; as independent trader, 289n7

Faribault, David, Jr., 175, 198, 219, 227–28, 246–47; challenges conviction, 264–65, 273

Faribault, Jean Baptiste, 18, 23, 32

Faribault, Minn., 47, 158

Faribault Central Republican, 174

Faribault County, 158

Farnsworth, Julia E., 146

Favorite (steamer), 276–77

Fifth Minnesota Regiment (volunteers), 97, 135, 142

Fillmore, Millard, 30

Fink, Martin, 95

Fisherbauer, John, 95

Flandrau, Charles, 55–56, 58–59, 61, 62, 109, 115; and relief of New Ulm, 150–55, 157–58, 175, 308n61–62

Folwell, William Watts, 191, 270

Forbes, William, 84

Forest City, Minn., 47, 55, 71, 78, 107, 146–47, 158–59; burning of, 171–72, 224, 273–74

Forester Building, 151

Fort Abercrombie, 136, 173, 180, 274

Fort Garry, Manitoba, 194, 281–82

Fort Randall, 209, 224, 279

Fort Ridgely, 48–49, 52, 55, 61, 67, 72, 78–79, 88, 92, 98, 101–3, 107, 135, 137–38; first battle of, 140–42; second battle of, 144–45, 146, 148, 150, 155–56, 161–63, 166–67, 169, 174–75, 177–78, 181, 190–91, 198–99, 201–2, 220, 227, 249, 273–75, 282

Fort Ripley, 135, 159

Fort Snelling, Minn., 5, 7, 11, 18, 20–21, 24, 58, 63, 81, 135–38, 155, 196, 224, 229, 233, 242, 245, 255–56, 266–67, 272–73, 276, 278; and death rate among Dakota Indians while incarcerated, 330n18

Fort St. Anthony, Minn., 7

Frazier, Jack, 18, 27, 139, 143, 233

Frenier, Antoine, 54

Frenier, Javier, 32

Frenier, Susan, 64

Friend, Andrew, 152

Galbraith, Thomas, 73–77, 79–81, 94, 102, 141, 169, 221–25, 270; and corruption of administration, 74–77, 297n43

Galpin, Charles E., 160, 208, 209

Garden City, Minn., 47, 78, 147

Gardner, Abbie, 58–59

Gardner, Roland, 57–58

Geister, David, 133

Georgetown (Washington, D.C.), 66

Gere, Thomas Mark, 97, 139, 143, 145, 194; and military honors, 306n17

German Lutheran Church, 92

German settlements, 17–18, 47, 54, 93–94, 99, 100, 143, 151, 162, 197–98, 204, 207, 209–10, 217, 228, 249, 259, 266

Ghost That Walks on Ice (Wayapamani), 265, 266

gift giving (reciprocity), 19

Gleason, George, 100–101, 204, 263

Glencoe, Minn., 47, 55, 71, 78, 90, 146–48, 158, 162, 170, 273, 274

Godfrey, Joseph, 94, 213, 217–19, 227–28, 253

Good Boy (Hakewaśte), 25

Good Day, 206–7

Good Road, 78, 278

Good Thunder (Wakiŋyaŋwaśte), 178–79, 204

Gorman, James, 141, 143, 194

Gorman, Willis, 48, 58, 63

Grand River, 209

Grant, Hiram P., as captain of Sixth Minnesota Regiment, 167–69; in command at Birch Coulee, 312n28

Grant, Ulysses S., 277

Grass, John, 58

Great Lakes, 5, 192

Green Bay and Prairie du Chien Papers (Dousman's records), Wisconsin State Archives, 31

Greenleaf Point, U.S. arsenal at, 65

Grey Bird (Zitkadaŋhota), 166

Grizzly Bear, 104–5, 207

Hahn, Margareta Holl, 93–94

Halleck, Henry, 180, 182, 214

Hallock, Mary Ann Marston,
147–48
Hapa, 204–5
Hapan, 266
Harney, W. S., 59
Harrington, Lewis, 147
Hartman, Florian, 93
Hastings, Minn., 249
Hastings Independent, 174
Hatch, Charles, 104–5
Hatch, Edwin, 284
Hawk Creek, 78, 87
Hay, John, 74, 231
Hayden, John, 52
Hazatoŋwiŋ, 143
Hazelwood/Hazelwood Republic,
49–51, 53–54, 60, 64, 70, 78,
164–65, 195, 246
head chief, 22
Heard, Isaac V. D., 191, 214, 216,
218, 229, 254
He Charges His Dwelling
(Tiwanata), 219
Henderson, Jonathan, 89–91, 93,
168–69
Henderson, Minn., 47, 54–55, 78,
102, 146, 158, 173
Henderson Democrat (newspaper),
63
Henle, Anton, 94
Henle, Athanas, 93–94
Henle, Theresa, 95
Henton, R. B., 109–10
Hepan (Second Son), 237
Hermak, Casimir, 93
Hicks, Marcus, 271
Hicks, Mrs., 272
Hinman, Samuel, 71, 74, 76, 82, 85,
97, 204, 272, 278
His Own Thunder
(Wakinyaŋtawa), 266
His Own Tree Bud (Ciŋkpatawa),
265

His People (Oyatetawa), 218
His Red Weapon (Tawotawaduta),
265
His Sacred Moccasin
(Tahaŋpiwakaŋ), 230
Holmes, Charles, 199
Holmes, Thomas, 171
Holt, Joseph, 251, 332n61
Hopkins, Robert, 206, 230, 245,
247, 255, 271–72, 277
Howard Lake, 283
Huebschmann, Francis, 52, 58
Huey, William, 152, 153
Huggan, Nancy McClure
Faribault, 138, 190, 198
Huggins, Amos, 206
Huggins, Sophia, 206
Hughes, Thomas, 73, 230
Humphrey, John, 86
Hunter, Marian, 198
hunting (of deer): deer taken,
288n26; hunting in "no-man's
land," 6; by Little Crow, 3;
Wakan men and hunting, 5
Hutchinson, Minn., 47, 55, 71, 78,
90, 102, 147, 158–59, 162, 167;
burning of, 170–72, 224, 273,
283

Ingalls, Amanda, 199–200
Ingalls, Jennie, 199–200
Iŋkpaduta (Scarlet End), 51, 56–63,
104, 150, 246
Intercourse Acts, 29
Iowa, 18, 20, 51
Ireland, Ellen, 126
Ireland, Roseanne, 126, 207
Ireland, Thomas, 104
Iron Elk, 202
Iron Gourd (Mazawamnuha),
165–66
Isabella (steamer), 278
Ives, Luther, 108–9

Jackson, Andrew, 18–19
Jackson, Minn., 47, 107, 111, 274
Jacques (also Jacobs), John, 104
James River, 31, 223
Johnson, Eric, 106
Jones, John, 140–41, 144
Jones, Robertson, 80
Juni, Benedict, 88–89

Kandiyohi County, Minn., 107
Kaposia, 3, 5
Katpantpanu, 88
Kettle Lake, 67
Kewaŋke, Joseph, 217, 233, 273
Kingston, Minn., 273
kinship, 4, 8, 10, 13, 93, 100–101
Kirkwood, Samuel J., 276
Kit Fox Society (Tokadaŋti), 13
Kittson, Norman, 281
Kitzman, Paul, 99–100
Knight, Albert, 155
Kreiger, Justina, 99–100, 125, 168, 197

LaBathe, Francois, 84
La Crescent, 174
Lac qui Parle River, 78, 177
Lac qui Parle, 13, 20–21, 23, 53, 64, 78, 185, 197, 206, 223
LaFramboise, Joseph, Jr., 18, 23, 31–32, 164, 190–91, 228, 233, 273
LaFramboise, Julia, 213
Lake Benton, 61
Lake Herman (aka Skunk Lake), 58
Lake Pepin, 20
Lake Shetek, 78, 104–6, 108, 126, 207, 246, 253, 262, 285
Lake Traverse, 8–9, 20–21, 24, 29, 32, 67, 78, 177, 180–81, 197, 280
Lamb, John, 85
Lamson, Nathan and Chauncey, 283
land cession, 22, 25

Lansing, Minn., 174
Larson, Inger, 106
Larson, L. J., 106
Larson, Pehr, 106
Lawrence, Lorenzo (Toŋwaŋitetoŋ), 54, 69, 177, 190, 233, 269, 278
Laying Up Buffalo (Taźu), 201–2, 218, 259
Lean Bear, 61
Leavenworth Expedition, 102–3, 107, 143, 150; not encouraged by Sheriff Roos, 304n61
Le Beau, Marcella R. Ryan, and Dakota hymns, 261
Lee, Francis, 48
Leech Building, 250, 258, 260
Le Sueur, Minn., 47, 153, 263
Lightning Blanket, 138
Limping Devil (Itewakiŋyaŋ; Sisseton), 8–9, 51
Lincoln, Abraham, 72, 74, 155, 161, 228–29, 231, 241, 243–48, 250–52, 253–57, 263–64, 277
Lincoln, Mary Todd, 275
Little Crow II (Petite Corbeau; Mdewakanton Dakota), 3
Little Crow III (Taoyateduta; Mdewakanton Dakota), 3–10, 16, 19–21, 23–29, 48–49, 52–53, 60–61, 63, 65–66, 68–69, 71, 76–79, 82–83, 85, 94, 101, 107, 138, 140–41, 143, 145, 163–67, 171–72, 175, 177–84, 186–87, 189, 197–202, 205, 208, 212, 223, 227, 230, 257, 259, 278; last days of, 280–84
Little Rock River, 27, 29, 31
Little Six (Śakpedaŋ), 7–8, 16, 69, 72, 76, 78–81, 83, 88, 92–93, 101, 138, 141, 163–67, 173, 180, 199, 284

Lone Tree Lake, 182, 184–85, 188–89, 215, 223
Long Lake, 284
Lott, Henry, 57
Lower Agency, or Redwood, 51–53, 64, 67, 69, 71, 75–76, 79–80, 83, 97, 99, 101, 107, 135, 137, 140, 144, 162, 167–68, 180–81, 194, 196, 198, 221, 224–25, 230
Lundborgs, 107
Lynd, James, 84

Madelia, Minn., 47, 78, 147, 232
Madison, John, 214
Magner, John, 98
Magua (Cooper novel character), 87
Maḣpiyahdinape, Henock, 53–54, 70, 195
"Maiden's Feast," or "Virgin Feast," 251–52, 318n34
Maine Prairie, Minn., 158
Mankato, Minn., 47, 49, 53–54, 58, 71–72, 78, 104, 106, 148, 150–51, 155, 157–58, 165, 185, 229, 233, 238–39, 242–43, 245, 248–50, 254–57, 262, 264, 266, 268, 270–72, 275, 276–77
Mankato (also Makato; Blue Earth), 65, 82–83, 166–67, 180–81, 194
Mankato Independent (newspaper), 158, 162, 174
Mankato Weekly Record, 162, 256
Mankato Semi-Weekly Record, 243
Manannah, Minn., 273
Manypenny, George, 51–52, 55, 64
Marble, Margaret, 58
Marsh, John, 77, 79, 97–98, 116, 138–39, 266; and explanation for lack of caution, 302n45

Marshall, William, 136, 169, 184–85, 214, 222–23, 225, 233, 256
Martell, Oliver, 85, 97
Massapust, Franz, 93–94
Mauley, Jacob, 85, 97
Mayer, Frank Blackwell, 11, 24
Mayo, William, 154, 263
Mazakutemani, Paul, 25, 53–54, 58, 60, 65–66, 102, 164–66, 175–77; attempt to rescue captive women, 205–7, 219, 233; and debate with the soldiers' lodge, 180–81, 186; and revival at Fort Snelling, 269, 272–73
McClellan, Patrick, 84
McFall, Orlando, 77
McGrew, James, 141–42, 144
McKenzie, Kenneth, 32
McKusick, William, 273
McLean, James C., 139
McLean, Nathaniel, 28–29, 48
McLeod, George, 167
McLeod, Martin, 23–24, 28, 32
McLeod County, Minn., 107
McNarin, John, 86
McPhail, Samuel, 156, 169–70
McSasen, W. T., 224–25
mde (lake), 6
Mdewakanton Dakota, 3, 5–10, 12, 16, 19–21, 23, 25–31, 48, 51, 55, 60–61, 64–65, 67–69, 71, 76, 79, 80, 82, 97, 99–100, 110–11, 138, 163–66, 173, 175–78, 180–84, 186–87, 189, 195, 196, 199, 205, 208, 211, 217, 220, 222–23, 230, 233, 255, 268, 271, 279, 281, 284
Meagher, John Ford, 263
Medicine Bottle, 27, 173, 284
Medicine Dance, 15, 69–70, 80, 208, 261, 289n14

medicine men (aka *Wićaśta Wakaŋs*), 6, 10, 13–14
medicine sack, 15, 54
Medicine Society, 13–15; and feasts, 22, 271
Meeker County, Minn., 107
Mendota, Minn., 18, 25–26, 65, 135, 273
Mesquakie people, 3, 6–7, 15, 56; Black Hawk's Mesquakies, 30
Métis, 281–82
Meyers, Aaron, 104–5, 108–9, 154
Middle Creek, 87, 91–93, 99, 101
Middle Creek Township, 78
Milford Township, 55, 78, 93–94, 96–97, 102, 107, 150, 152, 201, 217, 259, 266, 275
military commission trials, 217–20, 224–28; brevity of, 216–18, 324nn69–70, 324n74; critics of the trials, 229–31, 321n13, 321n16, 321n8, 321n27; Dakota Indians as "prisoners of war," 248, 325n12, 327n43; defenders of, 229, 265, 321n12; judge advocate general's rejection of Sibley's as illegal, 332n61; trials of April 1863, 265–66, 328n69
Millard, Henry, 259
Mille Lacs Lake, 6, 20
Miller, Stephen, 235, 241–44, 248–50, 254, 257–59, 260, 262–64, 276, 285
Millier, Hubert, 85
Minnesota Haus (hotel), 151, 154
Minnesota Pioneer (newspaper), 29
Minnesota River, 3, 6–10, 13, 20, 24–25, 27, 29, 47, 49–50, 54, 61, 64–67, 71–73, 77–78, 83, 87, 99, 101–2, 107, 135–36, 146, 148, 153–54, 158–59, 162, 181, 184, 186, 197, 219, 230, 244, 262, 268–69, 273–74

Minnesota Territory, 17, 22, 29
missionaries, 5, 14, 29, 31, 48–49, 63, 71, 85, 118
Mississippi River, 4–7, 20, 22, 24, 26–28, 47–48, 78, 94, 107, 135, 149, 159, 173, 192, 275–77
Missouri River, 105, 208, 224, 275, 279
Mitchell, William B., 159
Mix, Charles E., 64, 66–67, 74–75
Monkey Dance, 70
Monroe, James, 18
Montgomery, Sarah Purcell, 232
Monticello, Minn., 149
Mooers, John, 60, 96, 195, 206, 233
Morris, W. W., 71–72
Morton, Minn., 78
Murphey, Robert, 48–52, 54, 55, 64, 74
Myrick, Andrew, 50, 67, 79–80, 137, 168, 175, 195; and "let them eat grass," 299n66
Myrick, Nathanial, 67, 137, 168

Nat Turner Rebellion, 305n86
Nelson, A. D., 157
Nelson, C. C., 106
New Auburn, Minn., 139, 143
Newman, Mrs. John, 177, 185
New Sweden, Minn., 55
New Ulm, Minn., 47, 55, 58, 71–72, 78, 80, 85, 93–96; evacuation of New Ulm, 155; first battle of, 103–5, 108–9, 131, 140, 143, 147–48; reoccupation, 157–59, 162–63, 167, 177–78, 201, 207, 224, 226–27, 232, 249–50, 274–75, 282; second battle of, 150–54
New York Evangelist (newspaper), 271
New York Times, 231–32, 241, 251

Nicolay, John G., 161
Nicolay, Jonathan, 275
Nicollet, Joseph, 13
Nix, Jacob, 103, 154
Nobel, Lydia, 58–59
Norseland, Minn., 55
Northerner (steamer), 278
North Fork, 78
Norway Lake, 107, 146
Norwegian Grove, 106–7
Norwegians, 55, 106–7, 172

Ojibwes (Chippewas;
    Anishinaabes), 6
Old Aunt Judy, 143
Old Bets, 129, 143
Old Sarah, 71
Olin, R. C., 184, 218, 228, 244
One Who Forbids His House (aka
    Tihdonića), 202, 217–18, 236,
    259
Orphan (Wamdenica), 25
Otherday, John (Aŋpetutokeca),
    54, 58, 65–66, 78, 102, 113, 185,
    217, 233, 269; as "hero" in St.
    Paul, 303n59
Ottertail Lake, 70
Ottertail Road, 180
Owatonna, Minn., 158

Pajutazi (also Peźihutazi; Yellow
    Medicine), 49–50, 78
Passing Hail, 49, 278
Patoile, Francois, 96, 137, 200, 217,
    218
patrifocal family, 5
Patterson Rapids, 31
Pawn, 104–5, 207–8
Paynesville, Minn., 146, 273
Pelzl, Carl, 93
Pembina, N.Dak., 32, 194, 277, 284
Penetion (Mdewakanton), 7;
    village of, 20

Peteler, Francois, 274
Pettit, George F., 274
Pfeiffer, Richard, 151
Pfenninger, Jacob, 71
Pickett, Eli, 260
Pierce, Franklin, 49
Pierre, S.Dak., 224
Pierson, A. T. C., 75
Pine Tree (Wazi), 259
Pipestone Quarry, 61
Poinsett, Joel, 19
Pomeroy (steamer), 136
Pond, Gideon, 21, 271
Pond, Samuel, 21, 48, 69, 196
Pope, John, 179, 180–81, 182, 187,
    214–17, 220–21, 223–24, 224,
    229, 231–32, 241, 244–46,
    249–50, 253, 265, 267, 273, 276,
    285; and "extermination" of the
    Dakota people, 315n76
Porter, John J., 150
Potter, Theodore, 55
Prairie du Chien, Wisc., 32
Pratt, H. C., 61
Preemption Act, 72
Presbyterians, 21, 54, 66, 71, 245,
    254, 271
Prescott, Philander, 8–9, 11, 16, 19,
    51–52, 80, 85, 195
Provençalle, Louis, 18, 23, 195

Quinn, George, 140–41
Quinn, Peter, 97–98
Quinn, William L., 167, 223

Ramsdell, S., 158
Ramsey, Alexander, 17–18, 21–33,
    47–48, 72, 76, 90, 97, 135–36,
    143, 145–47, 149–50; orders
    wagons, horses, and supplies
    pressed into service, 155–62,
    170, 173–74, 187–88, 213, 221,
    224, 241, 244–45, 250–53, 269,

285, 310nn88–89; demands funds from Sibley during his investigation, 291n49

rape, 240–46, 257–58, 260, 269–70, 272–73, 276–78, 285, 288, 326–329, 316n5; and "fate worse than death," 319n52, 319n55

Rattling Runner (Ḣdaiŋyaŋka), 176, 183, 200, 219, 262

Ravoux, S., 258, 260, 271

Red All Over (Siŋtomniduta), 56–57

Redfield, D. R., 157

Red Iron (Mazaduta; Wahpeton), 9, 22, 25, 31, 50, 54, 58, 64–65, 77–78, 163–64, 177–78, 180, 183, 206, 217, 242, 259

Red Legs (Huśaśa; Wapekute), 65, 78, 166–67

Red Middle Voice (Hocokayaduta), 8, 16, 27, 49, 61, 69, 72, 76, 78–81, 83, 92, 137, 163, 166, 180, 284

Red Owl (Hiŋhaŋduta), 65, 76

Red River valley, 136

Red Wing village, 20

Redwood, Minn. (lower agency), 51

Redwood Agency, 56

Redwood River, 78

refugee problem, 137, 143–44, 146–50, 155–60, 173–74, 268–70, 275

Renville, Gabriel, 23–24, 53–54, 60, 64–65, 67, 72, 102, 121, 164–65, 175–76, 178, 180, 183, 195, 217, 222, 224, 227–28, 233, 242, 269, 273, 279–80

Renville, John B., 53, 164, 176, 205

Renville, Joseph (Akipa), 54, 64–65, 78, 101, 122, 163–64, 183, 217, 242, 259, 269

Renville, Joseph, 8, 12, 18, 21–23

Renville, Mary, 205

Renville, Michael, 102, 228

Renville, Victor, 12

Renville brothers, 60, 80, 273

Renville Rangers, 80, 94, 140–42, 169, 185

Republican Party, 18, 72, 74, 174, 233, 241, 244, 257

"Revival" at Mankato and Fort Snelling prisons, 255–56, 258–60, 271–73

Reynolds, Joseph, 86, 96, 101

Rhodes, A., 104–5

Rice, Henry, 22, 29–30, 248, 269

Rice Creek, 69, 81, 137, 140–41, 145, 163, 204–5

Riggs, Mary, 21, 246, 278

Riggs, Stephen Return, 21, 23–25, 49–51, 53–54, 58, 69–70, 75, 102, 156, 164, 175, 190–91, 193–95, 202, 210, 213, 222–23, 229–30, 244, 246–48, 254–56, 258–59, 263–67, 271–72; charges Joseph Brown with corruption, 297n45

Roaring Cloud, 58–59

Roberts, Louis (trader), 67, 84

Robertson, Andrew, 64, 80, 87, 89, 198, 233

Robertson, Angus, 218

Robertson, Thomas, 88–89, 175, 177–78, 195, 198, 202–3, 206, 210, 218, 227, 264

Robinson, Thomas, 177–78, 233

Rock Island, Ill., 256–57

Roebke, Mrs., 275

Rolette, Joseph, 18

Roos, Charles, 94–97, 157, 232, 274

Round Wind (Tatemima), 259

Ruggles, Francis H., 251

Ryan, Mary Schmitz, 152

Rykke, Asbjorn, 107

Sac and Fox (Mesquakie), 3, 8–9

Sacred Heart, Minn., 78, 87, 93, 99, 100–101

Saint Croix River, 20

Śakpe's village (also Shakopee's village), 20, 78

Santee Indian Reservation, 279, 283

Satterlee, Marion P., 203

Sauk Centre, Minn., 158, 274

Scalp Dance, 11, 53, 70, 72

Scandinavian, 18, 91, 106, 107, 146

Scantlebury, Louisa, 149

Scarlet End (Iŋkpaduta), 51, 56–57

Scarlet Plum (Sisseton), 50–51, 64–65, 67–68, 78, 101, 144, 180, 280–81

Scarlet Shooter (Wahpeduta), 218

Schilling family, 95

Schmitz, Anna, 151

Schoolcraft, Henry Rowe, 5, 192

Schwandt, August, 99

Schwandt, John, 99

Schwandt, Mary, 96, 134, 200–201, 203–4, 207, 217, 252, 256

Schwendinger, Alexander, 132

Scott, Winfield, 215

Senate investigation of Ramsey, 33

Sentzke, Mrs. Leopold, 124, 275

Seventh Minnesota Volunteers, 136

Shakopee, Minn., 47–48, 136–37, 146, 174

Shakopee (Śakpe, Six), 7–8, 10, 12–13, 16, 25, 27–28, 48–49, 61, 65, 78, 204

Sheehan, Timothy, 77, 117, 135, 139, 140–45, 149, 169, 194

Sherman, T. W., 59, 67–68

Sibley, Fred, 23, 25, 32

Sibley, Henry Hastings (Wapetoŋhaŋska), 18–19, 23, 25–26, 28–33, 50, 54, 63, 67, 72,
135–37, 141, 145–46, 149, 155–56, 160–63, 166–70, 174–75, 177–85, 187–91, 202–3, 207, 210, 211–16, 218–23, 226, 228–32, 241–42, 244–46, 248–50, 252–55, 257–59, 262, 264–65, 266–67, 269–70, 273, 275–76, 278, 280, 282–83, 285; exchange with Hercules Dousman re treaties, 291n43; exchange with Jack Frazier regarding afterlife, 287n7; as lobbyist for Treaties of 1851, 290n18

Singer (Dowaŋsa), 219

Sioux Falls, S.Dak., 224

Sioux River, 223

Sisseton Dakota Indians, 4, 8–9, 20–21, 23–24, 29–33, 48–52, 58–60, 64, 67–68, 77, 97, 100, 102–4, 107, 144, 162–66, 172, 176–77, 180, 186, 199, 207–8, 217, 223, 268–69, 279–81

Sitting Bull, 144

Sixth Minnesota Regiment, 136, 145

Skaro, A. K., 221

Skunk Lake (aka Lake Herman), 58, 60

Slaughter Slough, 130

Sleepy Eye (Iśtaĥba; Sisseton), 9, 25, 50–51, 56–59, 61, 65, 67, 208

Smith, Caleb, 244

Smith, John C., 245

Smith, Watson, 104–5, 108

Smithson, Captain, 147

Snelling, Josiah, 12, 81

Soldiers' Lodge, 9, 13, 138; as example of a "soldiers' kill," 288n28

South Bend, Minn., 232

South Fork River, 78

Spenser, George W., 50, 84, 177, 266

Sperry, Albert, 171

Spirit Lake, Iowa, and 1857 massacre, 56–61, 104, 207, 246, 293n46

St. Boniface, 281

St. Cloud, Minn., 157, 159, 172, 173

St. Cloud Democrat (newspaper), 159

St. Cloud Journal Press, 159

St. Croix Monitor, 234

St. Joseph, Manitoba, 281, 284

St. Louis, Mo., 26, 32, 180, 276, 278

St. Norbert, Manitoba, 281

St. Paul, Minn., 3, 5–7, 20, 22–23, 25, 29, 47, 55, 58, 81, 86, 90, 102, 146, 148–50, 157–58, 185, 241, 244, 247, 258–59, 262, 265, 284

St. Paul Daily Press (newspaper), 247–48

St. Paul Daily Union (newspaper), 275

St. Paul Journal, 162

St. Paul Pioneer and Democrat (newspaper), 150, 156, 254, 261

St. Paul Press (newspaper), 160, 162, 234, 241, 276

St. Peter, Minn., 47, 54, 58, 78, 103, 105–6, 109, 137, 140–41, 145–46, 148, 150, 155, 157–58, 170, 174, 221, 249, 263, 270

St. Peter Tribune, 249

Standing Buffalo (Tataŋkanaźiŋ; Sisseton), 9–10, 24–25, 50–51, 60, 65, 67–68, 77–78, 101, 112, 144, 180–81, 186, 223, 280–81

Standing Lodge (Tinaźiŋpi), 227

Stanton, Edwin (secretary of war), 161, 179

Stay, Ceclia Campbell, 201, 213

Stearns County, Minn., 71

Steele, Thomas, 55

Stein, John, 146

Stengel, Frank, 131

Stevens, John H. (general), 170, 171–72

Stocker, Joseph, 93, 95–96

Stone Man, 212

Strikes The Pawnee, 176

Strong Earth (Anishinaabe), 12

Strout, Richard, 158, 171–72, 181, 184, 224

Sun Dance, 9

Swan (Magataŋka), 229–30

Swan Lake, 219

Sweden, settlers from, 55

Sweet Corn (Wamnahezaskuya; Sisseton), 24–25, 50–51, 65, 78, 144, 281

Sweetser, Madison, 29–31

Swift, Henry A., 157–58

Swishelm, Jane, 174

Taché, Alexandre-Antonin, 281

Tainyanku, 219

takapsićapi (stick ball game), 24

Taliaferro, Lawrence, 18–19, 21; as honest agent, 289n3; on Indian chiefs and leadership in 1839, 288n14

Taopi (Wound), 49, 69, 71, 76, 86, 129, 143, 177–79, 186, 233, 264, 266, 273

Taoyateduta's village (aka Little Crow's village), 3–10, 16, 19–21, 23–28, 78

Tapetataŋka, Peter (His Big Fire), 54, 60, 186, 230, 245–47, 255, 269, 277

Tawasuota, 84

Taylor, Zachary, 17

Ten Mile Lake, 223

Tennyson, Alfred, 184

Territory of Minnesota, 16

Thatcher, Elizabeth, 58

Third Minnesota Regiment, 156
Thompson, Clark W., 73–74, 77, 80
Thoreau, Henry David, 76
Thul, Robert, 108–9
Tinkling (Snana), 204
tipsiŋna (also *tipsinah*; pomme de terre, turnip), 77
Tivoli, Minn., 274
Todd, J. B. S., 275
Tokadaŋti (Kit Fox Society), 13
traders, 8, 16, 18–19, 21–23, 27–29, 31–33, 50, 73, 77
Traveling Hail, 69, 76
Traverse des Sioux, Minn., 24–28, 31, 49, 53–54, 78, 198
Treat, Seliah B., 230, 246, 271
treaties of 1851, 23–24, 26–28, 32–33, 49, 66; debt from 1820s and 1830s associated with, 291n48; and five-year term of president's executive order, 292n9; Treaty of Traverse des Sioux, 31
Treaty of 1837, 19–21
Treaty of 1858, 65–67; and Little Crow's misunderstanding of 1851 treaty terms, 291n39
Troxel, C. P., 145
Twin Baby Boy (Hokśidaŋnoŋpa), 259
Two Kettle Lakota, 209
Two Stars, Solomon (Wićaŋhpinoŋpa; Wahpeton), 102, 164, 183, 217
Tyler, Hugh, 30–31

Uncle Calvin, 149
Union Army, 80, 94, 246
Union Hotel, 102
United States Arsenal, 65
Unktehi (also *Ukteri*; Great Mystery), 14, 16

Upper Agency (by Yellow Medicine River), 49, 51, 53, 56, 60, 64–65, 70, 77, 79–80, 100–102, 163–64, 184–85, 194, 197, 269
Upton, B. F., 240
Usher, John Palmer, 253–54, 276

Van der Horck, John, 172–73
Van Vorhes, A. J., 145, 150
Vernon Center, Minn., 147
"Virgin Feast," or "Maiden's Feast," 251–52, 318n34

Wabasha, Minn., 6, 47
Wabasha (also Wapaśa), 7, 9–10, 16, 23, 25–28, 30, 48–49, 65, 68–69, 71, 76, 78, 85–86, 94, 138, 143, 166, 176–79, 183, 200, 219, 233, 255, 264, 266, 276, 278
Wagner, A. H., 85
Wahpekute Dakota, 3, 10, 21, 28, 30–31, 49, 51, 56, 60, 65, 67, 166, 207
Wahpeton Dakota, 3–4, 8–9, 20–21, 23–25, 29–33, 48–51, 58, 60, 64, 67, 102, 143, 162–63, 165–66, 172, 176–77, 186, 268–69, 279–81
Wakaŋ (spiritual, mysterious, sacred), 6, 13
Wakefield, H. J., 174
Wakefield, Sarah, 100, 140, 163, 187, 204–5, 210, 212–13, 218, 262–64
Wakute (Mdewakanton), 7, 19, 49, 69, 85, 87, 94, 96, 138, 143, 166, 177–78, 200–201, 203, 219, 255–56, 269, 278
Wakute's village, 20, 48, 78, 227
Walking Iron (Mazamani), 25, 50, 64, 78, 163–65, 185–86

Walking Runner (also Running Walker; Iŋyaŋgmani; Wahpeton), 4, 9–10, 22, 25, 28, 50, 53–54, 56, 64, 71, 78, 186, 246, 259

Walking Spirit, 58, 78

Walks Among Stones (also Walker Among Stones; Tuŋkaŋmani), 167, 170, 227

Walks Clothed As An Owl (Hiŋhaŋshoonkayagmani), 198

Wapaśa village (also Wabasha), 20

War Dance, 11

Washington, D.C., 19, 26, 29–31, 48, 54, 57, 67, 69, 73–76, 161, 180, 215, 231, 245, 251–52, 285

Washington Monument, 4, 65

Watonwan County, Minn., 107, 158

Watonwan River, 274

Wauben, Charles, 104

Wauben, Clark, 104

Wawiyahiyewiŋ, Sarah, 56

Wege, 90

Welch, A. E., 184–85

Welles, Gideon, 231–32, 243

West, Emily, 85, 98

Whig Party, 17

Whipple, Henry Benjamin, 70–71, 74, 247–48, 252, 255, 264, 265, 269, 273; and corruption within Indian Bureau, 297n43, 297n48

Whipple, John, 141

whiskey trade, 19, 70–71, 81, 85, 98, 104, 174, 309n65

Whitcomb, George, 147, 171–72, 224; and possible tyrannical behavior, 312n36

White, Julia, 197–98

White, Mrs. N. D., 190–91, 197, 205–6, 210, 212

White, Urania S., 90, 134, 190–91, 197

White Dog (Śuŋkaska), 71, 85, 98, 266; pleadings of innocence, 303n47; and Satterlee's indictment of, 300n9

White Lodge (Sisseton), 50–51, 56–57, 59–61, 65, 67, 78, 102, 104, 107, 126, 176, 207–9, 223, 246

White Man (Waśicuŋ), 264

White Spider (Uŋktomiska), 197, 283–84

Whiting, George C., 251

Whitney, J. C., 221–22, 224–25

Wićaśta Wakaŋ (medicine man), 10–11, 13–14, 260, 271

Wilkinson, Morton Smith, 252–53, 256, 269–70

Williams, Mattie, 96, 191, 200–202, 205, 213, 218, 252, 256

Williamson, Jane, 77, 255

Williamson, John, 71, 79, 230–31, 256, 272, 277–79

Williamson, Thomas S., 21, 49, 64, 72, 102, 182, 230, 242, 245, 247, 255, 259–61, 265, 270–71, 277

Williston, William C., 249–50

Wilson, J. P., 173

Winchell, Newton H., 33

Wind Comes Home (Tatehdedaŋ), 206

Windom, William, 256

Winnebago Indians, 73–74, 229, 268, 274

Winnipeg, Manitoba, 281

Winona, Minn., 7, 174

Wiŋyaŋ, Elizabeth, 5, 14

Wisconsin, 4, 18–19, 149, 158, 174, 180, 182, 224, 242–44

Wise, John, 257

Wohler, Leopold, 199, 200

Wood, John Kingsley, 225

Wood, Sally, 173

Wood, Samuel, 56, 57
Wood Lake, battle of, 181, 185, 208, 285; casualties, 315n88
Workman, Harper, 108, 208
Wound (Taopi), 49, 69
Wowinape (Refuge), 82, 282–83
Wright, Eldora, 126, 208–9
Wright, John, 104
Wright, Julia, 105, 126, 208–9

Yanktonai Sioux, 9, 280–81
Yankton Sioux, 58–59, 67, 280–81
Yellow Medicine River, 49, 72, 78, 163–64, 167, 182–84, 186, 196, 212, 230

Yellow Medicine River Agency, 51, 97, 135, 156, 181, 197, 204, 205, 219, 221–22, 225
York, Frank, 110
Young, Antoine, 84

Zeller, Max, 93
Zettle, John, 93–95
Zierke, Robert (Dutch Charley), 108–9
Zimmerman, Mrs., 275